PARIS

teNeues

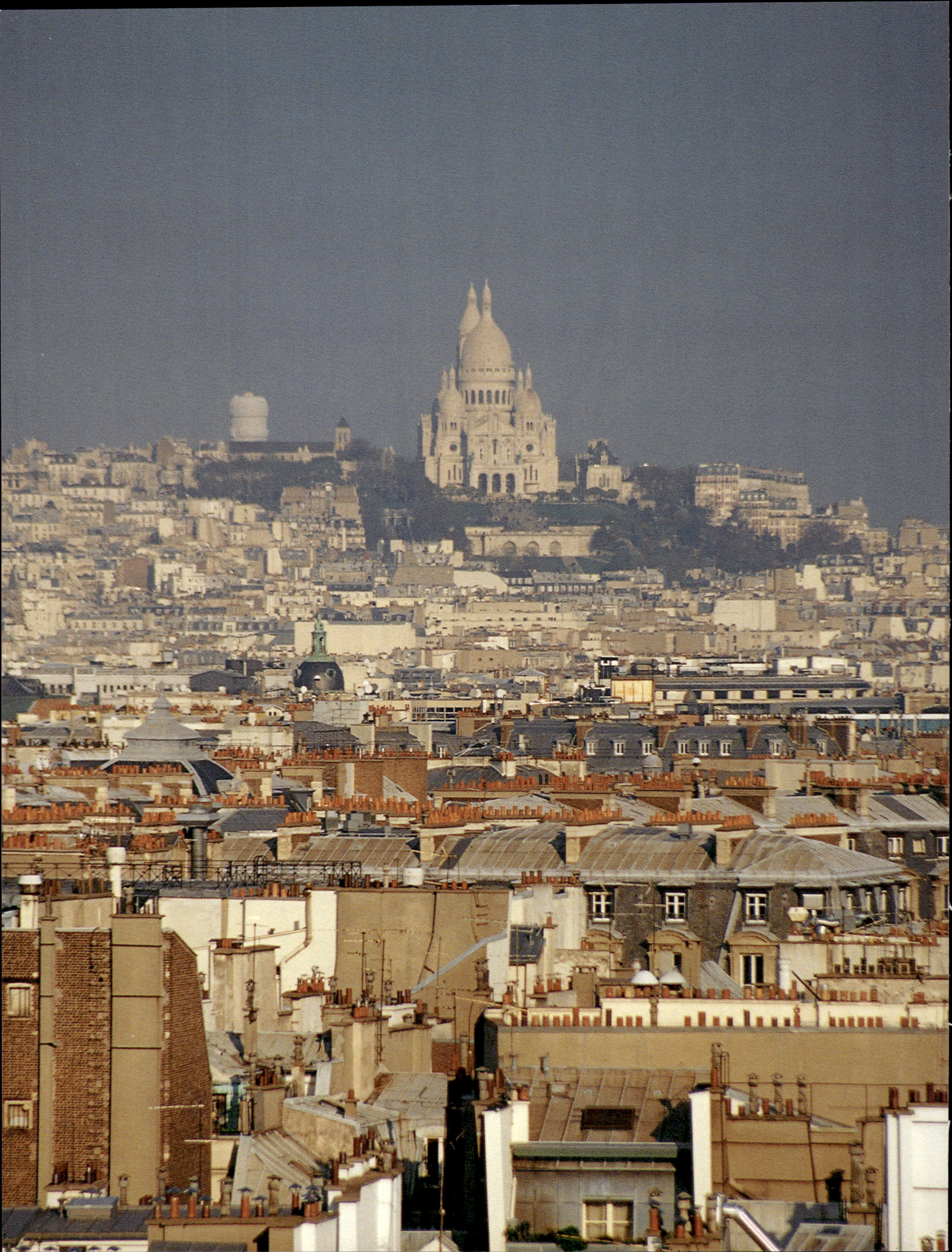

PARIS

Photographs by Tina and Horst Herzig
Text by Pierrette Stephan-Letondor

teNeues

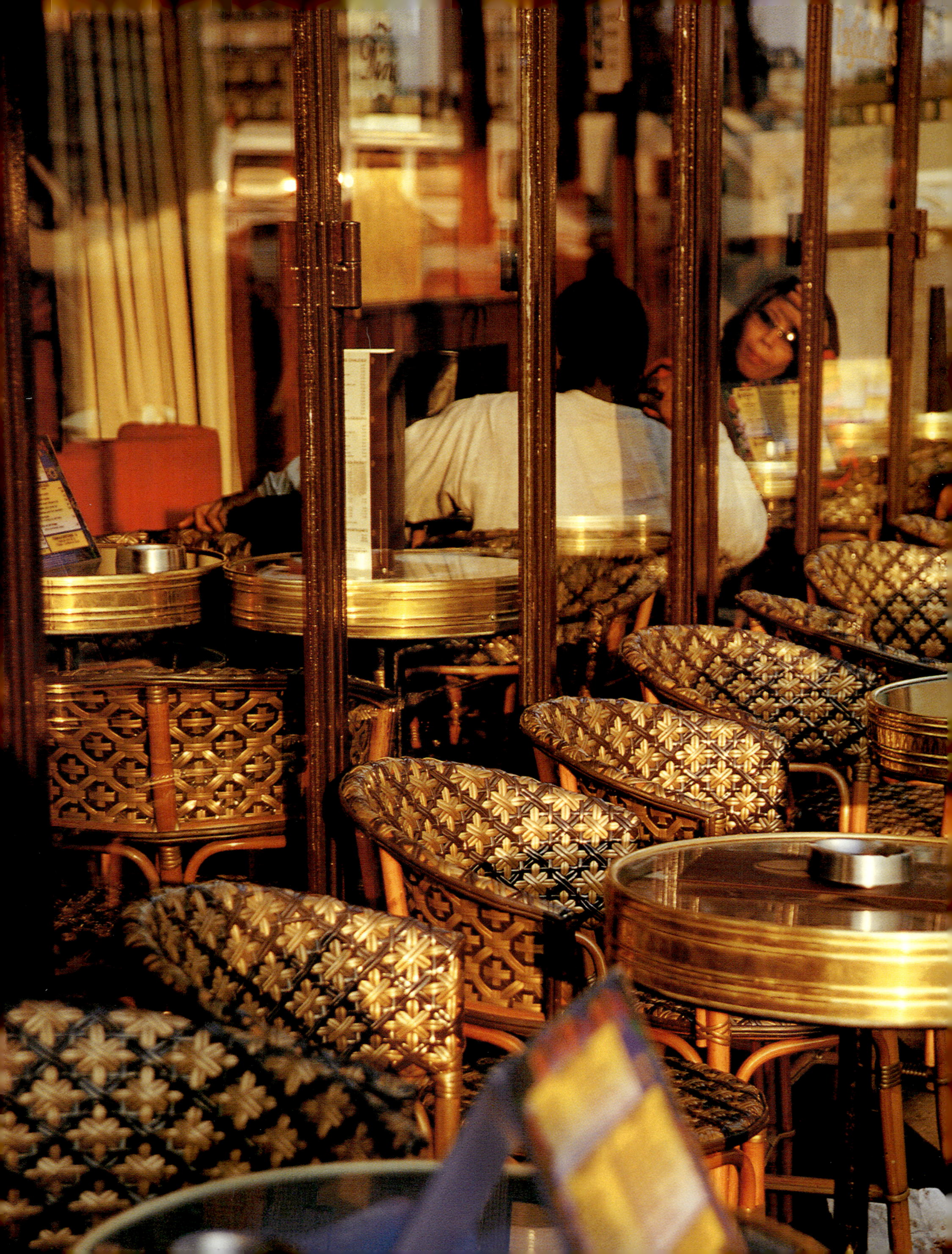

Les Français ne font pas dans la modestie quant à leur capitale : les Champs-Élysées sont la plus belle avenue, le Louvre, le musée le plus vaste, la mode est appelée haute couture et la restauration, haute gastronomie. Et comme si la Grande Arche de la Défense ne suffisait plus, on inventa récemment la TGB, la Très Grande Bibliothèque. Les chiffres leur donnent raison, Paris restant la capitale internationale la plus visitée.

Les superlatifs et la modernité ne font pas nécessairement la beauté d'un lieu. Elle accroche plus le regard le long du méandre langoureux que dessine la Seine d'est en ouest. Sa rive nord est ourlée des magnifiques façades des anciens palais royaux devenus musées, bordée d'authentiques jardins à la française où gambadèrent les futurs rois. C'est sur l'Ile de la Cité que les Parisi, bateliers gaulois, installèrent leurs huttes et que, treize siècles plus tard, le clergé et la noblesse y érigèrent Notre Dame. Cette promenade au « cœur de Paris » et sur sa voisine l'Ile Saint-Louis au site enchanteur, entre les ponts des Arts et de Sully, finissant le long des quais avec les immuables boîtes à livres vertes des bouquinistes, demeure une rencontre physique avec le Paris historique.

Un plaisir très sensuel, particulier à cette ville bâtie densément, est communiqué par l'océan gris blanc des toits en zinc hérissés de petites cheminées. Il faut donc prendre de la hauteur sur la Tour Eiffel, digne vieille dame de Paris, en montant avec l'escalator vertical et brisé de Beaubourg, gravir les marches abruptes de Montmartre, nostalgique des chevalets d'antan, s'extasier sur les terrasses des Grands Magasins ou, pour les puristes, toucher le ciel depuis la Tour Montparnasse, admirer un panorama sur lequel celle-ci n'apparaît pas.

Les balades urbaines dans le Marais, à Saint-Germain-des-Prés, Montparnasse, celles campagnardes à La Butte aux Cailles et aux Buttes Chaumont ou celle très végétale de la Promenade Plantée qui emprunte l'ancienne voie de chemin de fer (12e arrondissement) se font d'autant plus aisément que Paris intramuros avec un peu moins de deux millions d'habitants a une petite superficie de 48 km^2. On passe vite de la rive droite « chic » à la rive gauche « intellectuelle », on s'étonne de l'esprit village des rues Daguerre et Montorgueil, on découvre le quartier branché de la Bastille et tombe sur l'exotisme des quartiers chinois, africains, indiens.

Des milliers d'adresses pour découvrir le Paris gourmand et gourmet : restaurants et bistrots aux décors souvent classés, qui aguichent toute l'année avec les corbeilles de fruits de mer servies sur un plateau surélevé. Même les gares mettent le visiteur sur la voie de la bonne chair avec des brasseries phares, comme celle de la gare de Lyon, Le Train Bleu, « le plus beau buffet de gare du monde ».
Paris sans ses superlatifs ne serait plus Paris !

Pierrette Stephan-Letondor

When it comes to their capital city, the French are not exactly modest: for them the Champs-Élysées is the most attractive of all avenues, the Louvre is the biggest museum, fashion and food are classed here as haute-couture and haute-cuisine and belong to the fine arts. As if the biggest triumphal arch—the Grande Arche in the city's La Défense district—is not big enough they also recently opened the TGB, the Très Grande Bibliothèque, which means nothing short of the "very big library". The French are right, if you look at the visitor numbers—Paris still comes top of the world's most visited capitals.

Yet supremity and modernity are no firm guarantees of how attractive a place is. Beauty is more evident, if you look at the wide, meandering flow of the river Seine, as it cuts its way across country from east to west. The river's northern bank is lined by museums with magnificent façades of former royal palaces, which are still surrounded by the same French gardens, where the young princes and heirs once used to run riot amusing themselves. Thirteen centuries before royalty and clergy joined forces and began to build Notre Dame Cathedral, the Parisi, or Gallic river boatmen, built their huts on the Ile de la Cité. This enchanting promenade in the "heart of Paris" and on the neighbouring island of Saint-Louis is located between the two bridges of Pont des Arts and Pont de Sully. The riverside walk ends along the quay-side with the same green box-shaped stalls of the Bouquinistes, who are trading in second hand books. Take a walk here and you begin a journey to Paris as it used to be centuries ago.

A lasting impression for the senses is offered by the light gray ocean of tin rooves, dotted with chimney stacks, in this densely built city. Now let's climb up the Eiffel Tower (the dignified old lady of Paris), the striking escalator at the Pompidou Center, or the steep steps to Montmartre with the nostalgic atmosphere of painters at their easels. There is also a delightful view from the terraces of the great Parisian stores—and for real fans, you can reach for the sky on top of the Montparnasse tower and admire the panorama without this landmark.

It doesn't matter whether you take a walk through the city's districts, like the Marais quarter, or Saint-Germain-des-Prés or Montparnasse, whether you choose the more rural routes on the Butte aux Cailles and Buttes Chaumont, or whether you pick the "all-country route" of the Promenade Plantée, along the old railtrack (in the 12th district)—you never need waste too much energy, because with a population of a little less than two million, the center of Paris only covers a distance of 48 km^2. From the chic right bank, you can quickly move across to the intellectual left bank, you can admire the village charm of the avenues, Rue Daguerre and Rue Montorgueil, discover the trendy Bastille quarter and dive into the exotic Chinese, African and Indian quarters.

Paris also has thousands of places to visit for connoisseurs and gourmets: the restaurants and bistros often have interior decor to listed building standard and they tempt the customer all year round with baskets full of seafood. The shellfish is served on a platter that rests on a small pedestal. Even in the railway stations, visitors' every needs are well catered for: you can find excellent brasseries, like Le Train Bleu, the one at the Gare de Lyon, the "most fabulous railway restaurant in the world".
Without its superlative qualities, Paris would not be Paris!

Pierrette Stephan-Letondor

Wenn es um ihre Hauptstadt geht, sind die Franzosen nicht gerade bescheiden: Für sie sind die Champs-Élysées die schönste aller Straßen, der Louvre das größte Museum, Mode und Küche gehören hier als Haute-Couture und Haute-Cuisine zu den hohen Künsten, und als ob es dann mit dem größten Triumphbogen – dem Grande Arche de la Défense – nicht genug wäre, hat man unlängst auch noch die TGB eingerichtet, die Très Grande Bibliothèque, was nicht weniger bedeutet als die „sehr große Bibliothek". Die Besucherzahlen geben den Franzosen Recht, Paris ist international nach wie vor die am meisten besuchte Kapitale.

Doch Superlative und Modernität sind nicht unbedingt Garanten für die Schönheit eines Ortes. Diese zeigt sich vielmehr, wenn der Blick den ausladenden Mäandern folgt, welche die Seine auf ihrem Weg von Ost nach West in die Landschaft zeichnet. Das nördliche Flussufer wird von Museen mit großartigen Fassaden gesäumt, ehemaligen königlichen Palais, die noch heute von den gleichen Französischen Gärten umgeben sind, in denen einst die jungen Thronanwärter herumtollten. Auf der Ile de la Cité hatten dreizehn Jahrhunderte vor dem gemeinsam von Adel und Klerus unternommenen Bau der Kathedrale Notre Dame die gallischen Flussschiffer, die Parisi, ihre Hütten errichtet. Dieses „Herz von Paris" und die Insel Saint-Louis gegenüber liegen zauberhaft zwischen den Brücken Pont des Arts und Pont de Sully, die an der Uferstraße mit den immer gleichen grünen Kastenbuden der Bouquinisten (der Antiquariatsbuchhändler) enden. Wer hier spazieren geht, begibt sich auf eine Reise in das Paris vergangener Jahrhunderte.

Einen besonderen Sinneseindruck bietet der hellgraue Ozean der mit Schornsteinen gespickten Zinndächer in dieser dicht bebauten Stadt. Also hinauf auf den Eiffelturm (die ehrwürdige alte Dame von Paris), die bemerkenswerte Rolltreppe des Centre Pompidou oder die steilen Stufen des Montmartre mit den nostalgischen Staffeleien der Maler. Auch auf den Terrassen der Grands Magasins entzückt die Aussicht – und Puristen können auf dem Montparnasse-Turm nach dem Himmel greifen und das Panorama ohne dieses Wahrzeichen bestaunen.

Ganz gleich, ob man durch die städtische Umgebung des Marais-Viertels, von Saint-Germain-des-Prés oder des Montparnasse schlendert, die ländlicheren Wege auf die Butte aux Cailles und die Buttes Chaumont wählt oder sich für die „ganz naturnahe" Promenade Plantée entlang der alten Eisenbahnstrecke (im 12. Arrondissement) entscheidet – man muss sich nie überanstrengen, denn die Pariser Innenstadt mit etwas weniger als zwei Millionen Einwohnern erstreckt sich nur über 48 km^2. Vom „schicken" rechten Ufer gelangt man schnell zum „intellektuellen" linken Ufer, kann über den dörflichen Charme der Straßen Rue Daguerre und Rue Montorgueil staunen, das trendige Bastille-Viertel entdecken und in die exotischen Stadtteile der Chinesen, Afrikaner und Inder eintauchen.

Auch für Feinschmecker und Genießer gibt es in Paris Tausende von Anlaufstellen: Restaurants und Bistros mit oft denkmalgeschützter Ausstattung, die das ganze Jahr über mit Körben voller Meeresfrüchte locken. Diese werden auf einer Platte gereicht, die auf ein kleines Podest gestellt wird. Selbst auf den Bahnhöfen wird gut für das leibliche Wohl der Besucher gesorgt: Dort findet man herausragende Brasserien, wie etwa das Le Train Bleu am Gare de Lyon, das „schönste Bahnhofslokal der Welt".
Ohne seine Superlative wäre Paris nicht Paris!

Pierrette Stephan-Letondor

Cuando se trata de su capital los franceses no son precisamente modestos: Para ellos los Campos Elíseos son la avenida más bella, el Louvre el museo más grande, la moda es la alta costura y la cocina la alta gastronomía y como si no fuera suficiente con el mayor Arco de Triunfo –la Grande Arche de la Défense– aún fue creada recientemente la TGB, la Très Grande Bibliothèque, que no significa menos que la "biblioteca muy grande". Las cifras de visitantes dan la razón a los franceses; París continúa siendo internacionalmente la capital más visitada.

Pero el superlativo y la modernidad no tienen por qué garantizar la belleza de un lugar. Ésta se muestra más bien cuando la mirada sigue los amplios meandros que el Sena dibuja en el paisaje a su paso del este hacia el oeste. La orilla norte del río está bordada por museos de fachadas grandiosas, antiguos palacios reales que todavía hoy se hallan rodeados por los mismos jardines franceses por los que antaño corrían los jóvenes futuros reyes. Fue en la Ile de la Cité donde los navegantes galos, los Parisi, habían construido sus chozas, trece siglos antes de la construcción de la catedral de Notre Dame emprendida conjuntamente por la nobleza y el clero. Este "corazón de París" y la Isla de Saint-Louis enfrente se hallan situados de forma fascinante entre los puentes Pont des Arts y Pont de Sully que acaban en la carretera ribereña con las tiendecillas de los "bouquinistes" (los libreros de antigüedades) siempre verdes. Quien pasea por aquí reencuentra el París histórico.

Una impresión muy sensual, especialmente en esta ciudad densamente edificada, la ofrece el océano gris claro de los tejados de zinc salpicados de chimeneas. Pues a subir a la Torre Eiffel (la digna vieja dama de París), por las notables escalerillas mecánicas del Centro Pompidou o por las abruptas escaleras de Montmartre con los caballetes nostálgicos de los pintores. La vista embriaga también en las terrazas de los Grands Magasins y los puristas pueden tocar el cielo en la Torre de Montparnasse admirando el panorama sin este monumento característico.

Es igual si uno deambula por los barrios de Marais, de Saint-Germain-des-Prés o de Montparnasse, si elige los caminos más rurales de Butte aux Cailles y de Buttes Chaumont o se decide por la Promenade Plantée, "muy silvestre", a lo largo de la antigua vía de ferrocarril (en el 12° arrondissement), uno nunca necesita esforzarse demasiado pues el centro urbano parisino, con algo menos de dos millones de habitantes, se extiende sólo por 48 km^2. Desde la orilla derecha "chic" se llega rápidamente a la orilla izquierda "intelectual"; uno puede sorprenderse del encanto rústico de las calles Rue Daguerre y Rue Montorgueil, descubrir el barrio de moda de la Bastille y sumergirse en los exóticos barrios de chinos, africanos e indios.

También para amantes de la buena cocina hay miles de lugares en París: los restaurantes y los bistros, con una decoración interior a menudo monumento histórico, que atraen durante todo el año con cestos repletos de mariscos. Éstos son servidos en una bandeja colocada sobre una pequeña plataforma. Incluso en las estaciones de trenes se vela bien por el bienestar de los visitantes: Allí uno encuentra excelentes braserías como por ejemplo Le Train Bleu en la estación de Lyon, "el local de estación más bello del mundo". ¡Sin sus superlativos París no sería París!

Pierrette Stephan-Letondor

Gli Champs-Élysées sono il viale più bello del mondo, il Louvre il museo più grande, la moda si chiama "haute couture" e nei ristoranti si gusta l'alta gastronomia. E, come se non fosse già bastata la Grande Arche de la Défense, di recente si è inventata anche la TGB, la Très Grande Bibliothèque, che altro non significa che la "grandissima biblioteca". Quando parlano della loro capitale i francesi mettono completamente da parte la modestia. E le cifre danno loro ragione: Parigi è e resta la capitale più visitata in assoluto.

Ma i superlativi e la modernità non sono necessariamente una garanzia della bellezza di un luogo. Piuttosto questa si apprezza facendo scorrere lo sguardo lungo il meandro languido della Senna che si snoda da oriente ad occidente. La riva settentrionale è orlata dalle magnifiche facciate delle antiche residenze reali trasformate in musei, fiancheggiate dai giardini alla francese in cui un tempo scorrazzavano i futuri regnanti. Sull'Ile de la Cité, tredici secoli prima che il clero e la nobiltà vi erigessero la cattedrale di Notre Dame, dei pescatori e barcaioli della tribù celtica dei Parisi costruirono le loro capanne. Quest'affascinante passeggiata nel "cuore di Parigi" e sulla vicina Ile Saint-Louis, tra il Pont des Arts e il Pont de Sully, conduce poi sui lungofiumi con le immutabili bancarelle verdi dei venditori di libri usati (i bouquinistes) e regala un vero incontro con la Parigi storica.

Un piacere dei sensi particolare offerto da questa città così fittamente edificata è l'oceano bianco-grigio dei tetti in zinco punteggiati da piccoli comignoli. Si deve perciò salire in alto, sulla Tour Eiffel (dignitosa vecchia signora parigina), prendere le scale mobili che formano una linea spezzata sulla facciata del Centre Georges Pompidou (il Beaubourg), inerpicarsi su per i ripidi gradini di Montmartre, con la nostalgia per i cavalletti dei pittori d'un tempo, restare rapiti sulle terrazze dei grandi magazzini o, per i puristi, toccare il cielo con un dito dalla Tour Montparnasse, godendosi il panorama non alterato dalla torre stessa.

Le passeggiate cittadine al Marais, a Saint-Germain-des-Prés, a Montparnasse e quelle di campagna nelle strade della Butte aux Cailles e nel parco delle Buttes Chaumont o quella immersa nel verde della Promenade Plantée, che segue il percorso di una vecchia linea ferroviaria (nel 12° arrondissement), si fanno senza fatica, in quanto il centro di Parigi, che conta poco meno di due milioni di abitanti, ha una superficie di soli 48 km^2. Si passa rapidamente dalla riva destra della Senna, la riva dell'eleganza, alla riva sinistra, quella della cultura, ci si meraviglia del fascino paesano di rue Daguerre e rue Montorgueil, si scopre la zona alla moda della Bastille e ci si immerge nell'esotismo dei quartieri cinesi, africani o indiani.

E poi, migliaia di indirizzi per andare alla scoperta della Parigi dei buongustai: ristoranti e bistrot, spesso con interni dichiarati beni culturali da tutelare, che attraggono tutto l'anno con ceste di frutti di mare disposte in bella vista su vassoi con piedestallo. Persino le stazioni mettono i visitatori sulle tracce della buona cucina con dei locali di spicco, come quello della gare de Lyon, Le Train Bleu, "il bar-ristorante di stazione più bello del mondo".
Parigi senza superlativi non sarebbe più Parigi!

Pierrette Stephan-Letondor

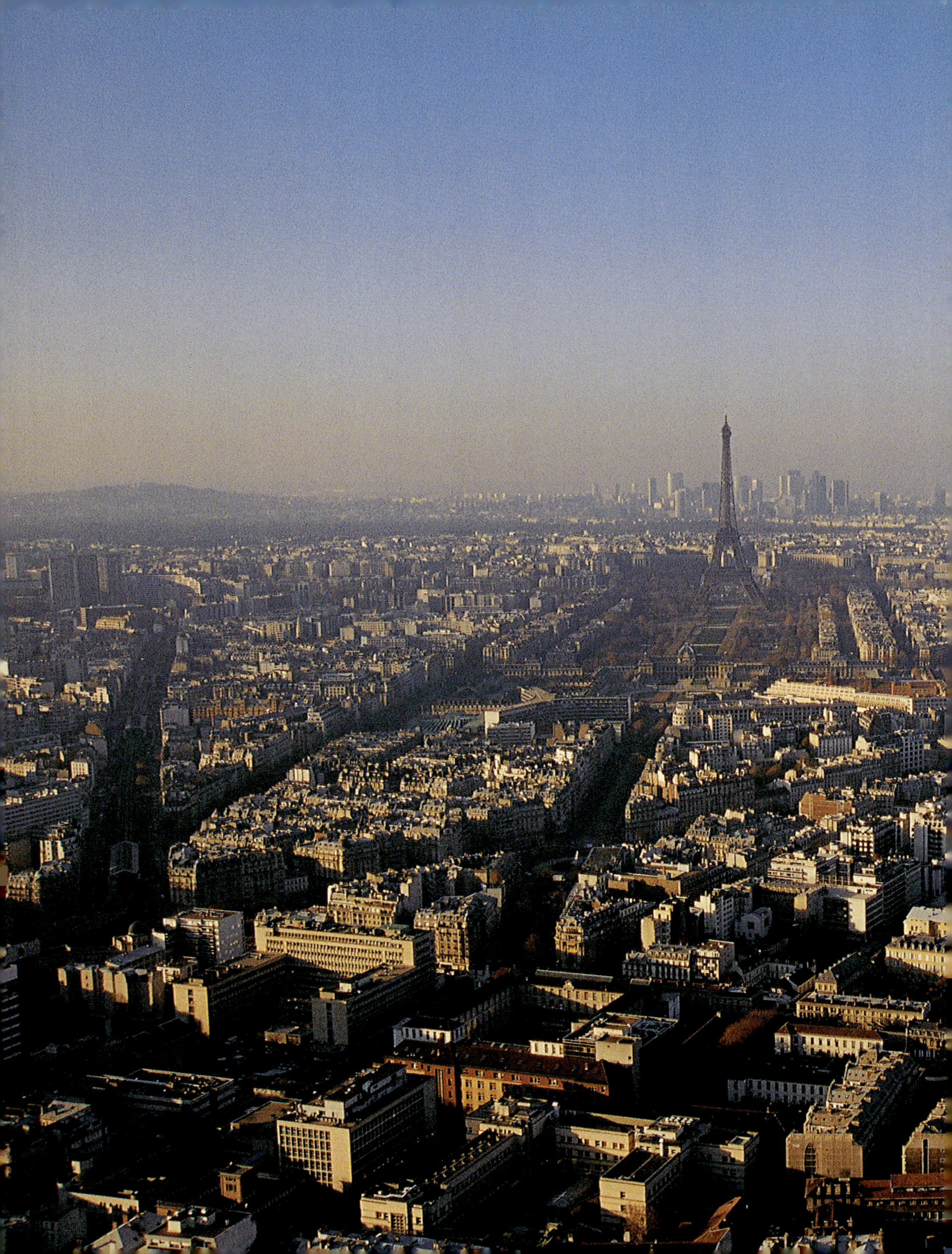

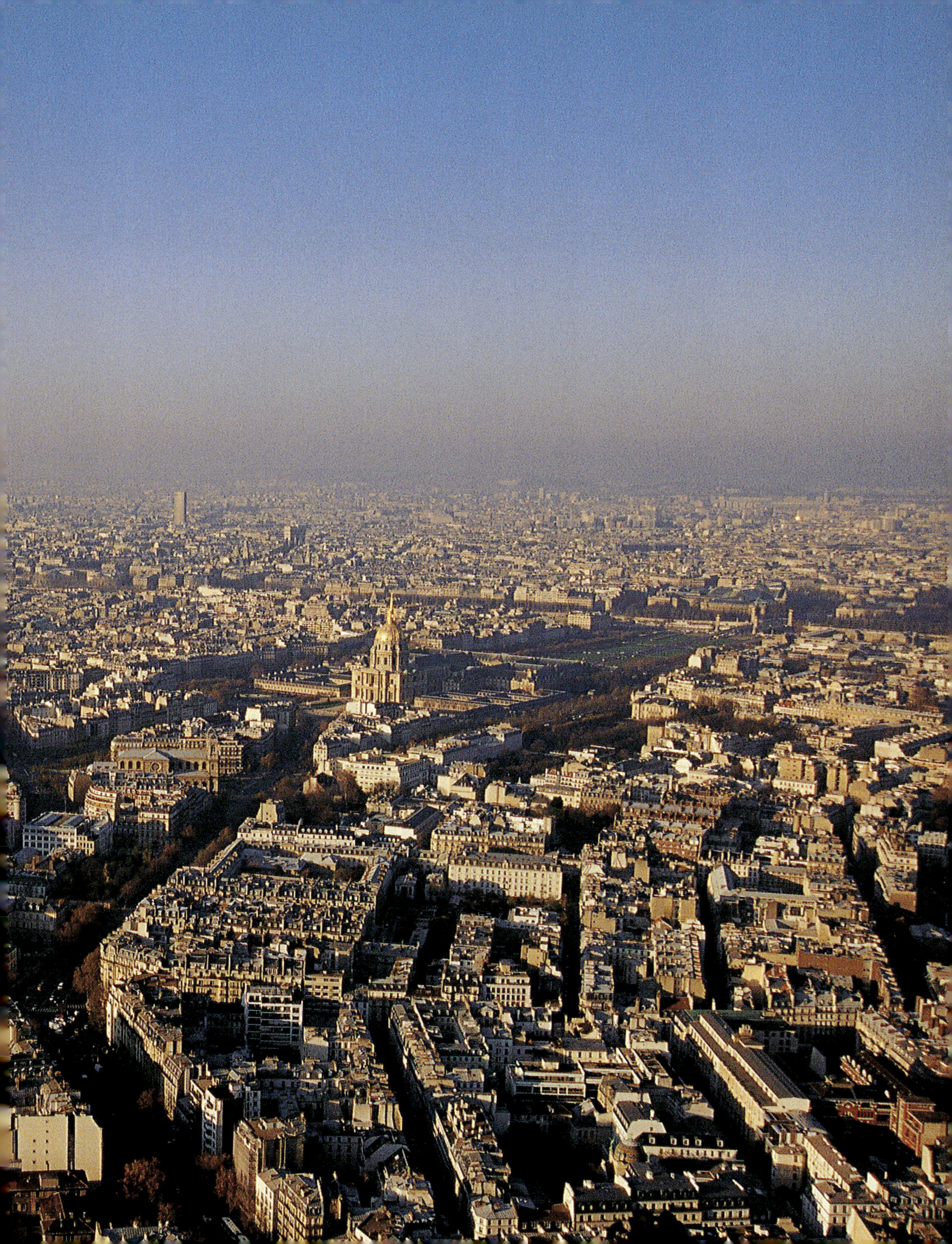

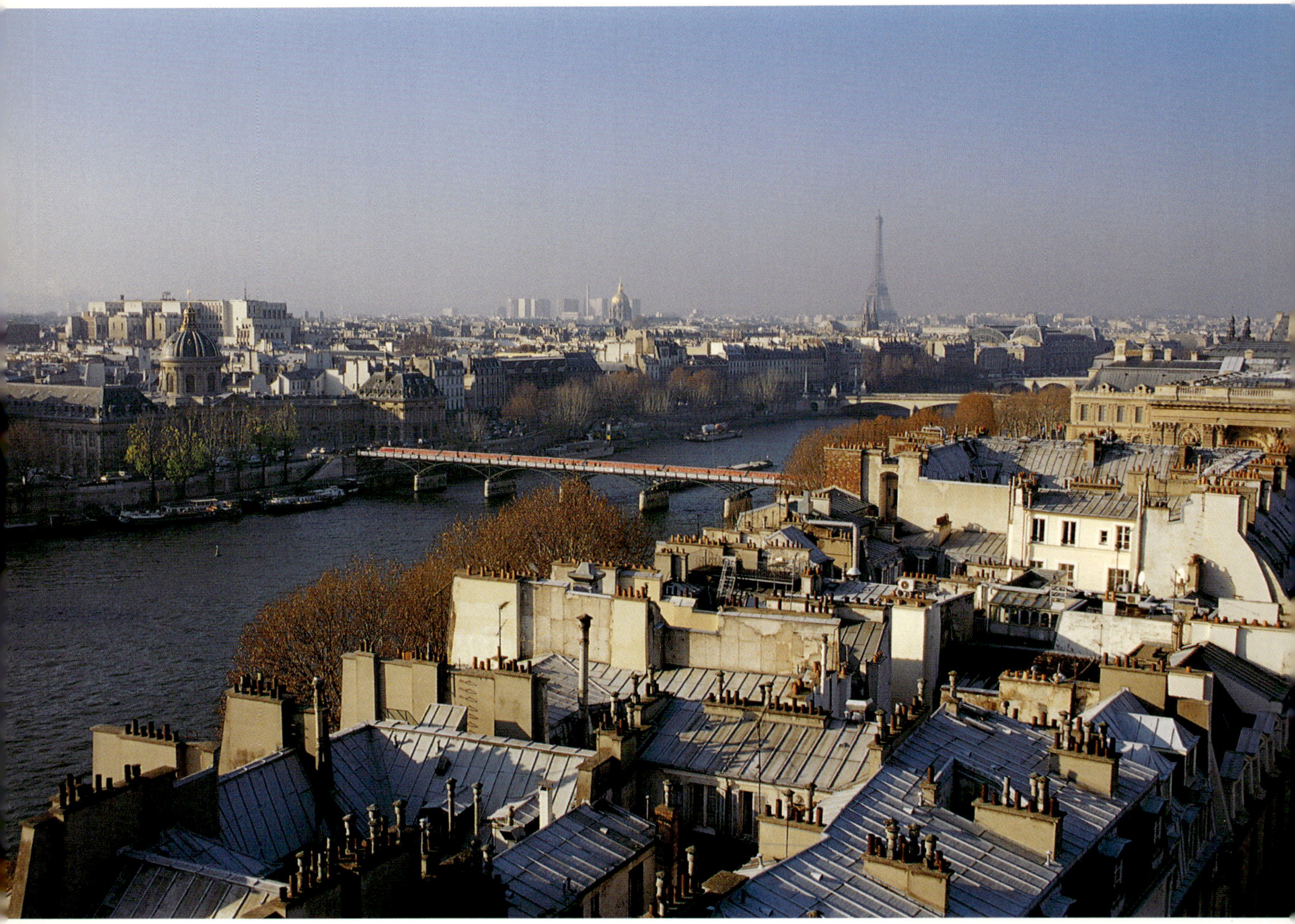

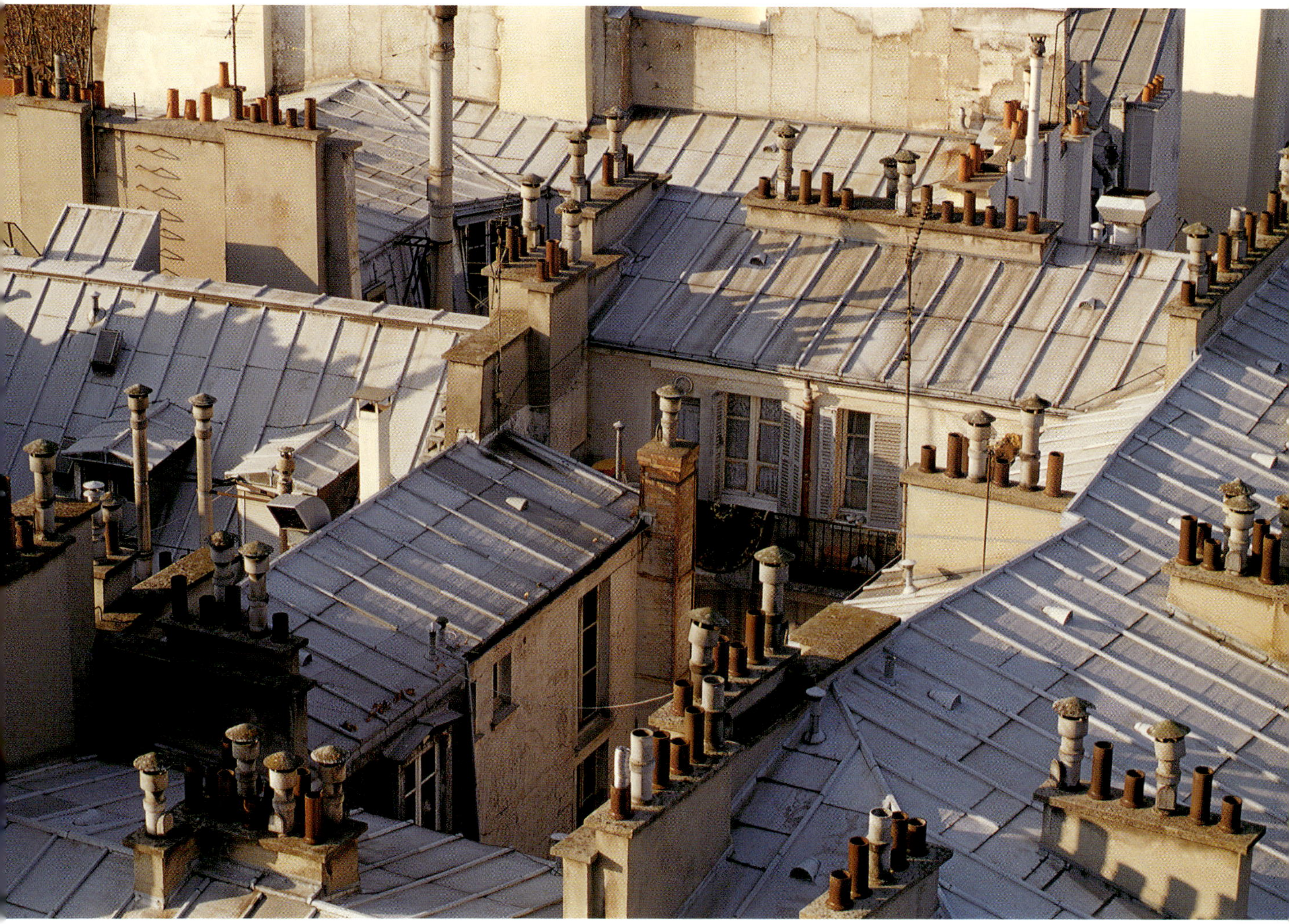

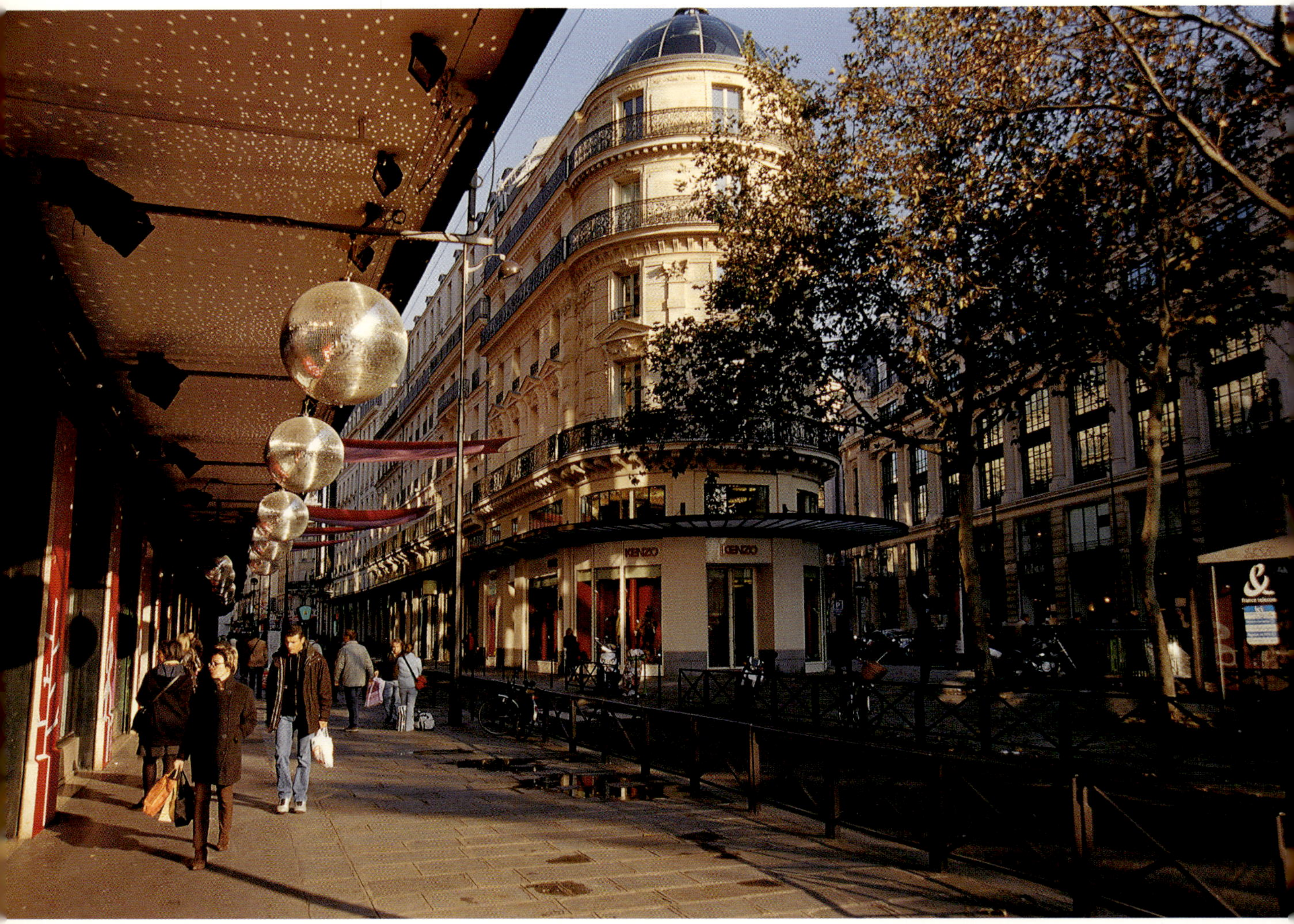
KENZO
KENZO

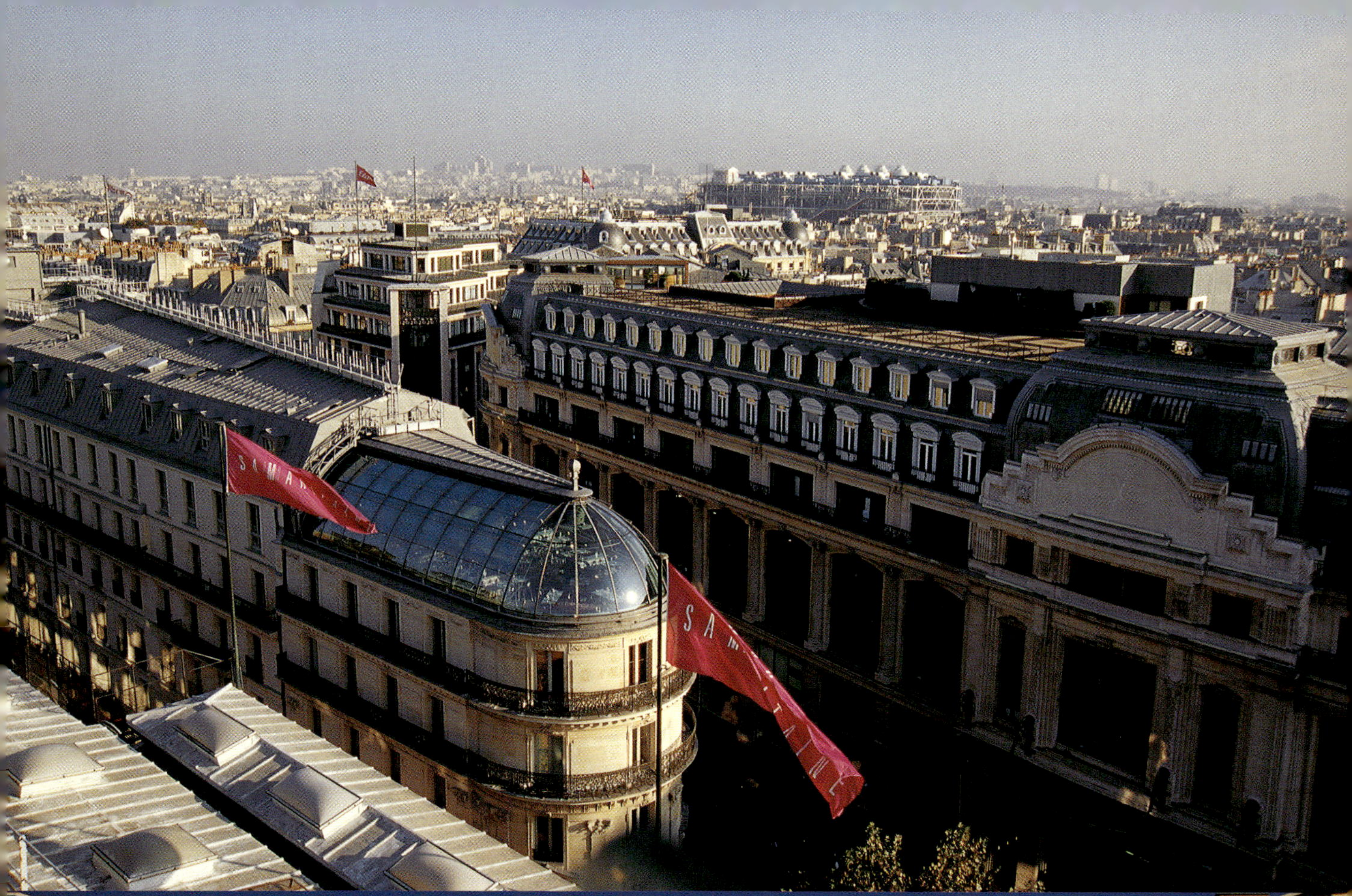

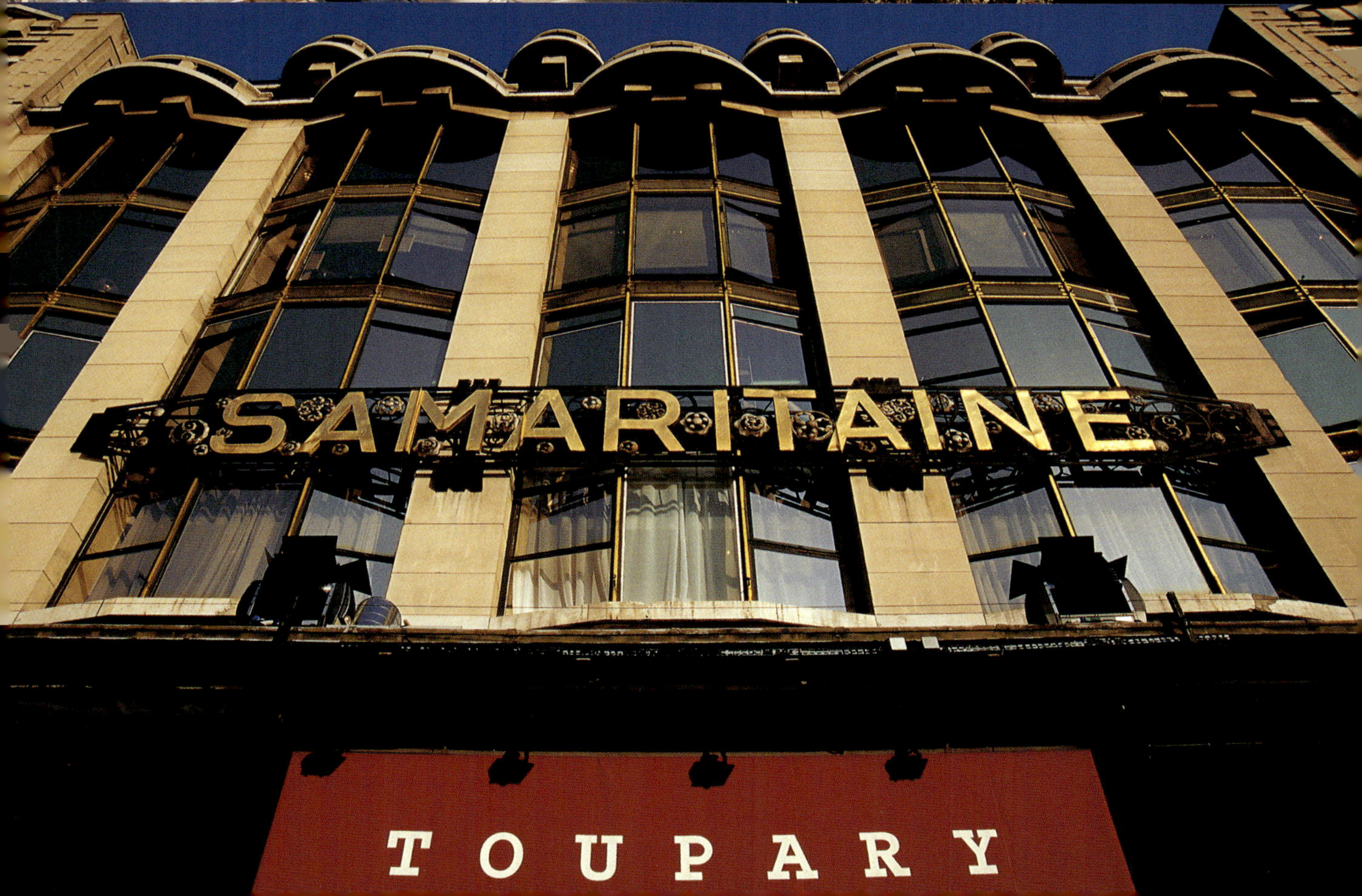
SAMARITAINE
TOUPARY

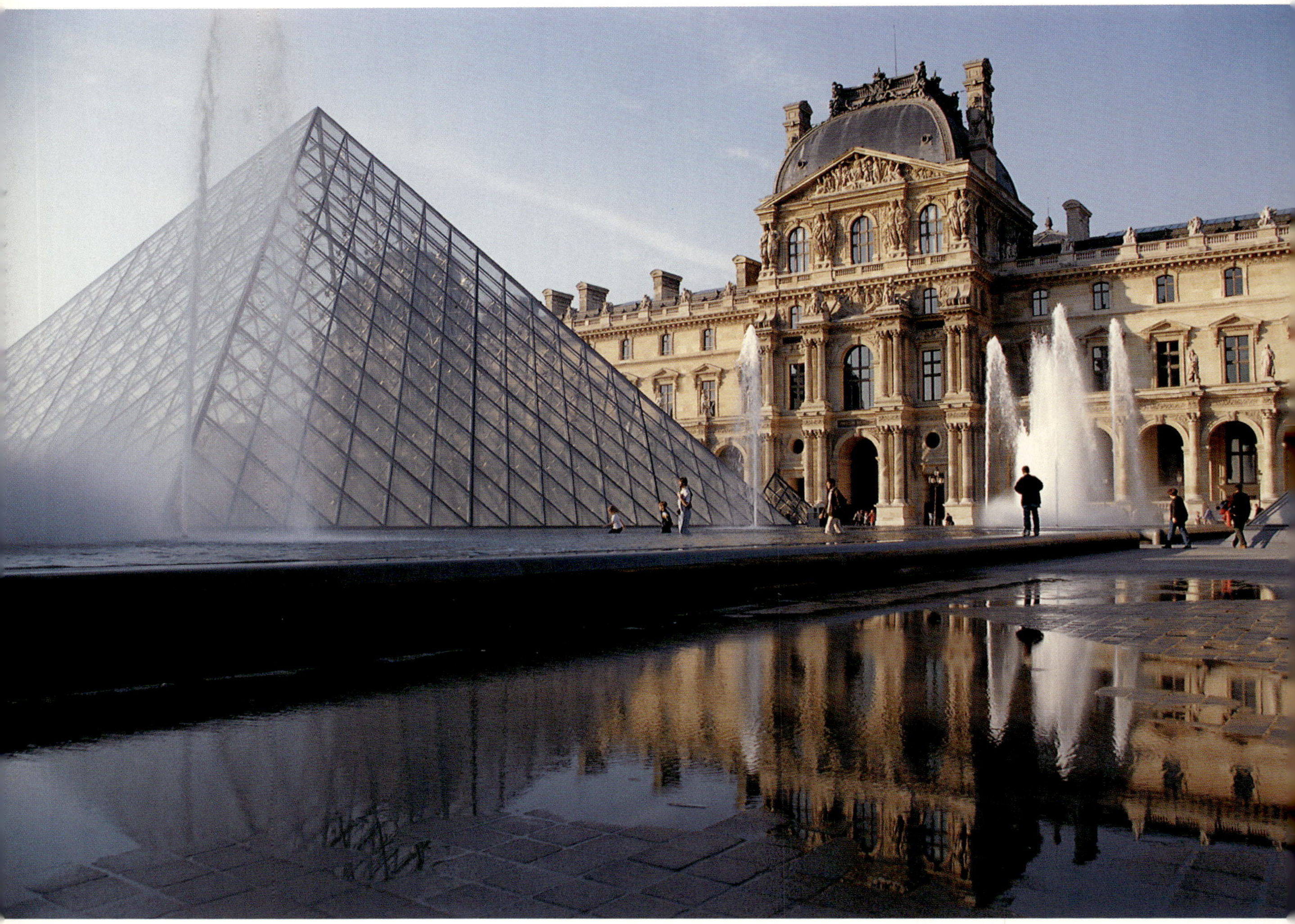

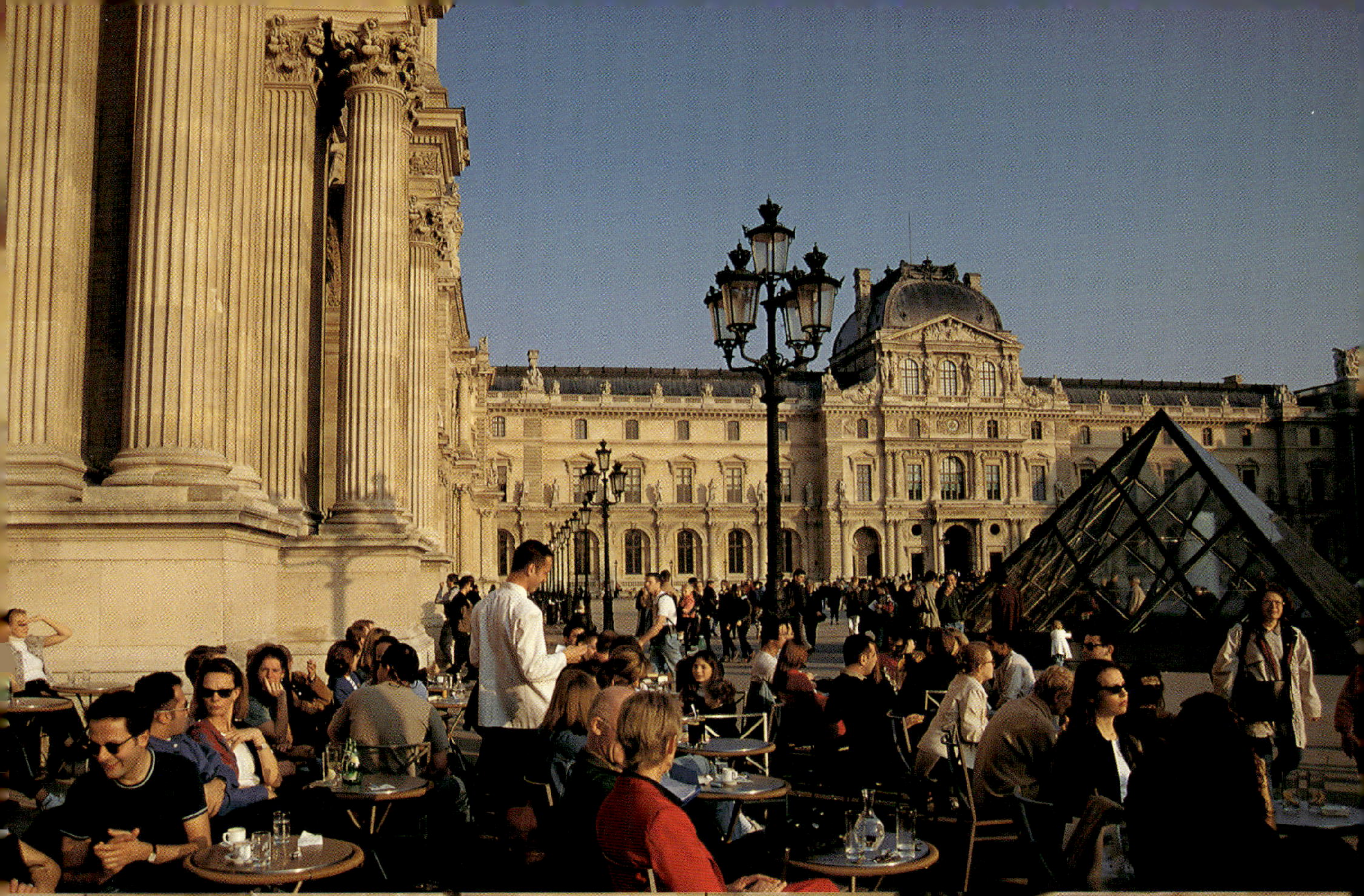
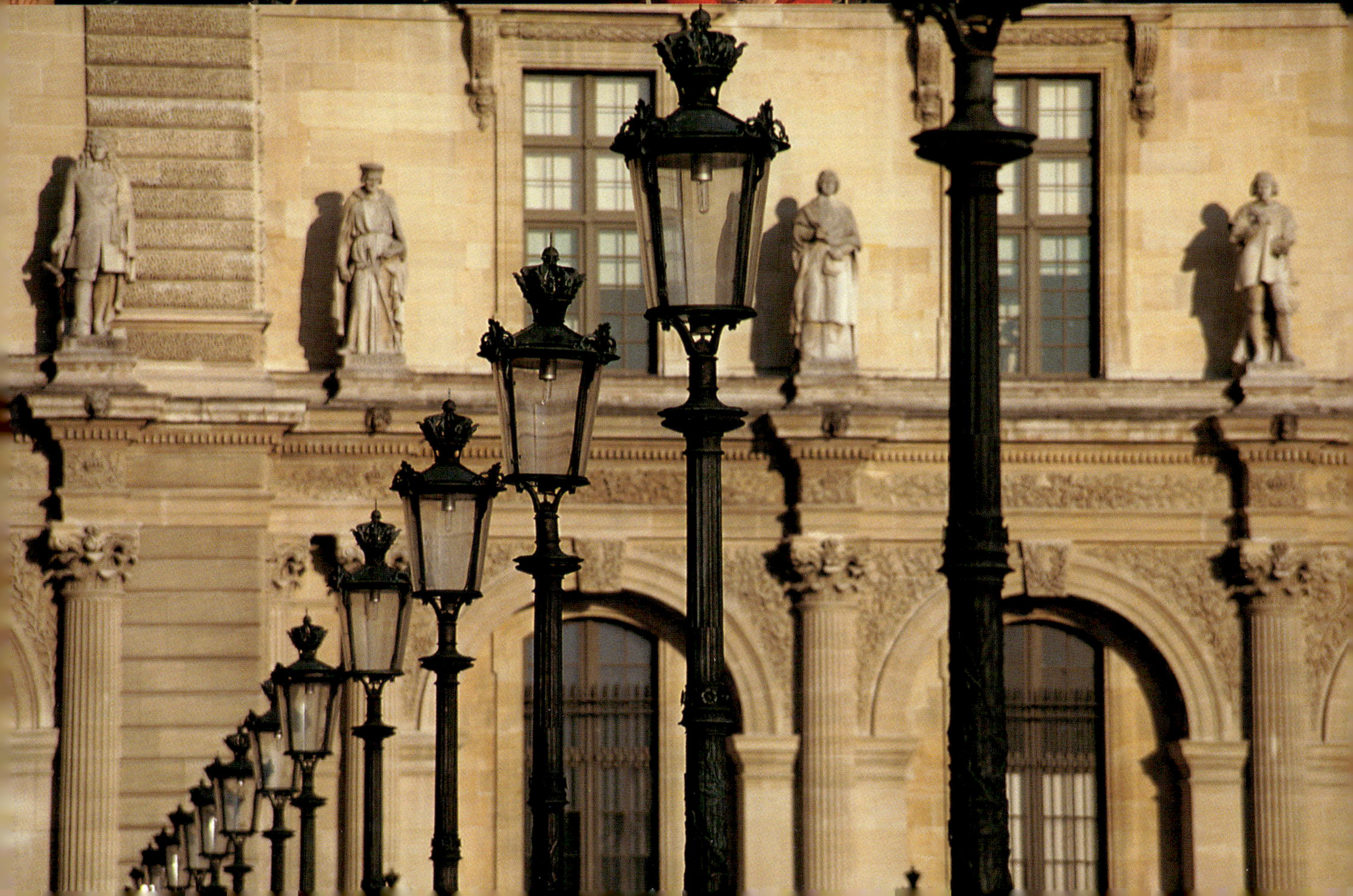

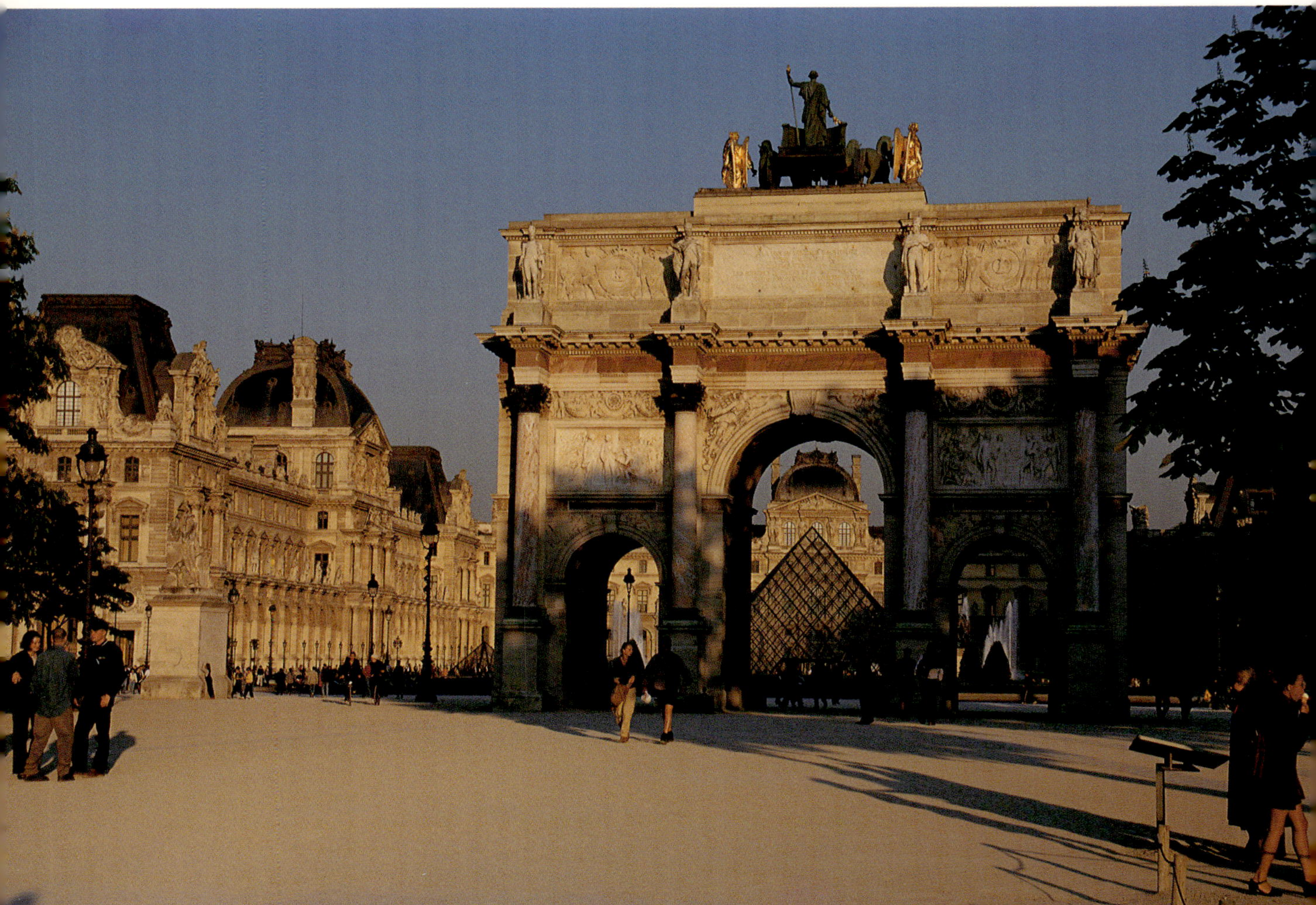

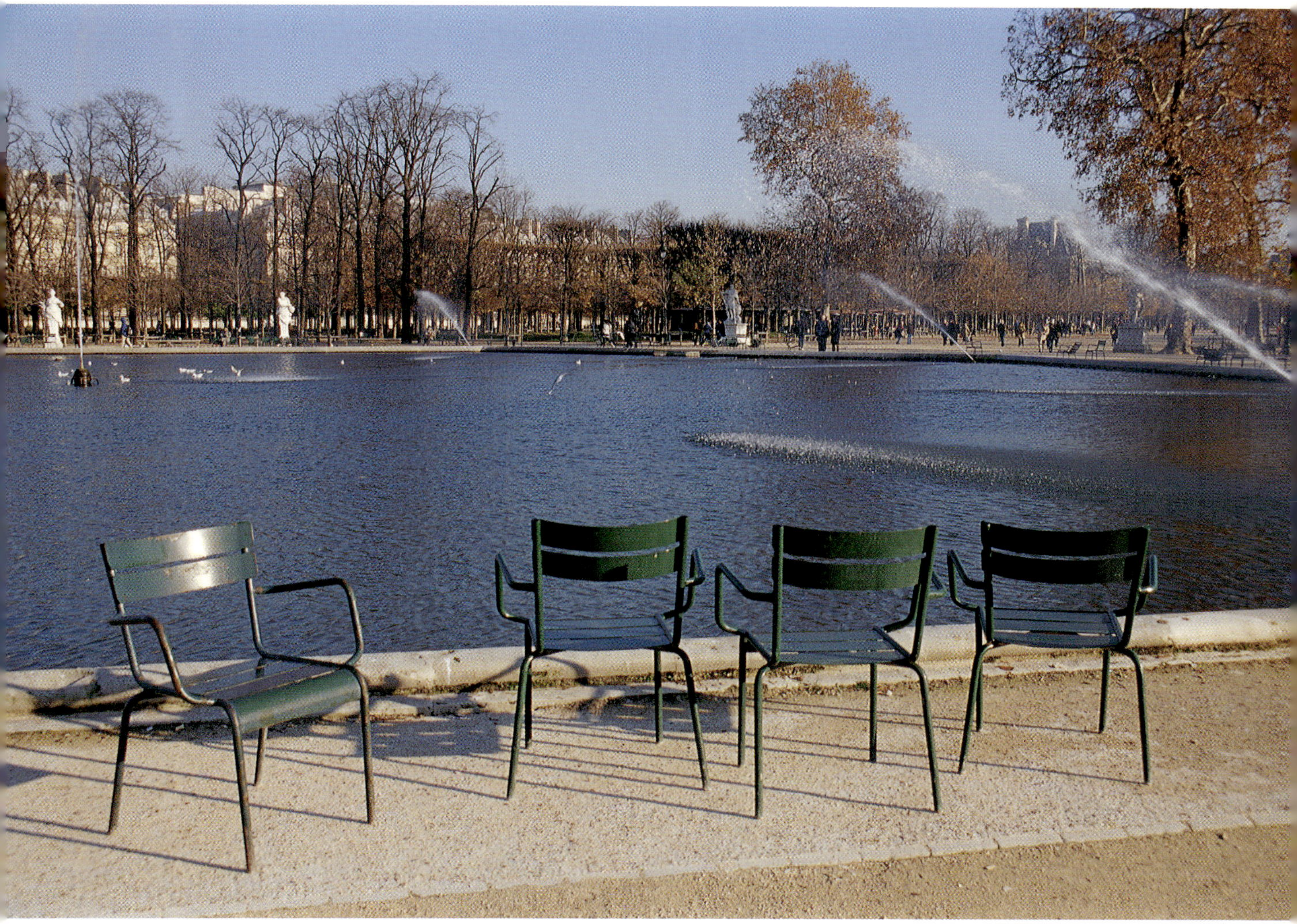

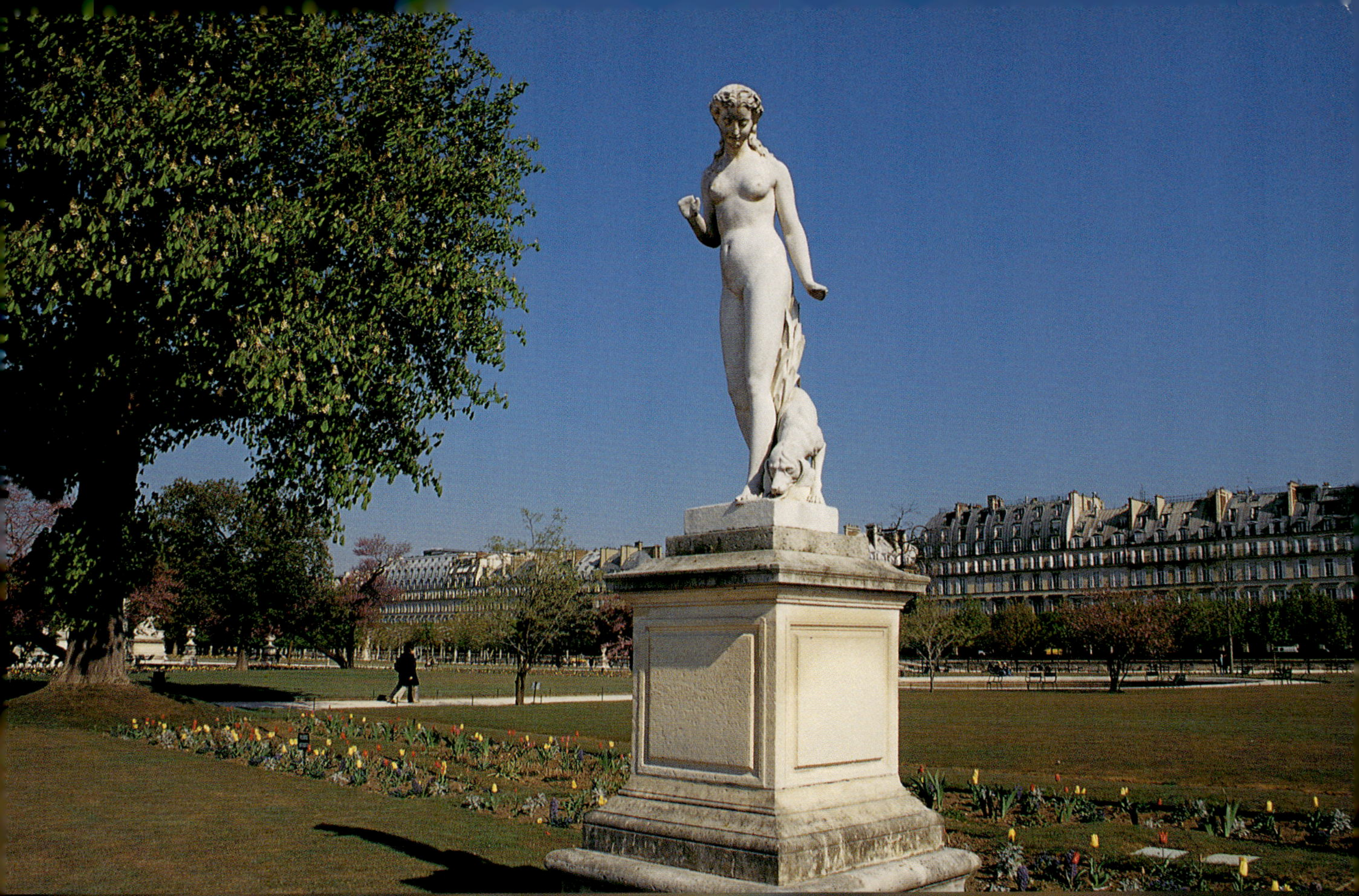

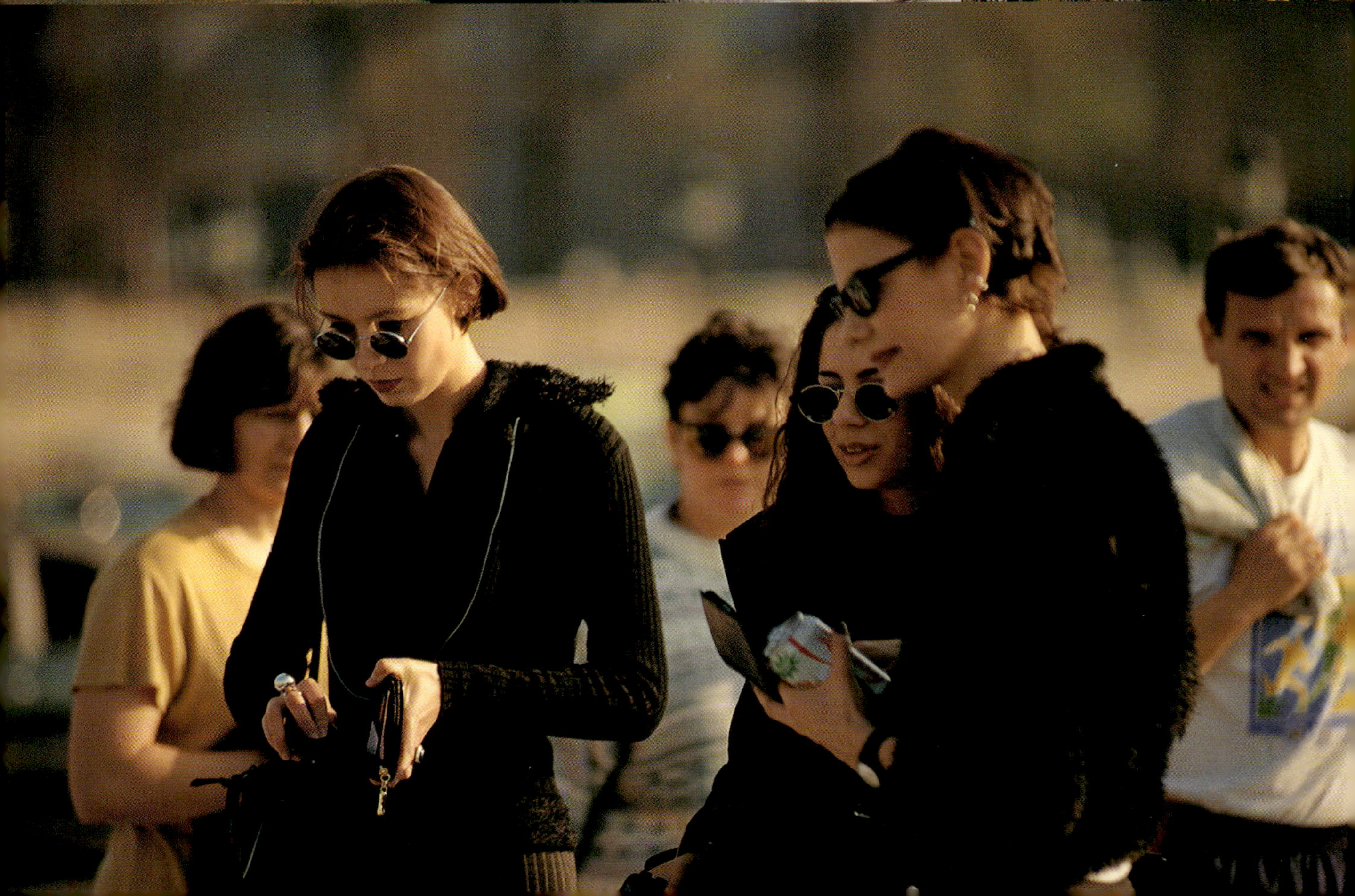

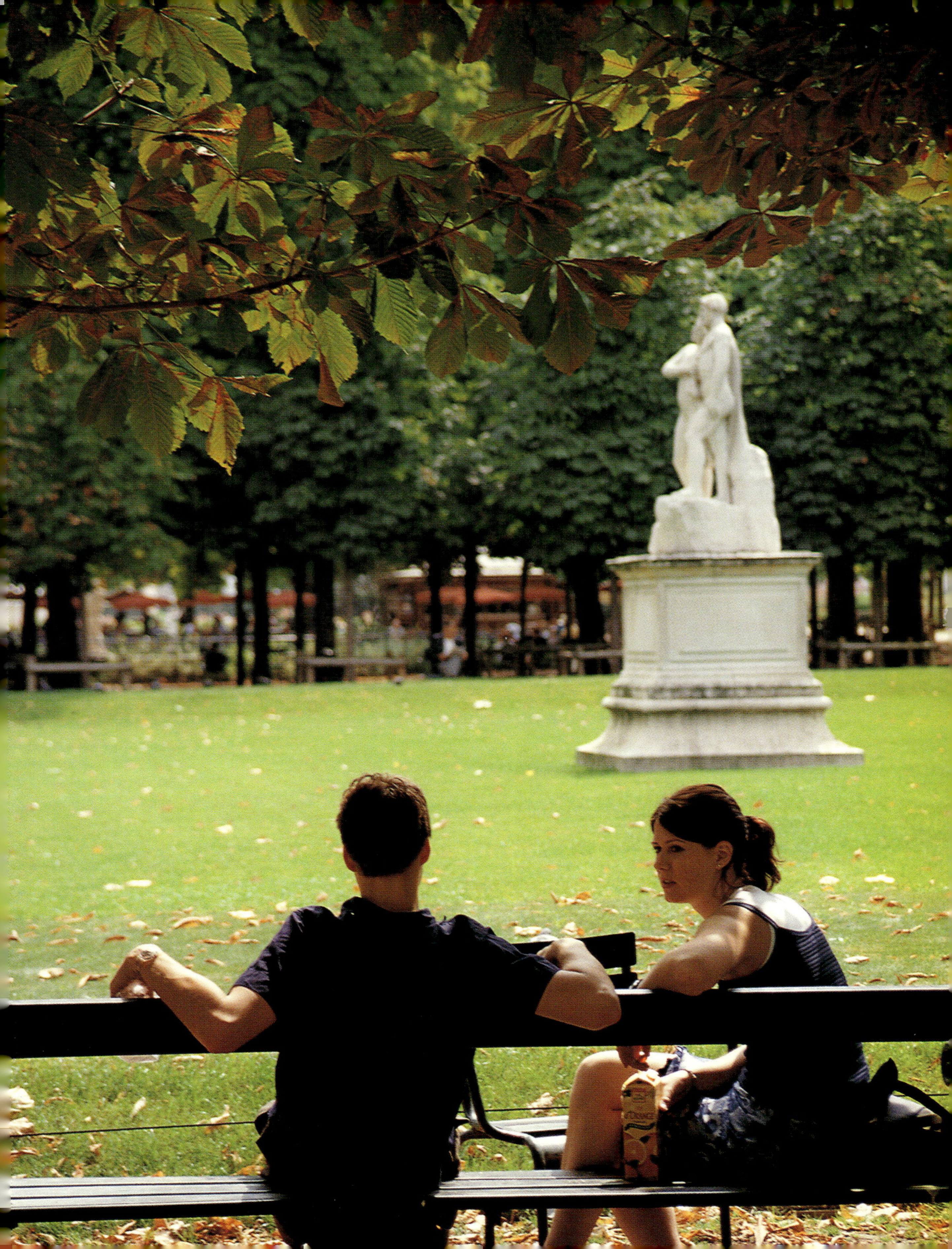

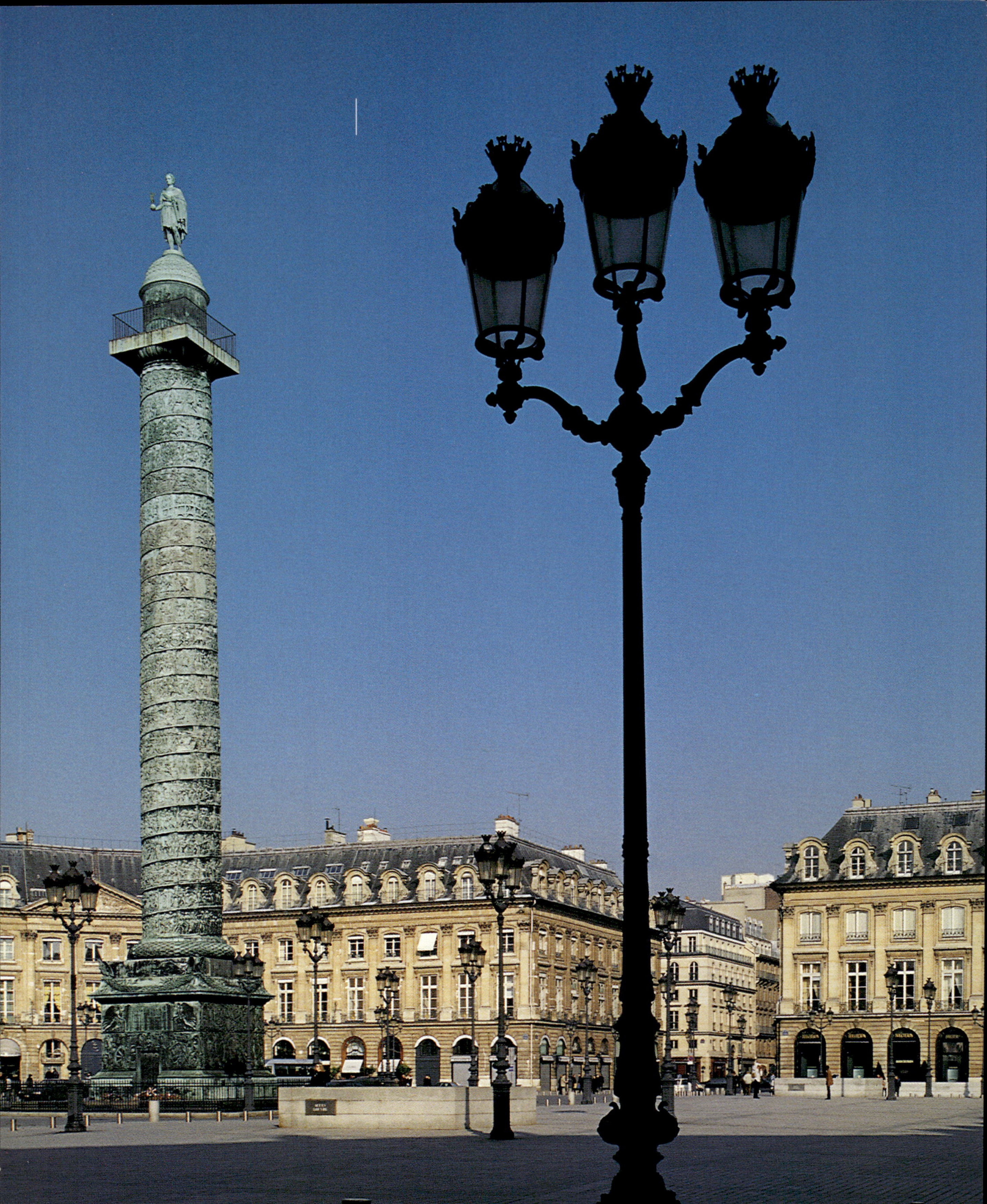

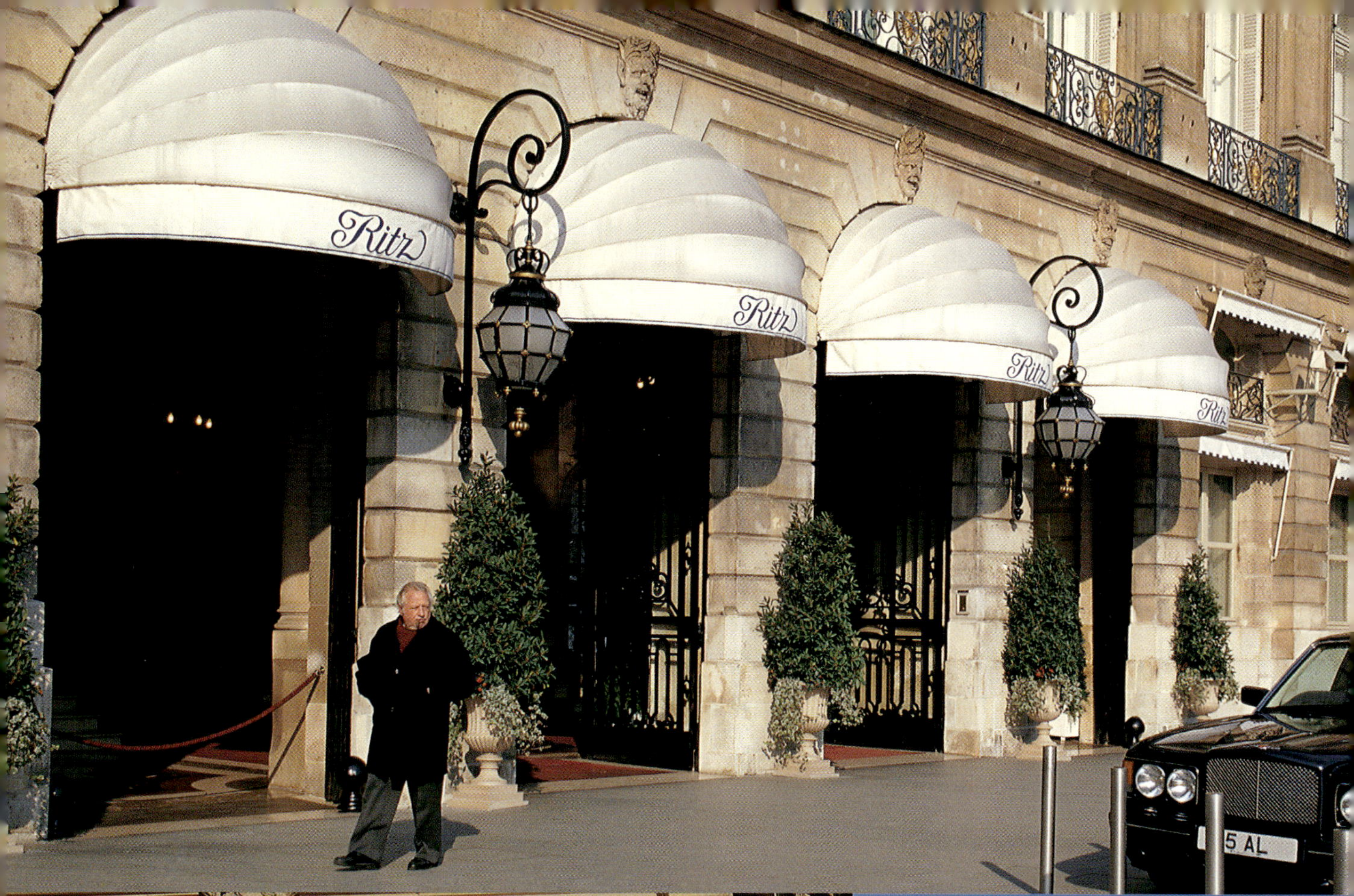
Ritz
Ritz
Ritz
Ritz

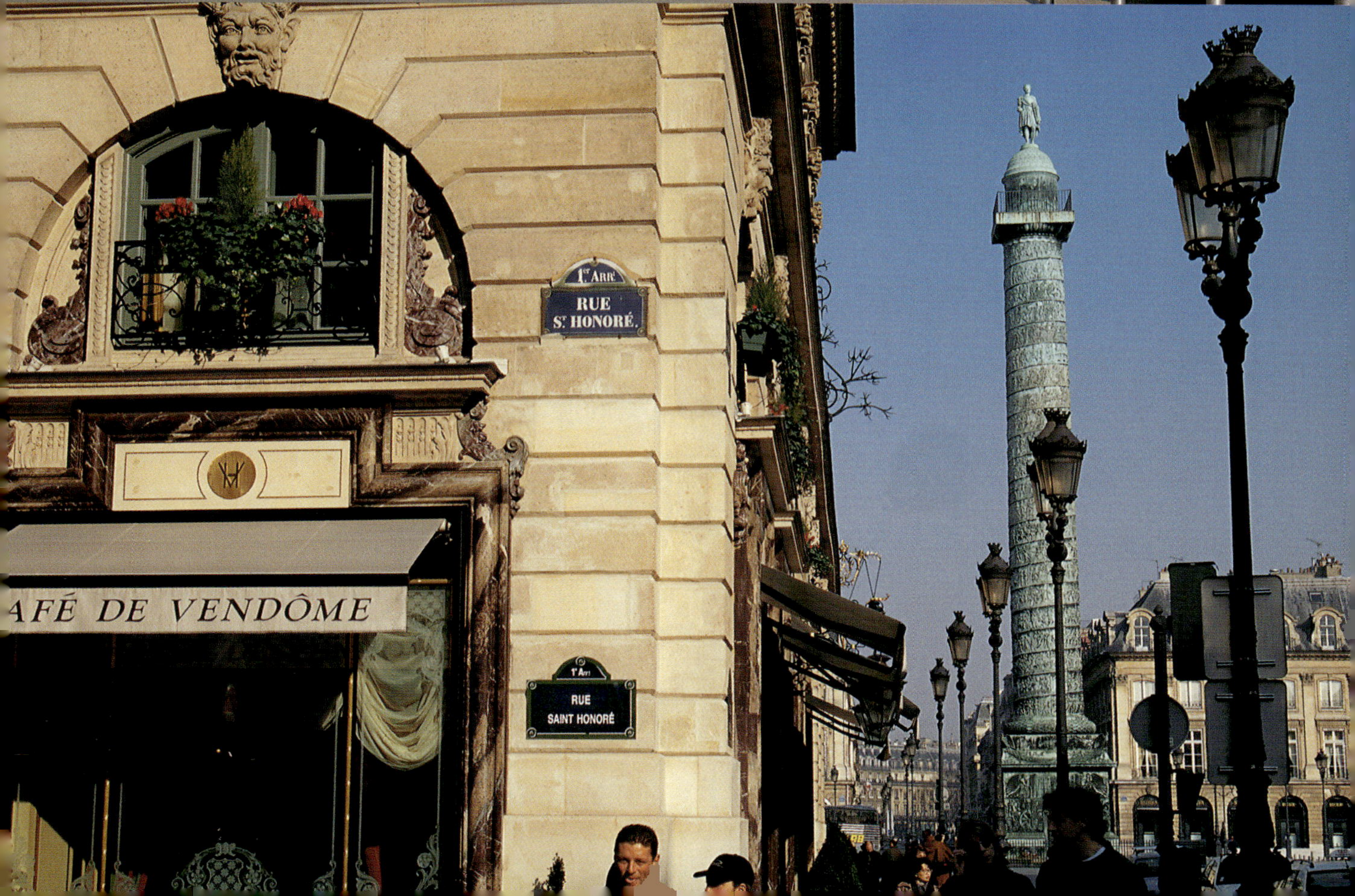
RUE
ST HONORÉ
AFÉ DE VENDÔME
RUE
SAINT HONORÉ

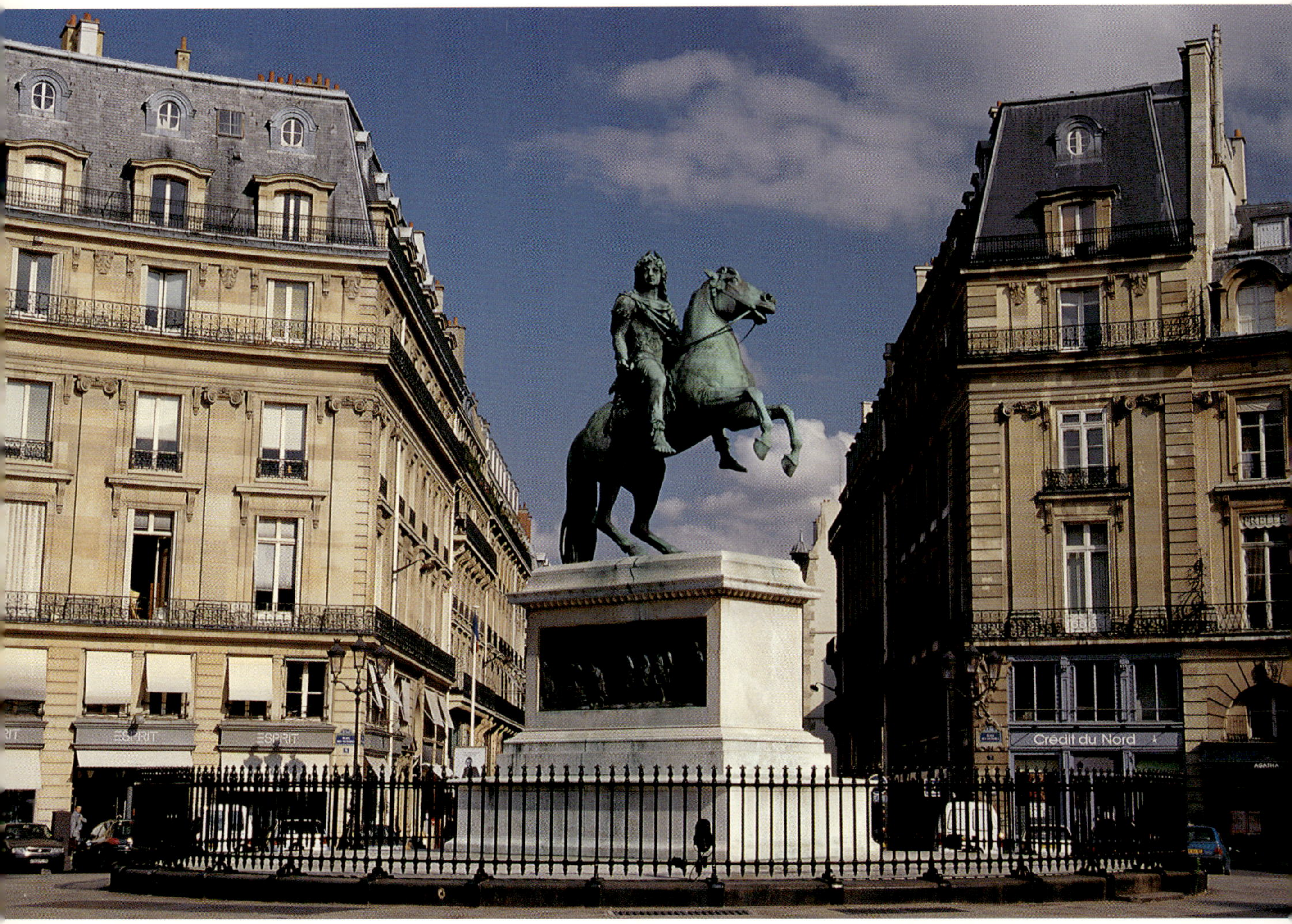
ESPRIT
ESPRIT
Crédit du Nord

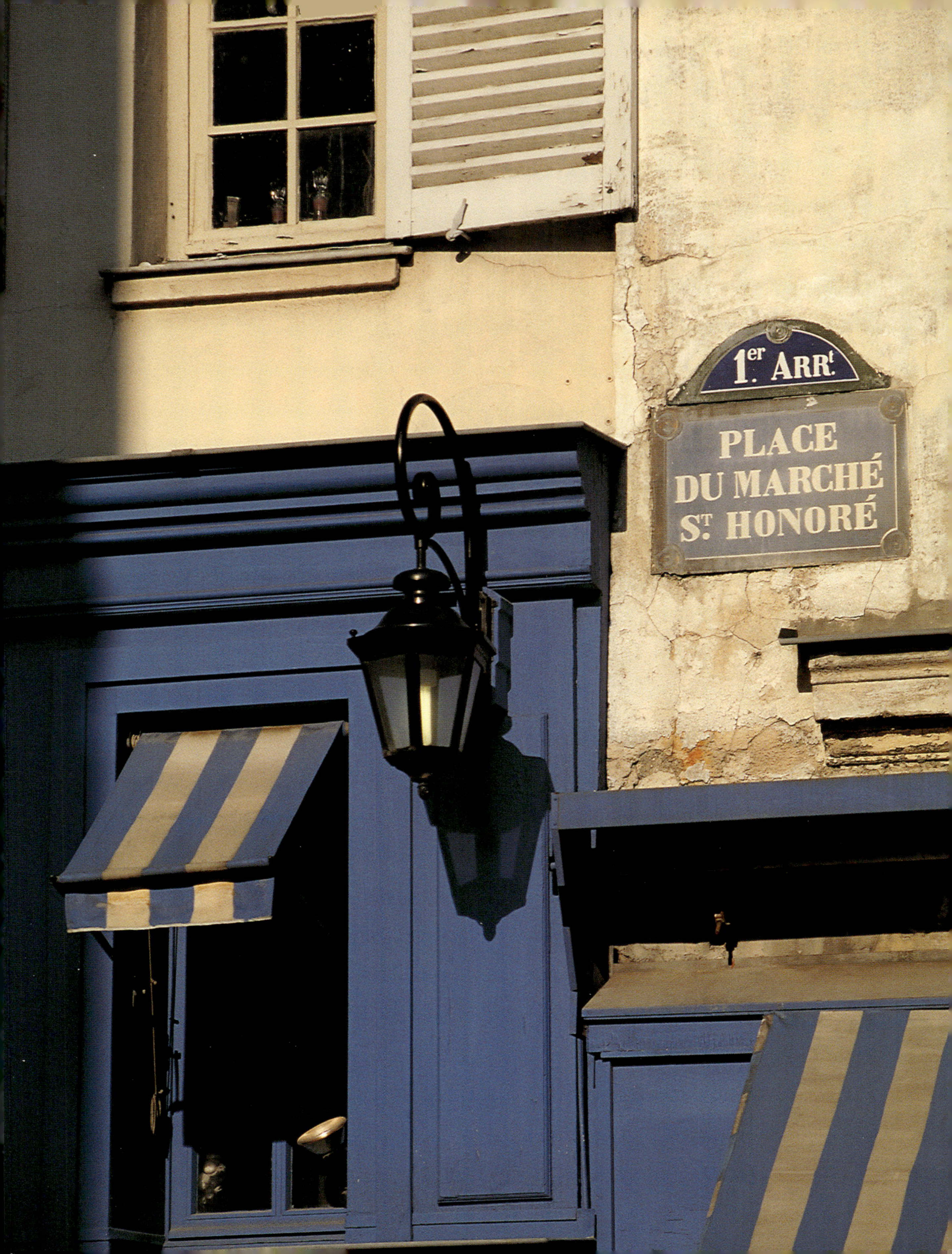
1er ARRt
PLACE
DU MARCHÉ
St HONORÉ

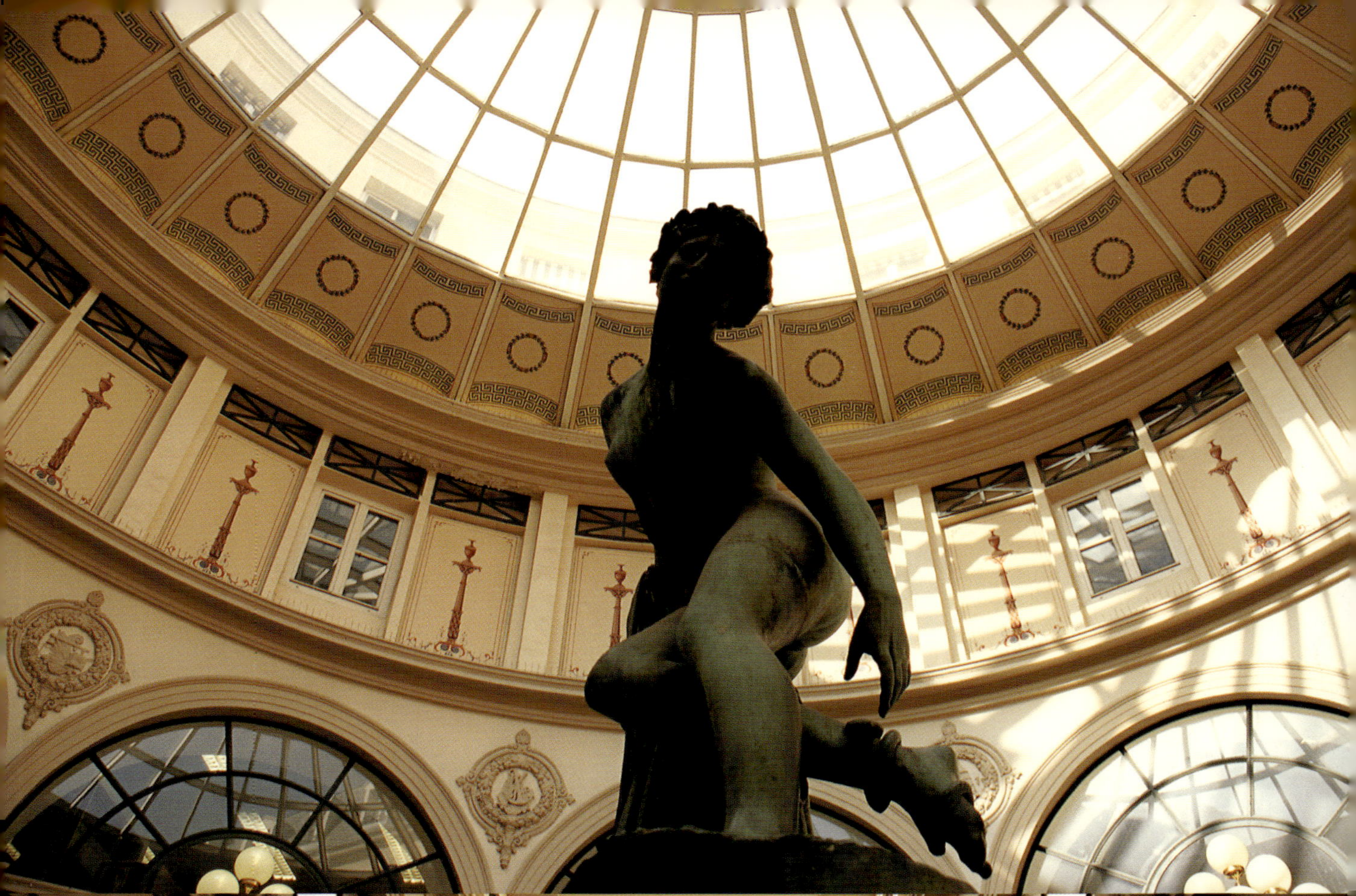
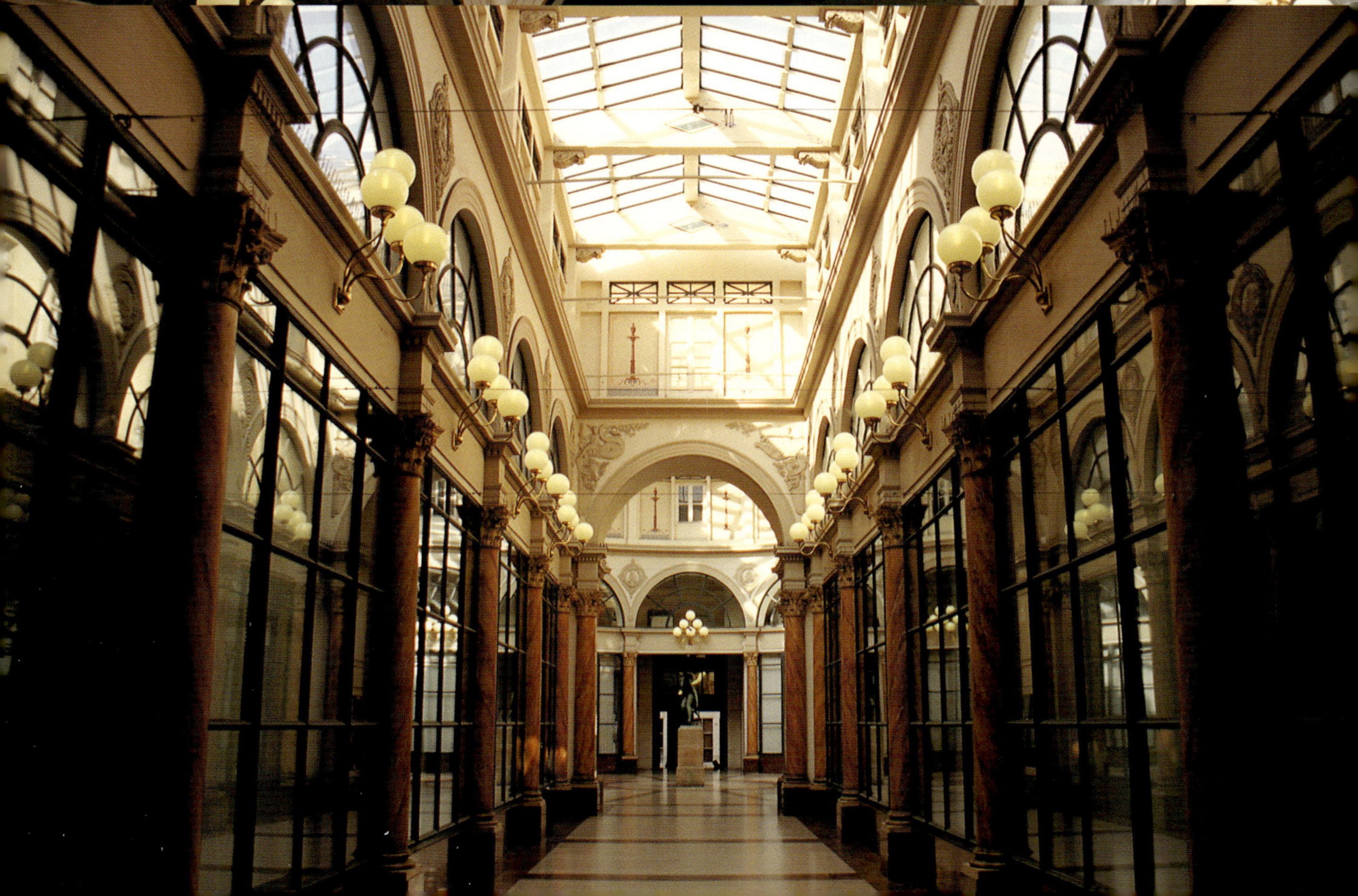

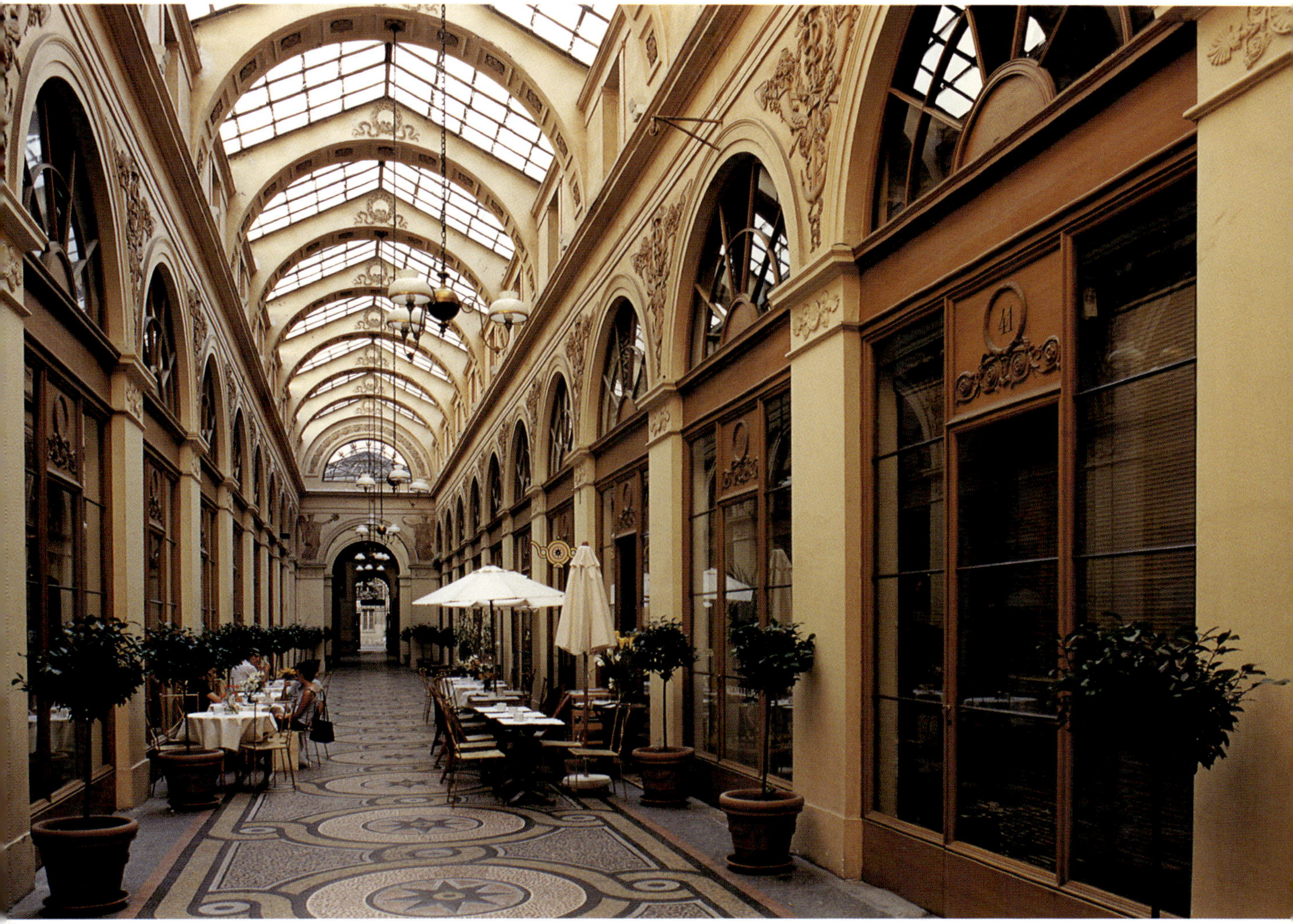
41

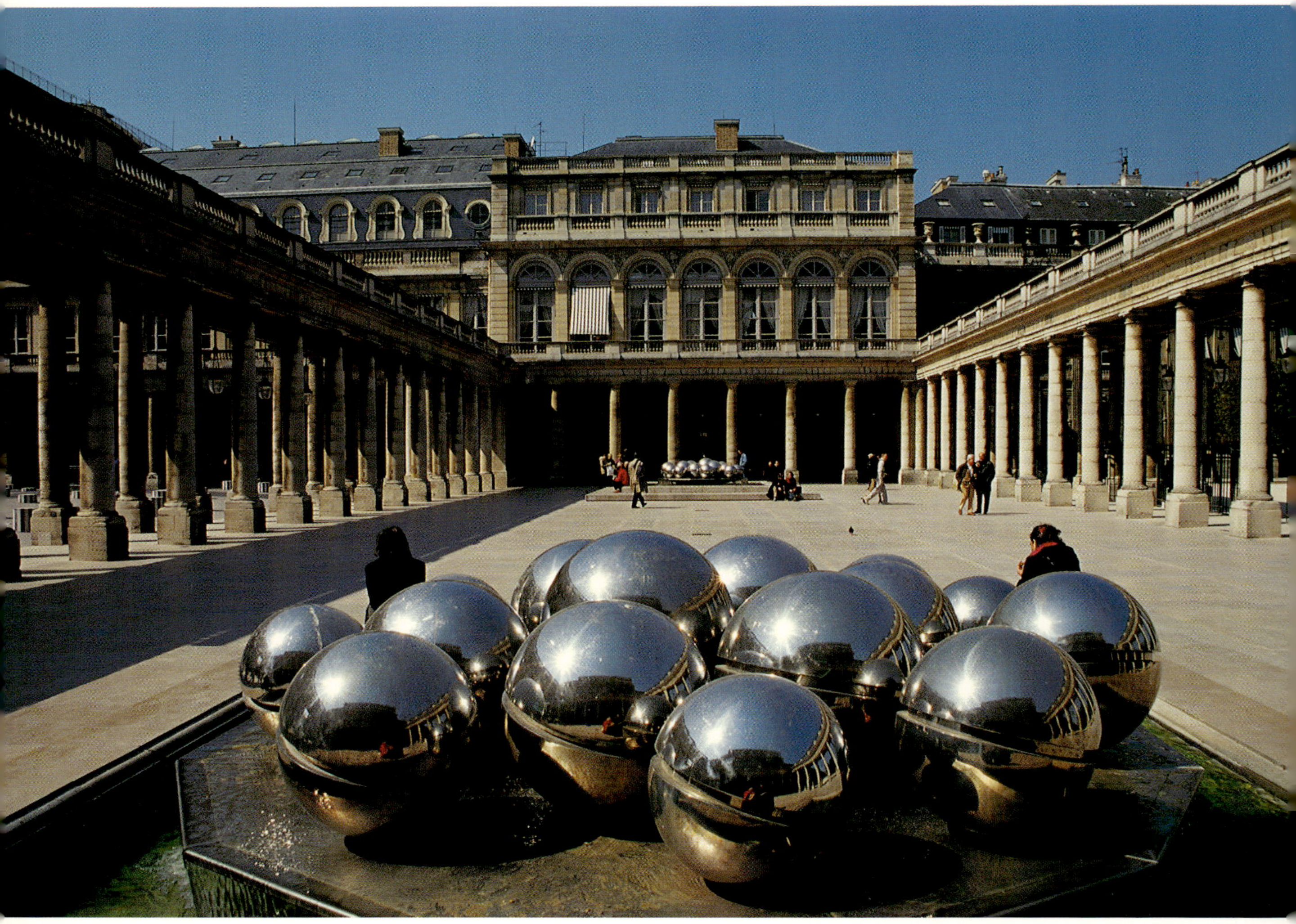

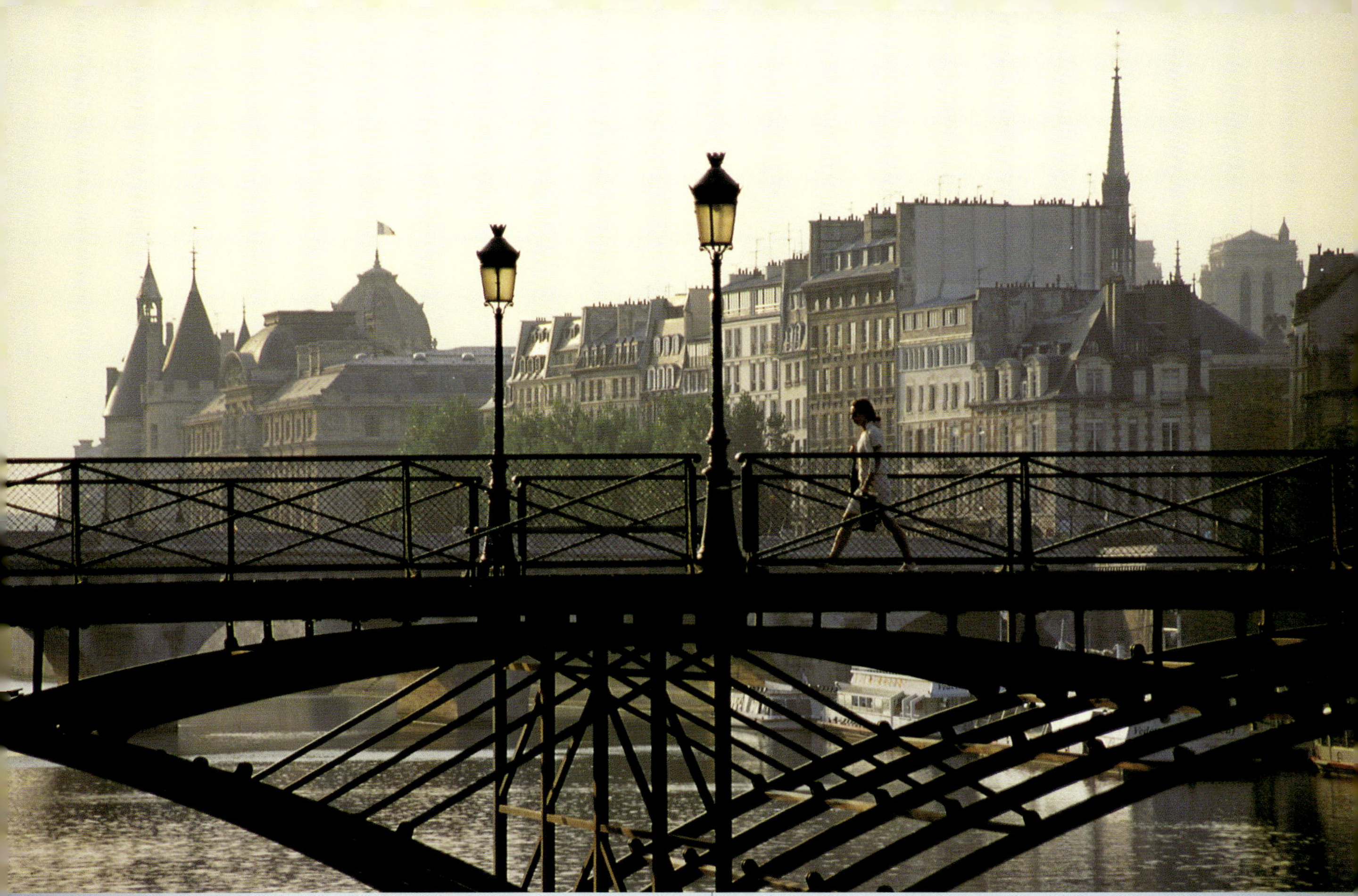

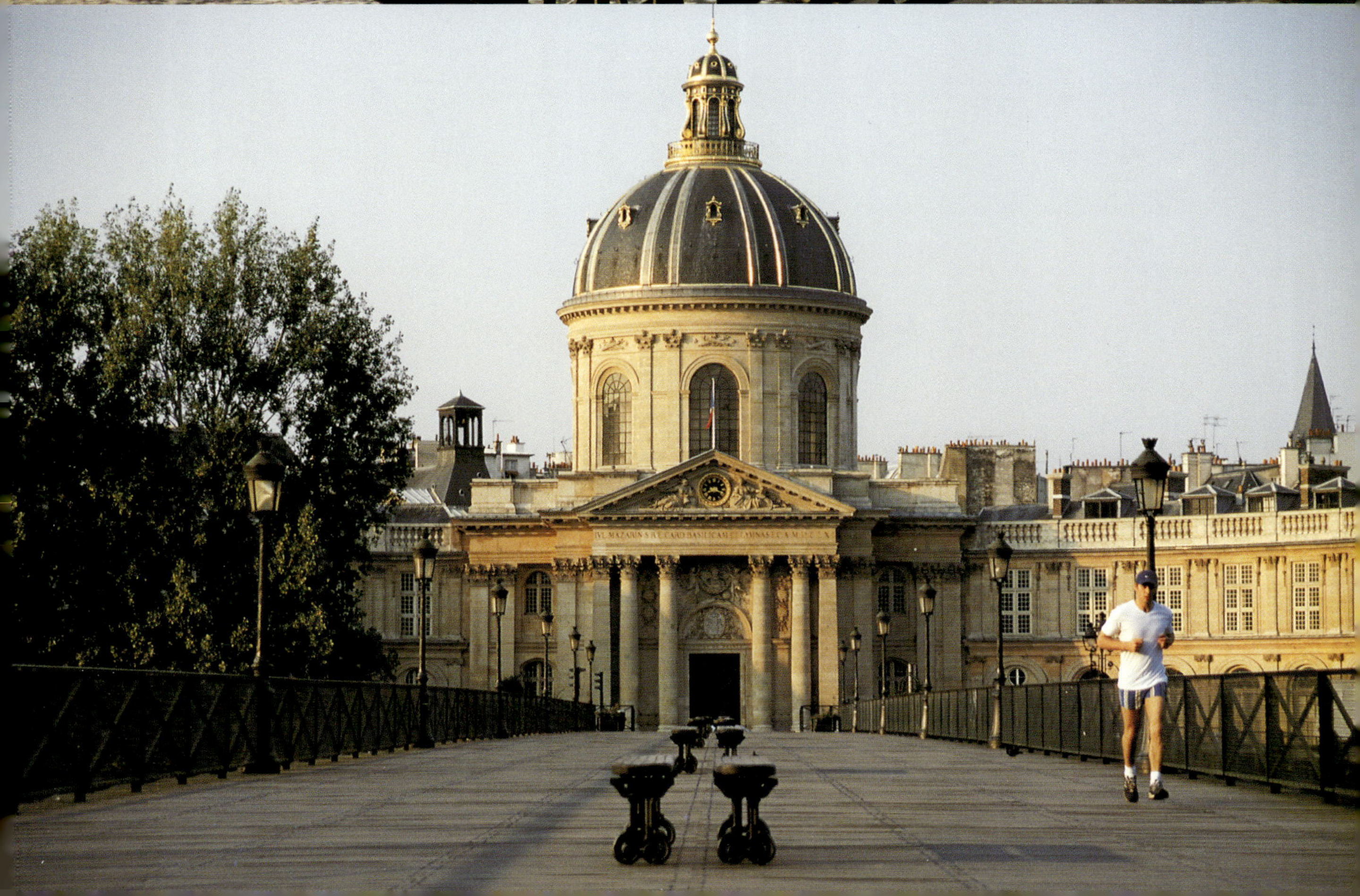

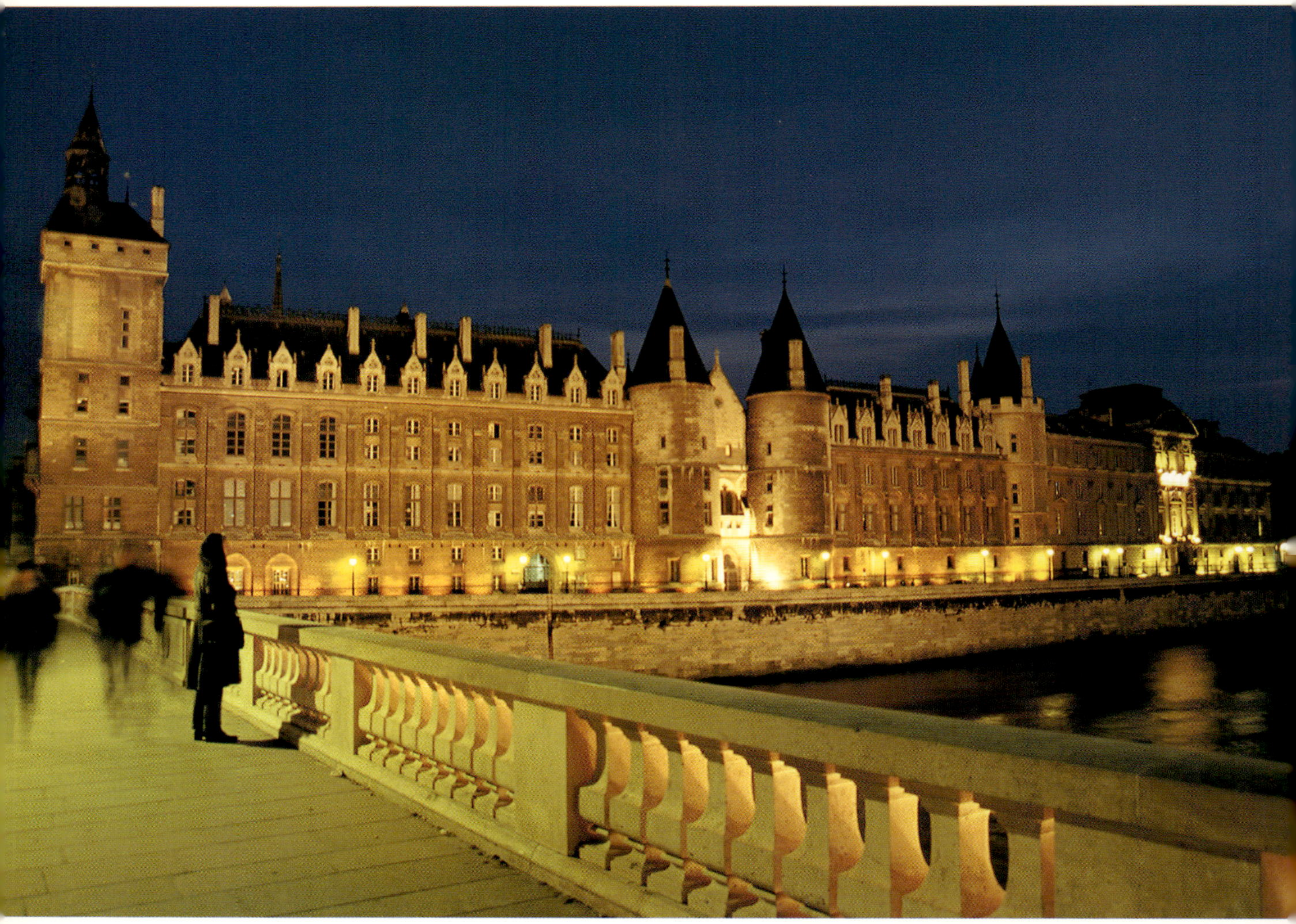

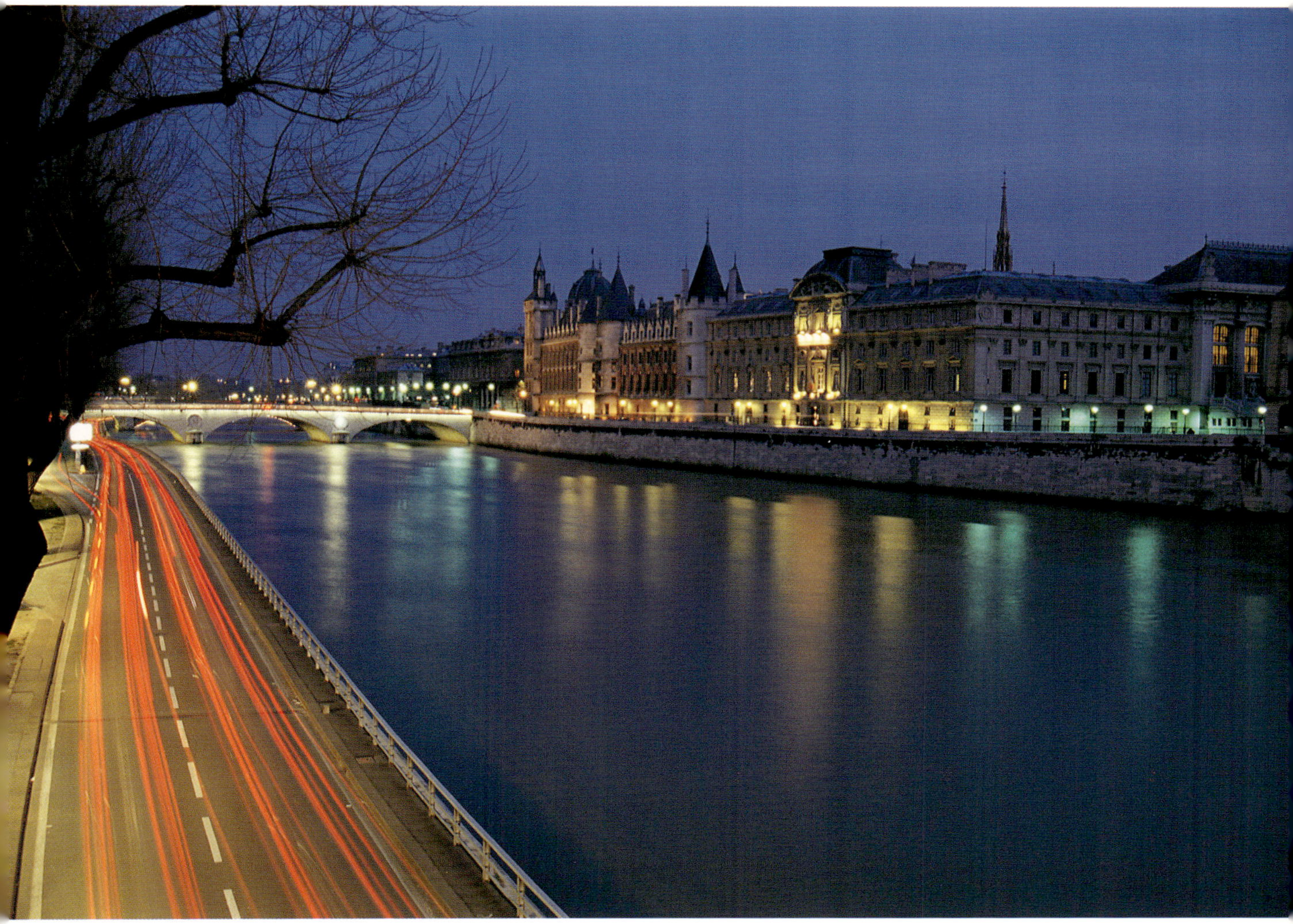

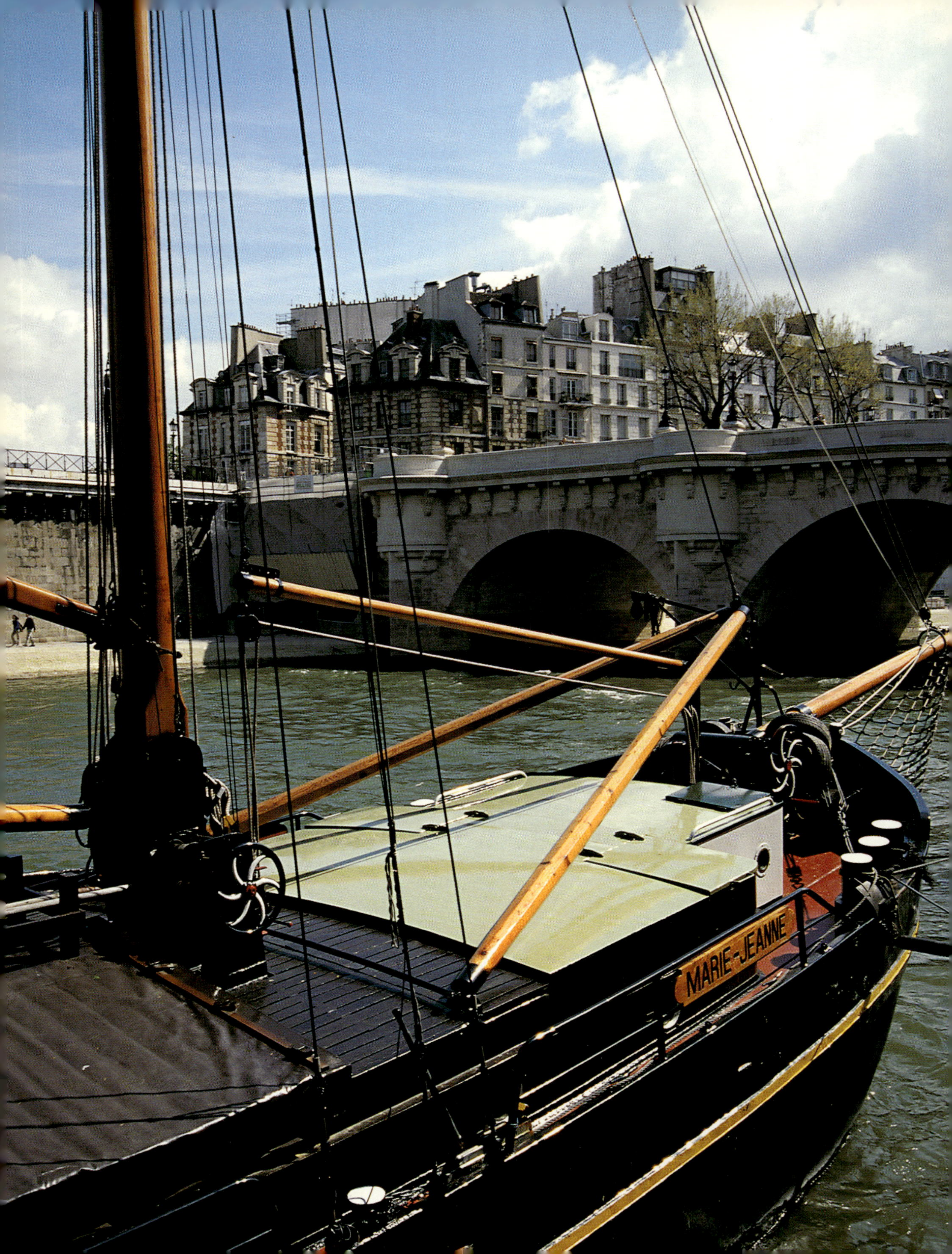
MARIE-JEANNE

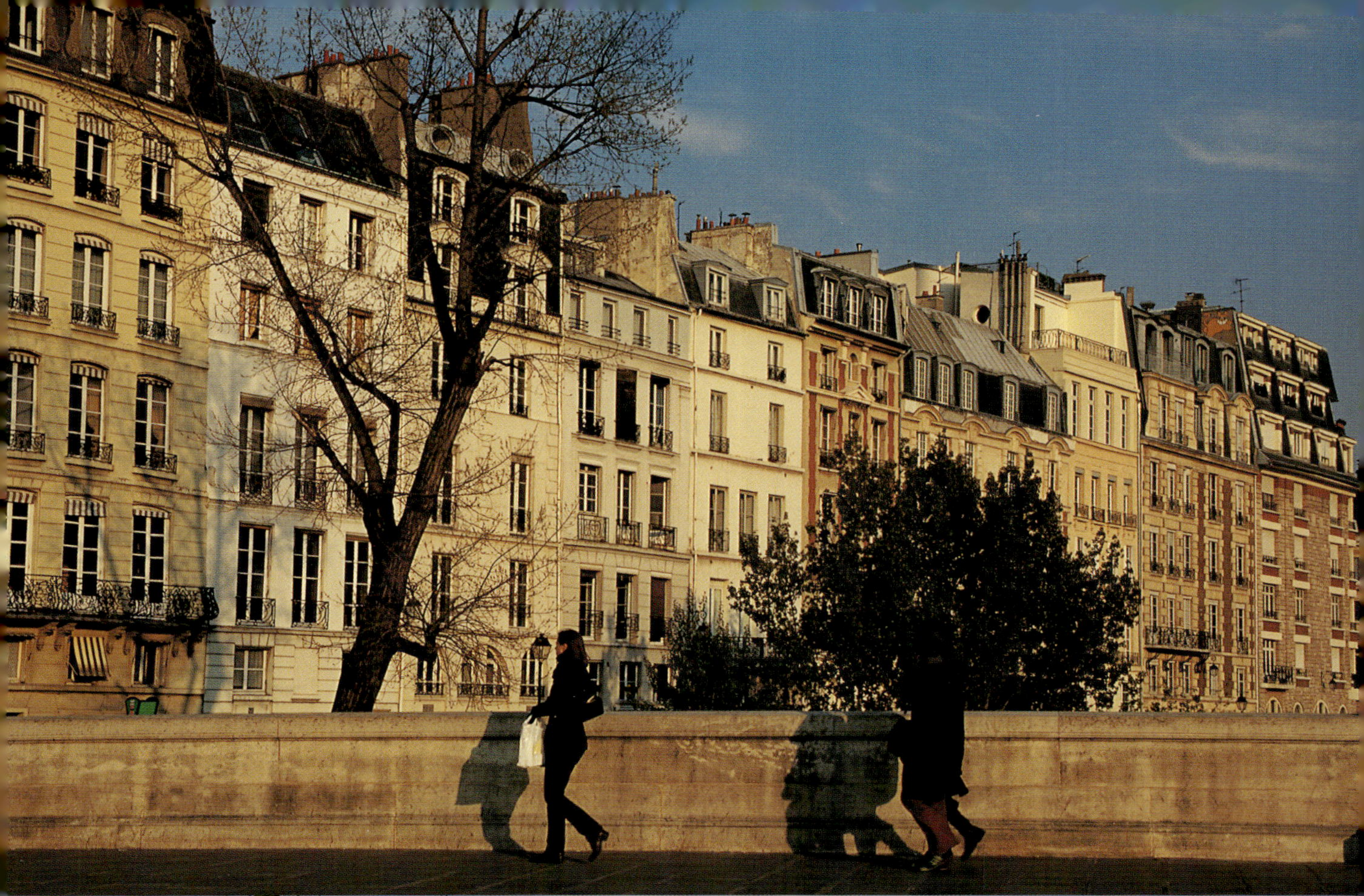

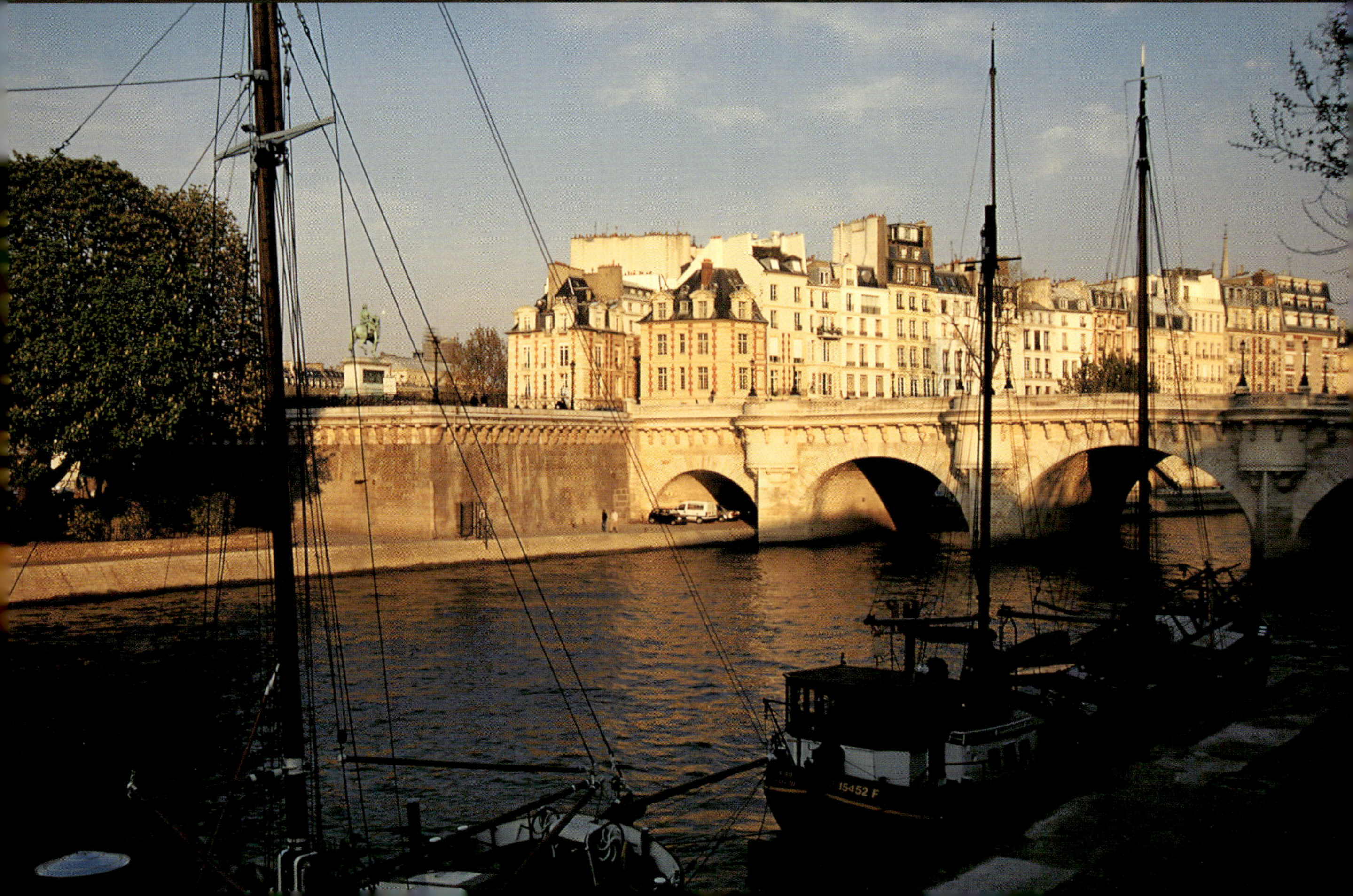

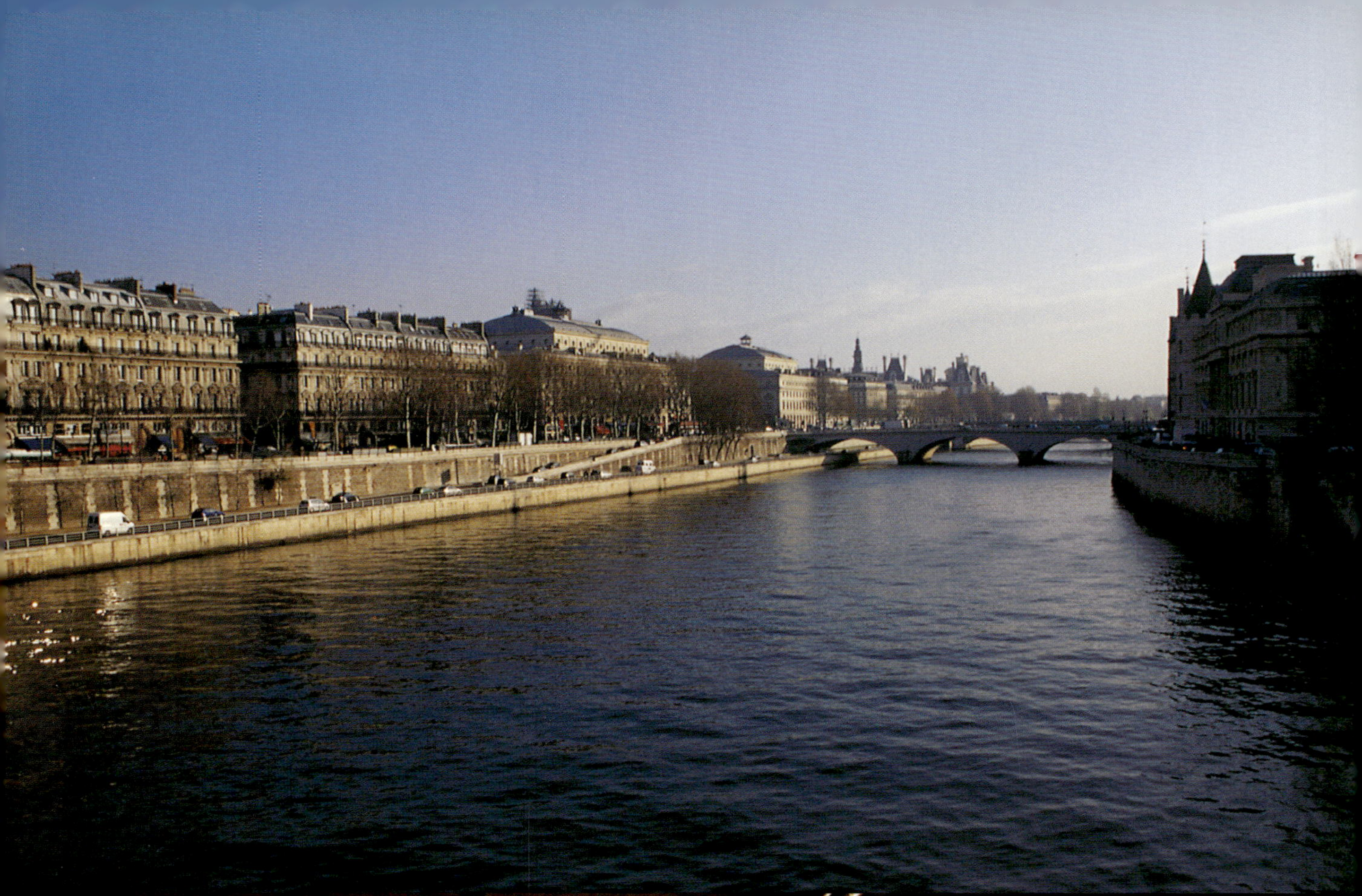

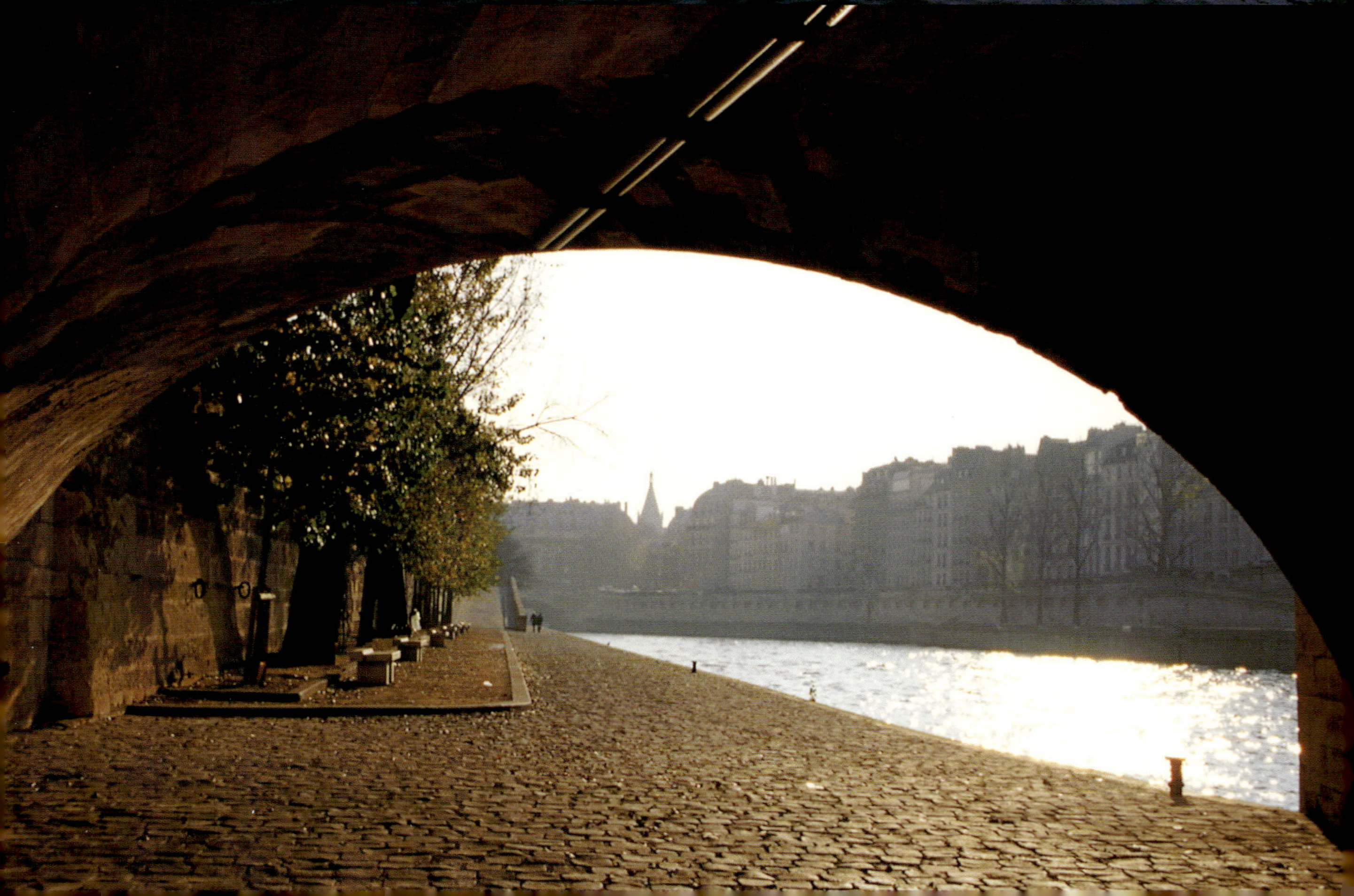

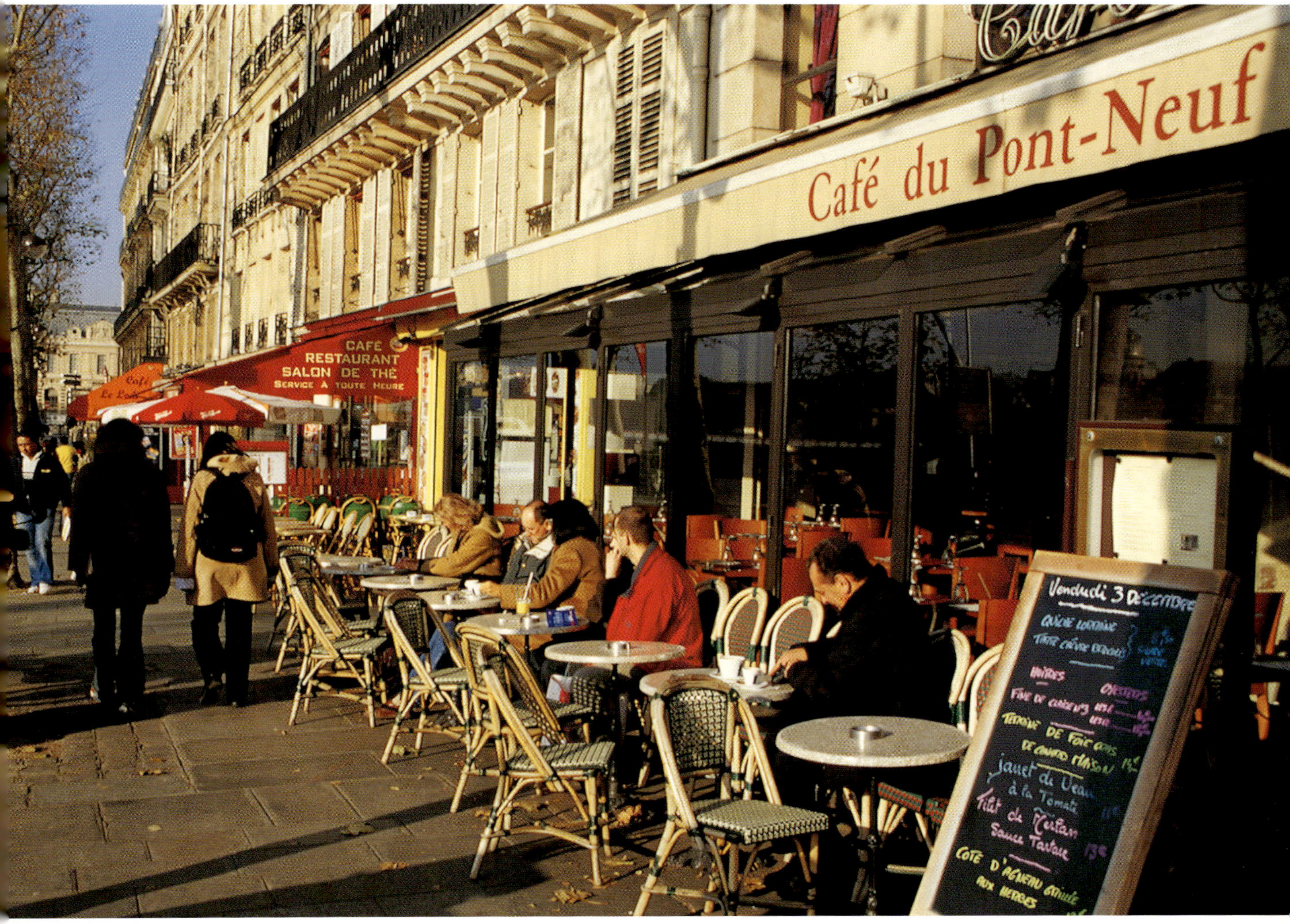
Café du Pont-Neuf
CAFÉ
RESTAURANT
SALON DE THÉ
SERVICE À TOUTE HEURE

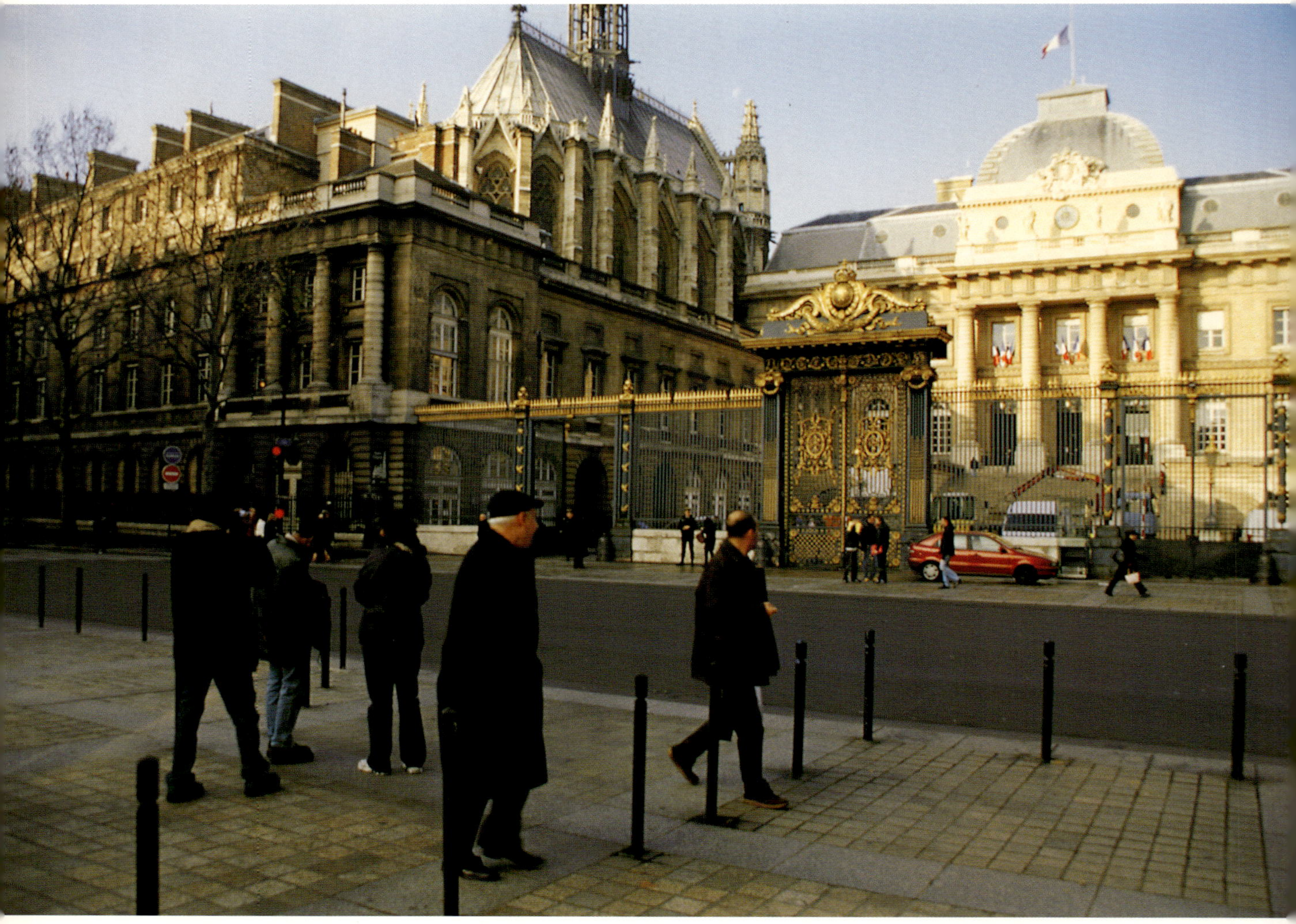

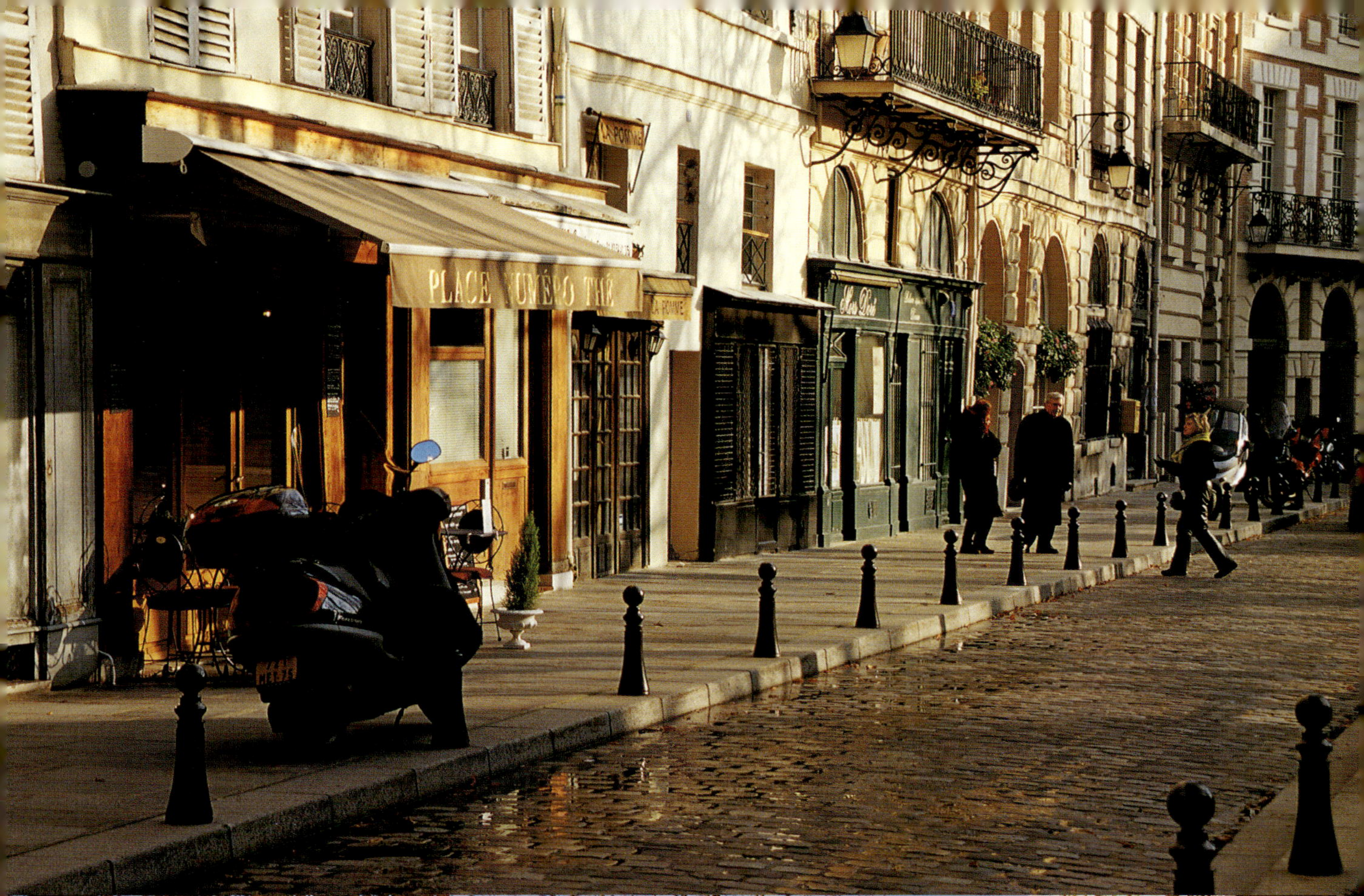
PLACE NUMÉRO THÉ

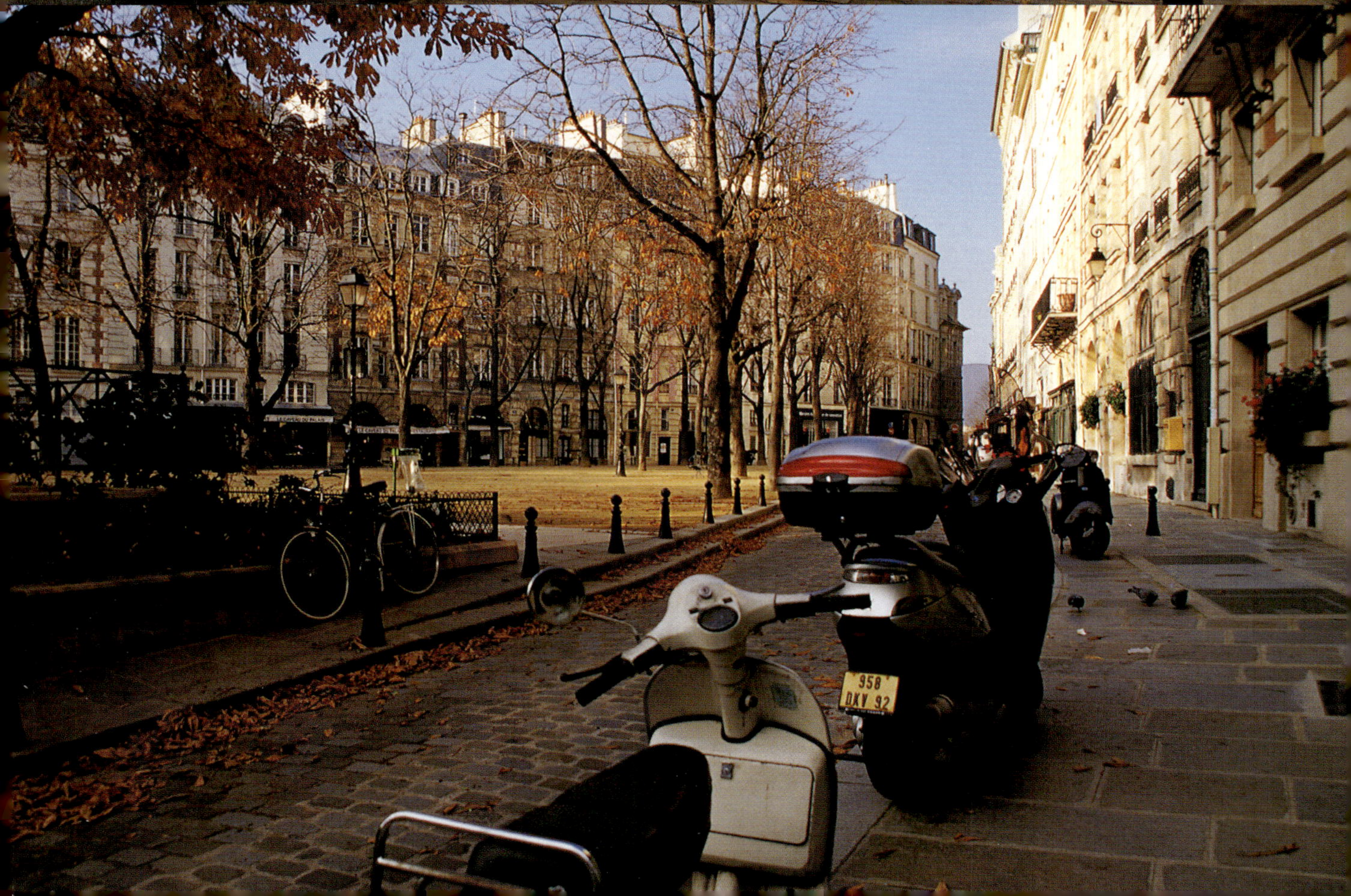
958
DKV 92

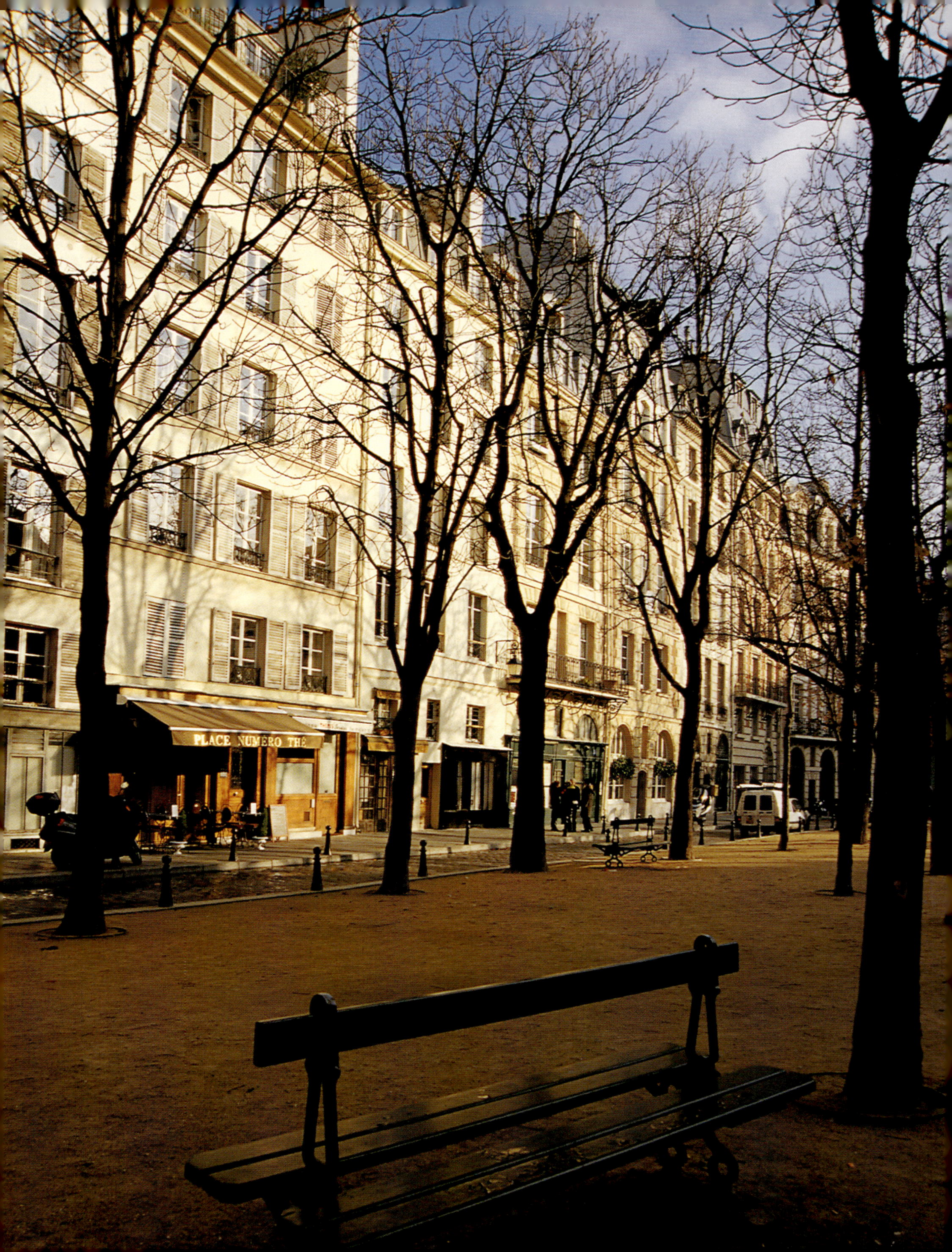
PLACE NUMERO THE

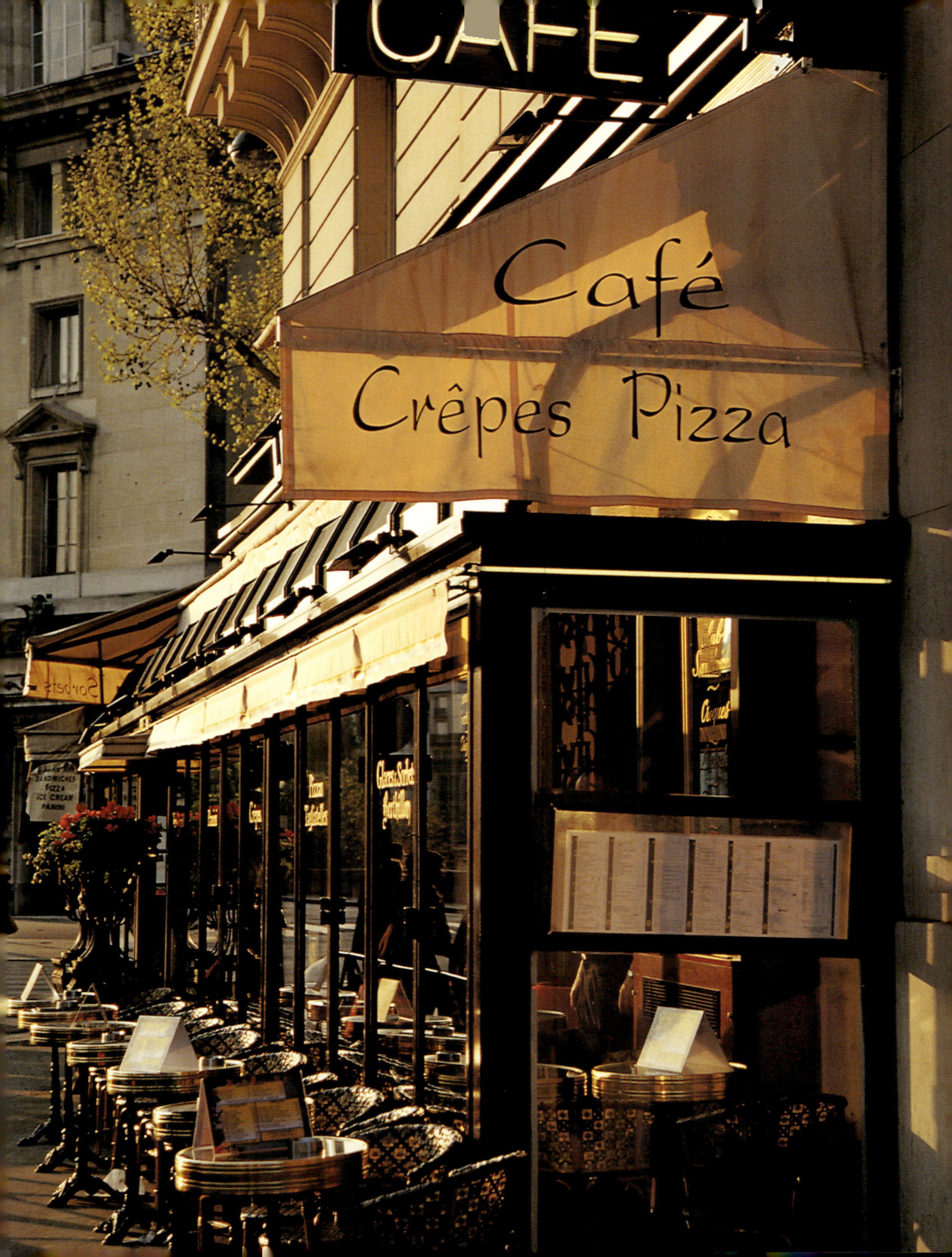
CAFE
Café
Crêpes Pizza
SANDWICHES
PIZZA
ICE CREAM
PANINI

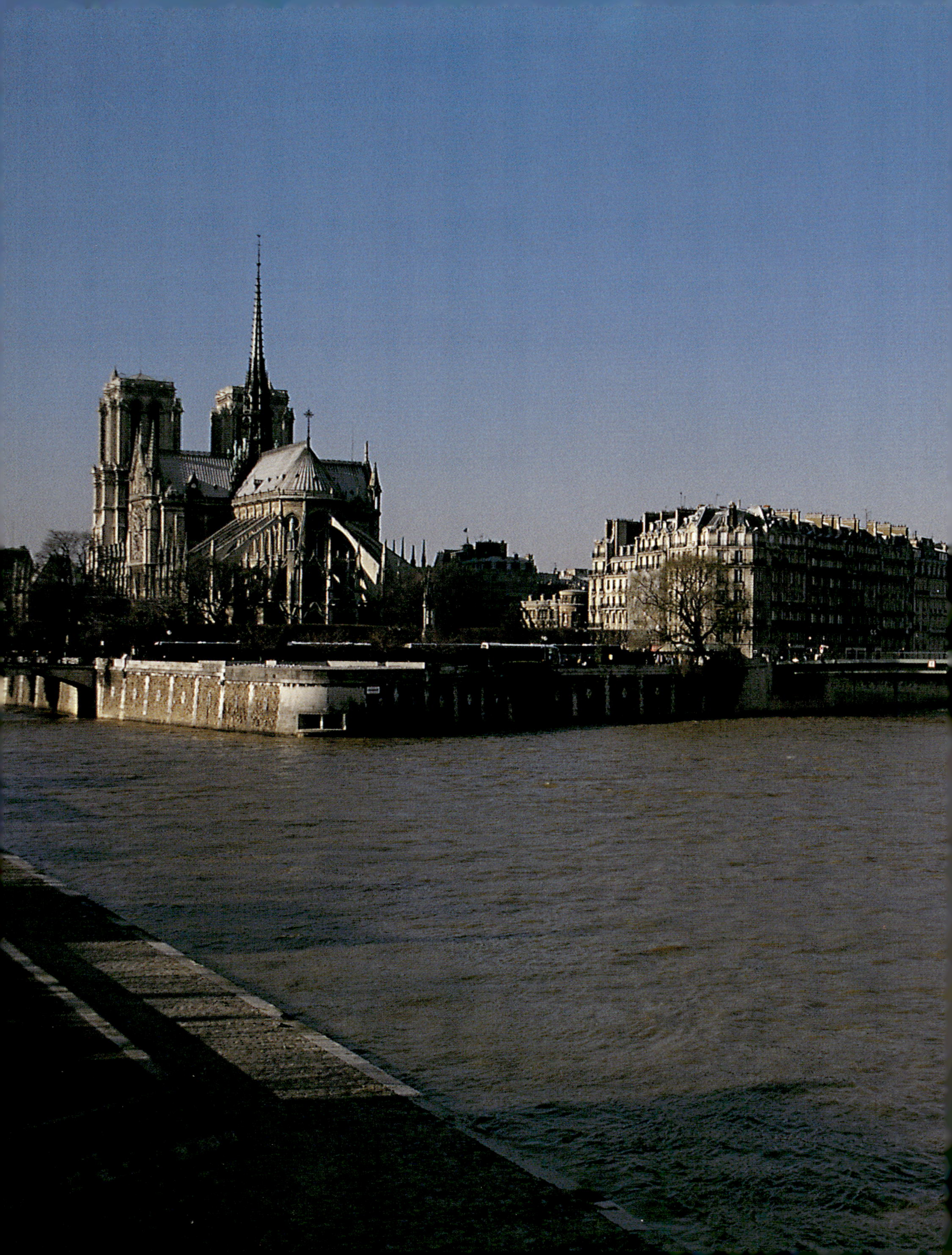

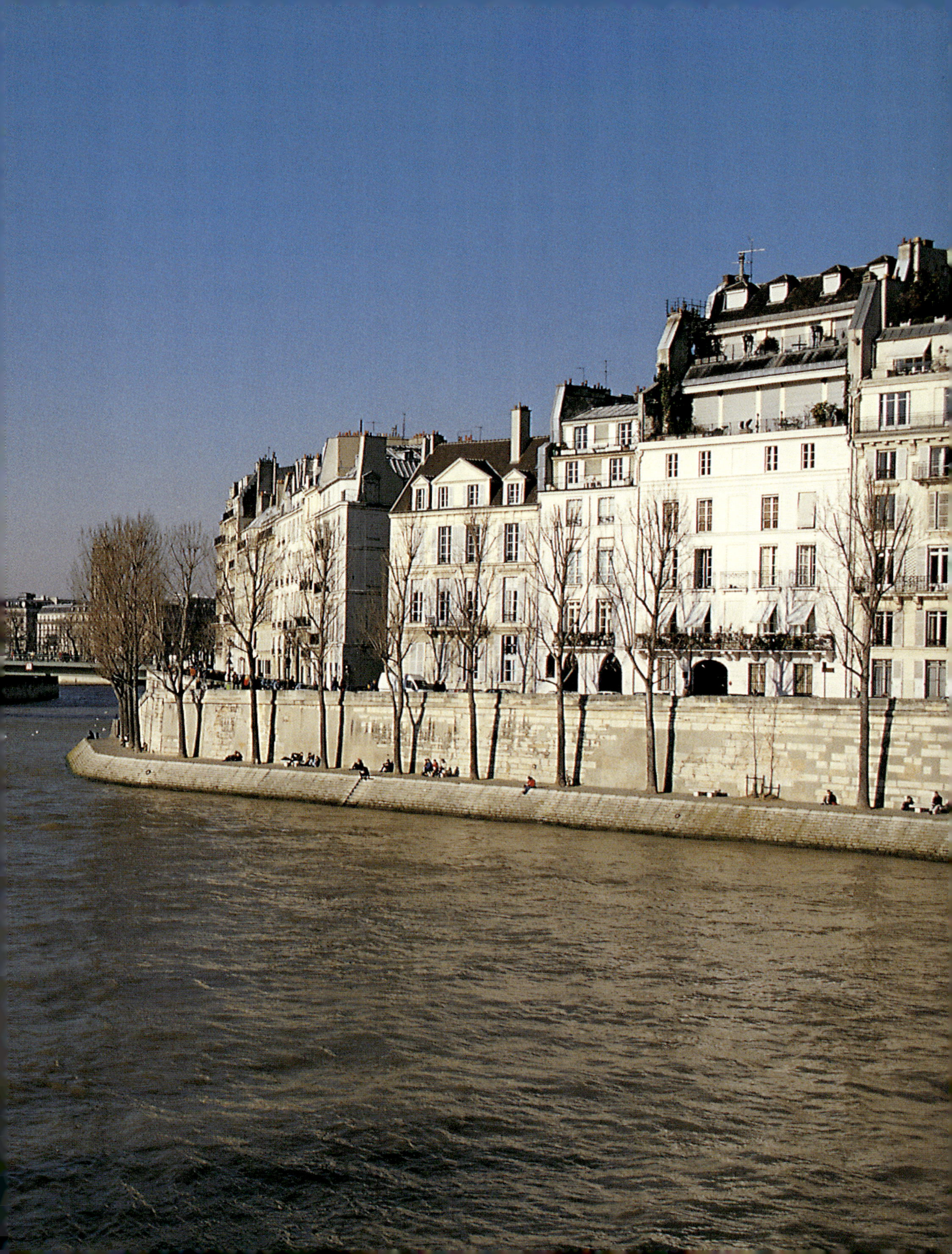

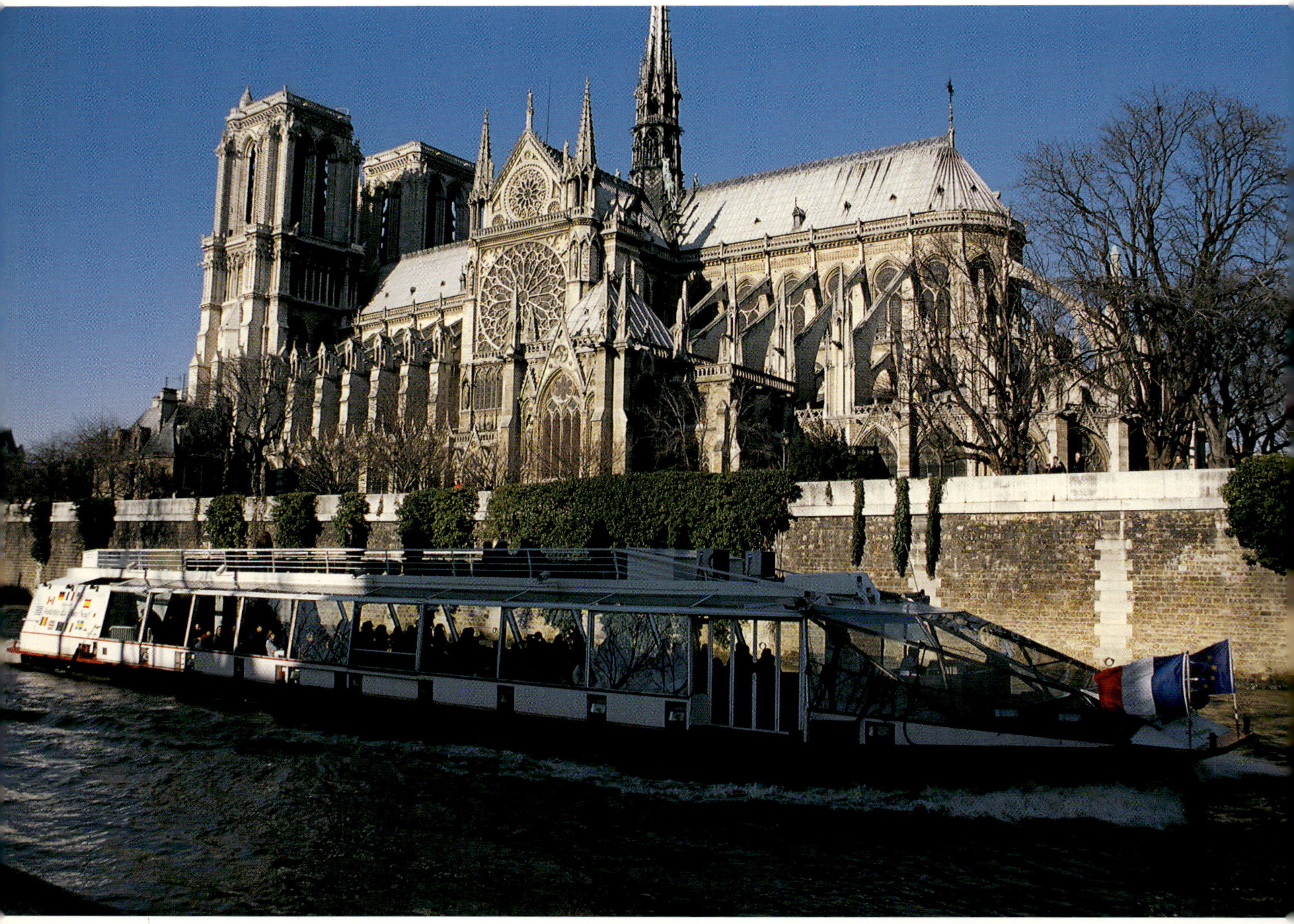

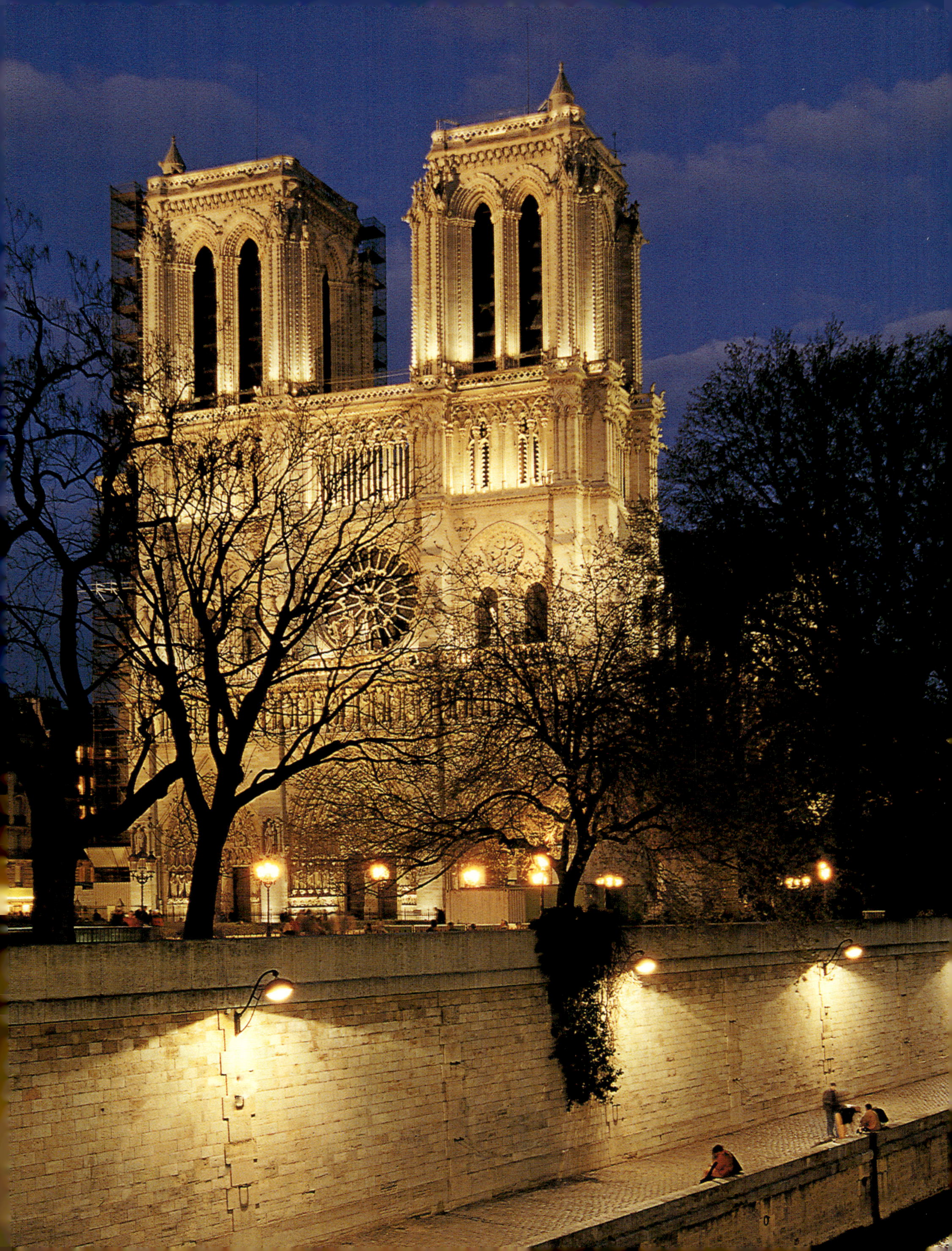

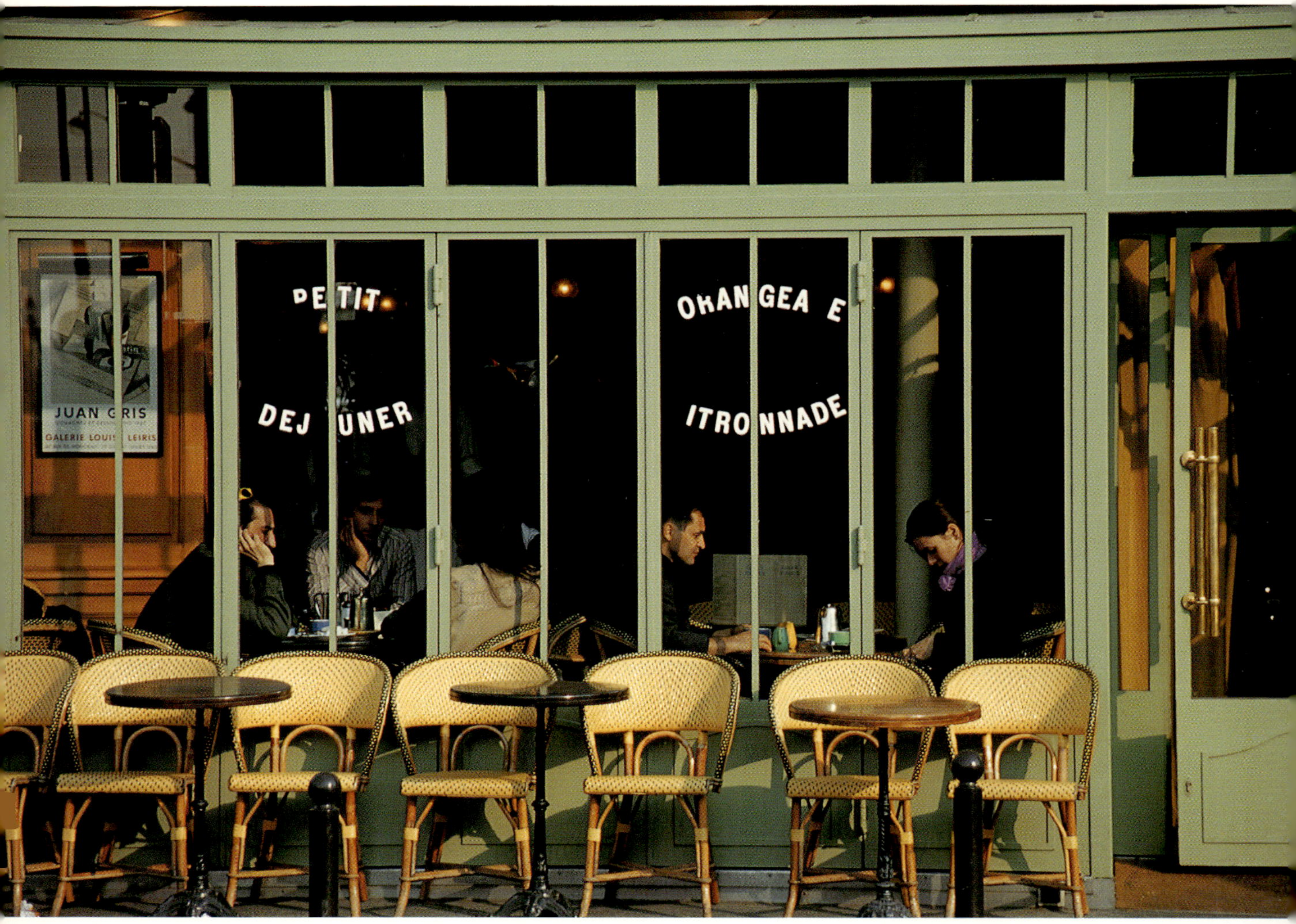
PETIT
JUAN GRIS

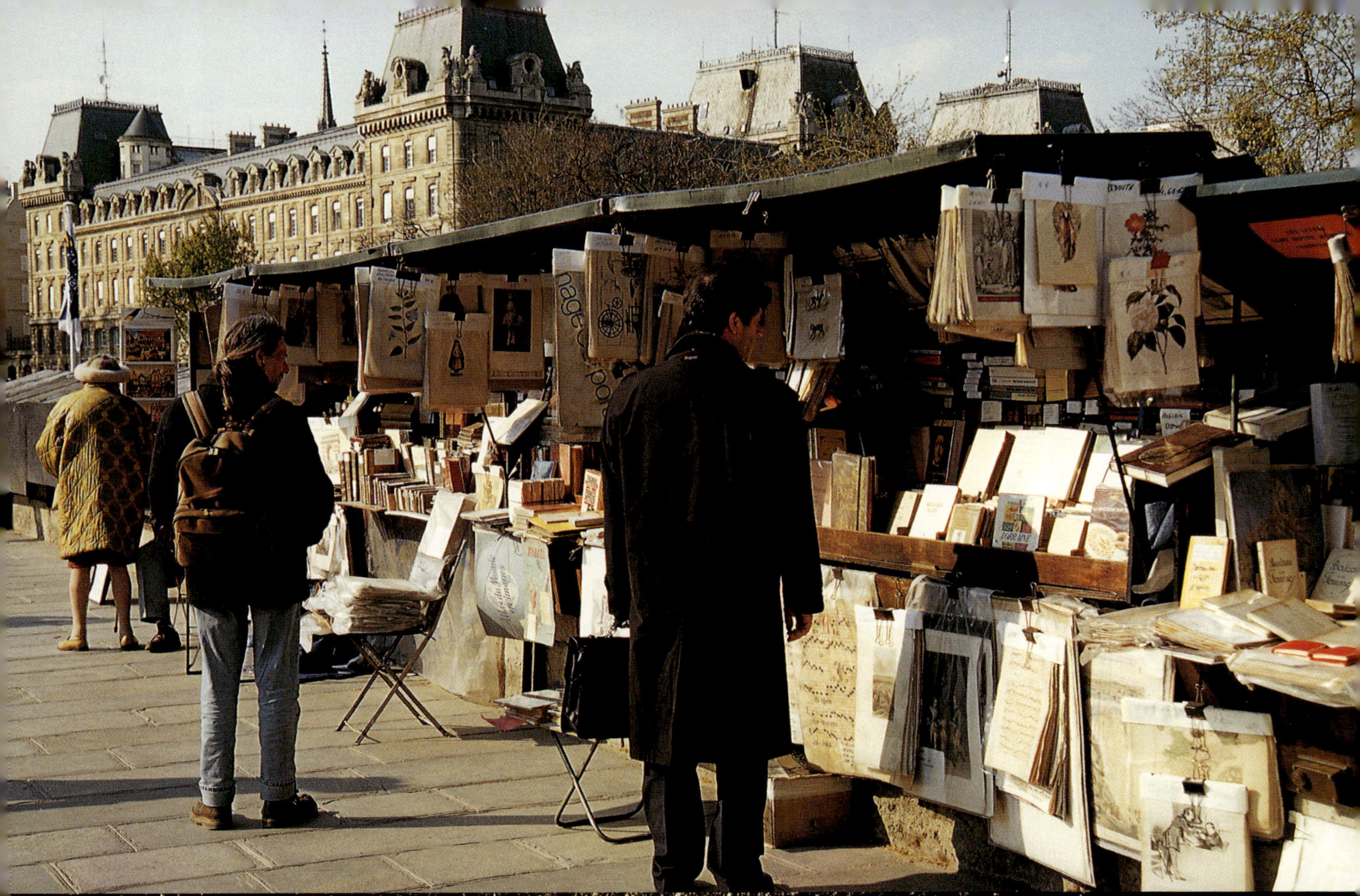

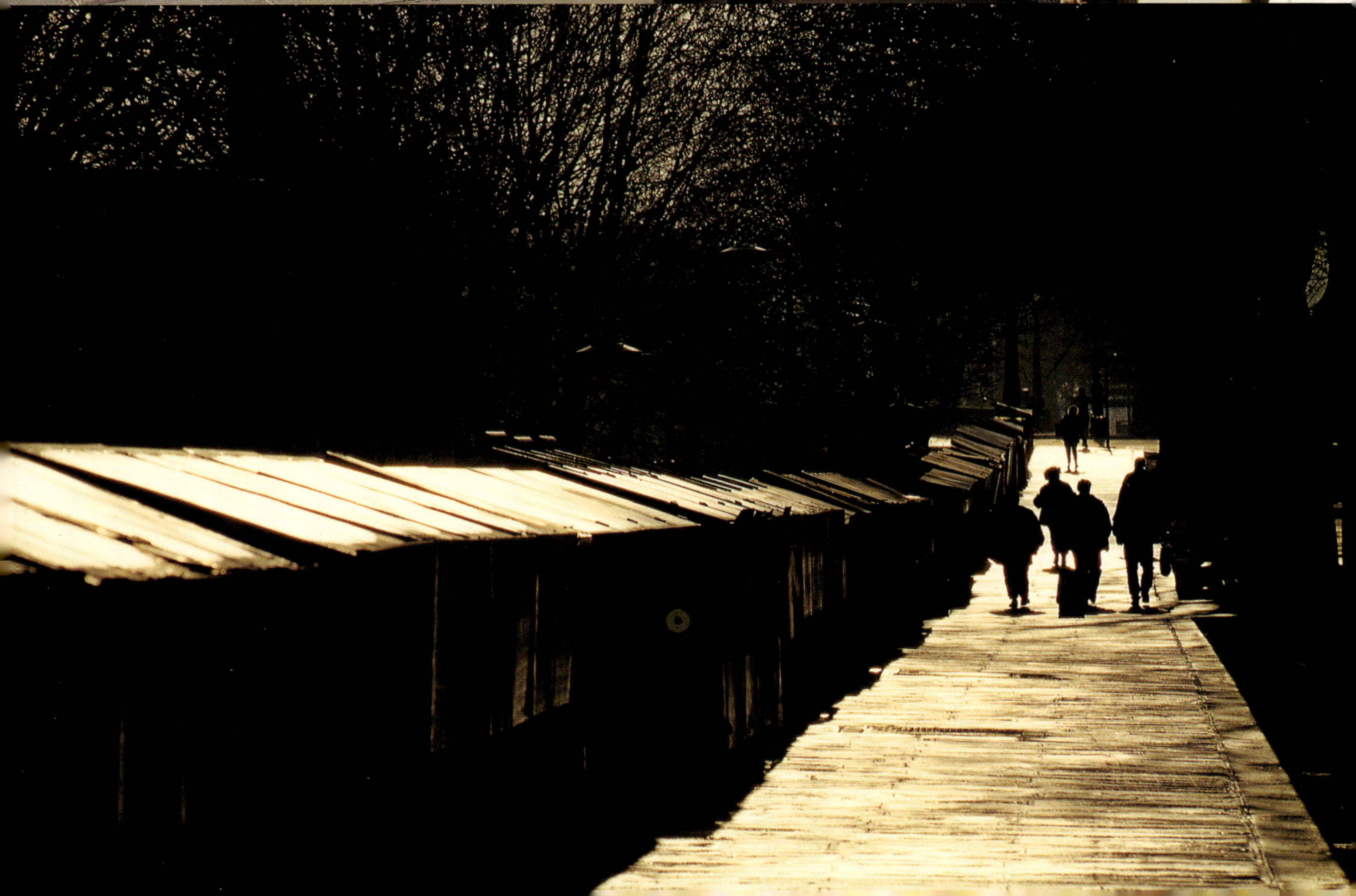

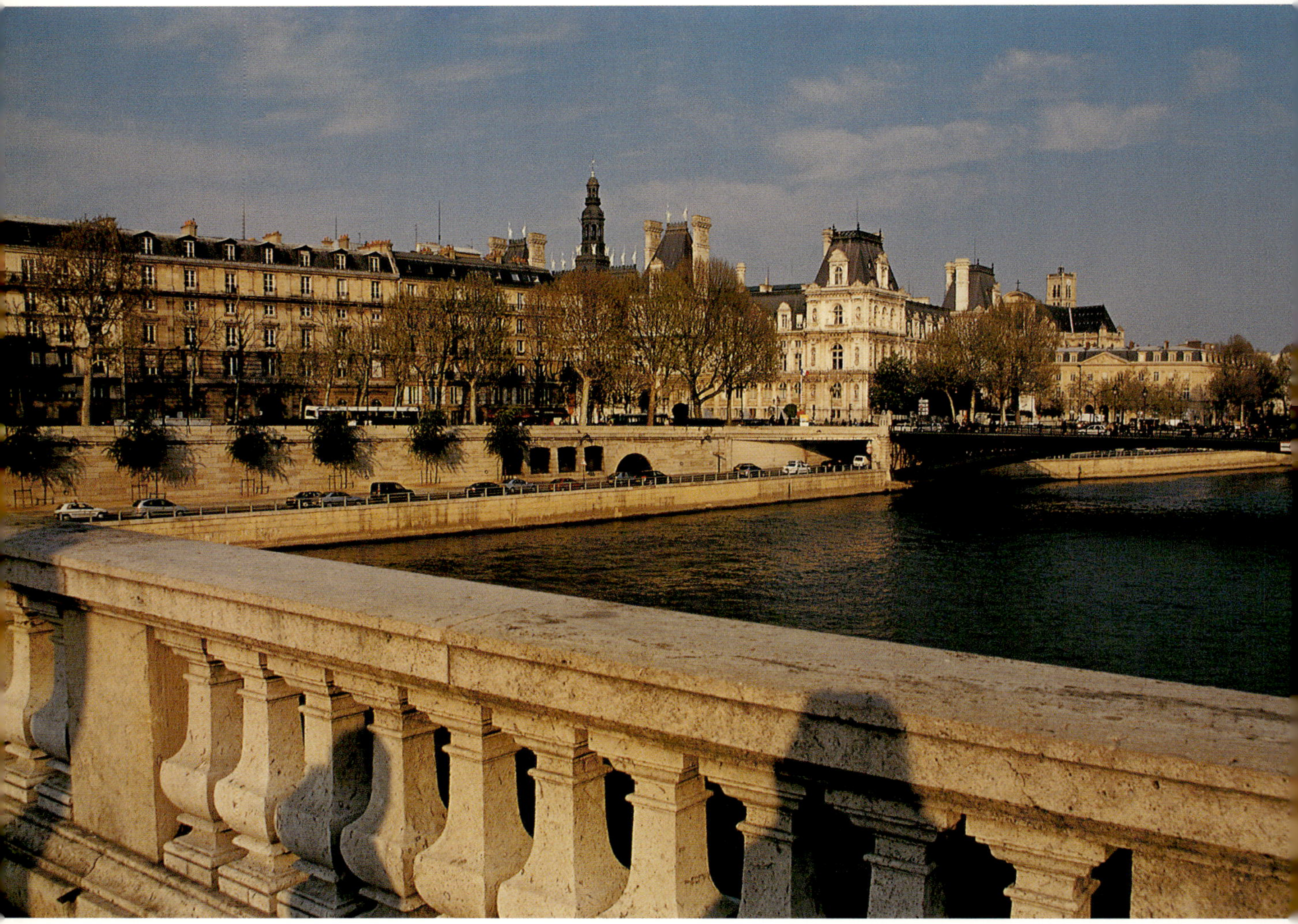

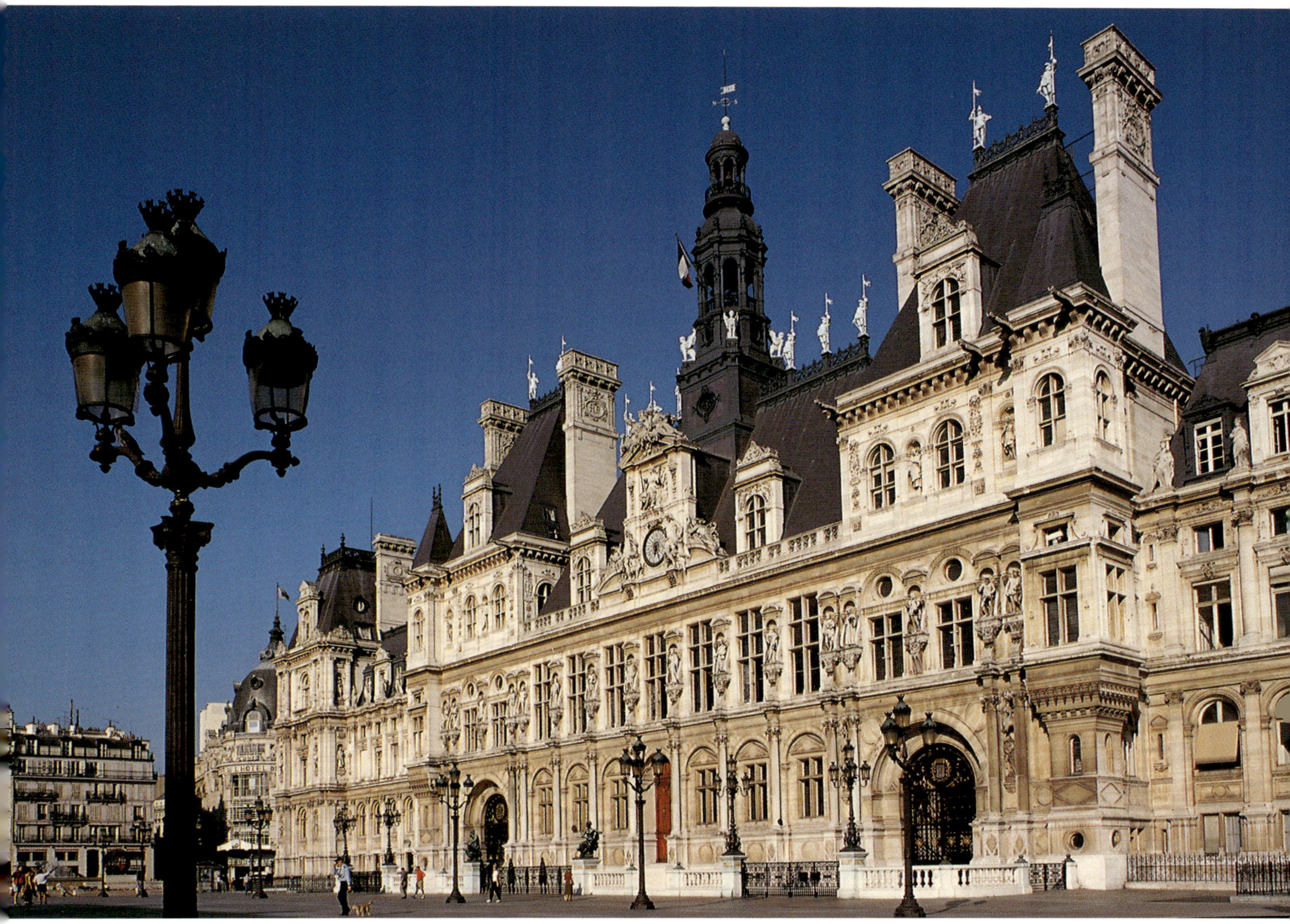

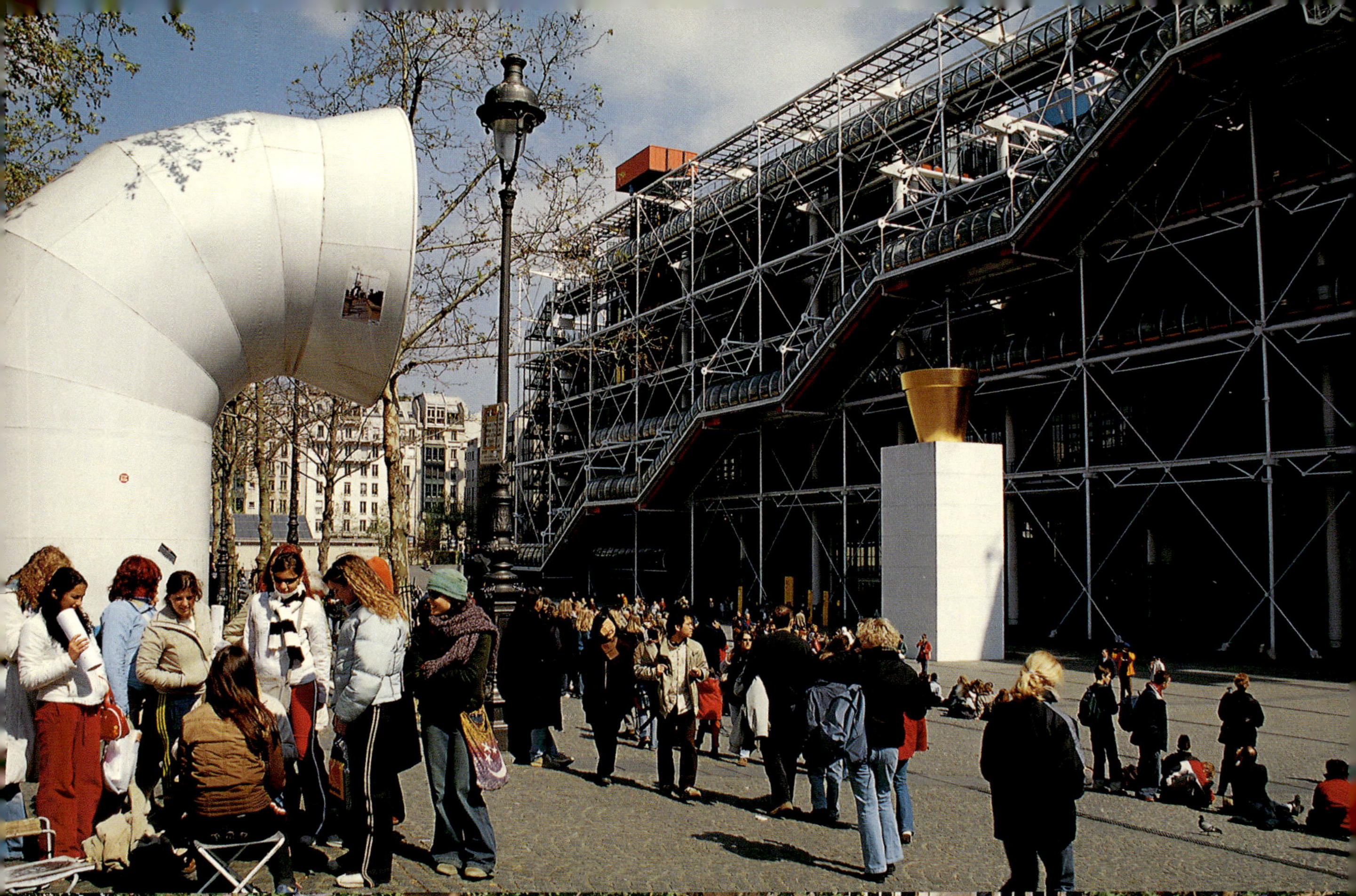

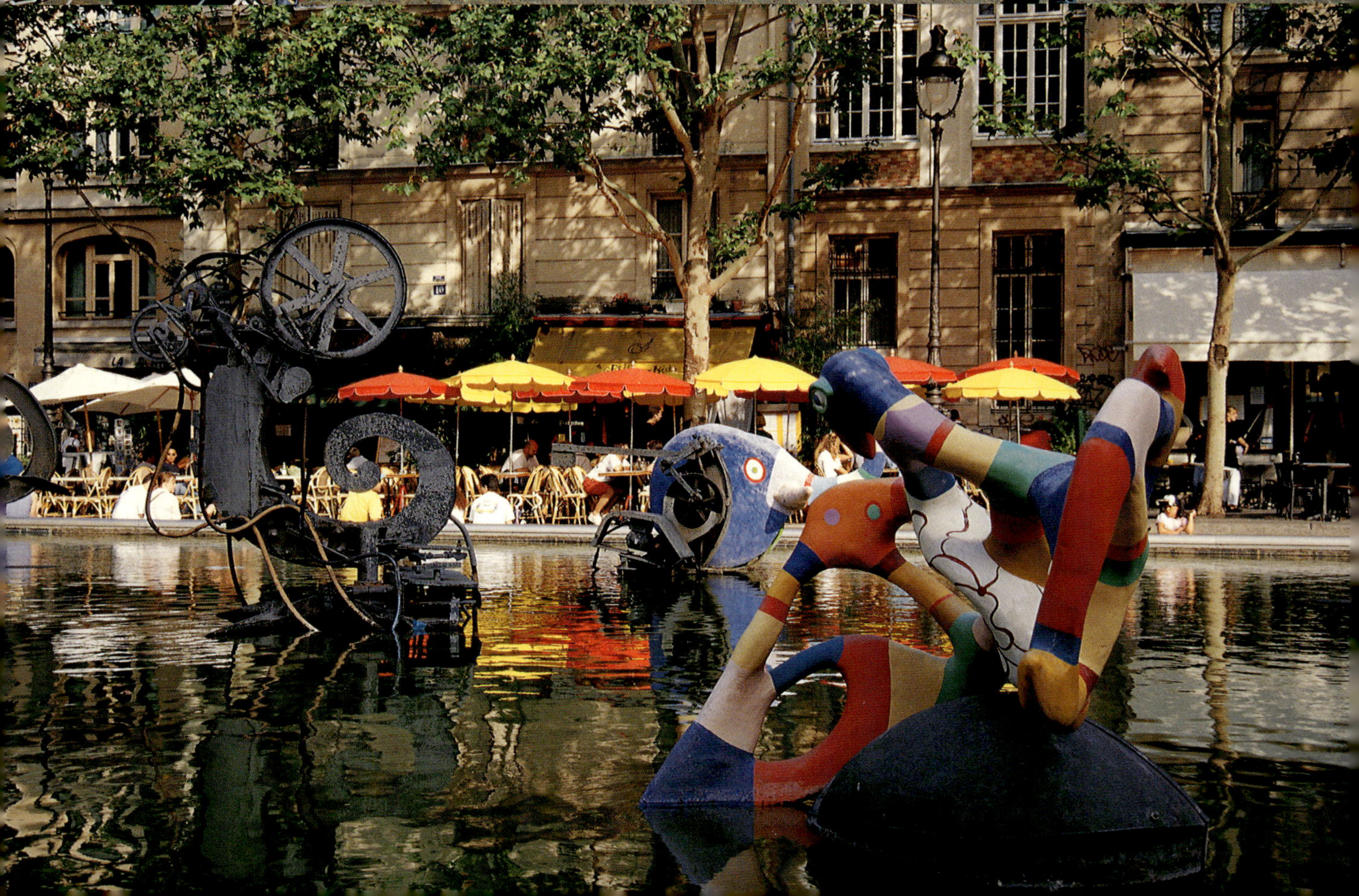

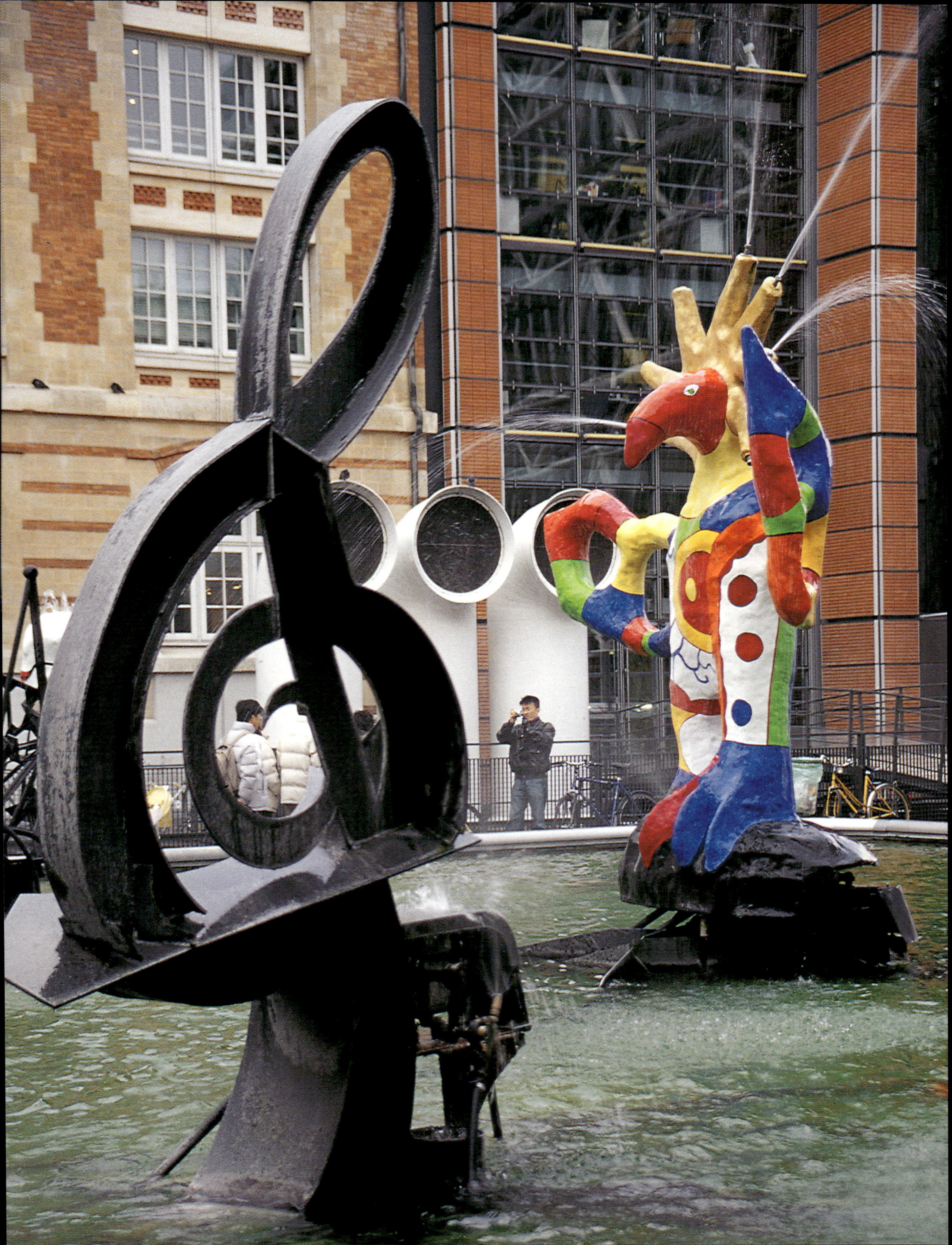

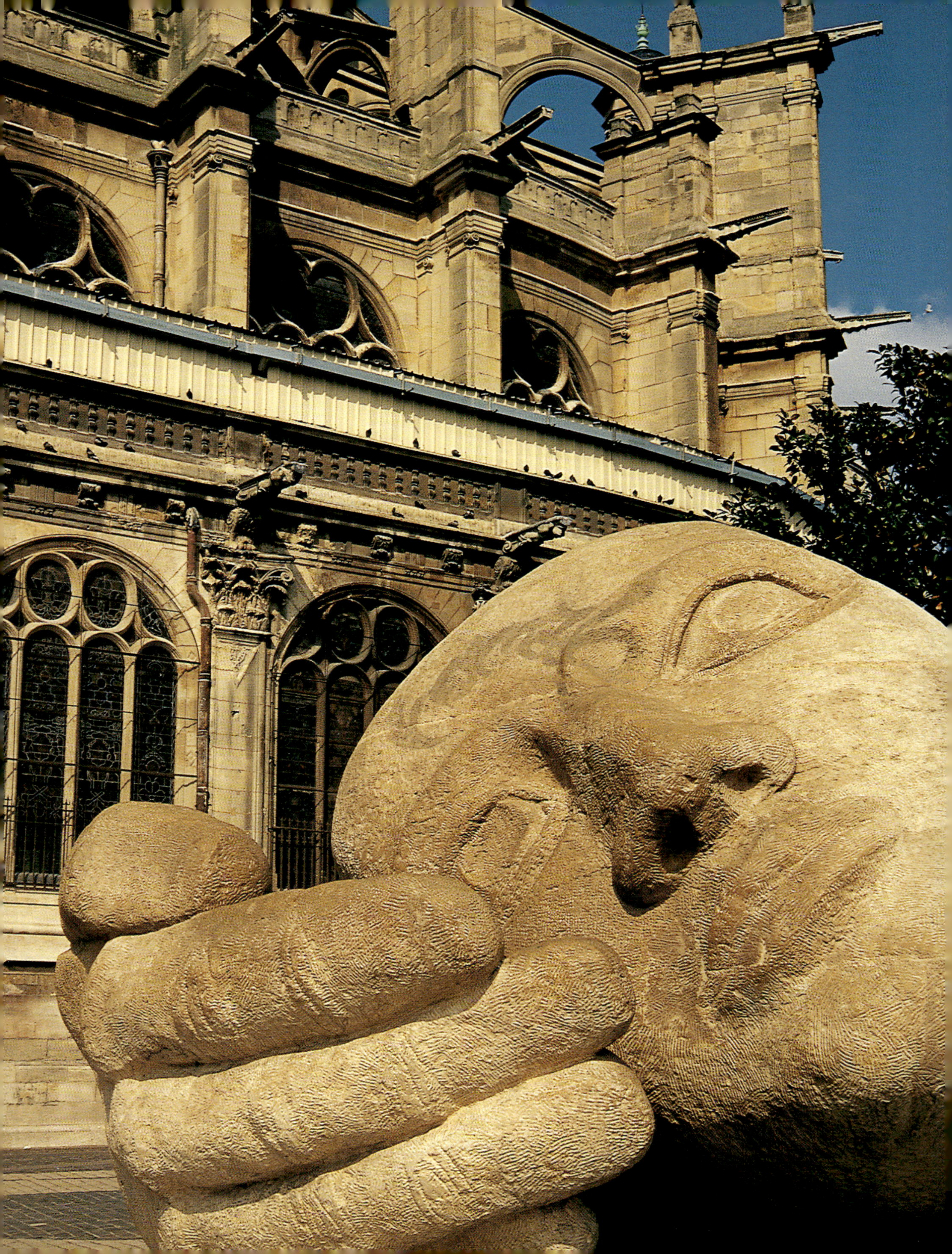

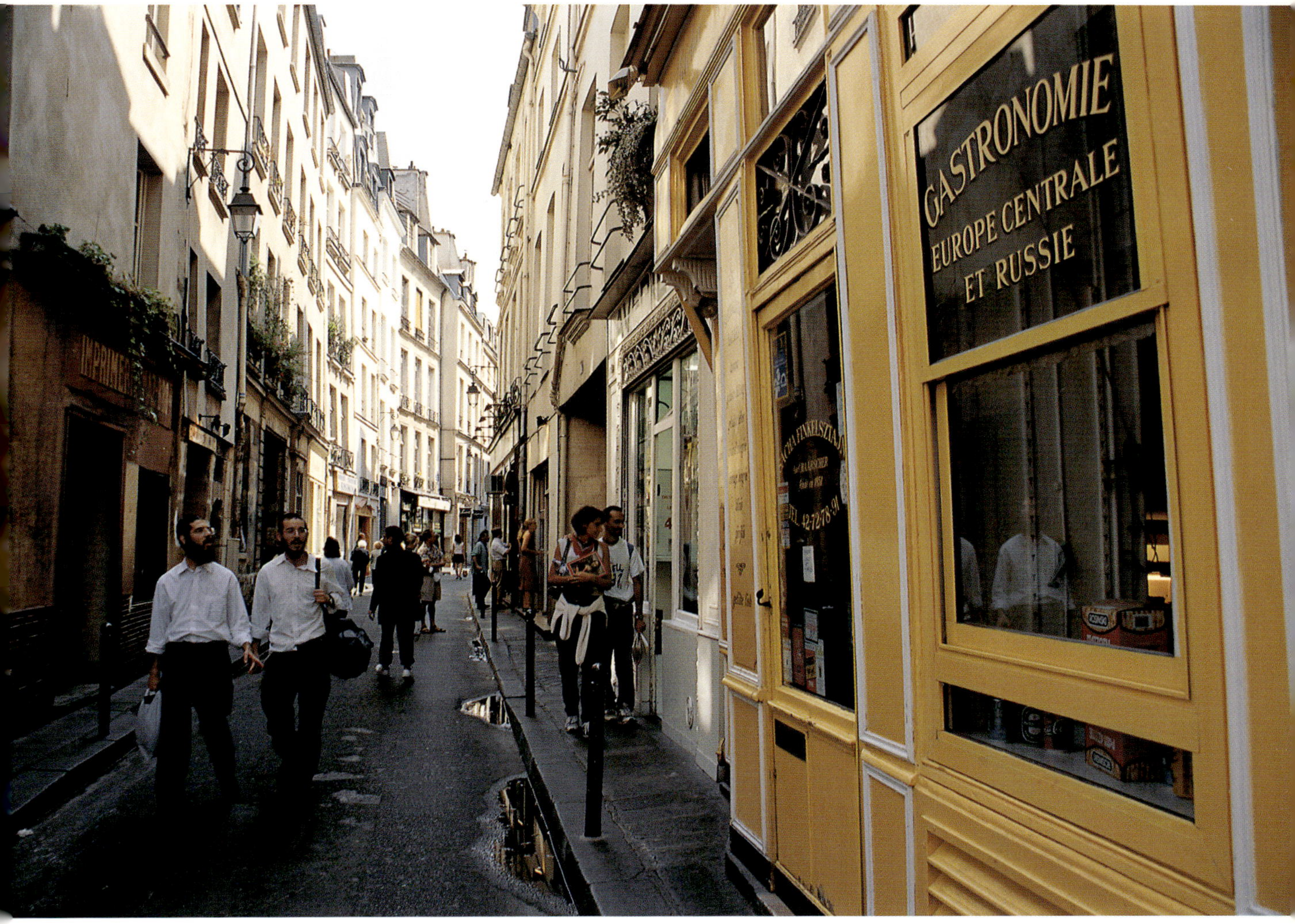
GASTRONOMIE
EUROPE CENTRALE
ET RUSSIE

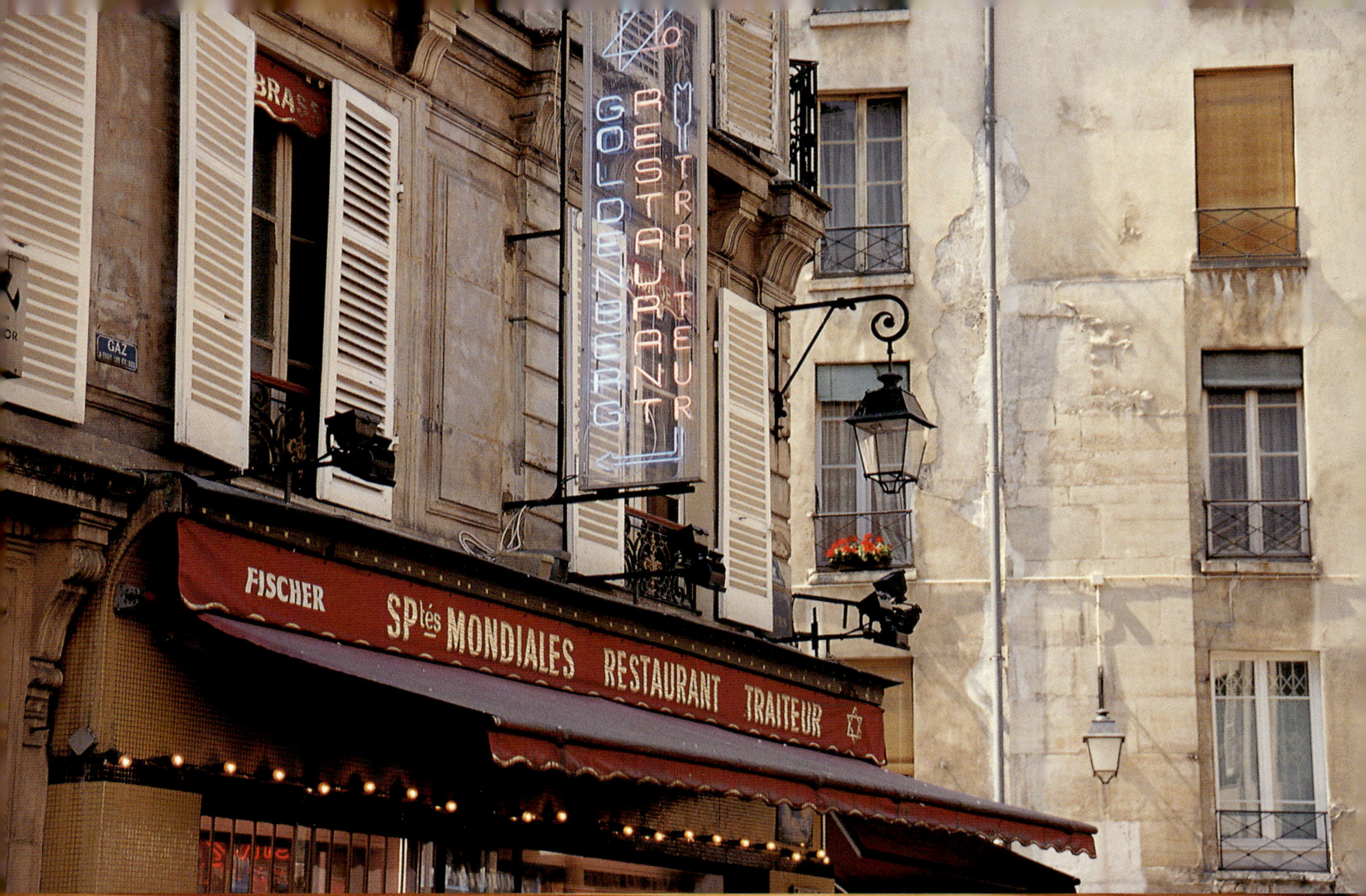
GAZ
RESTAURANT
TRAITEUR
FISCHER
SPtés MONDIALES RESTAURANT TRAITEUR

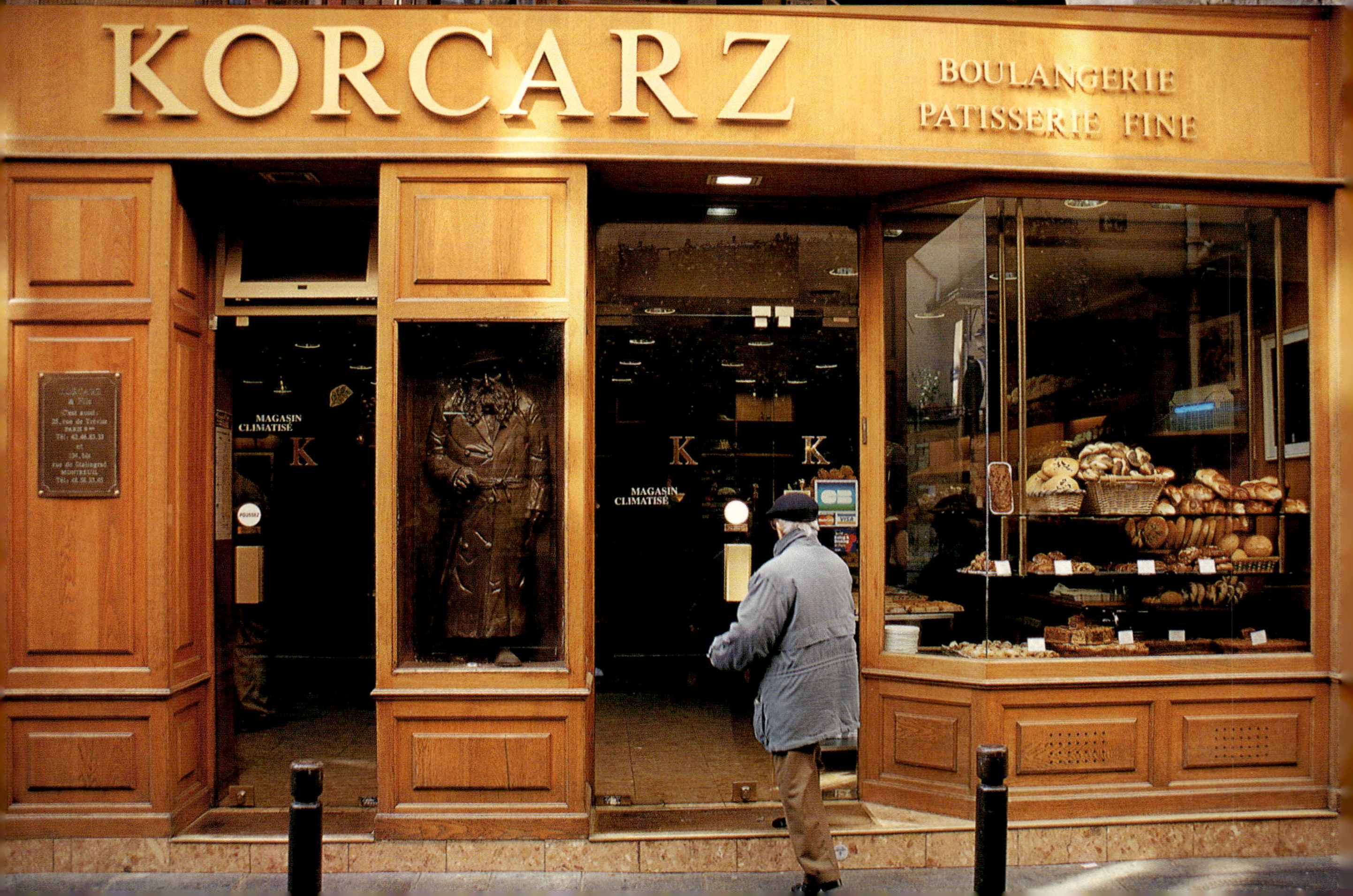
KORCARZ
BOULANGERIE
PATISSERIE FINE
MAGASIN
CLIMATISÉ
MAGASIN
CLIMATISÉ

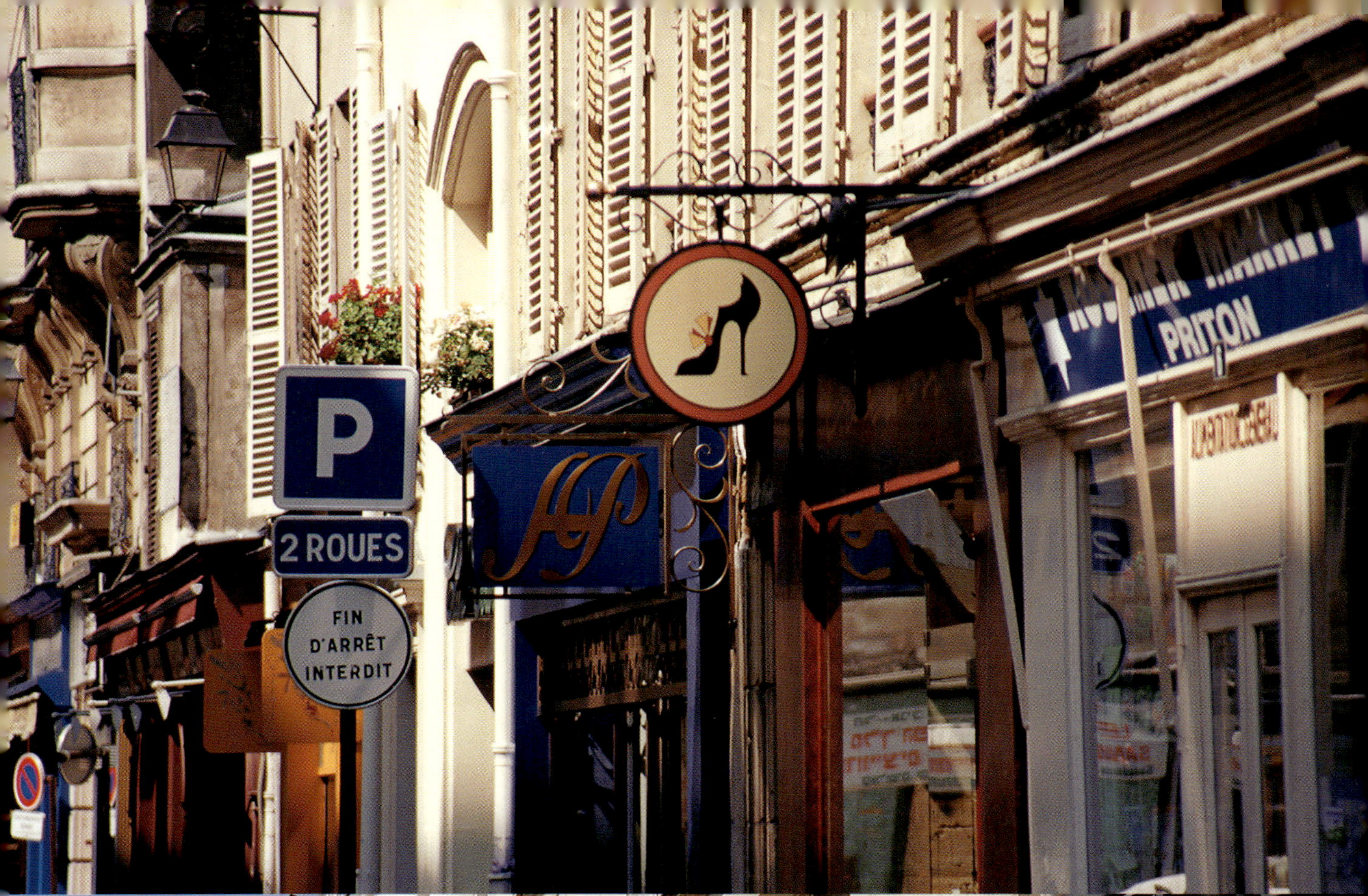
P
2 ROUES
FIN
D'ARRÊT
INTERDIT
PRITON

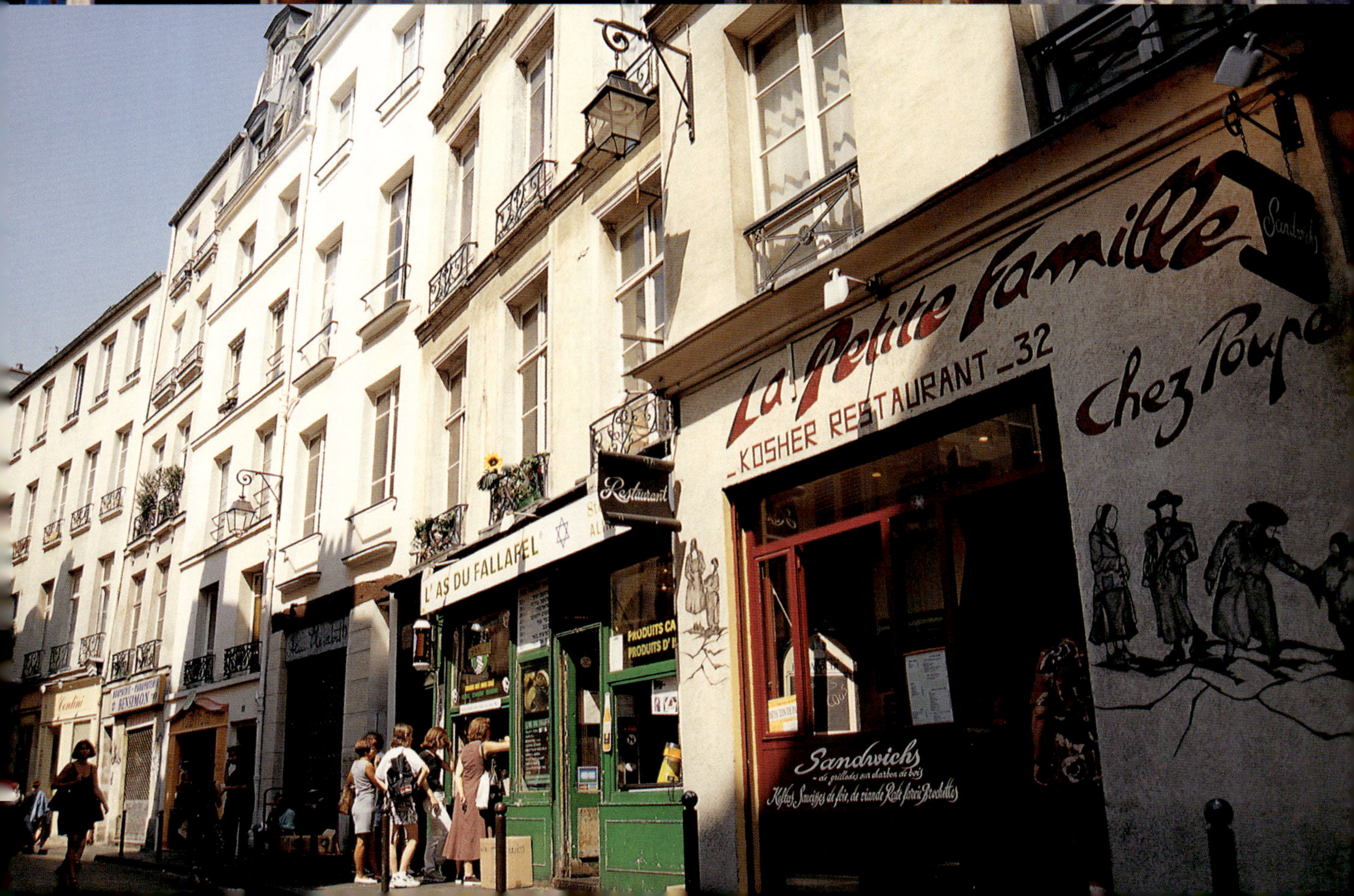
La Petite Famille
KOSHER RESTAURANT _32
L'AS DU FALLAFEL
Restaurant
Sandwichs

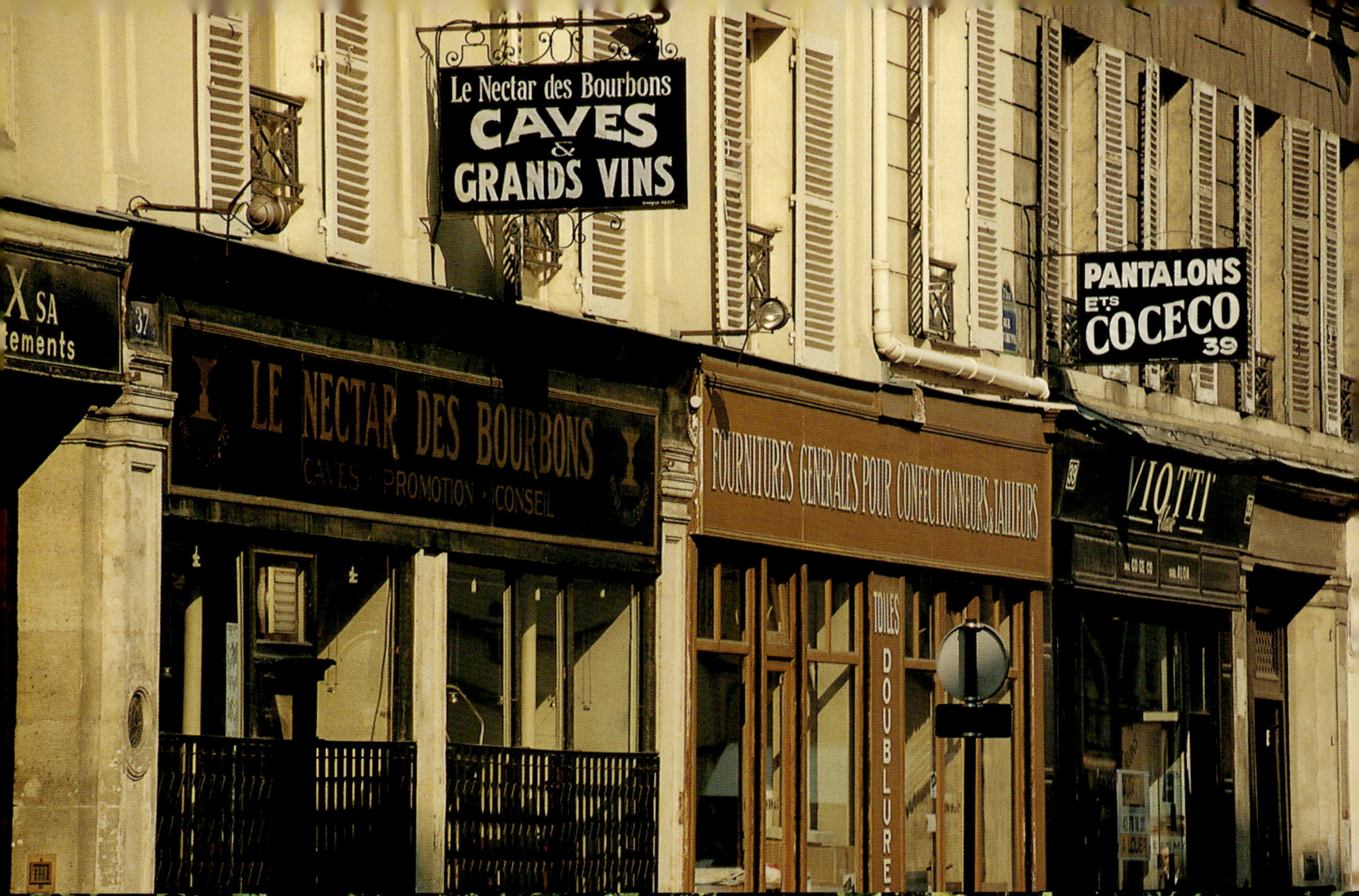
Le Nectar des Bourbons
CAVES & GRANDS VINS
PANTALONS
ETS COCECO
39
LE NECTAR DES BOURBONS
CAVES · PROMOTION · CONSEIL
FOURNITURES GENERALES POUR CONFECTIONNEURS & TAILLEURS
TOILES
DOUBLURES
VIOTTI

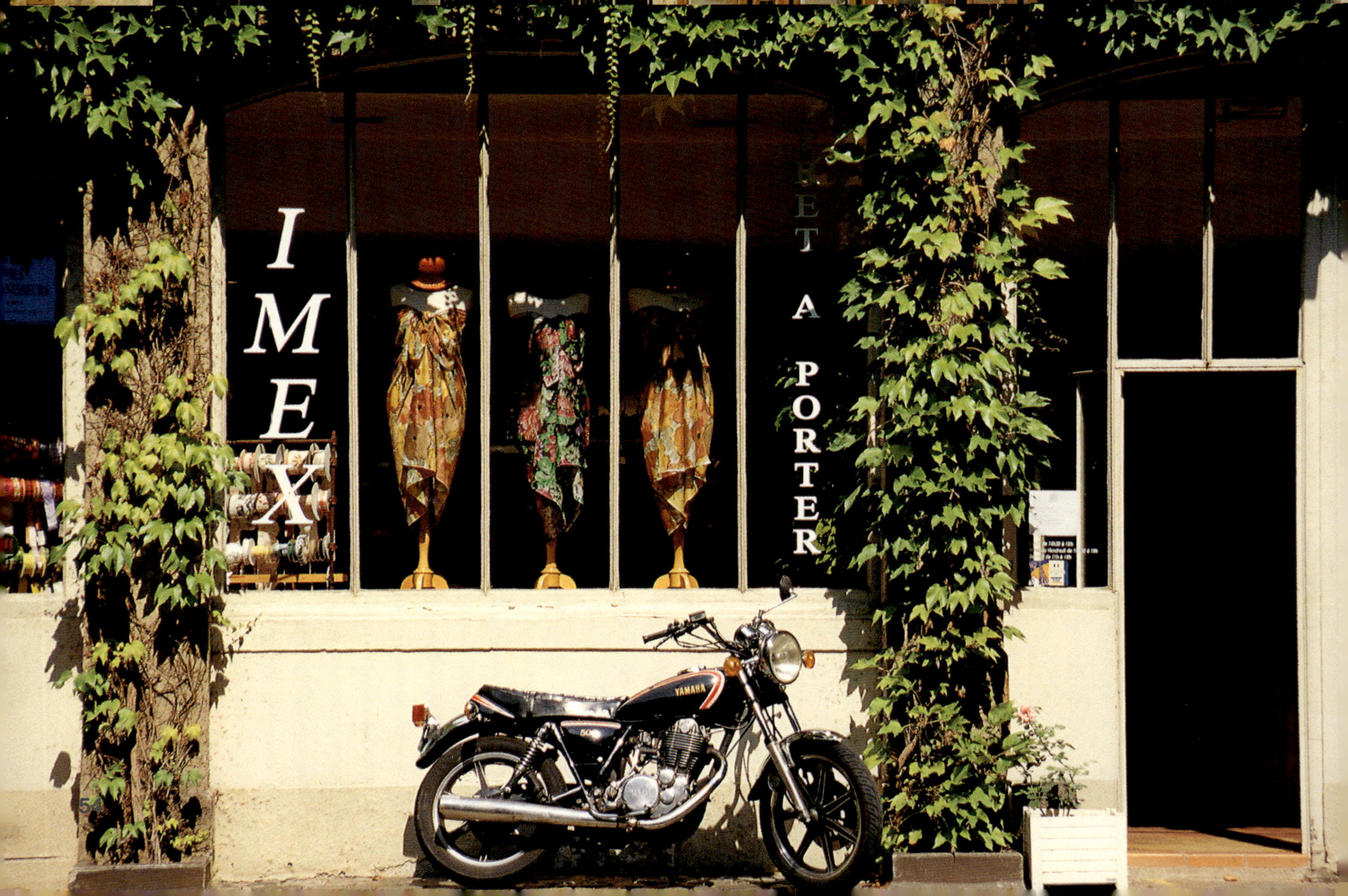
IMEX
PRET A PORTER
YAMAHA

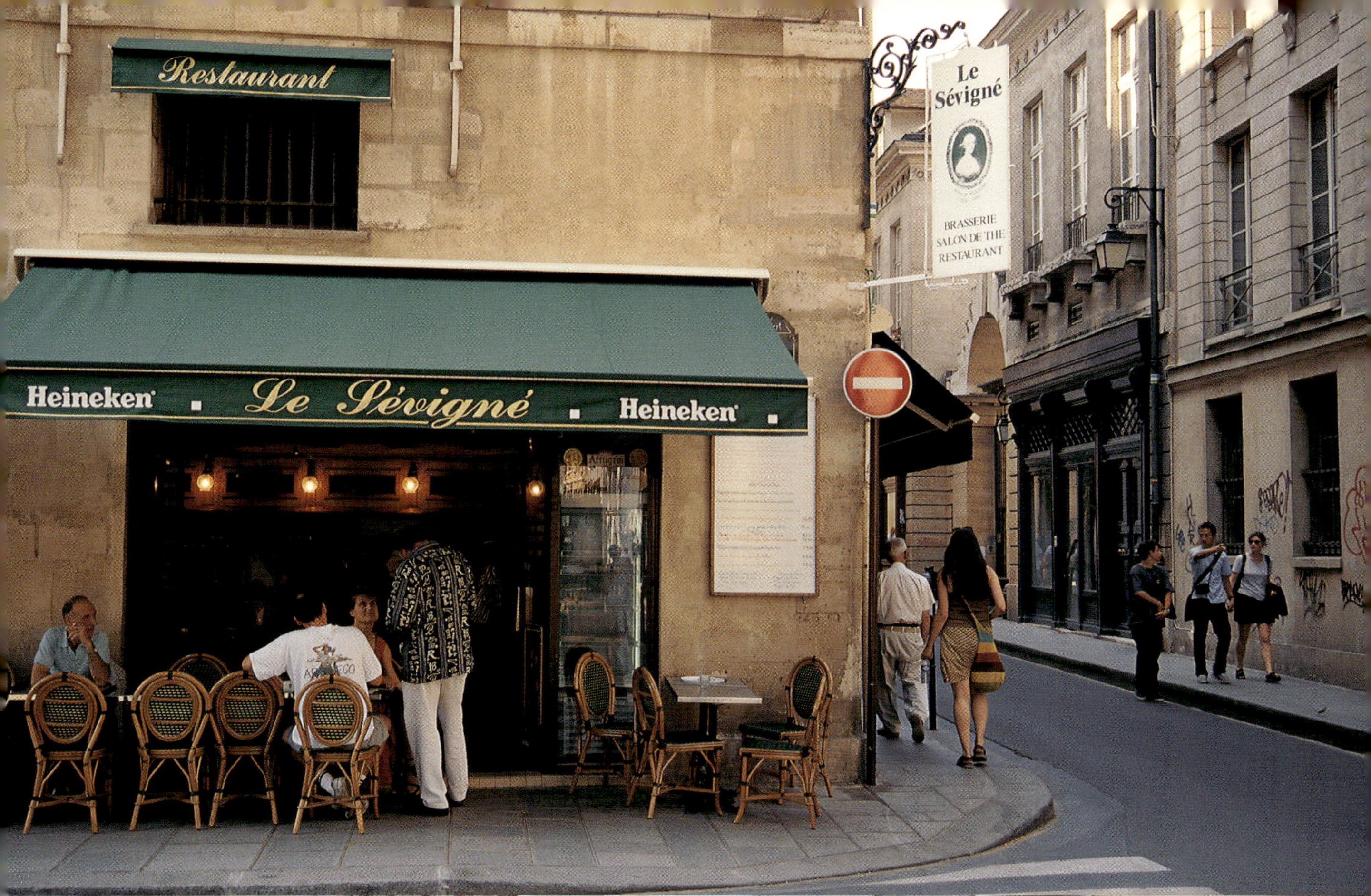
Restaurant
Heineken
Le Sévigné
Heineken
Le Sévigné
BRASSERIE
SALON DE THE
RESTAURANT

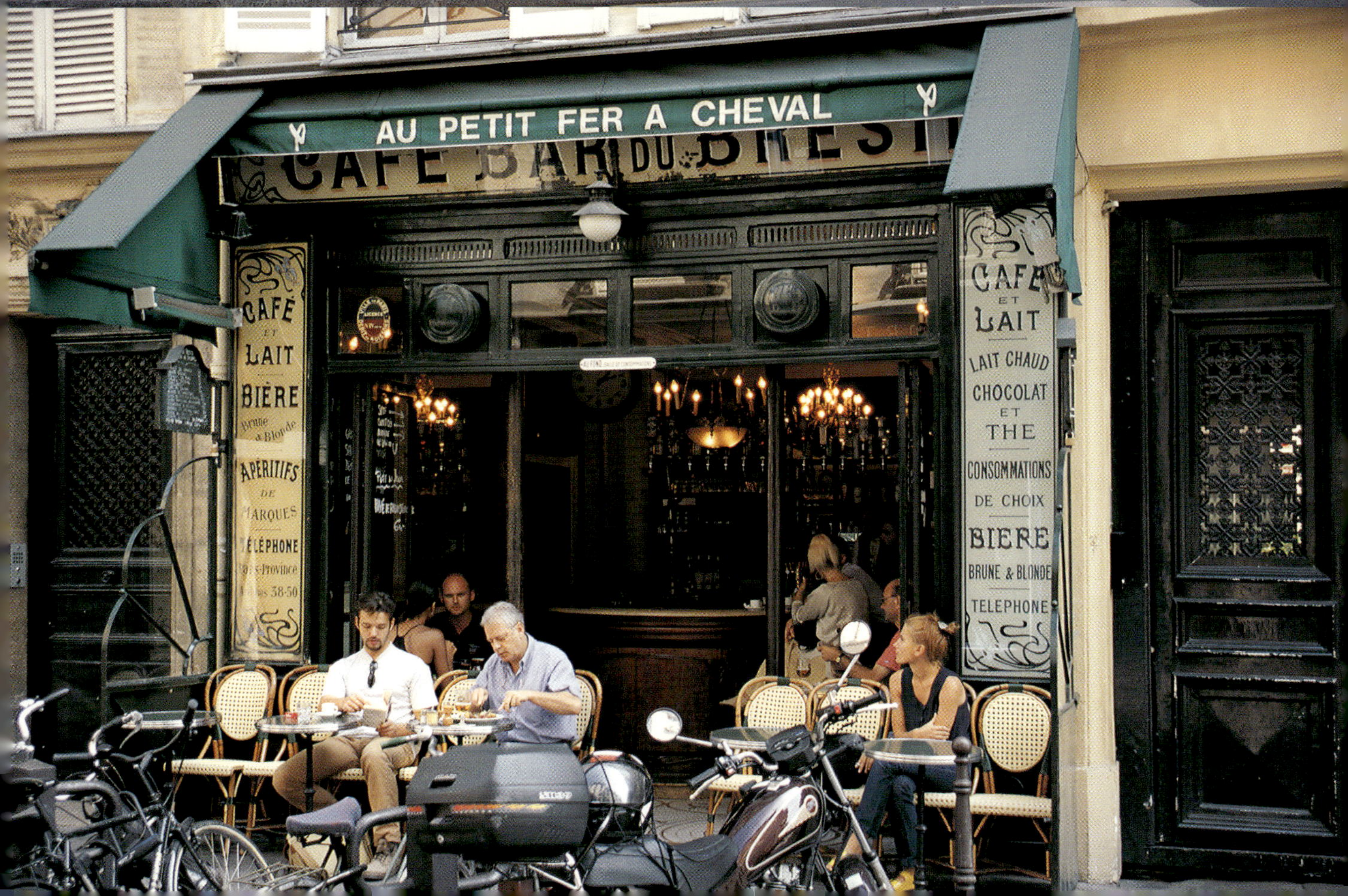
AU PETIT FER A CHEVAL
CAFE
CAFE
ET
LAIT
BIERE
Brune & Blonde
APERITIFS
DE
MARQUES
TELEPHONE
CAFE
ET
LAIT
LAIT CHAUD
CHOCOLAT
ET
THE
CONSOMMATIONS
DE CHOIX
BIERE
BRUNE & BLONDE
TELEPHONE

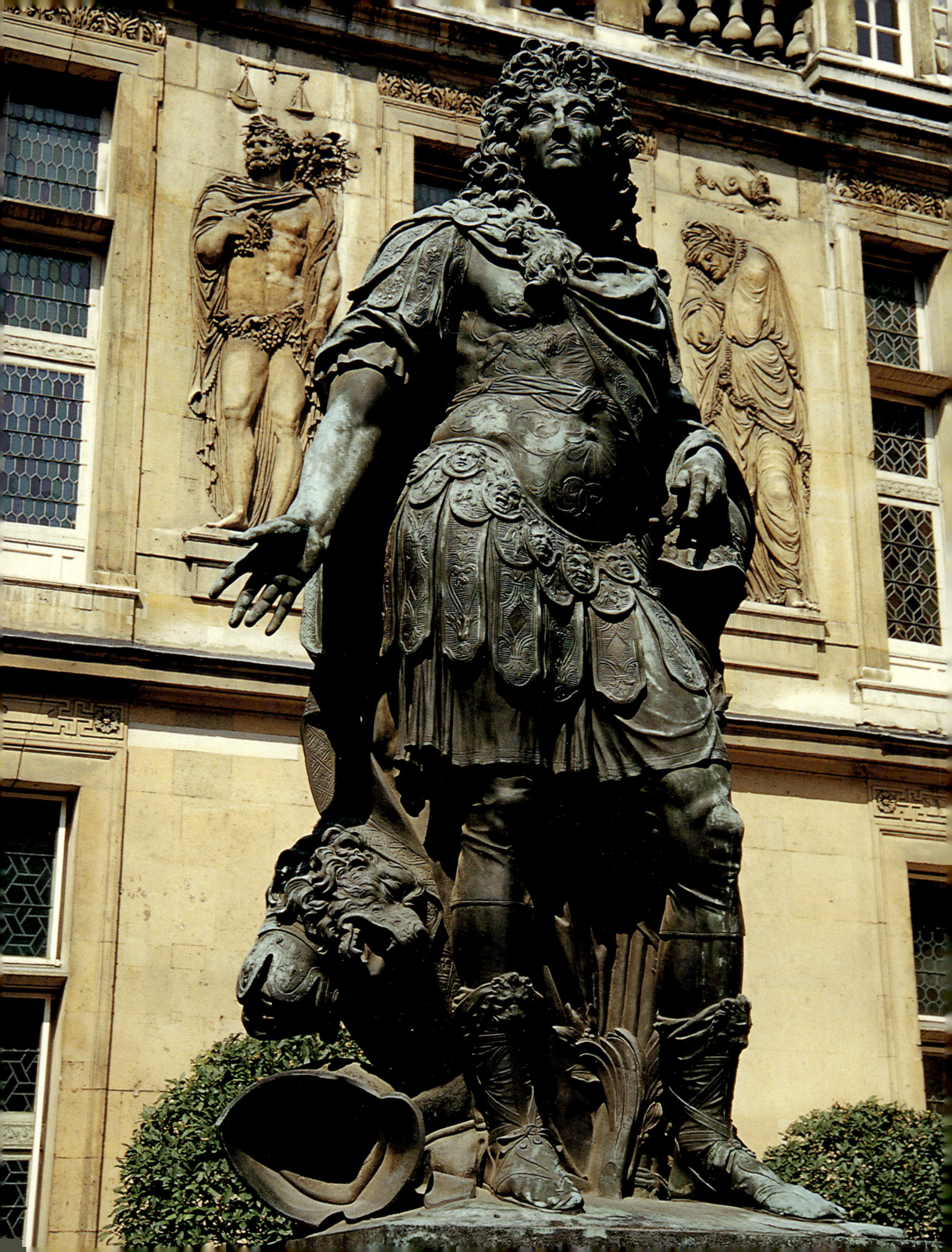

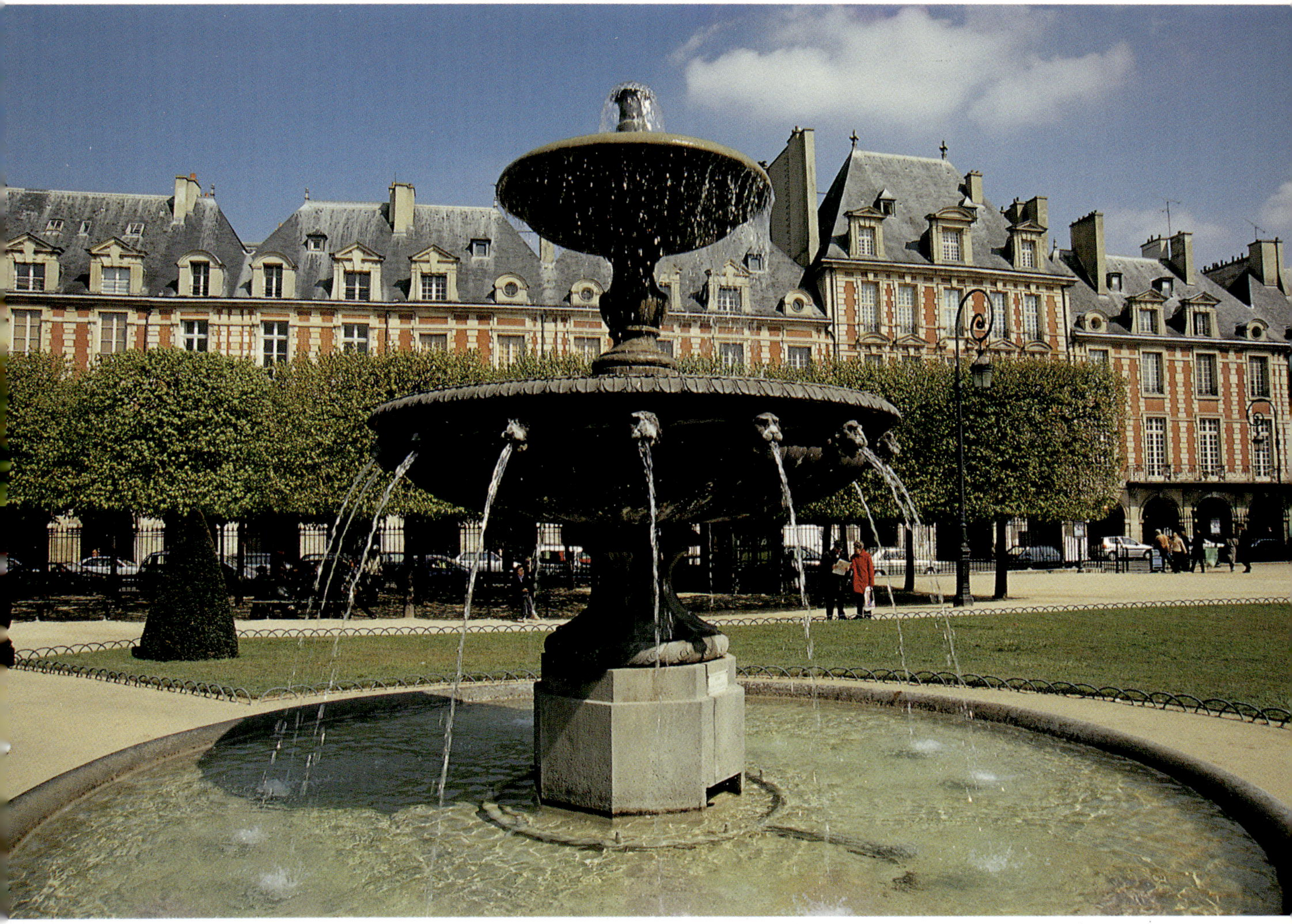

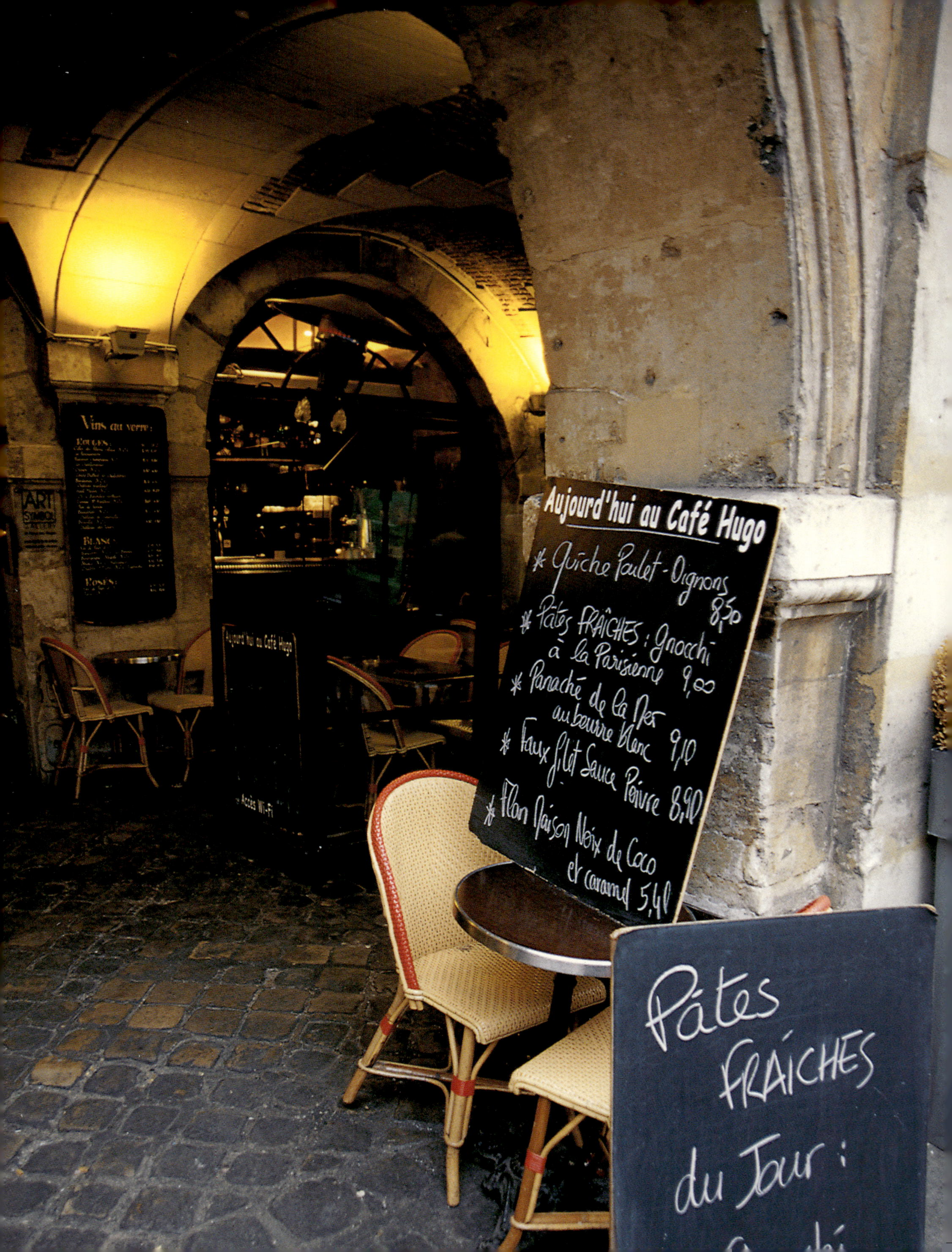
Vins au verre :
Aujourd'hui au Café Hugo
* Quiche Poulet - Oignons 8,50
* Pâtes FRAÎCHES : Gnocchi à la Parisienne 9,00
* Panaché de la Mer au beurre blanc 9,10
* Faux filet Sauce Poivre 8,90
* Flan Maison Noix de Coco et caramel 5,40
Pâtes FRAÎCHES du Jour :

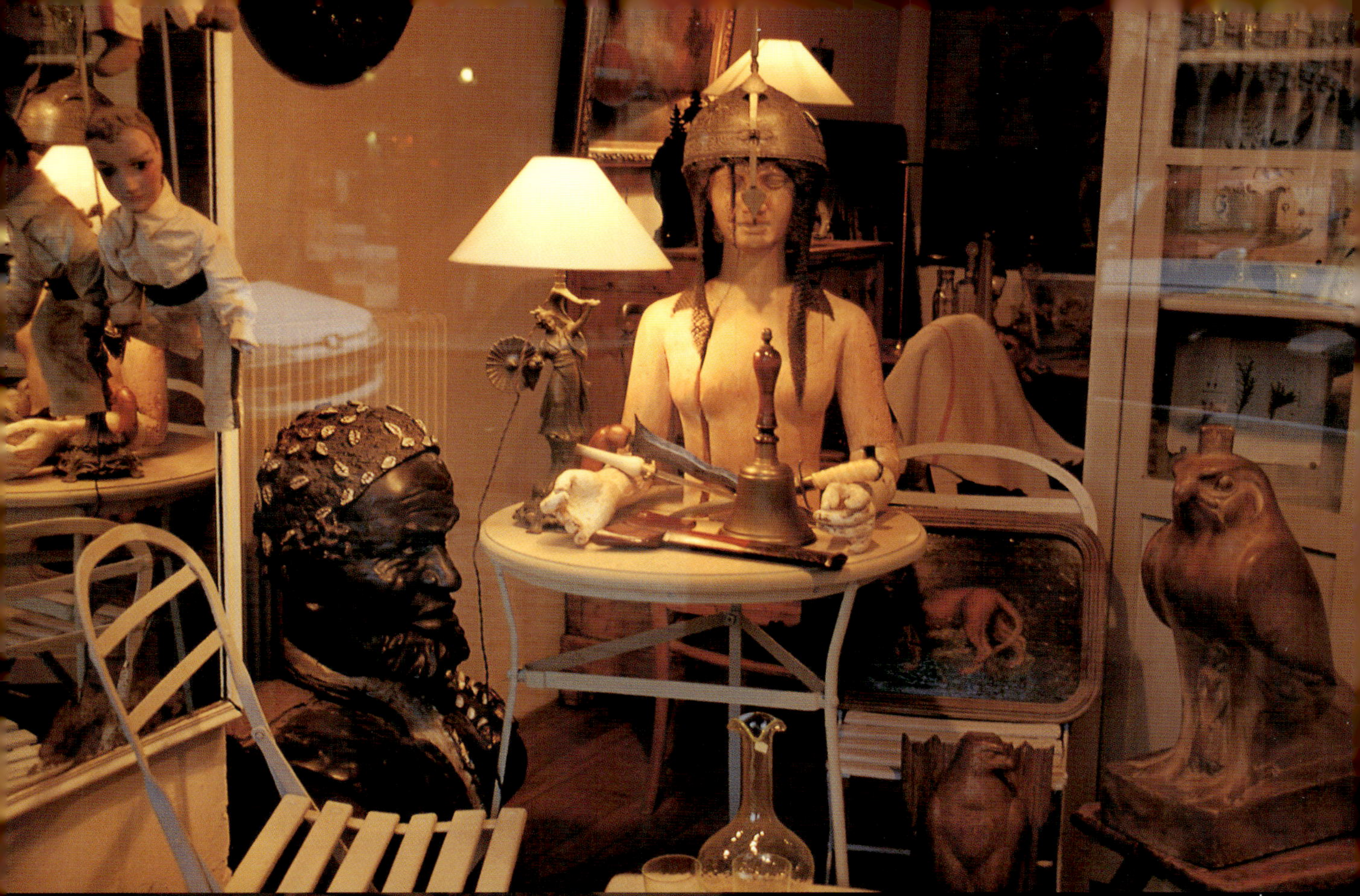

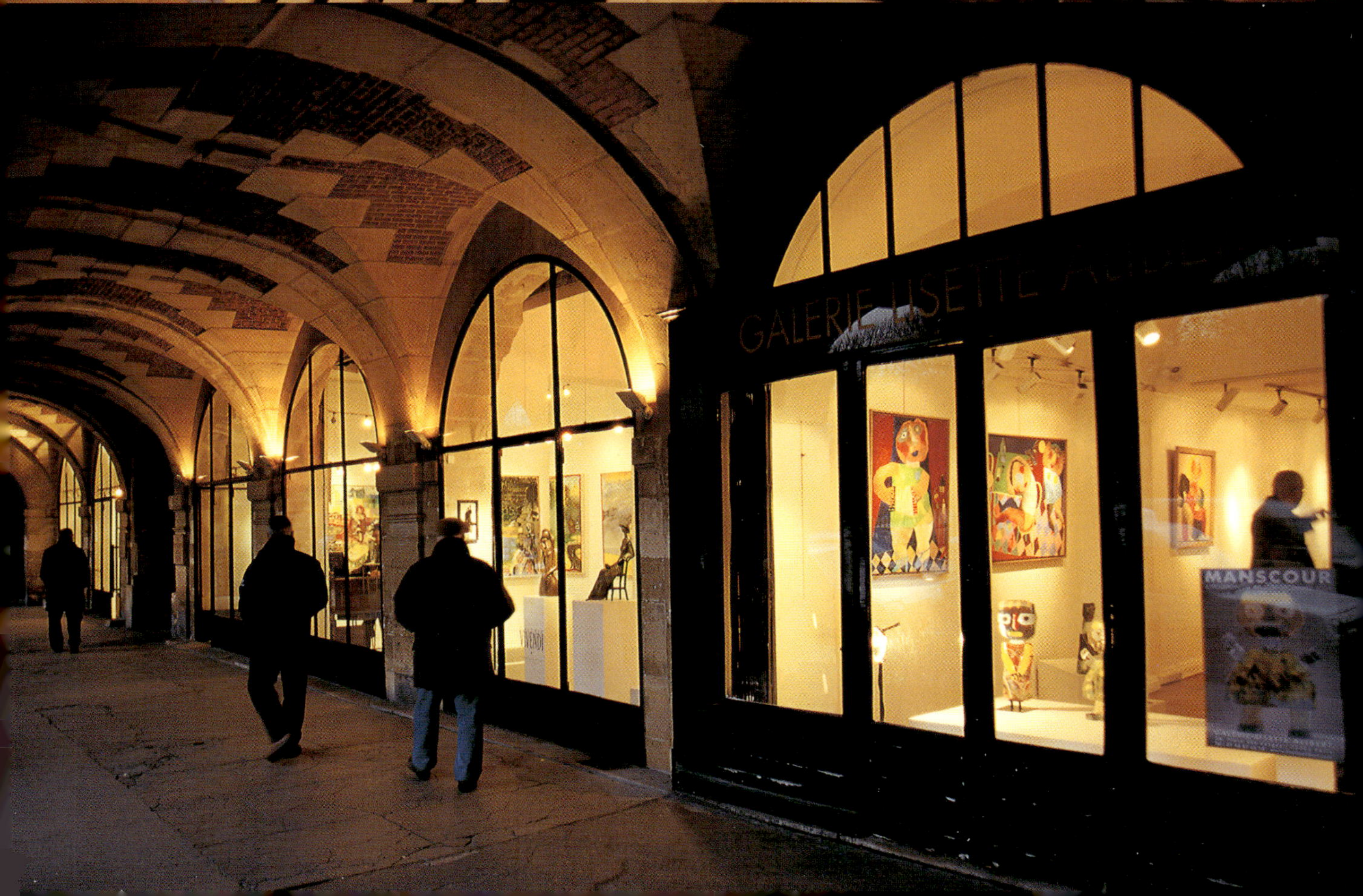
GALERIE LISETTE
MANSCOUR

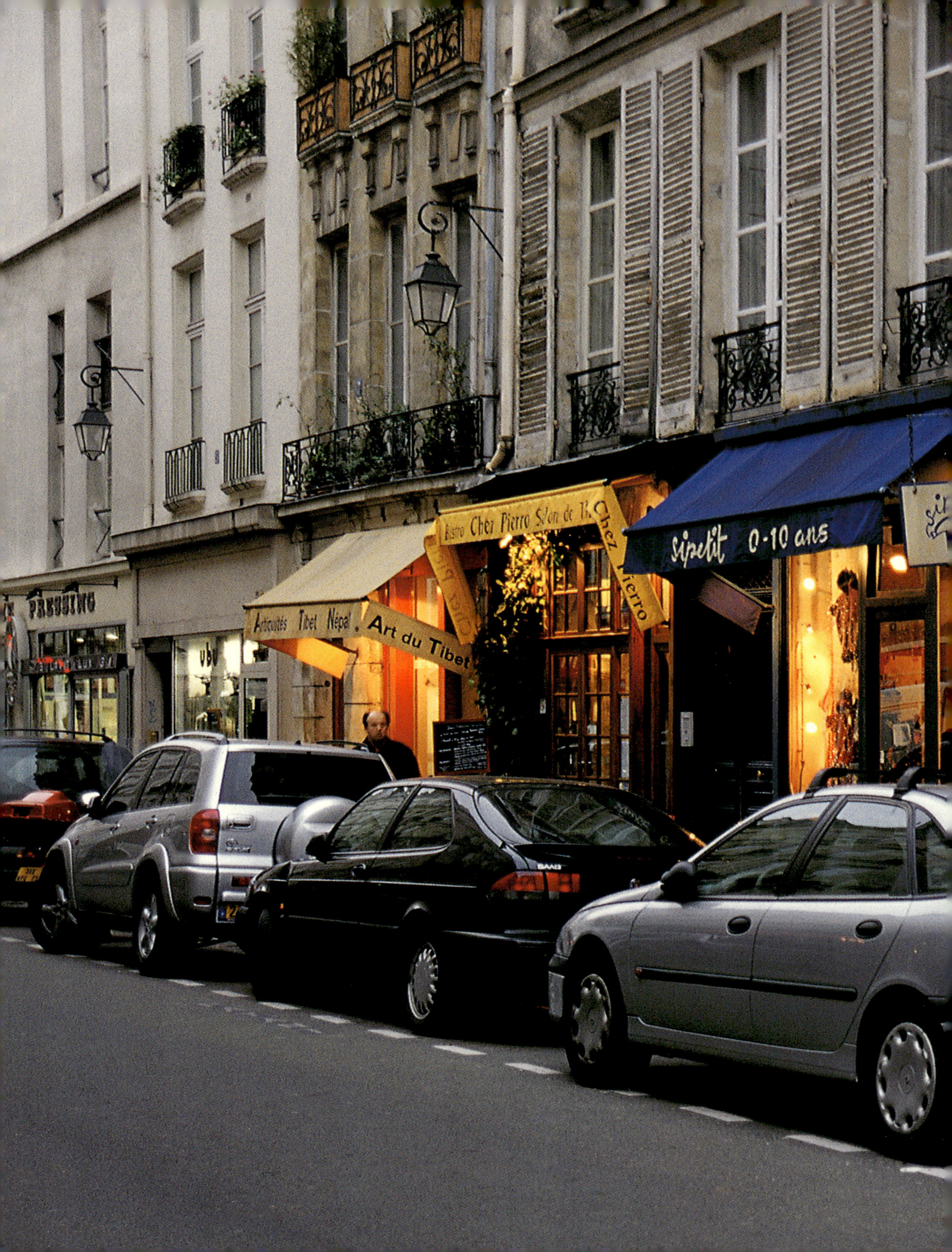
PRESSING
Artisanats Tibet Népal
Art du Tibet
Bistro Chez Pierro
Chez Pierro
sipetit 0-10 ans

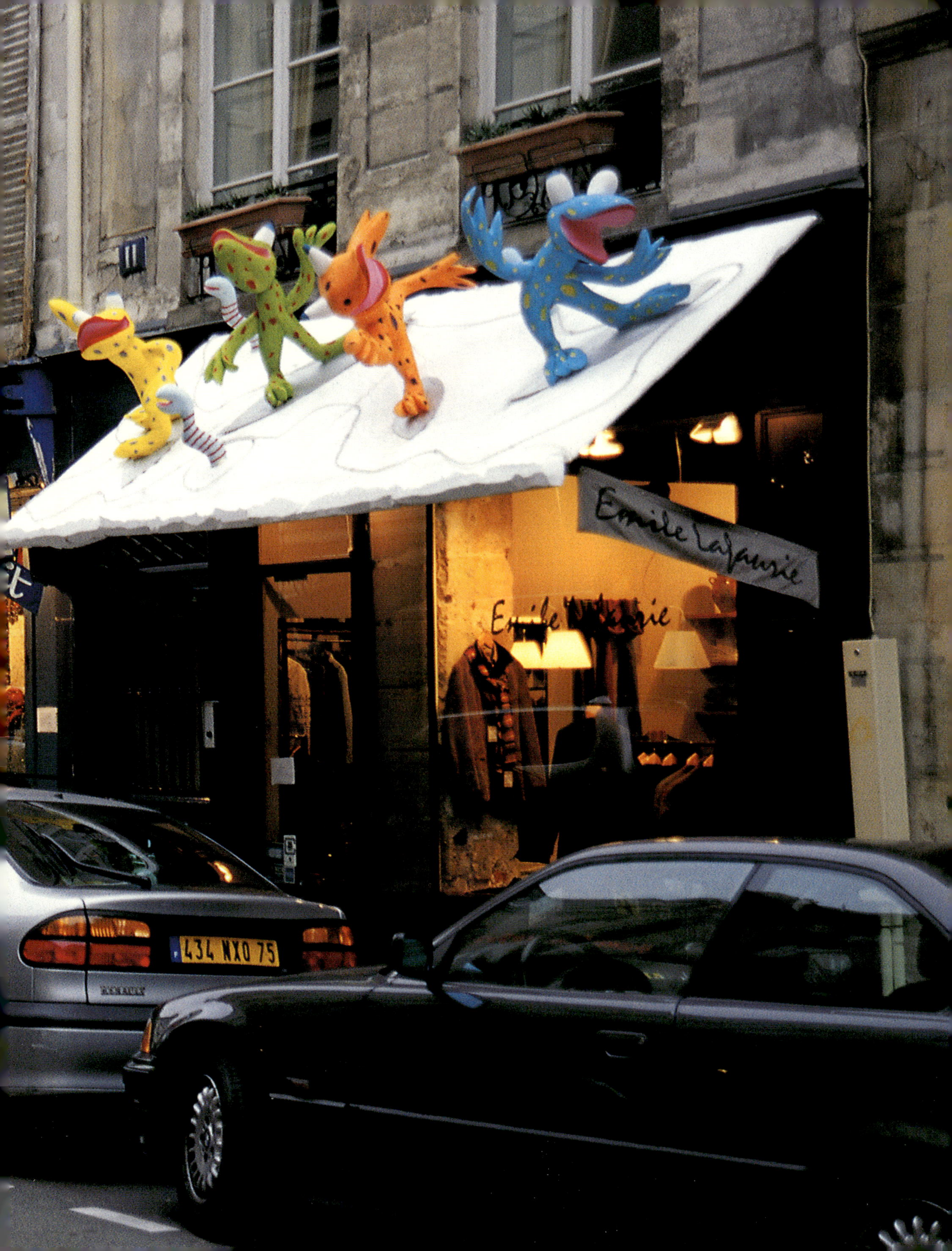
Emile Lafaurie
434 NXO 75

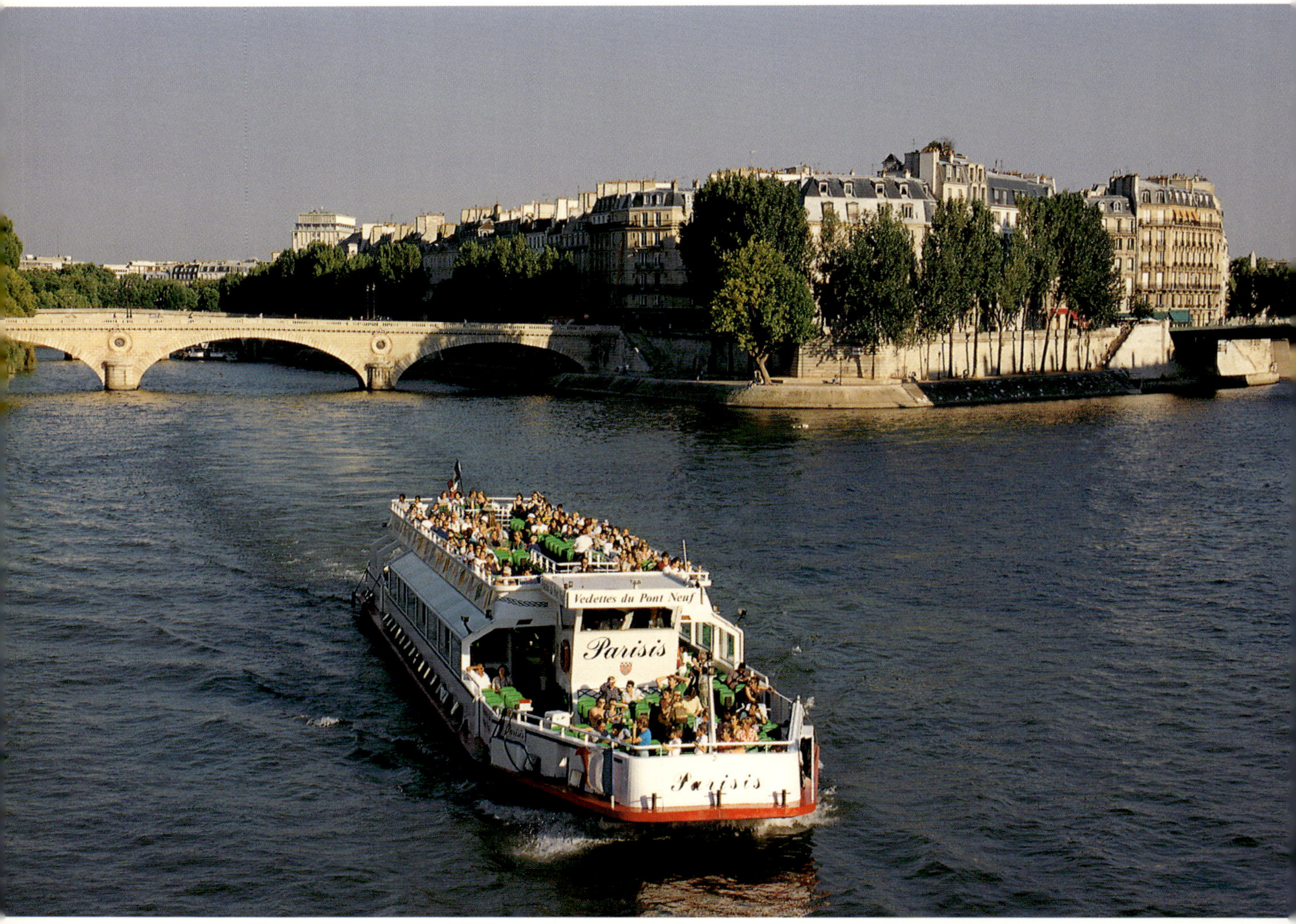
Vedettes du Pont Neuf
Parisis
Parisis

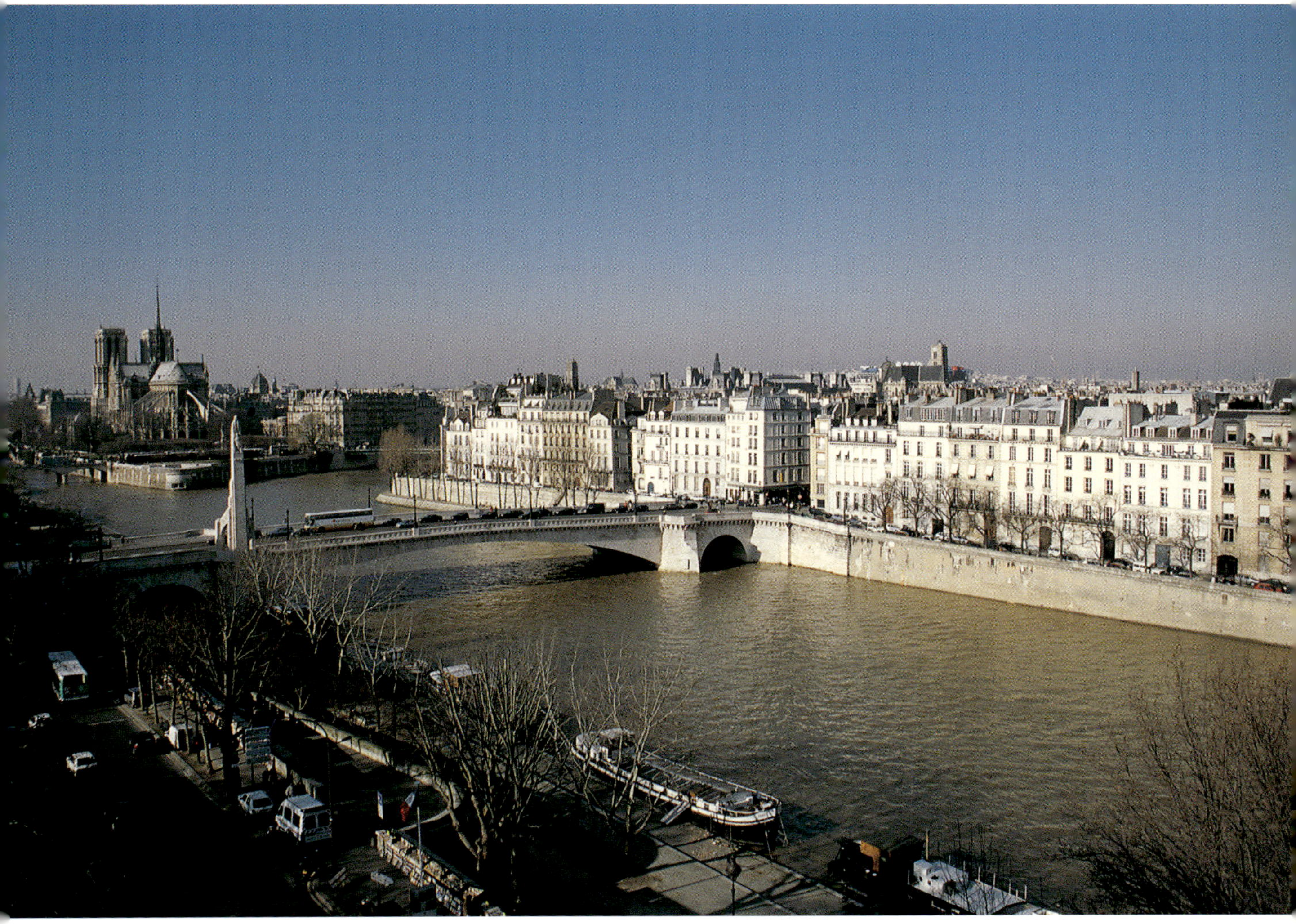

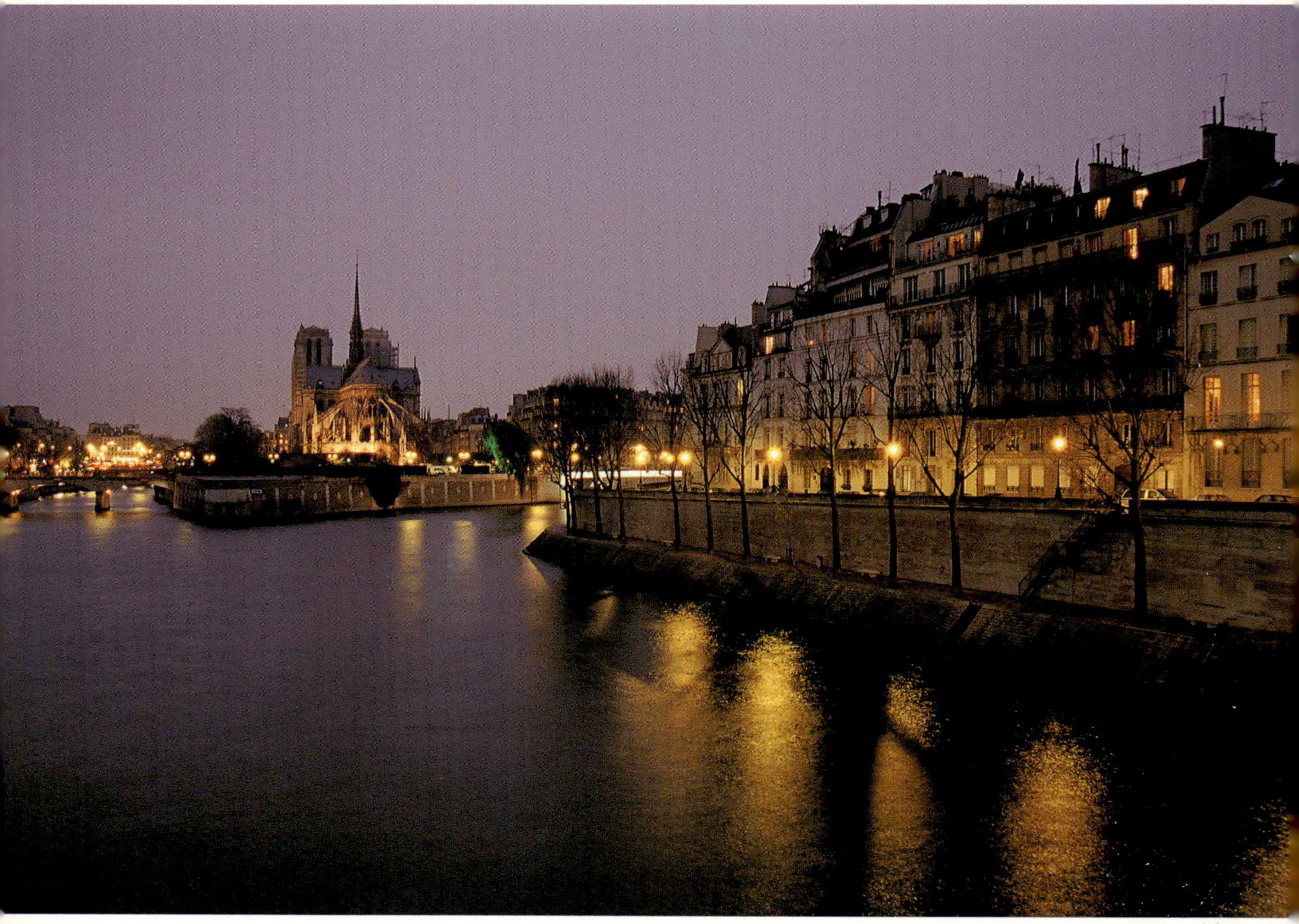

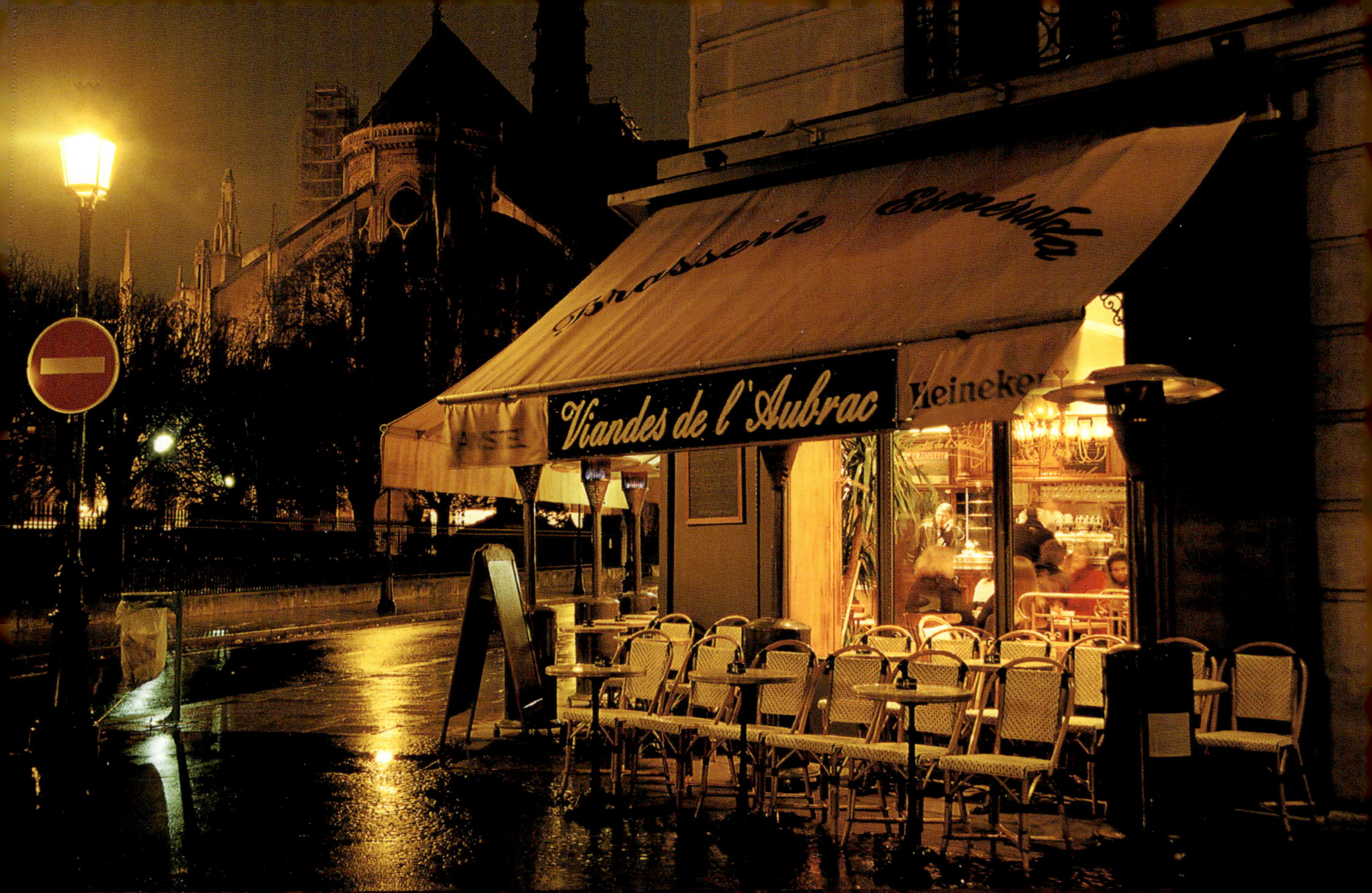
Brasserie
Esméralda
Viandes de l'Aubrac

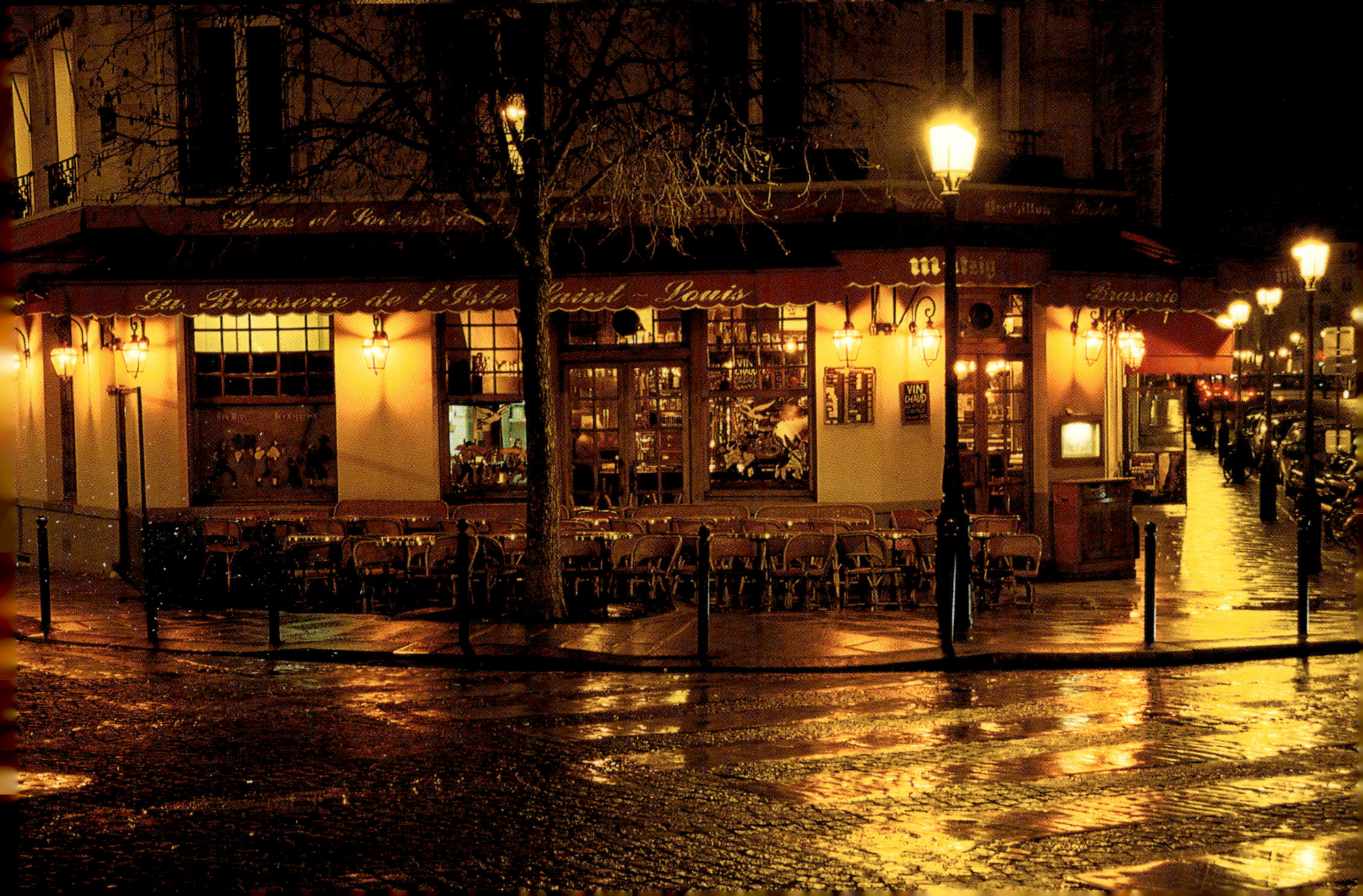
La Brasserie de l'Isle Saint-Louis
VIN CHAUD
Brasserie

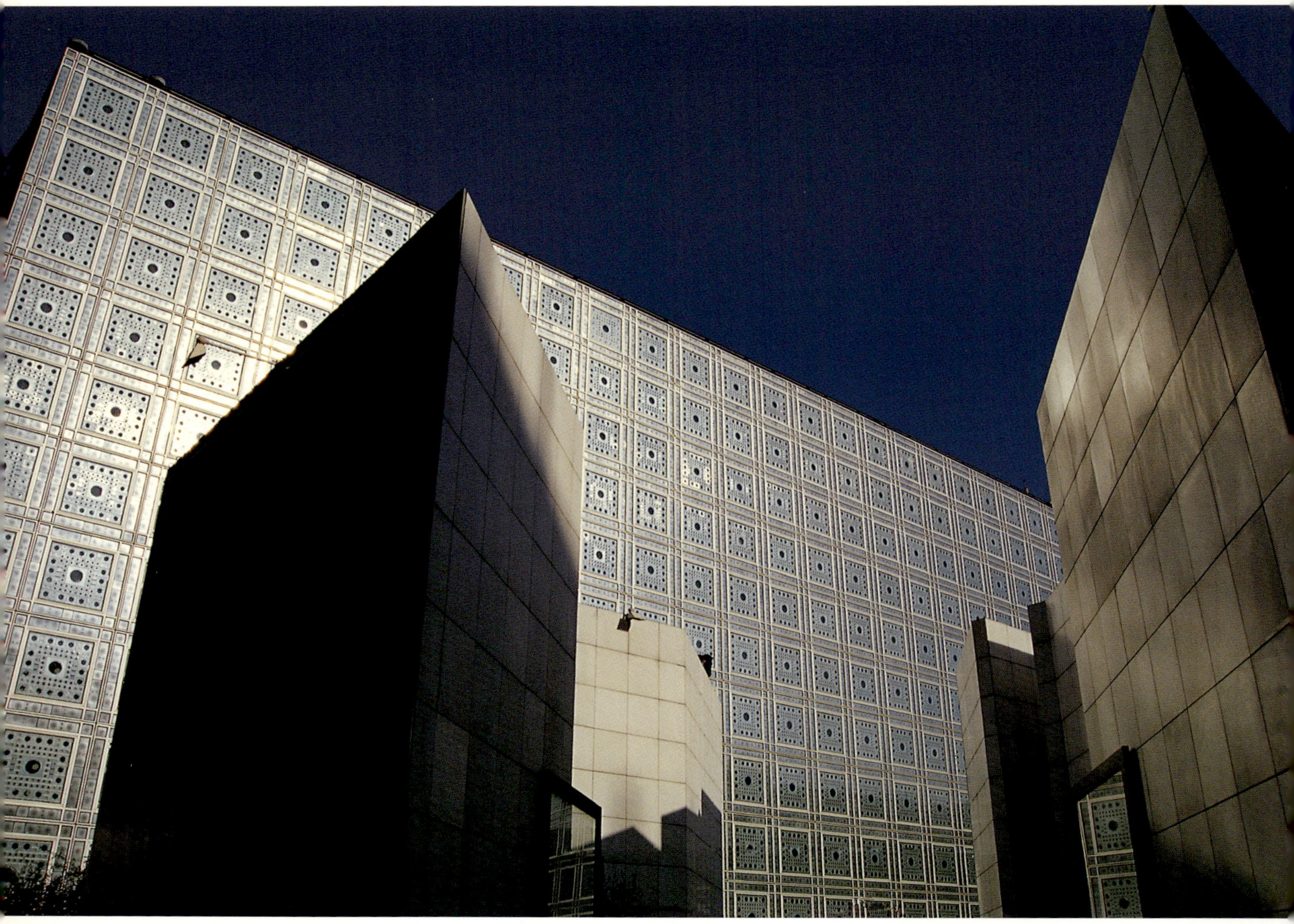

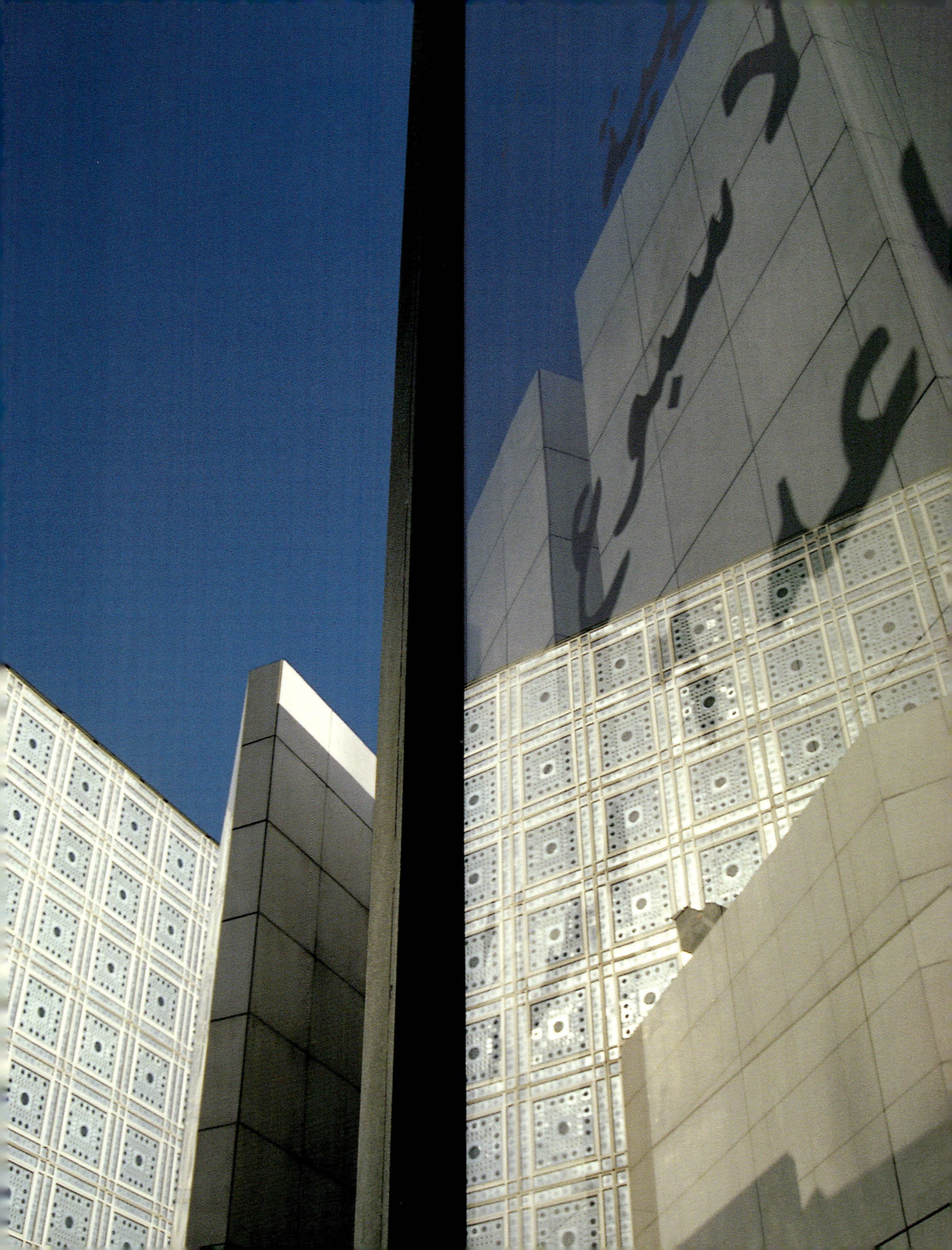

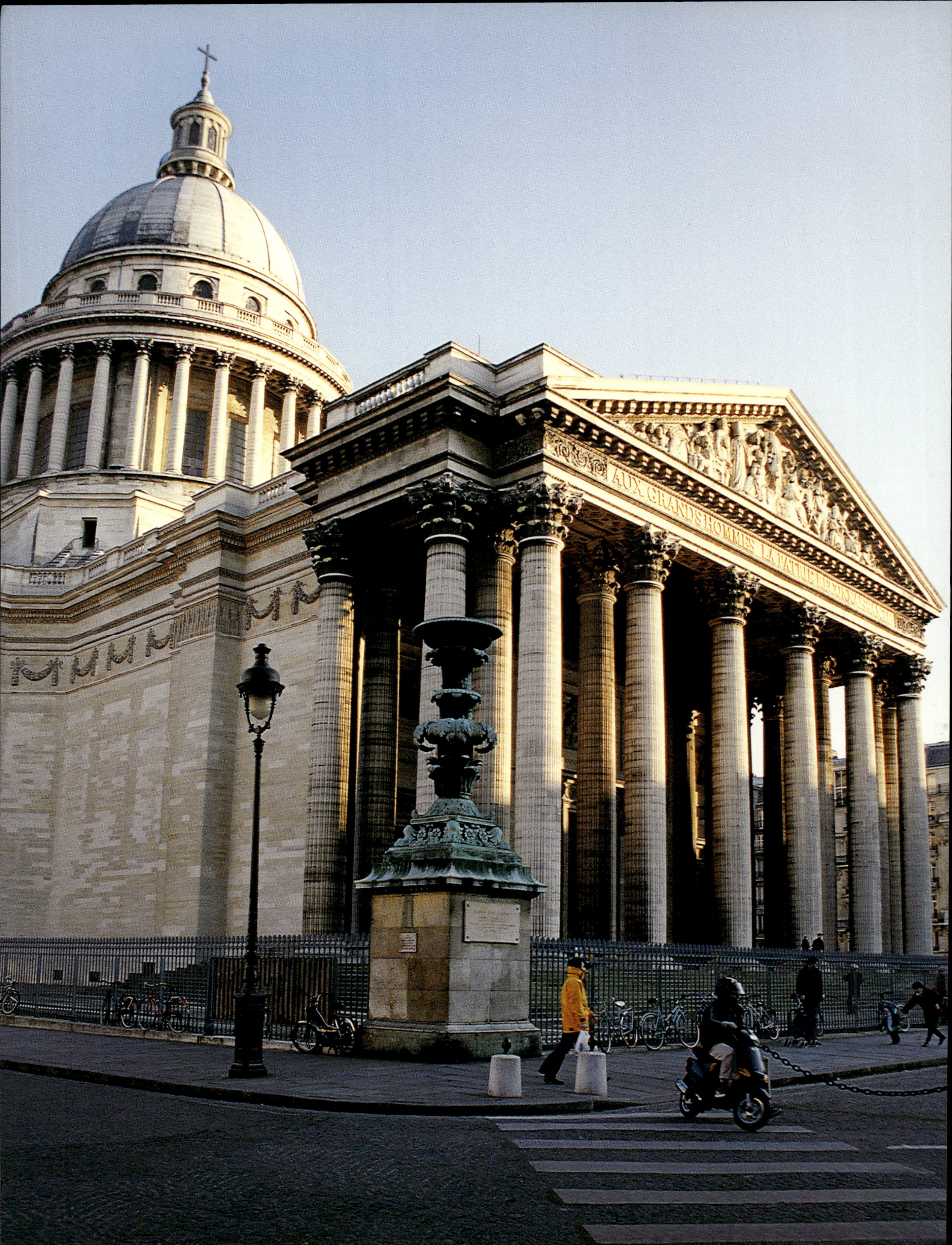
AUX GRANDS HOMMES LA PATRIE

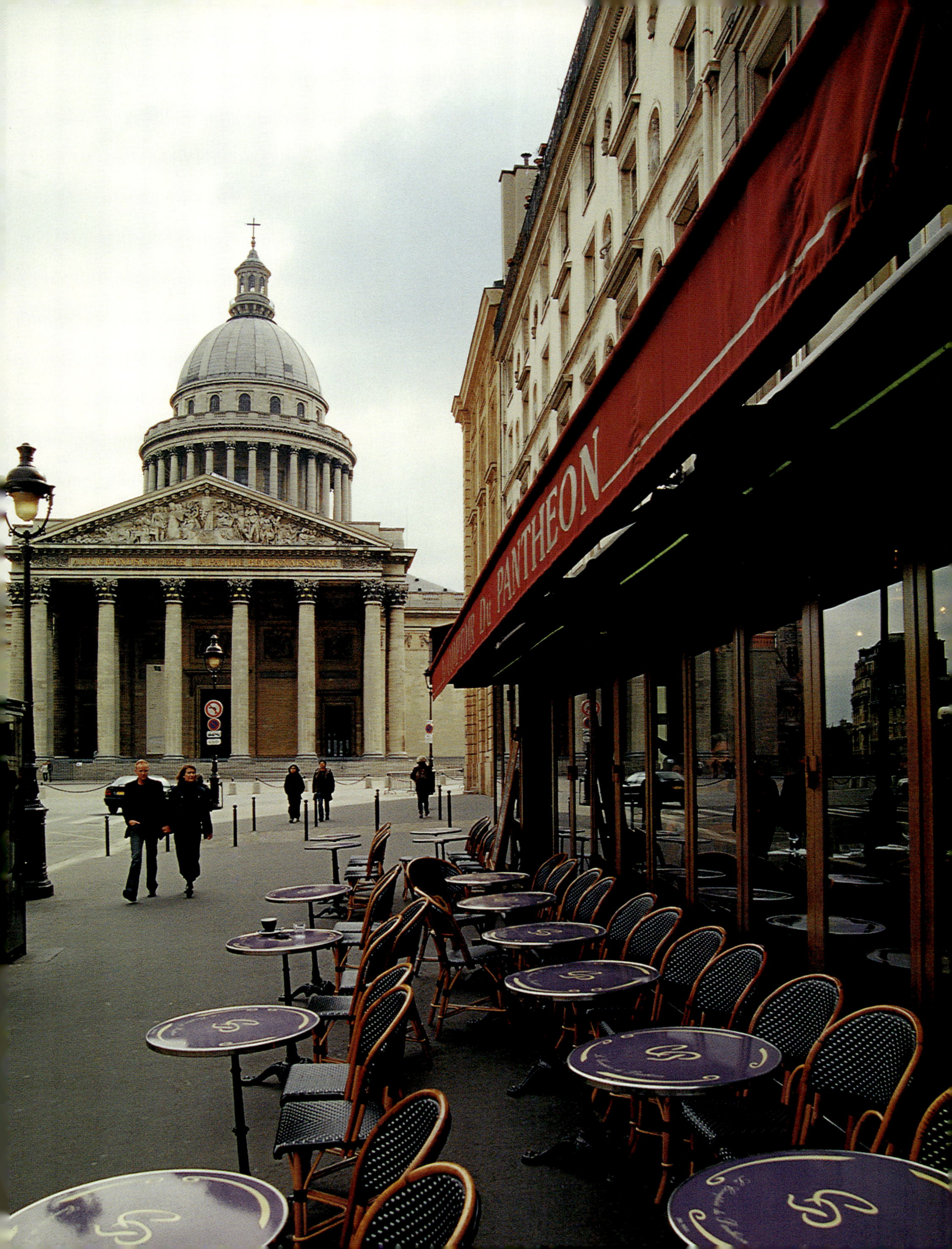
PANTHEON

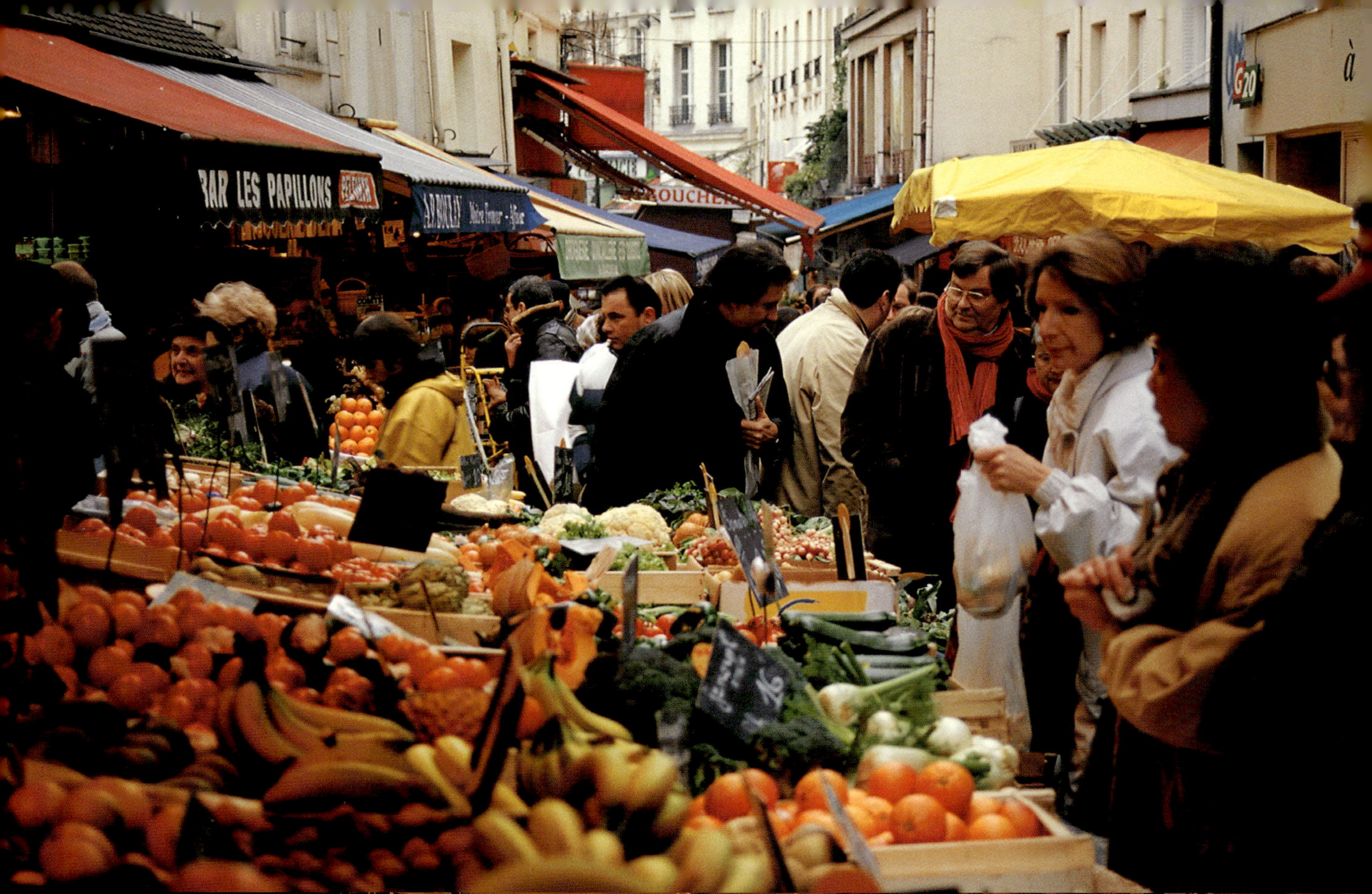
BAR LES PAPILLONS
G20

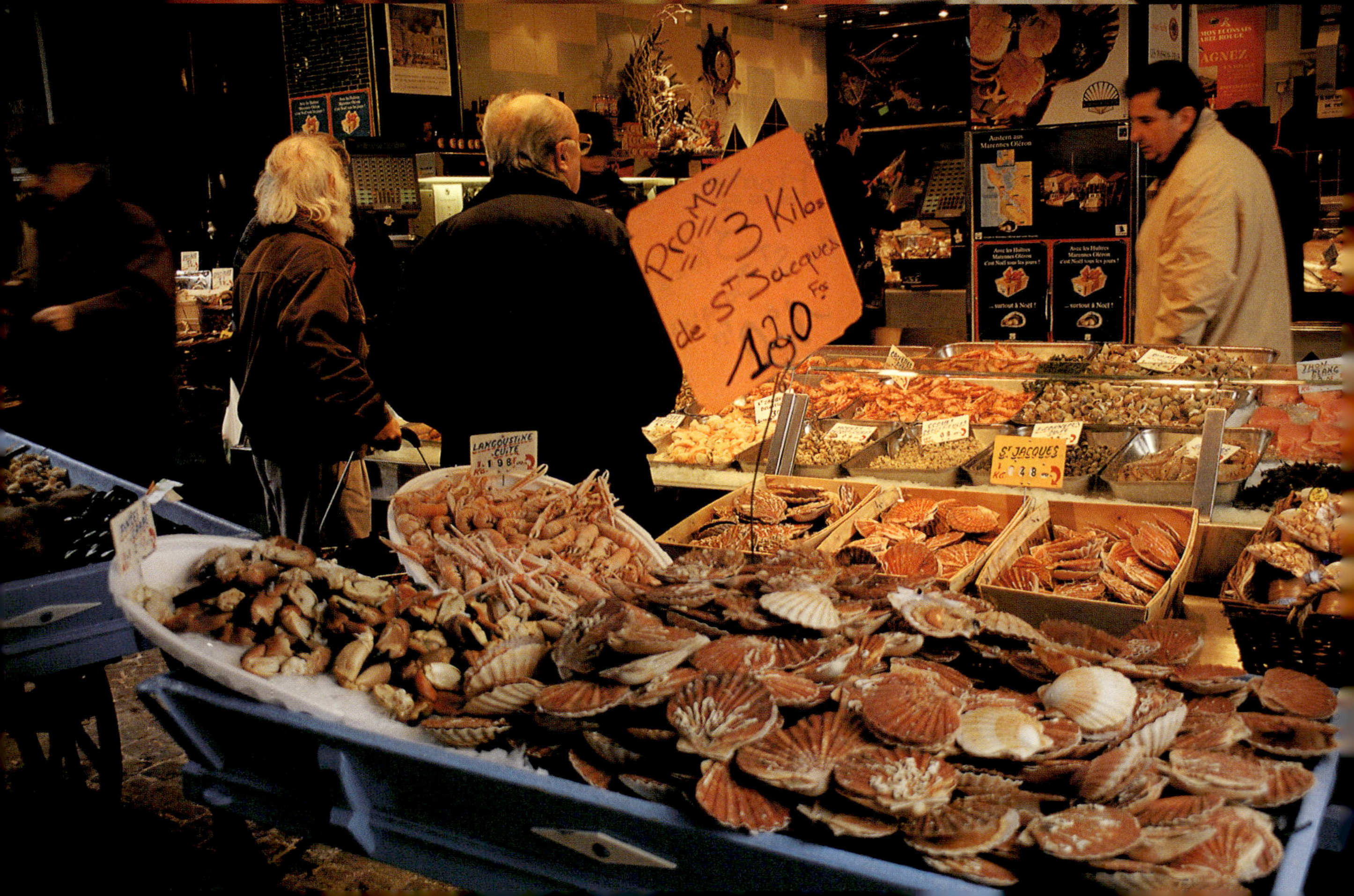
Promo!! 3 Kilos de St Jacques 120 Fs
LANGOUSTINE CUITE
St JACQUES

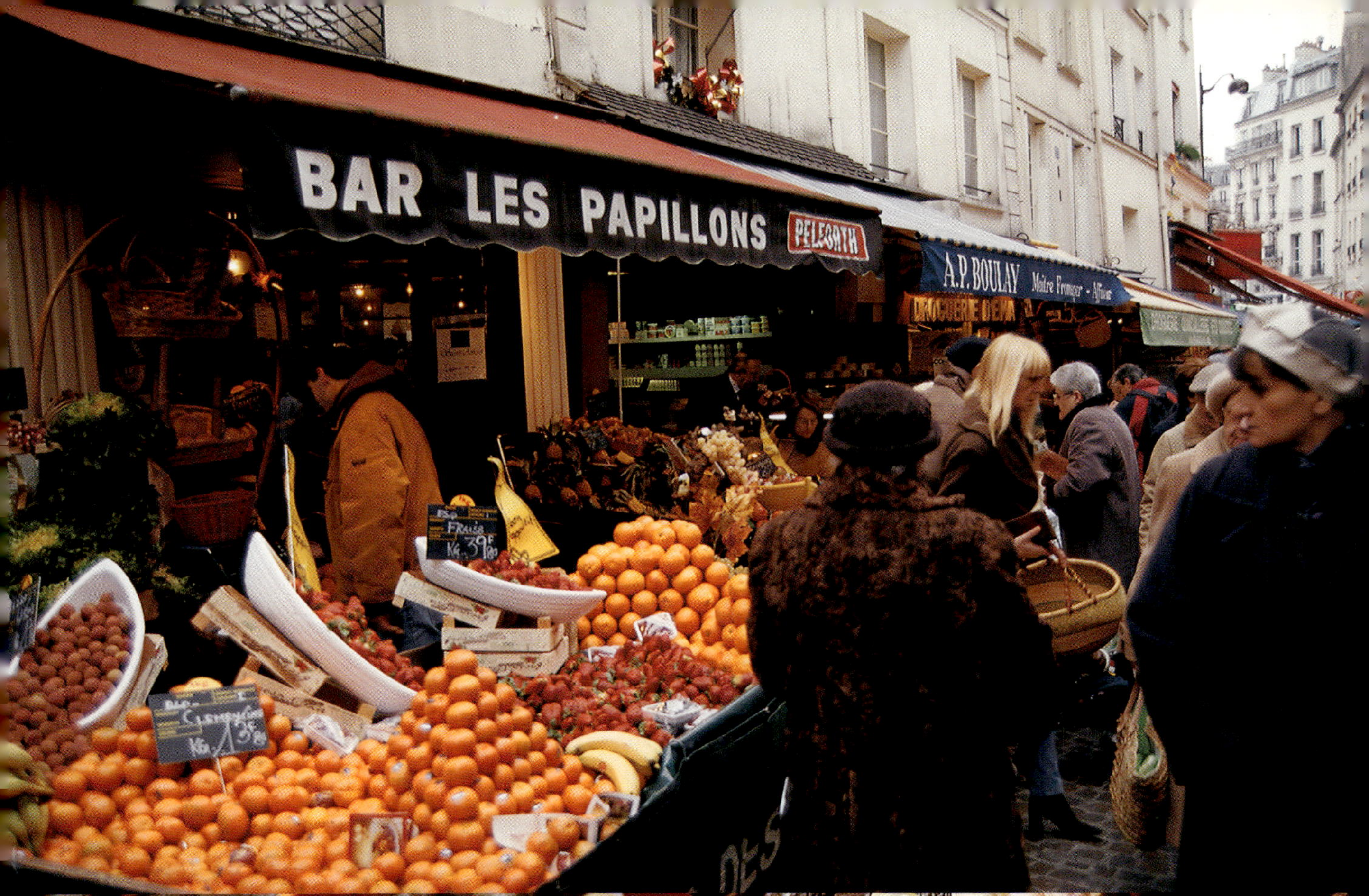
BAR LES PAPILLONS
PELFORTH
A.P. BOULAY

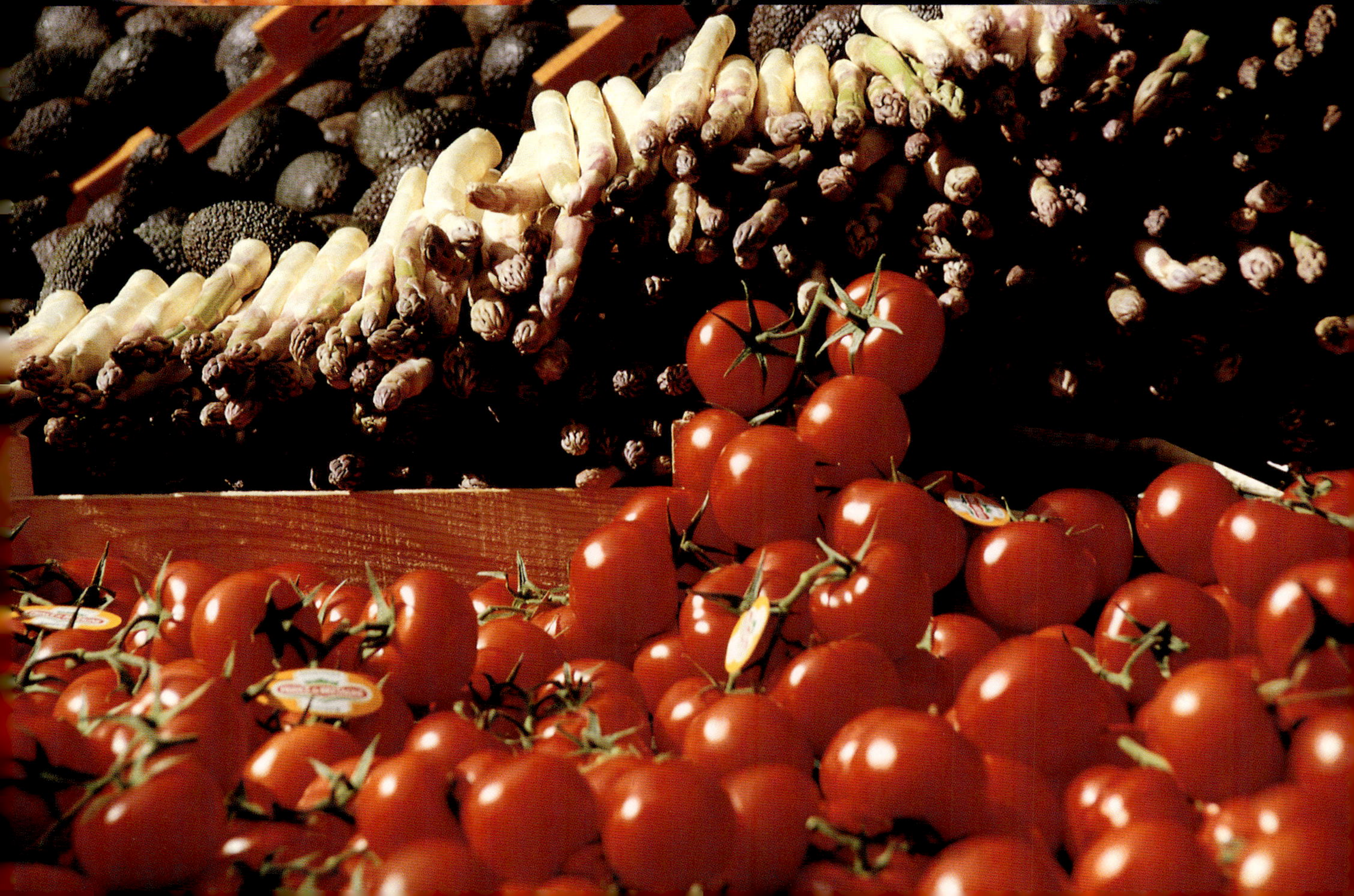

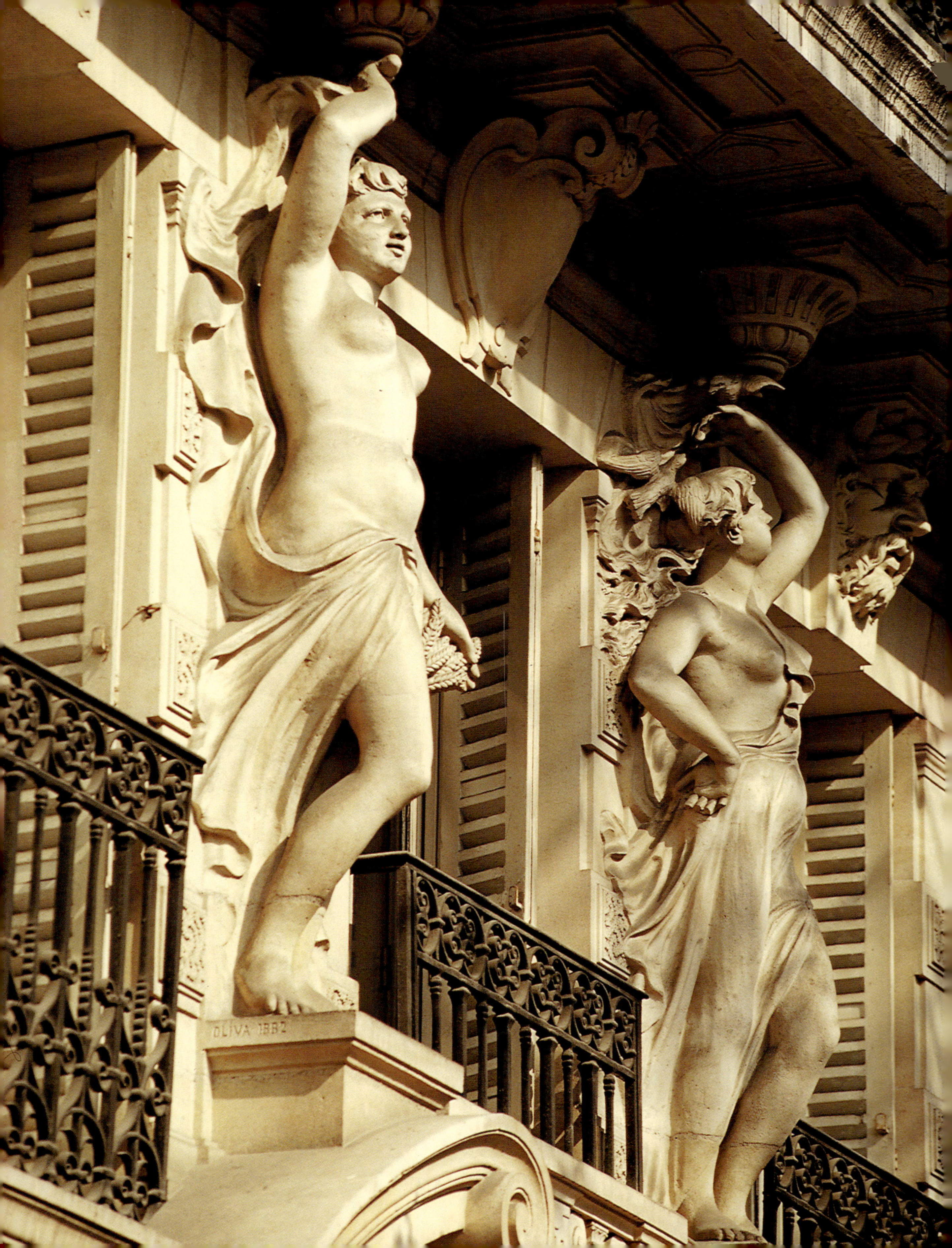
OLIVA 1882

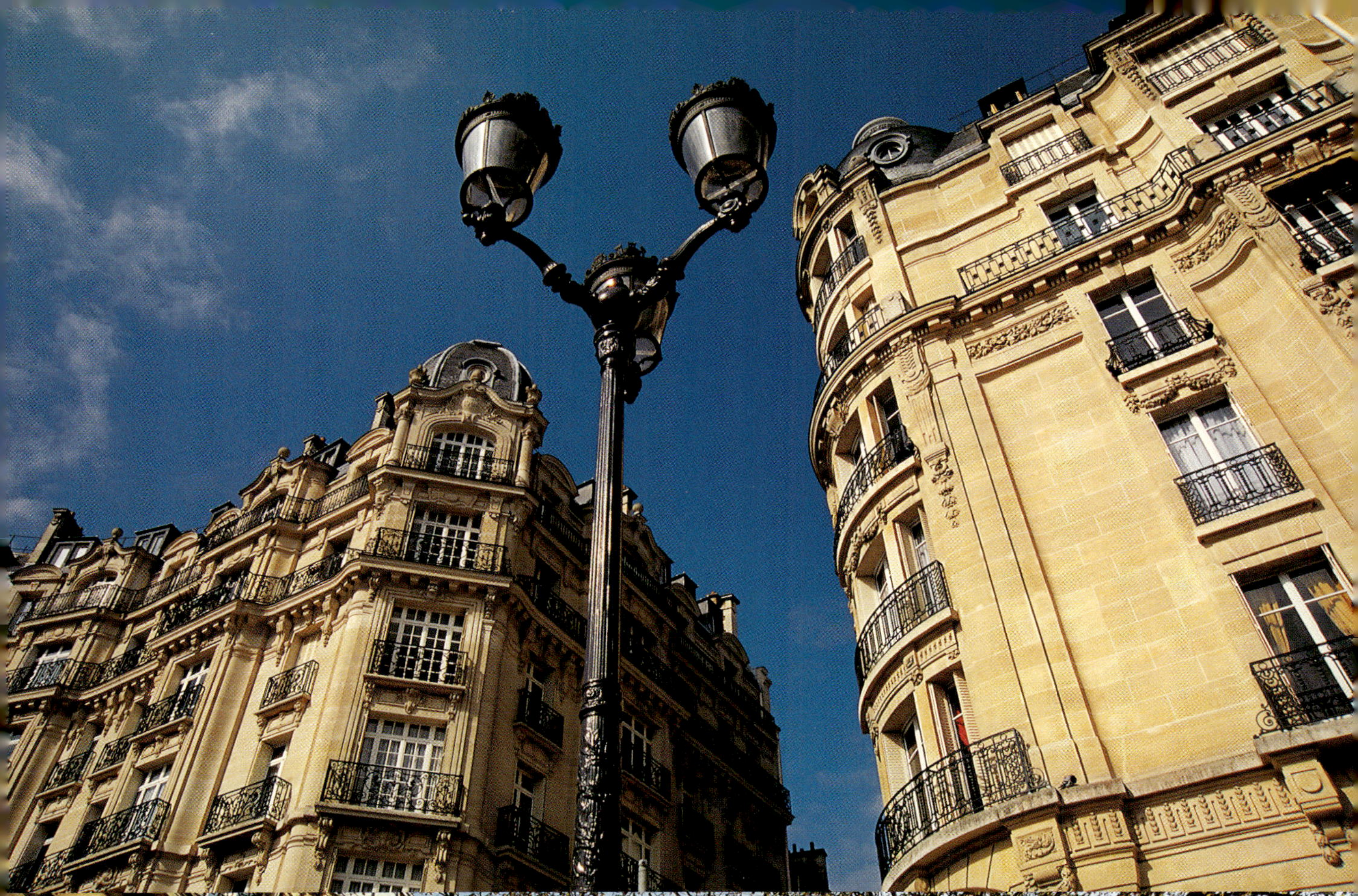

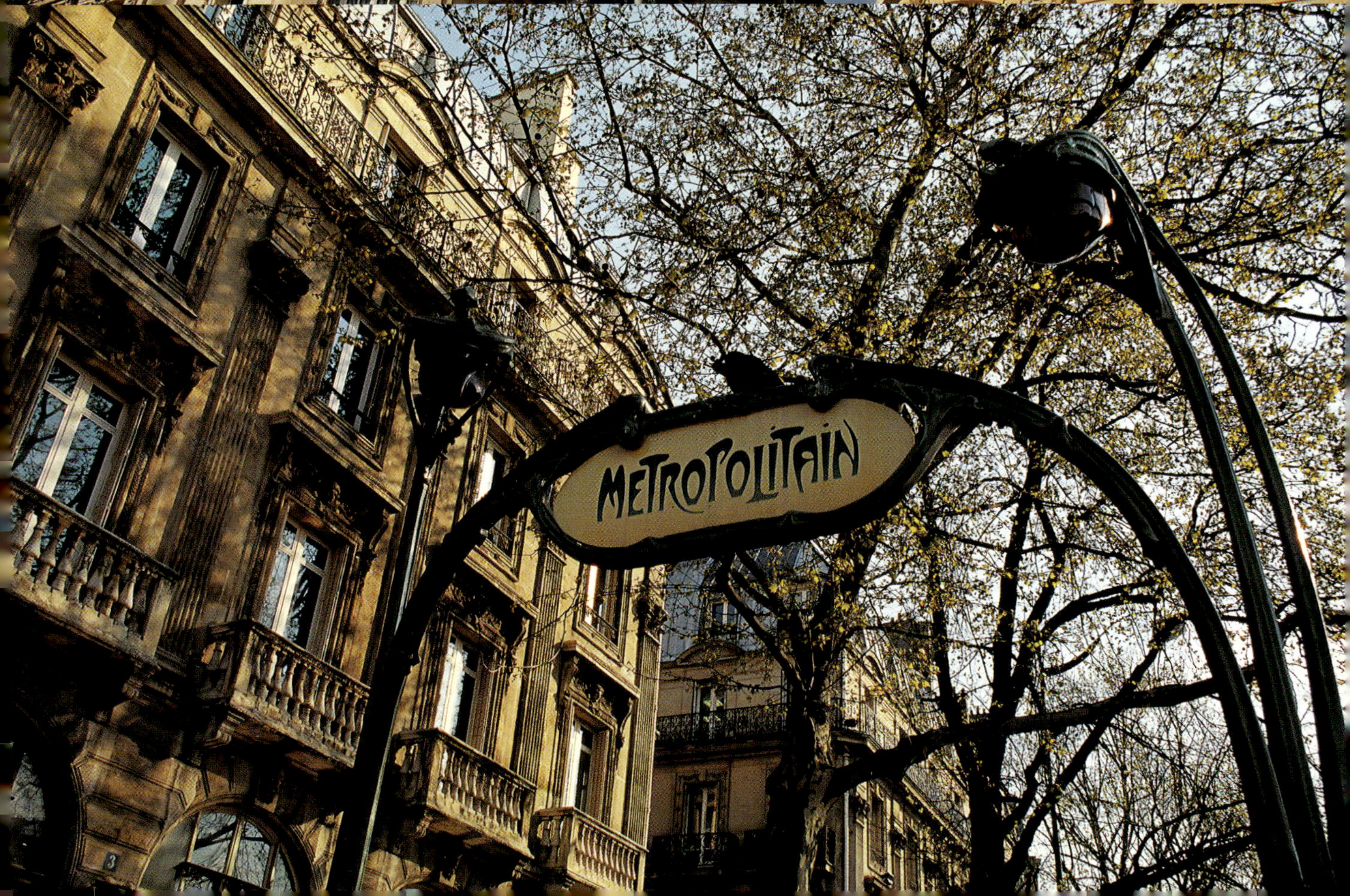
METROPOLITAIN

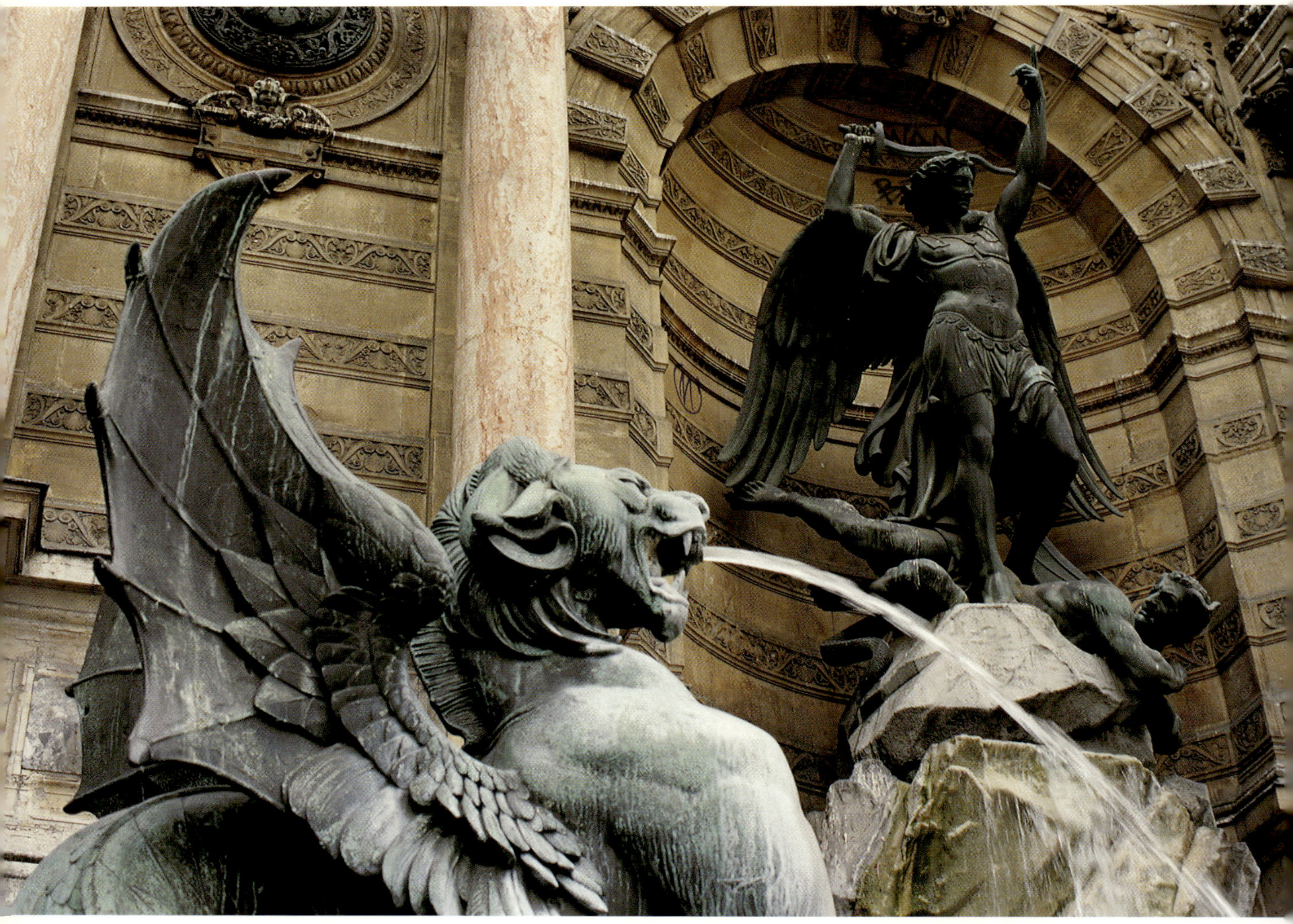

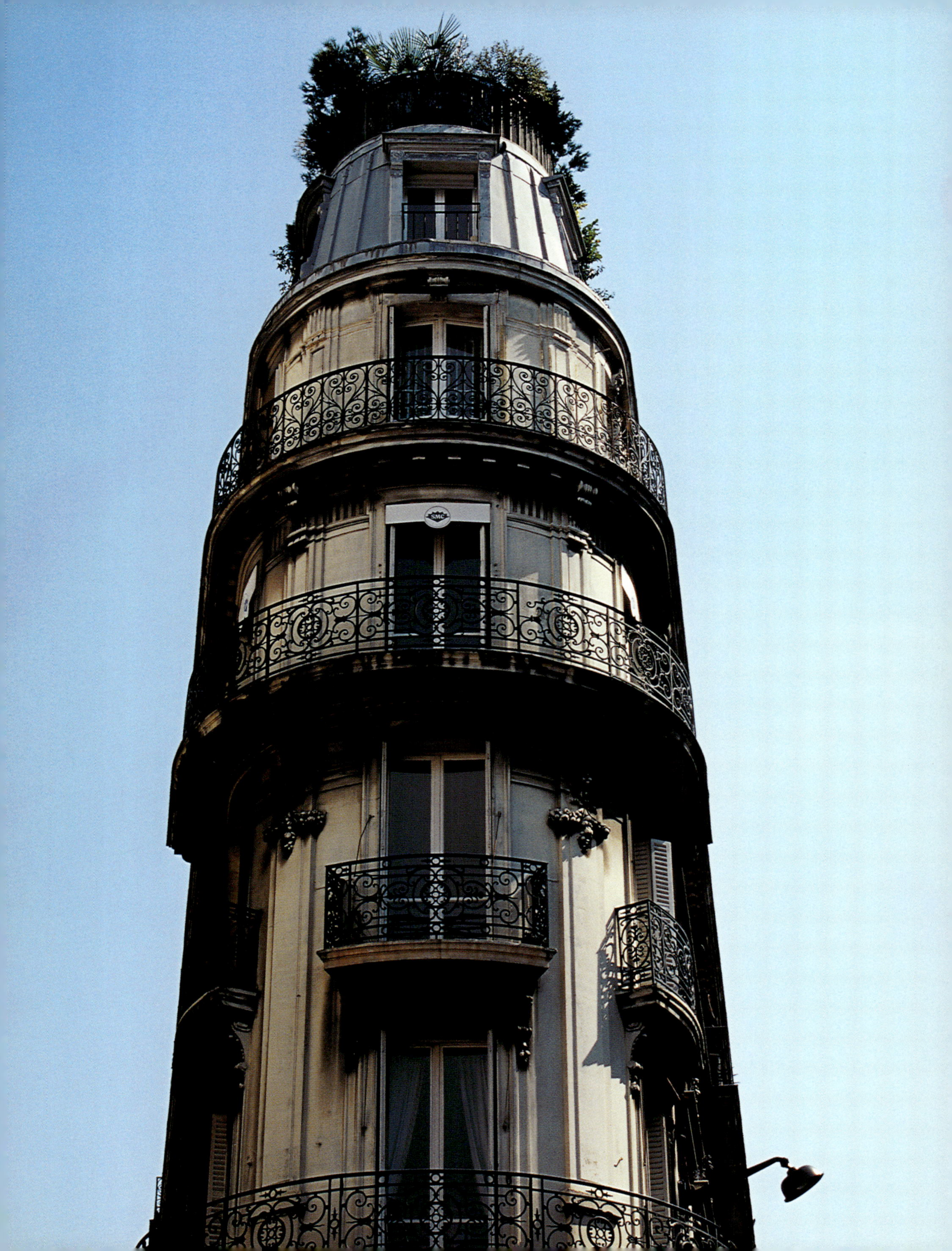
SMC

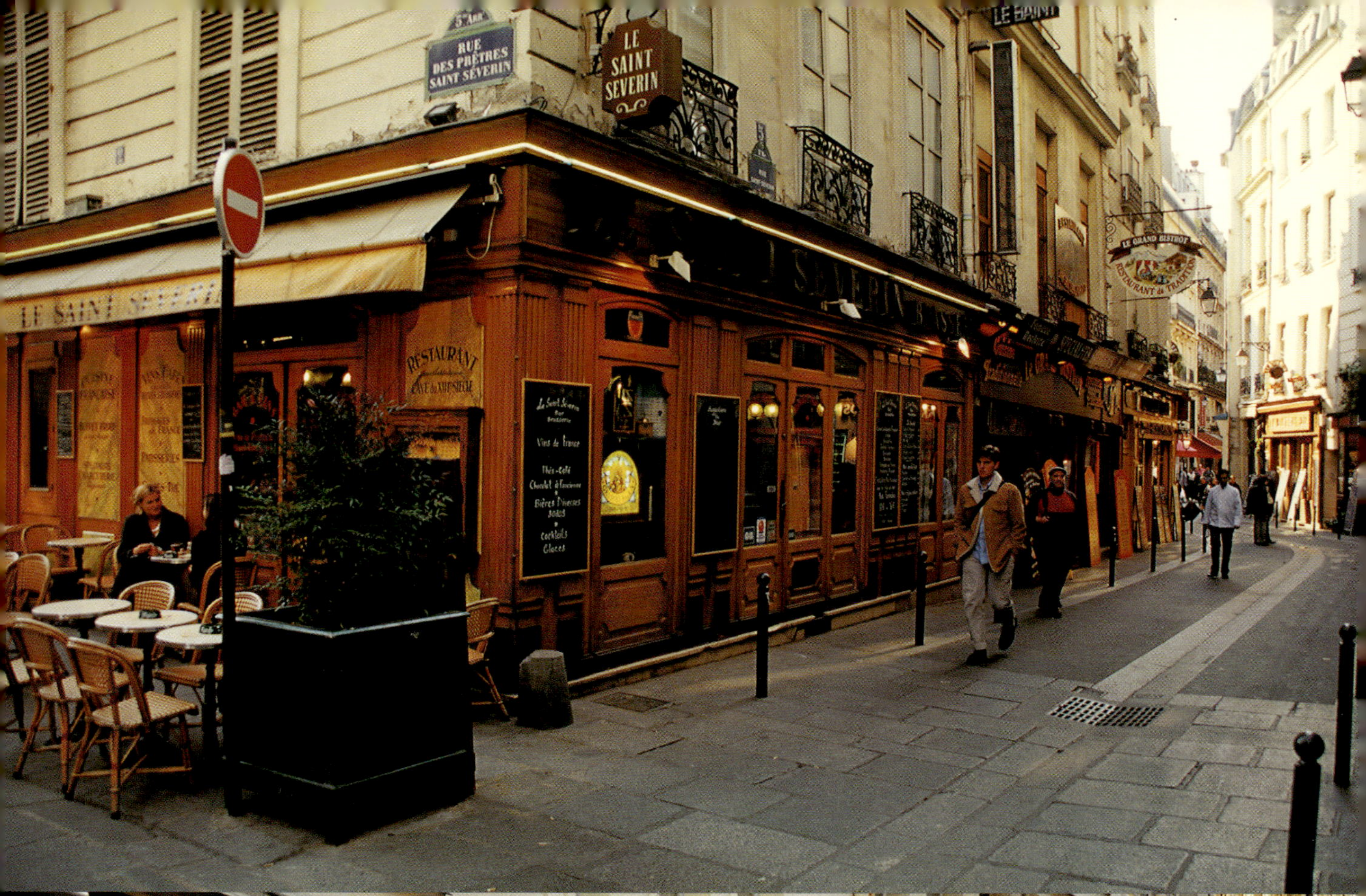
RUE DES PRÊTRES SAINT SÉVERIN
LE SAINT SEVERIN
RESTAURANT
LE GRAND BISTROT

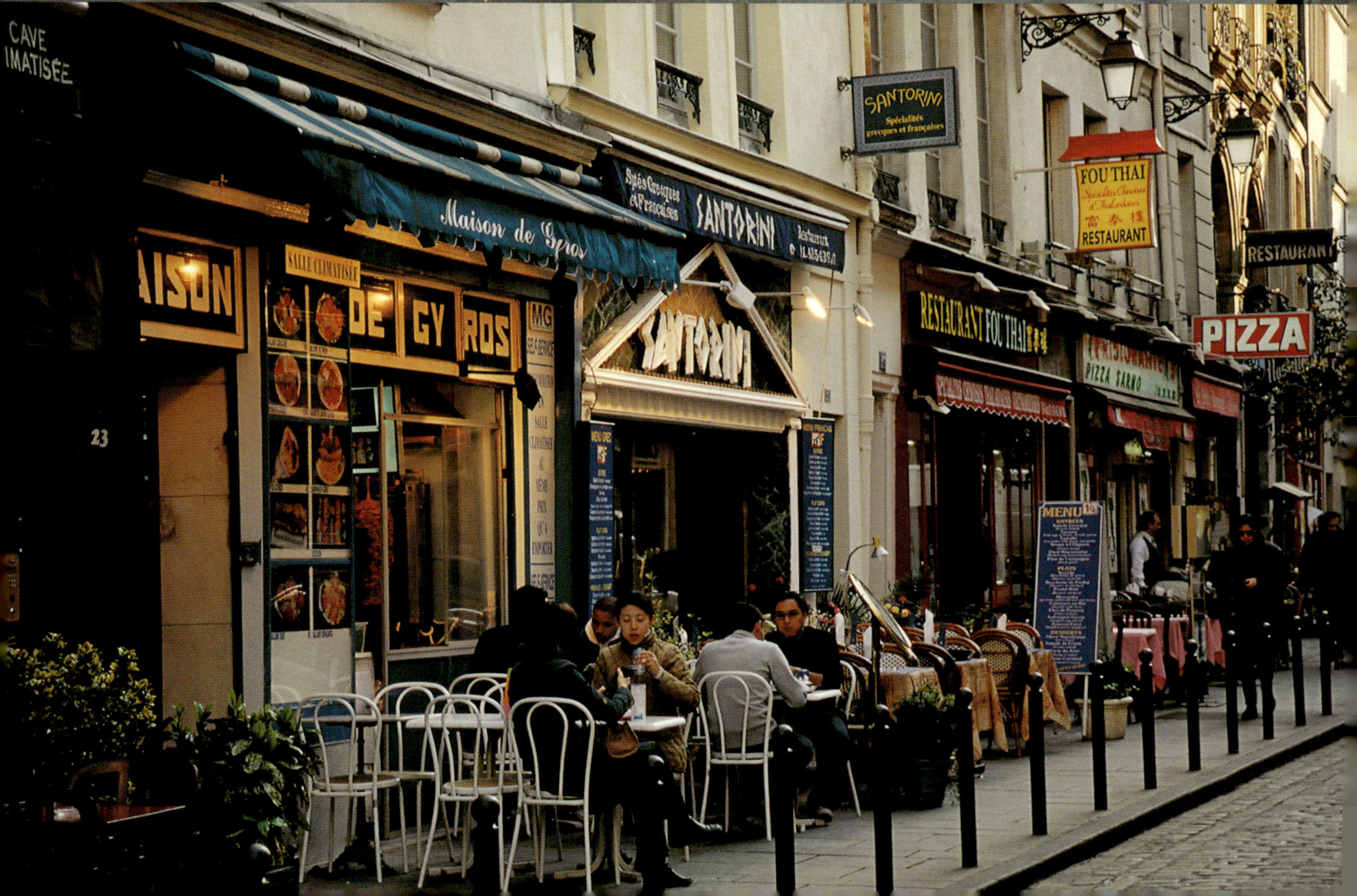
CAVE
SANTORINI
Spécialités grecques et françaises
FOU THAI
RESTAURANT
Maison de Gyros
SALLE CLIMATISÉE
DE GY ROS
SANTORINI
SANTORINI
RESTAURANT FOU THAI
RESTAURANT
PIZZA
PIZZA SARNO
MENU
23

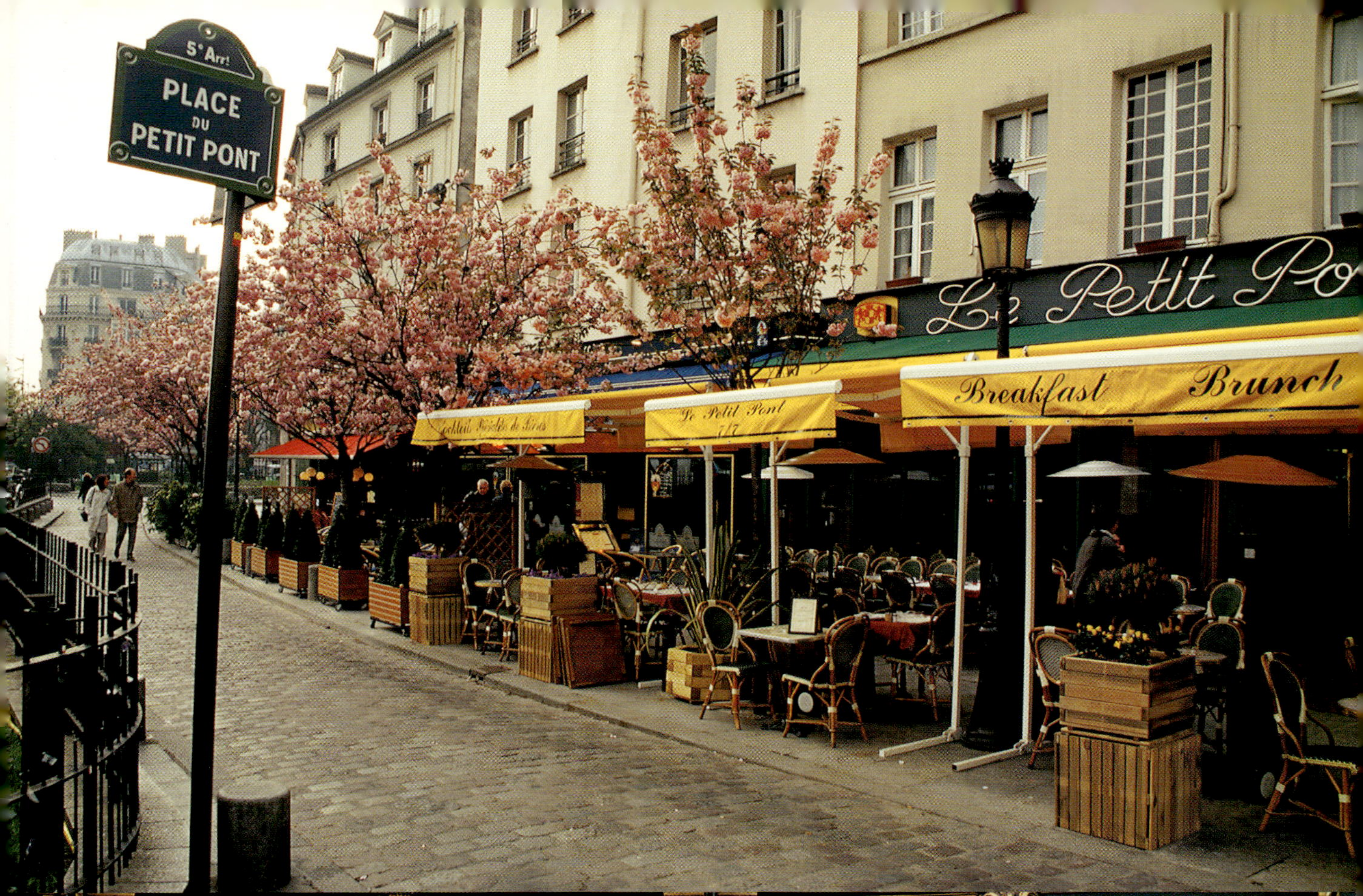
5e Arr!
PLACE DU PETIT PONT
Le Petit Po
Le Petit Pont
Breakfast
Brunch

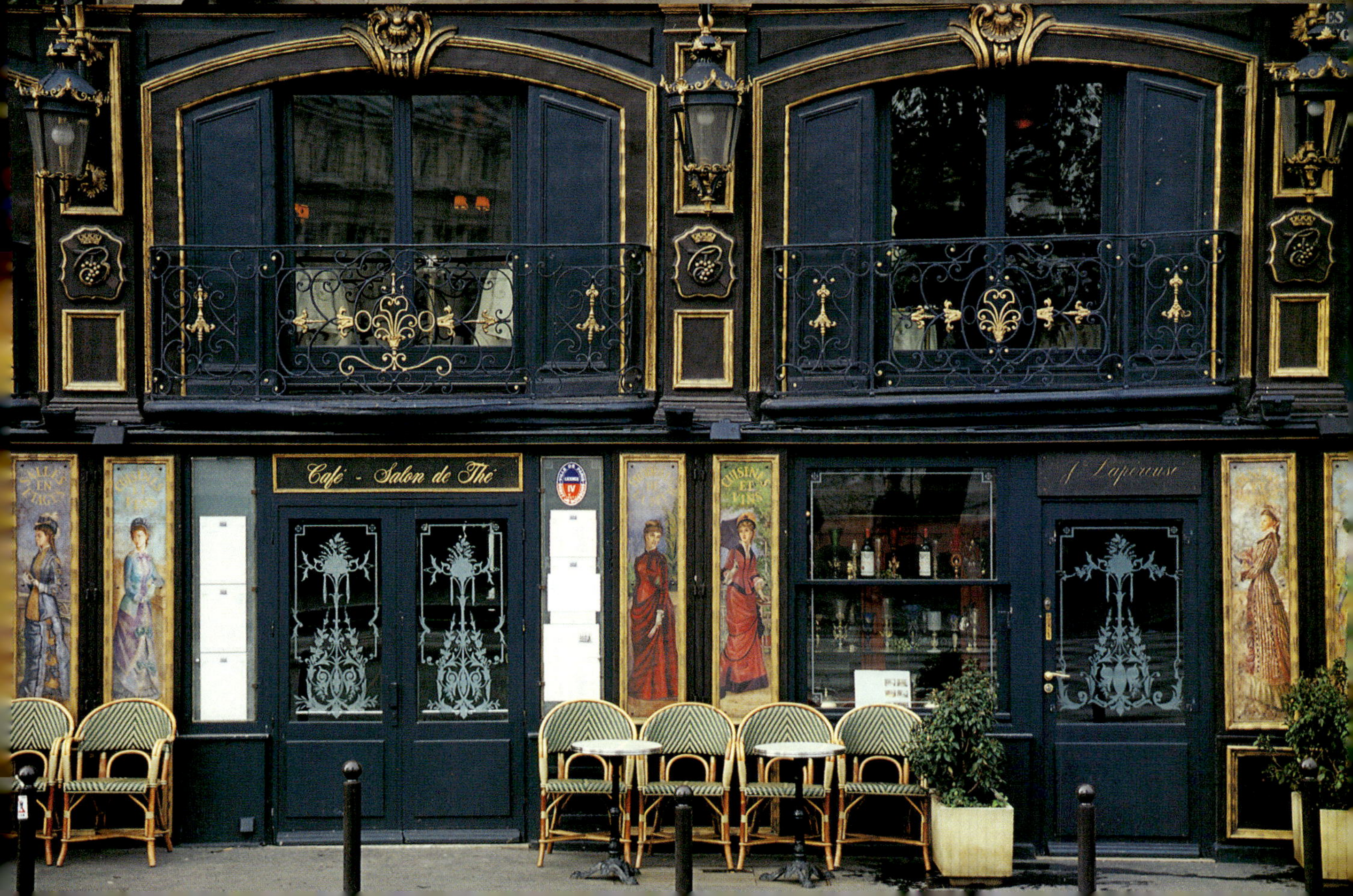
Café - Salon de Thé

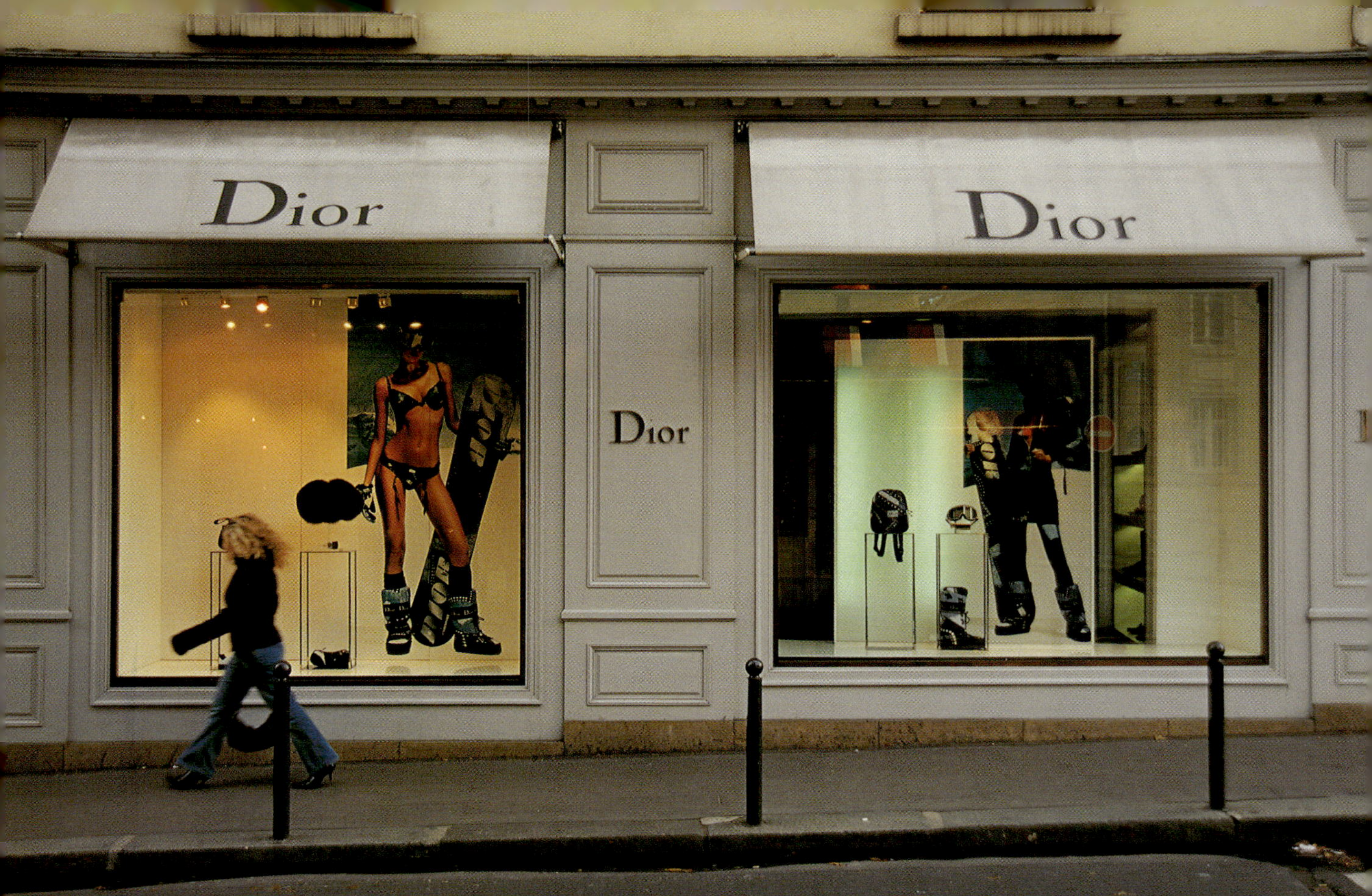
Dior
Dior
Dior

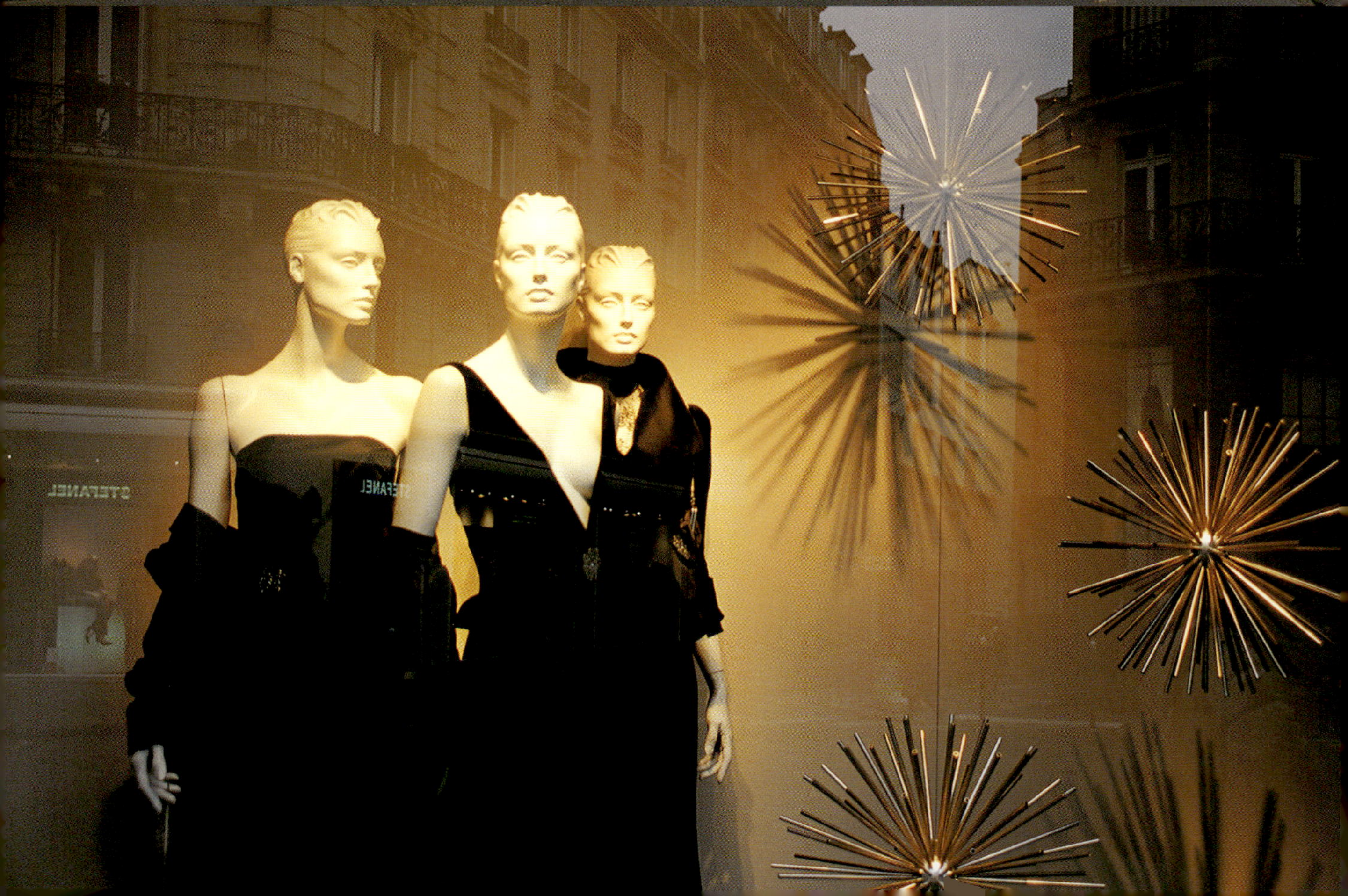

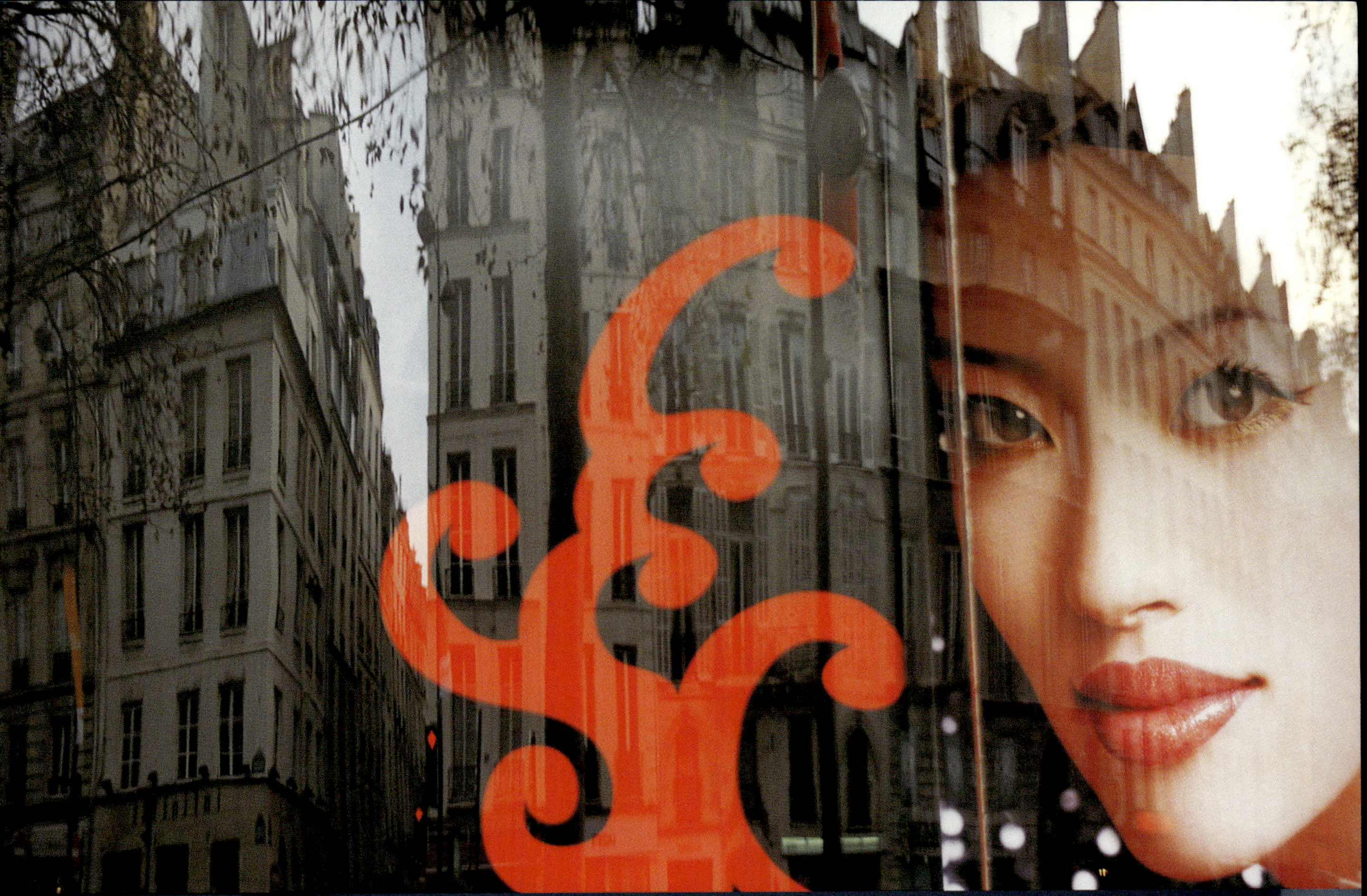

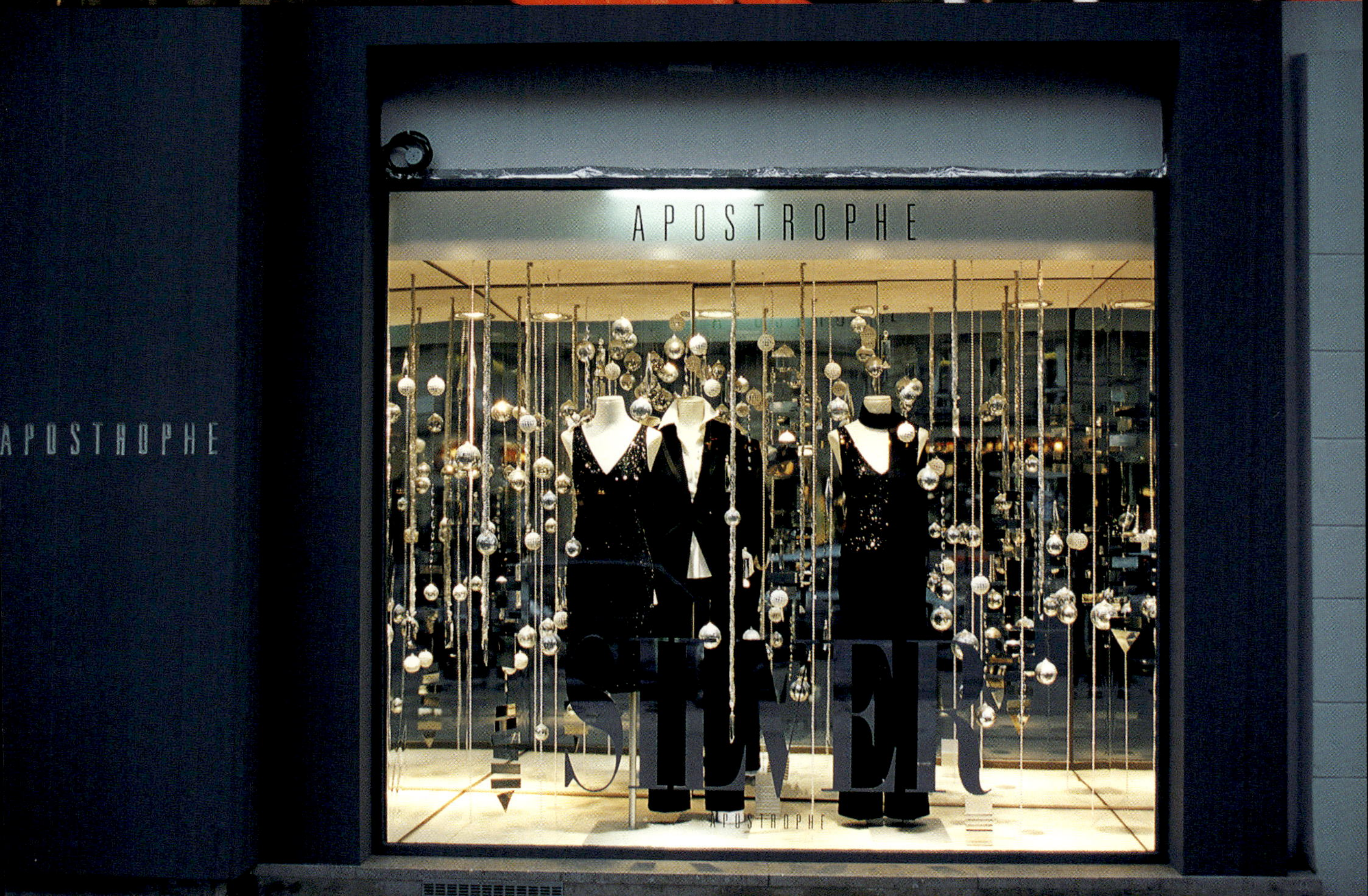
APOSTROPHE
APOSTROPHE
SILVER
APOSTROPHE

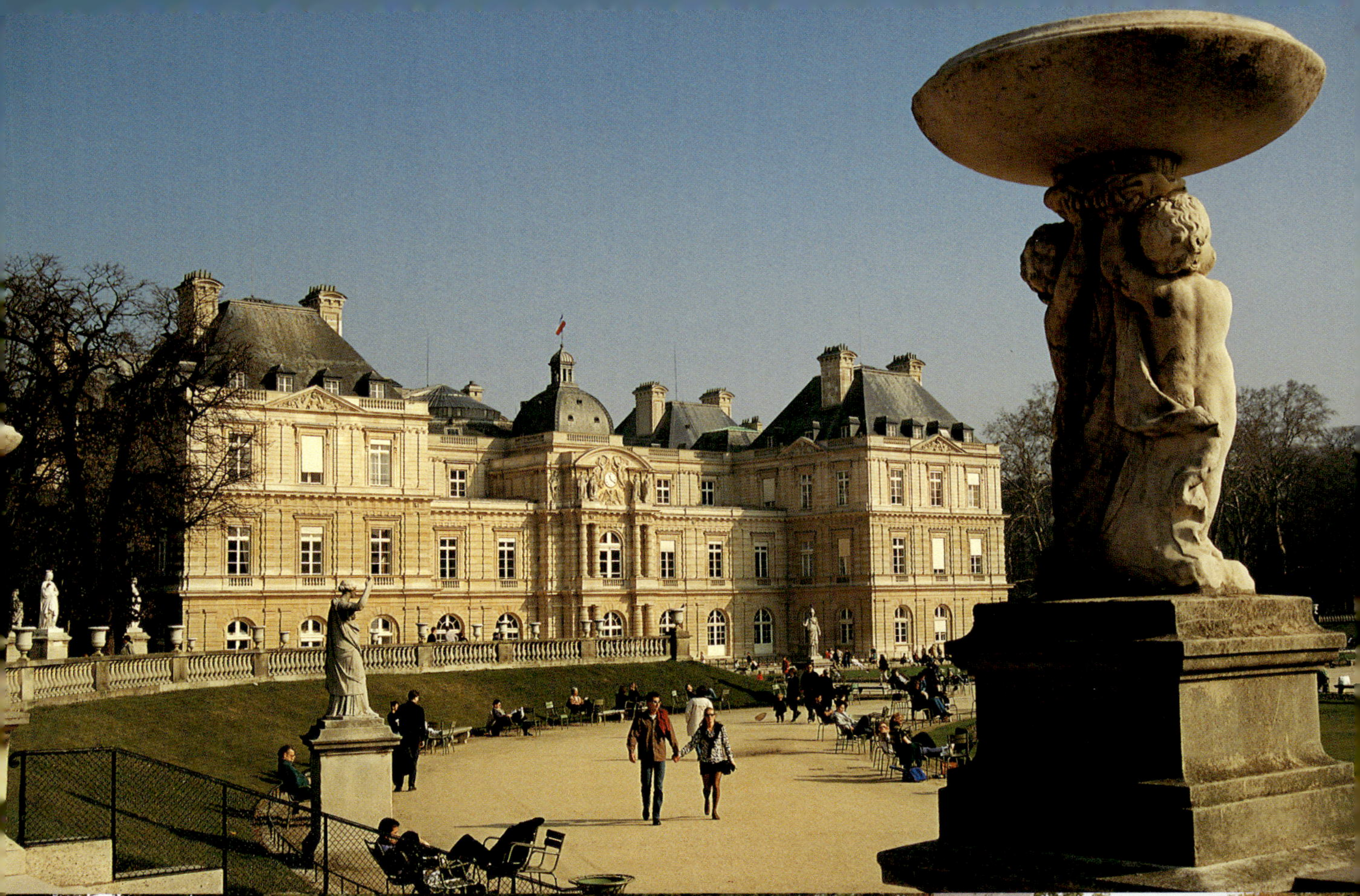

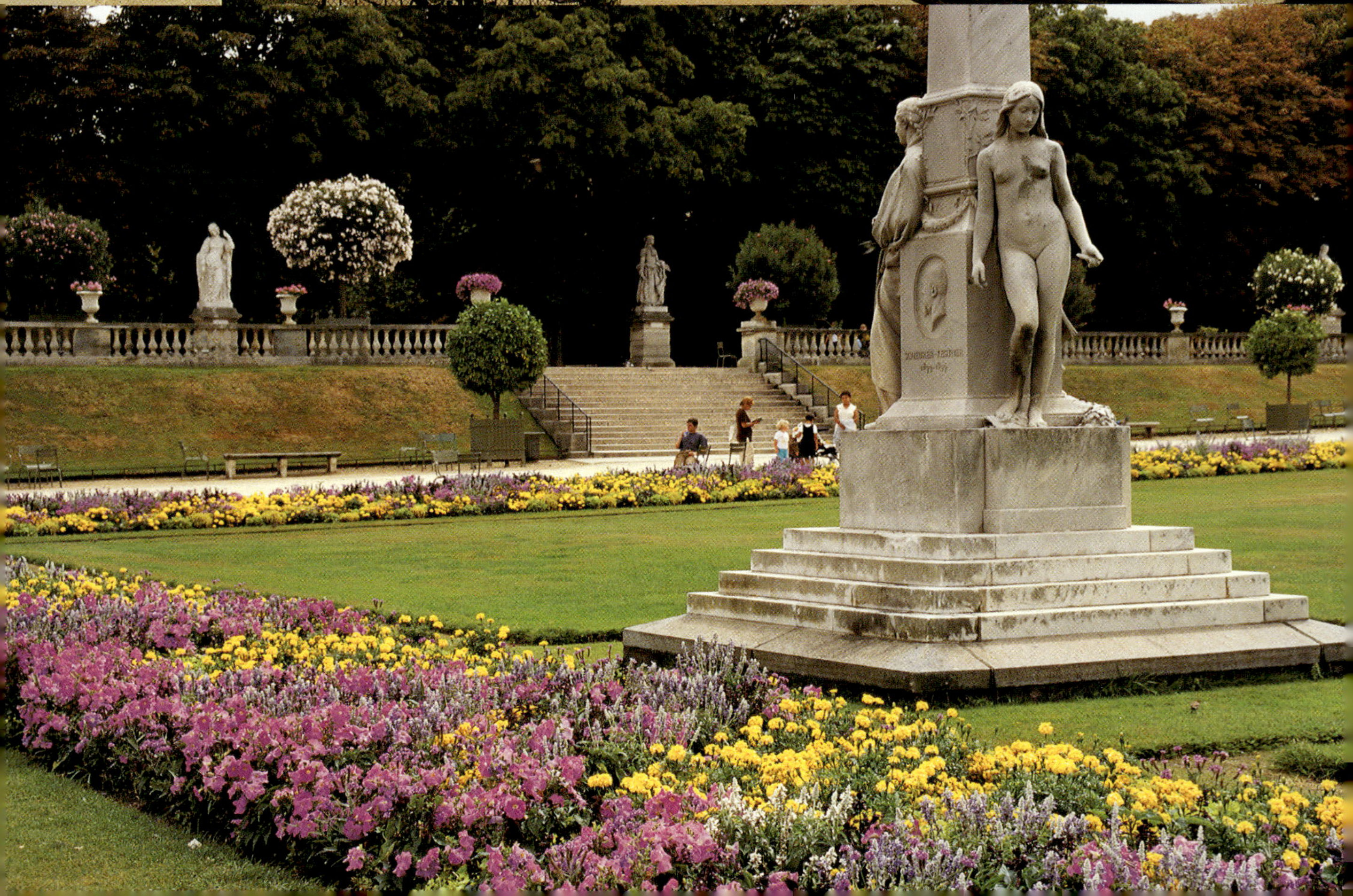

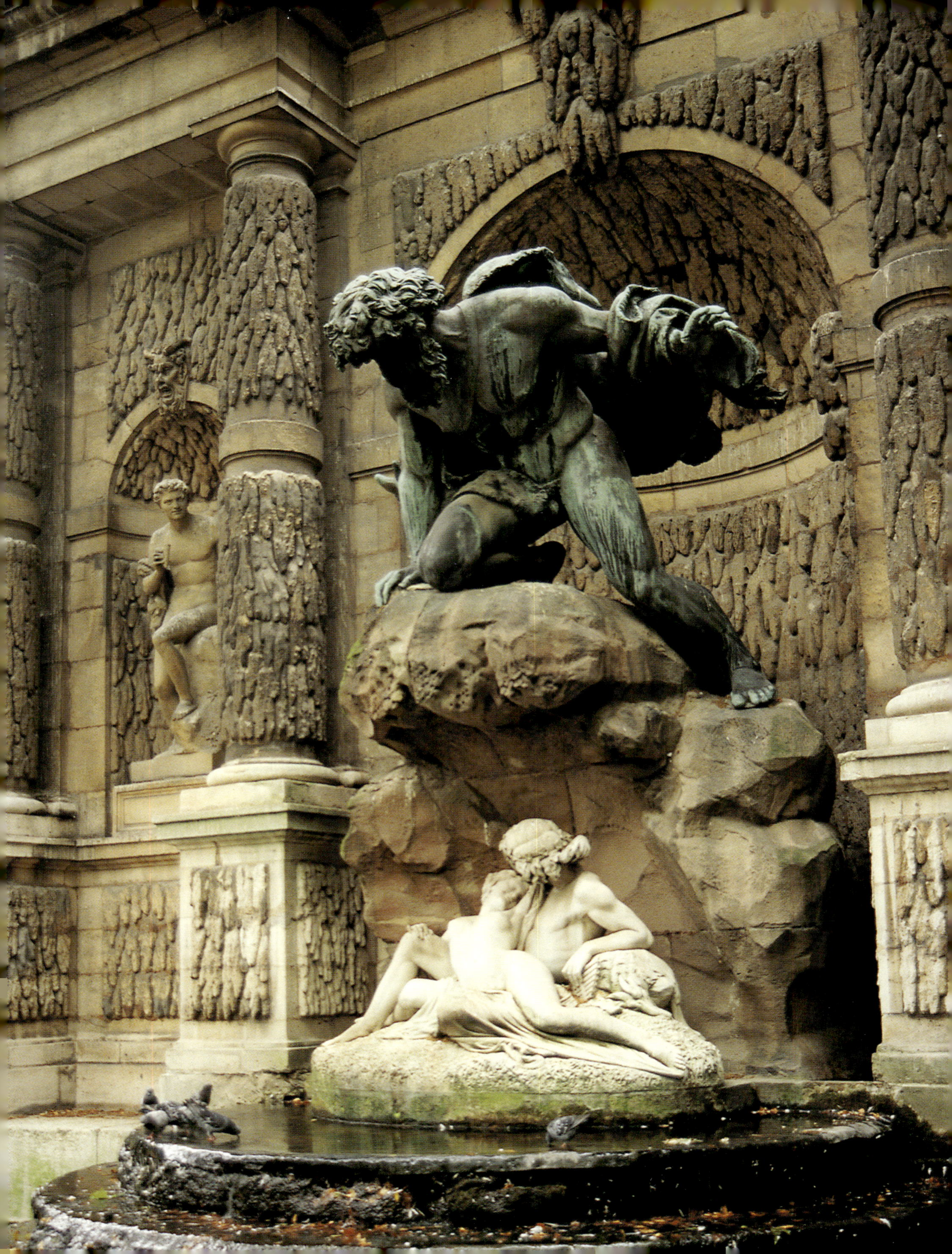

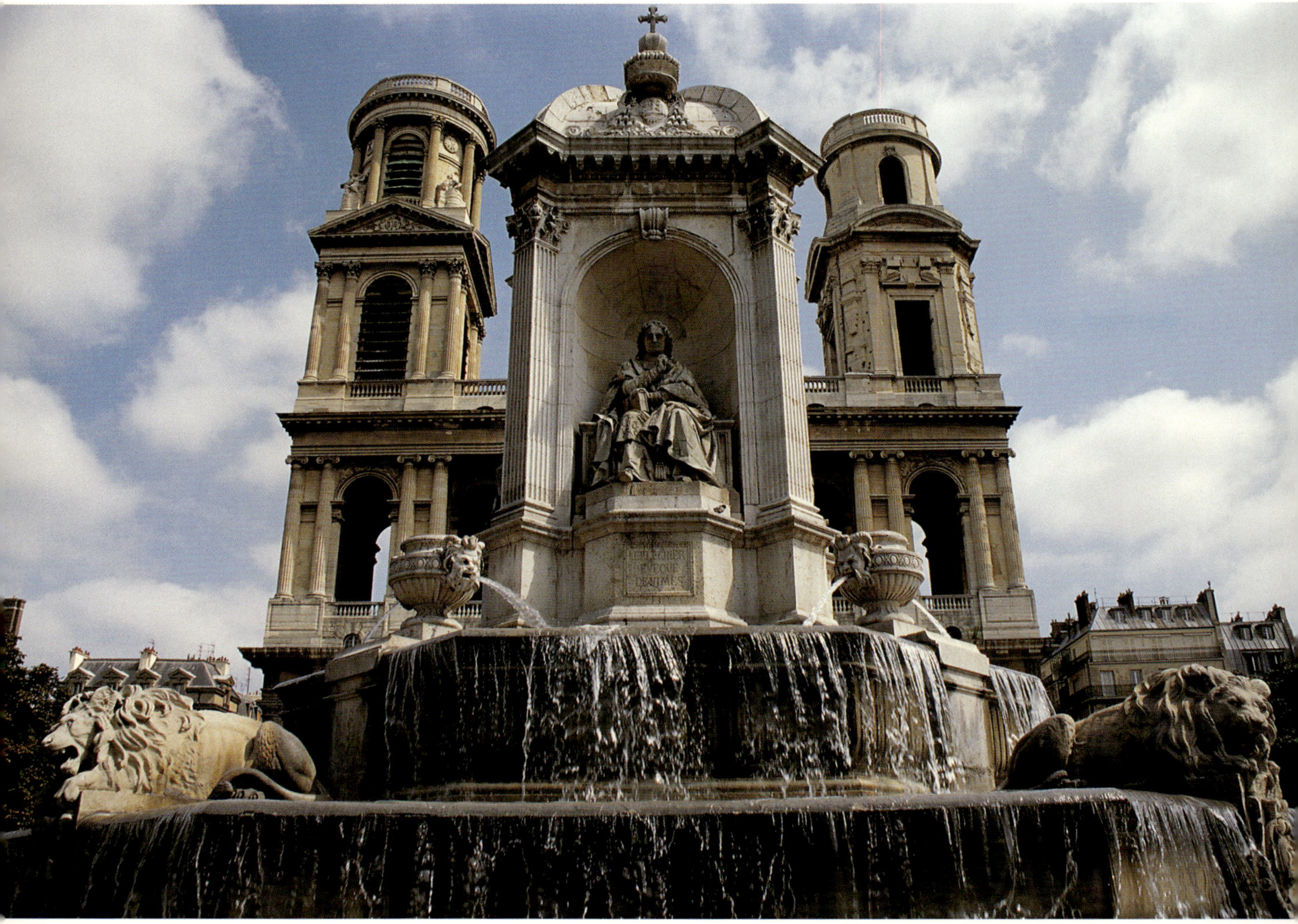

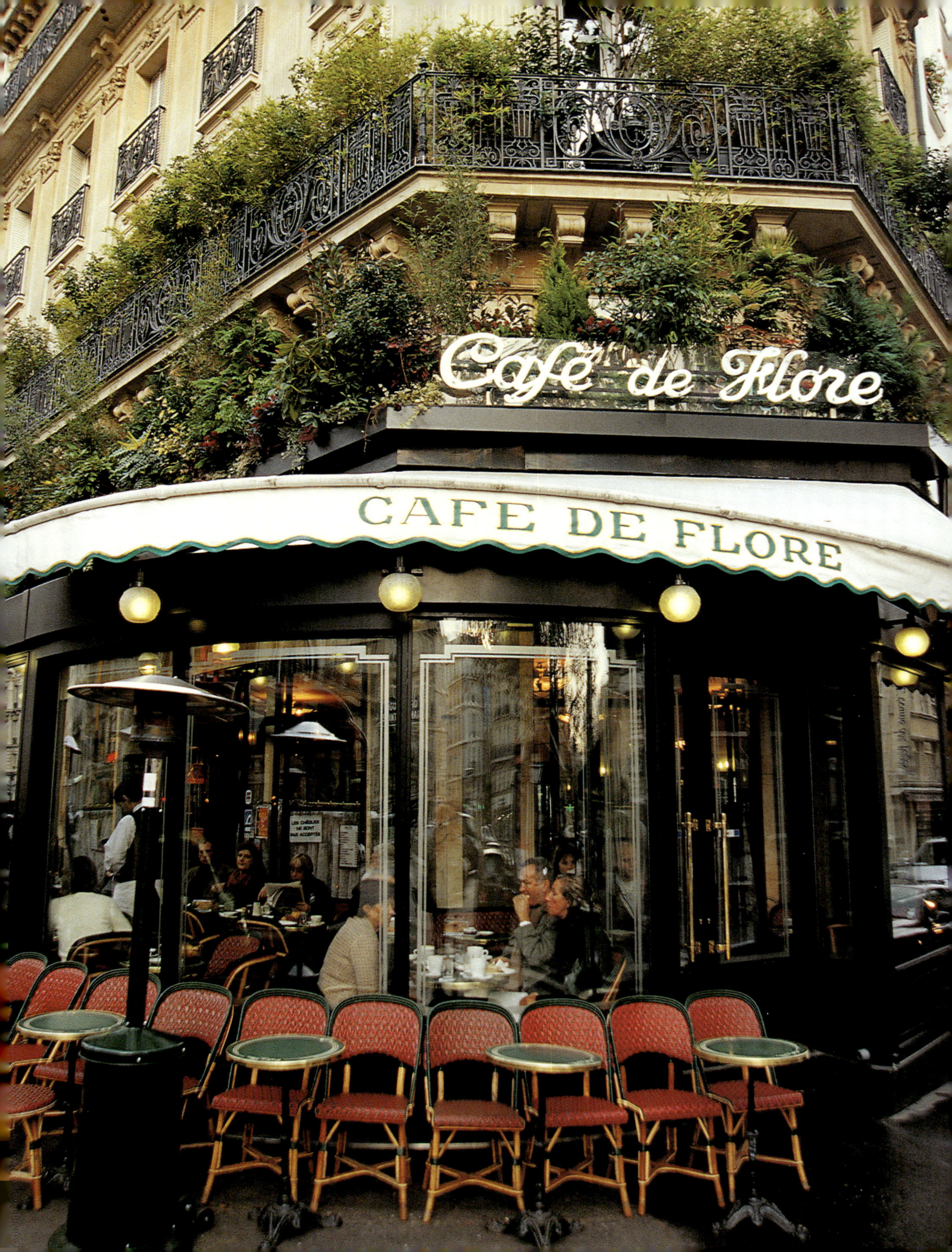

Café de Flore
CAFE DE FLORE
LES CHÈQUES NE SONT PAS ACCEPTÉS

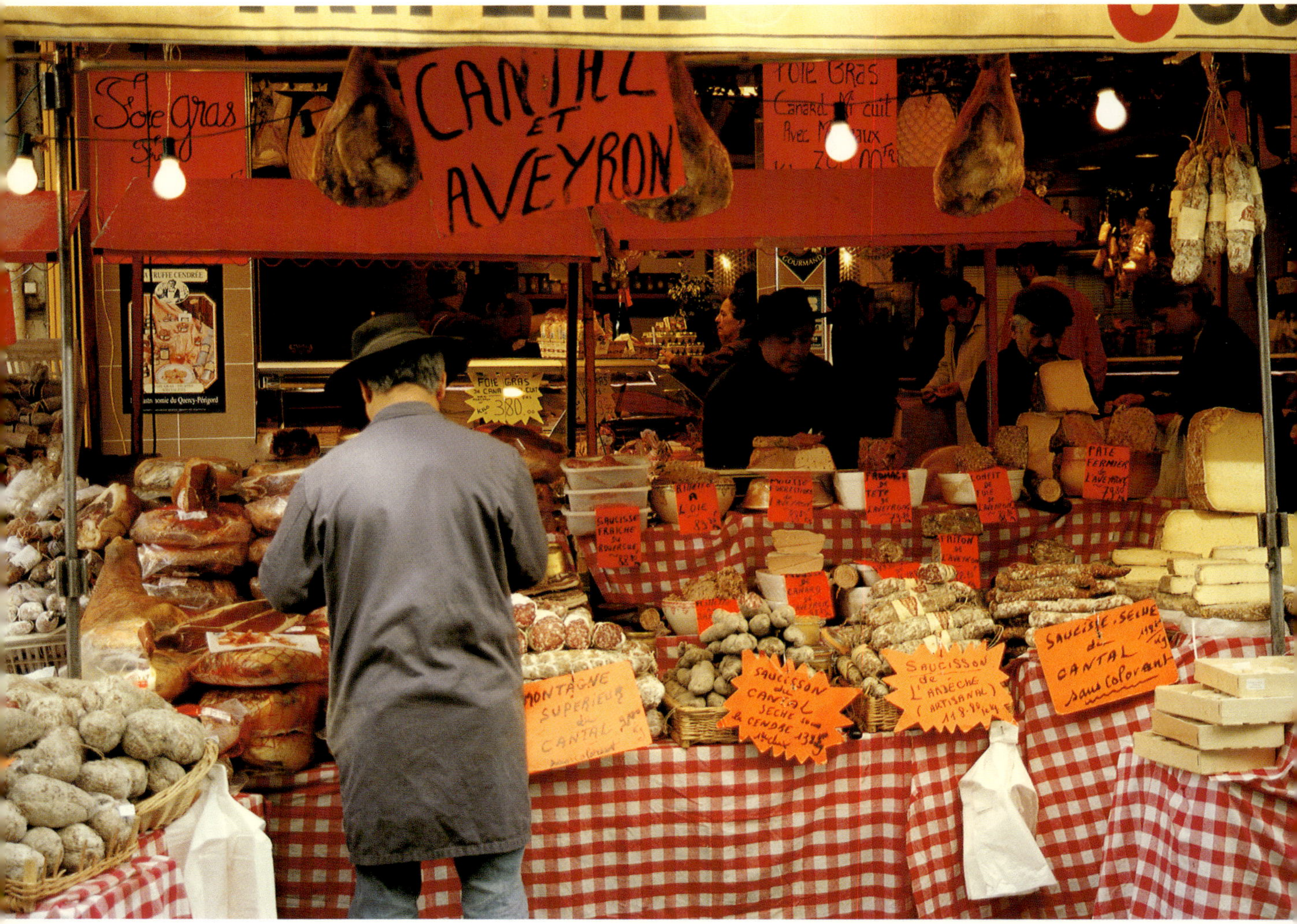
CANTAL
ET
AVEYRON
SAUCISSON de L'ARDECHE (ARTISANAL)
MONTAGNE SUPERIEUR du CANTAL

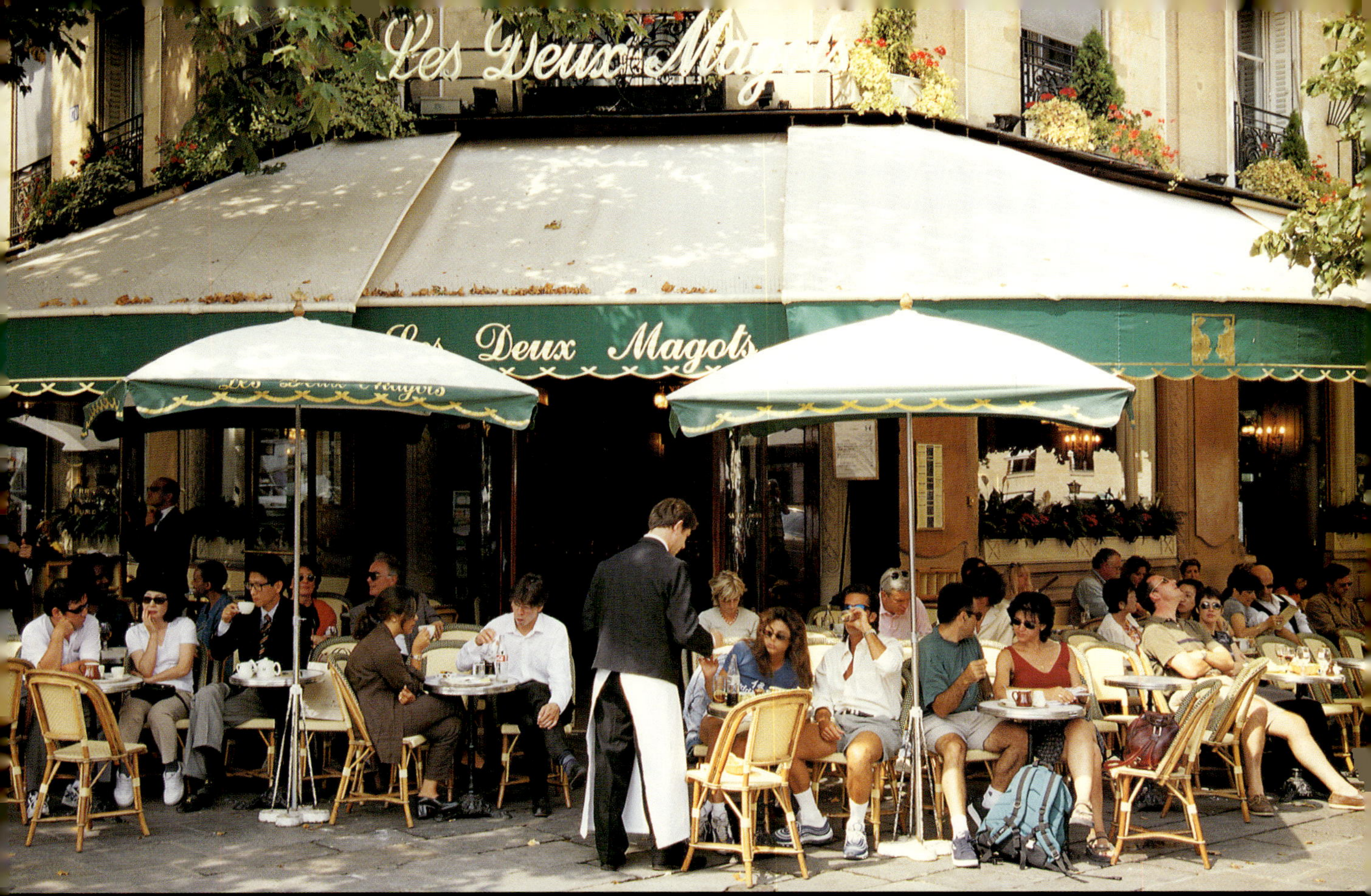
Les Deux Magots
Les Deux Magots

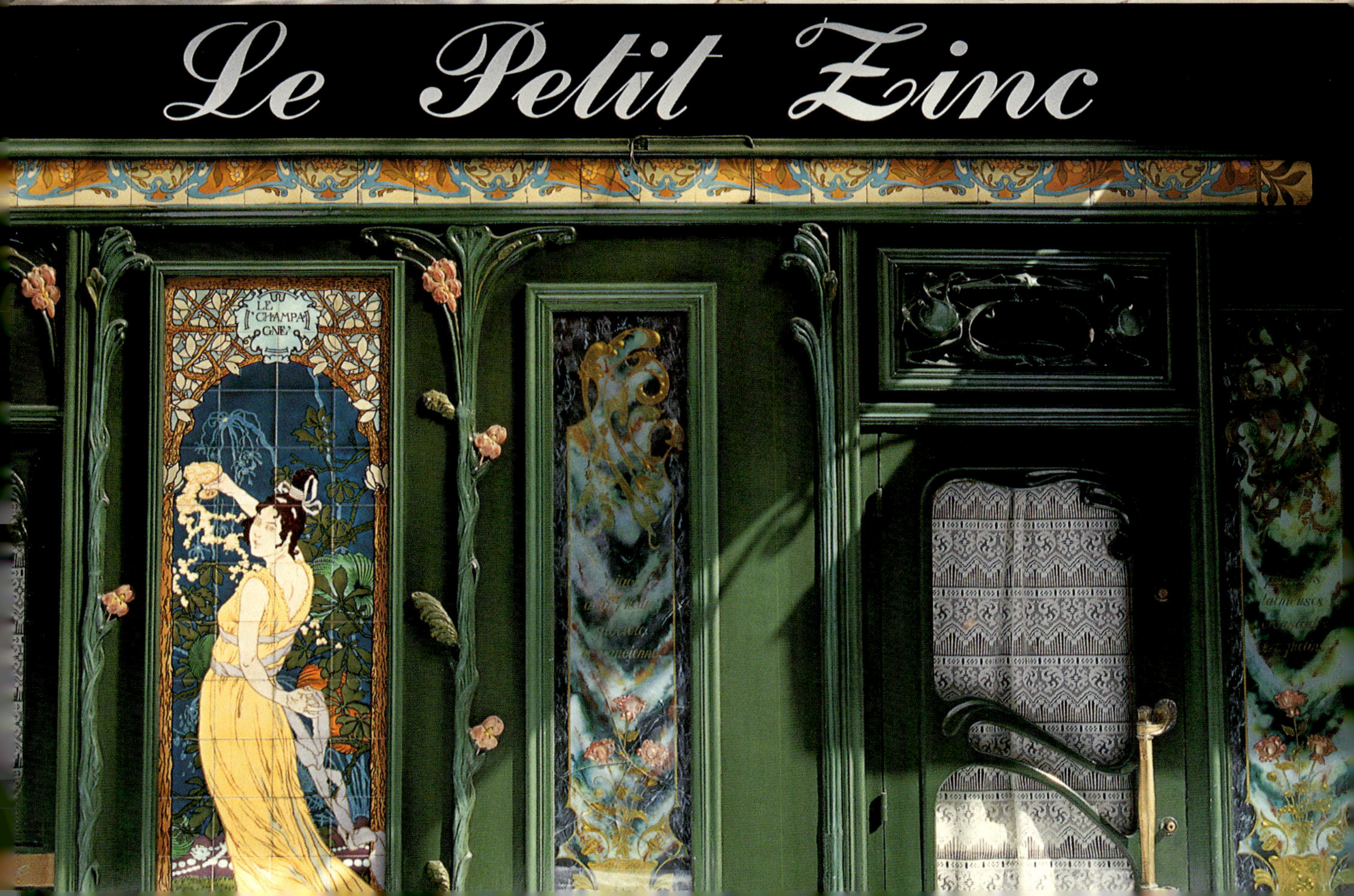
Le Petit Zinc
LE CHAMPAGNE

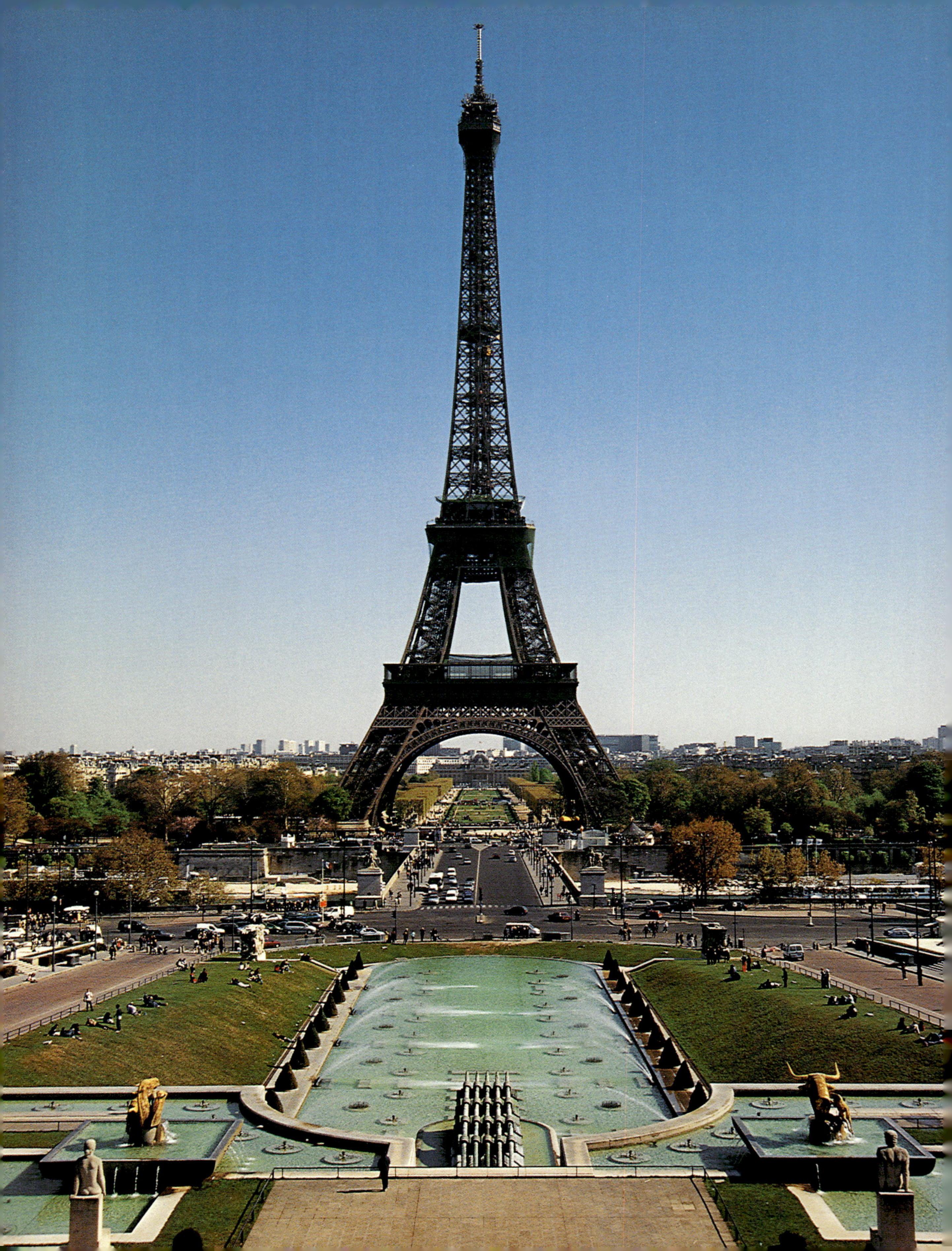

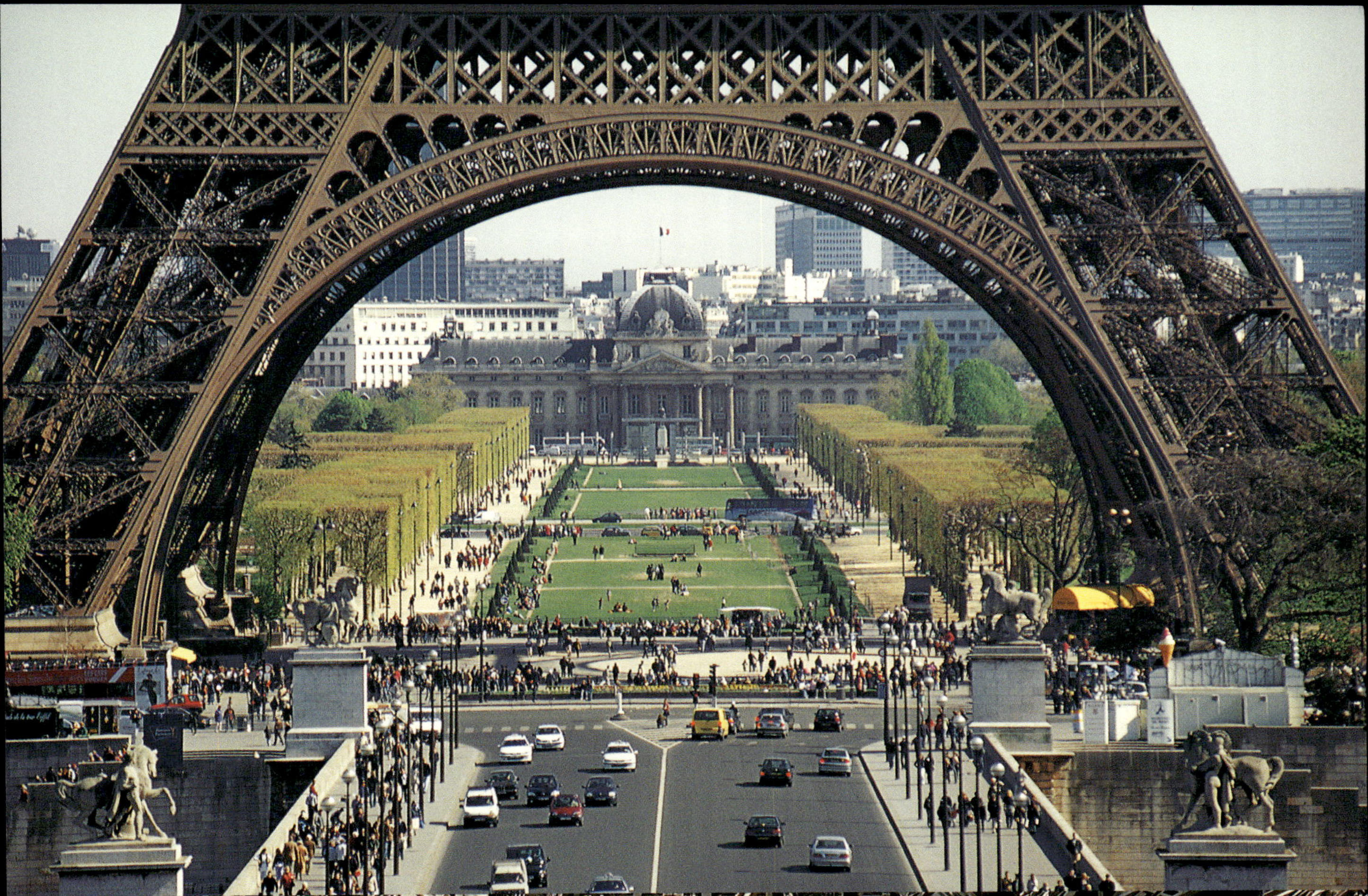

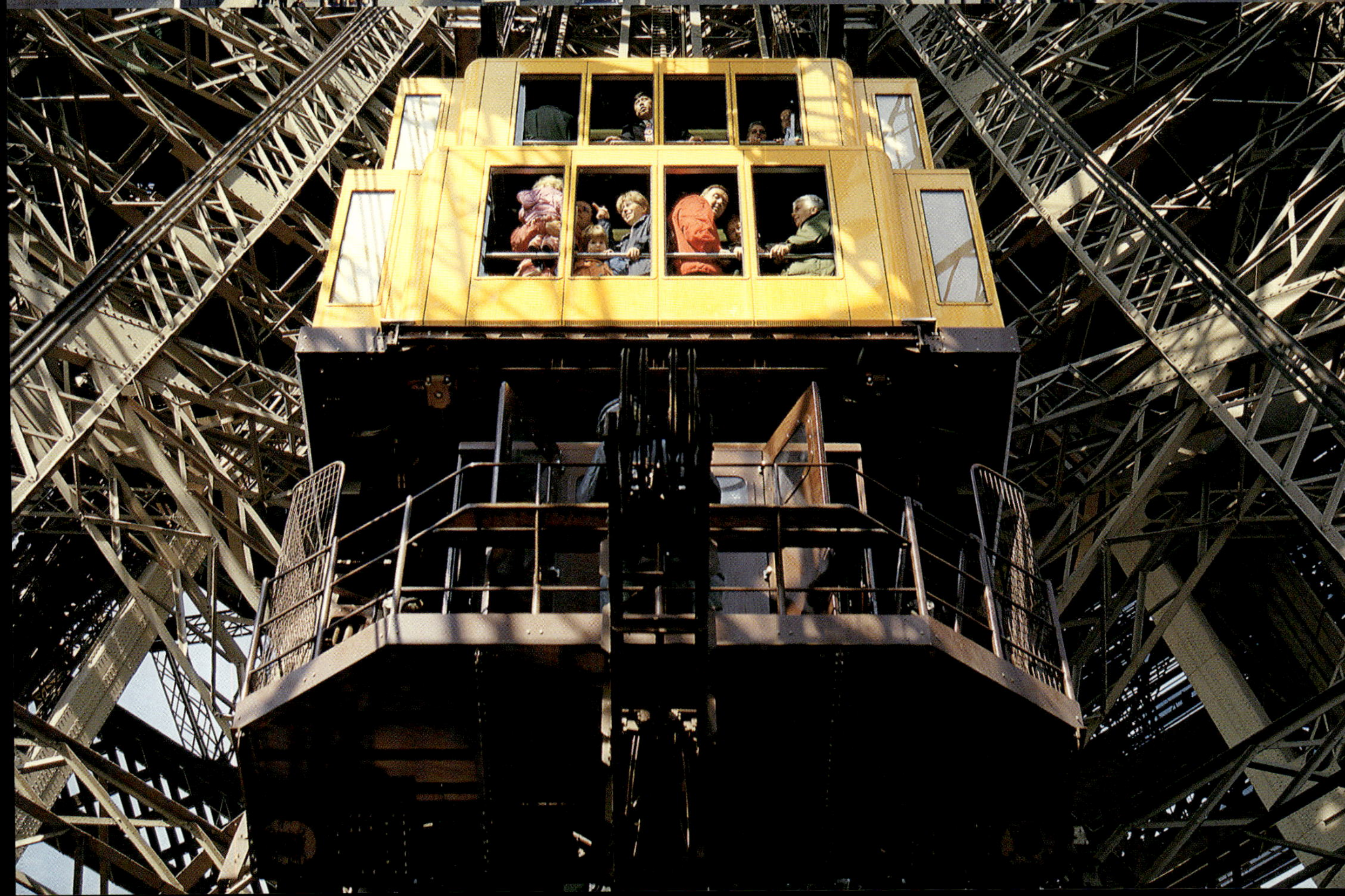

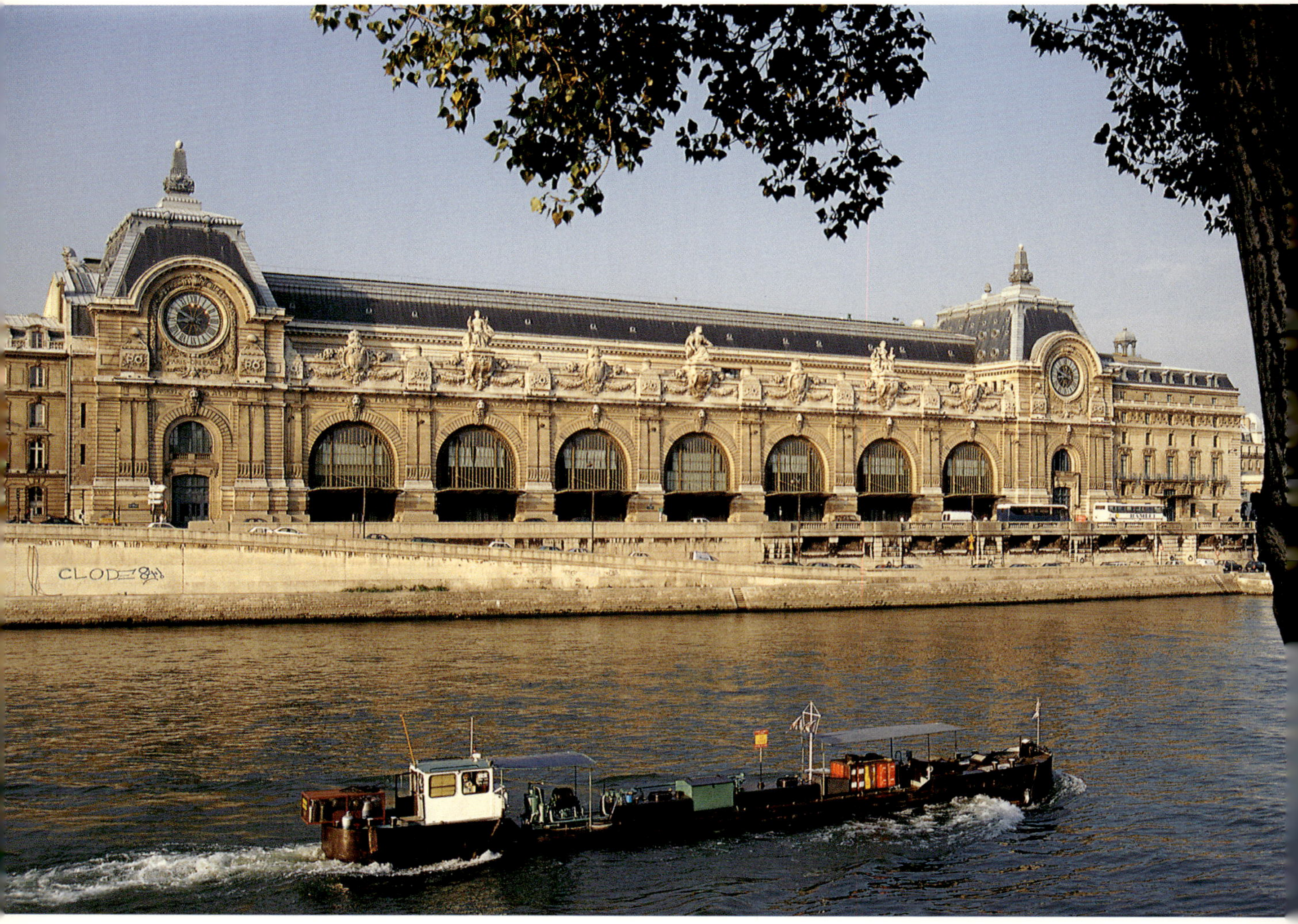

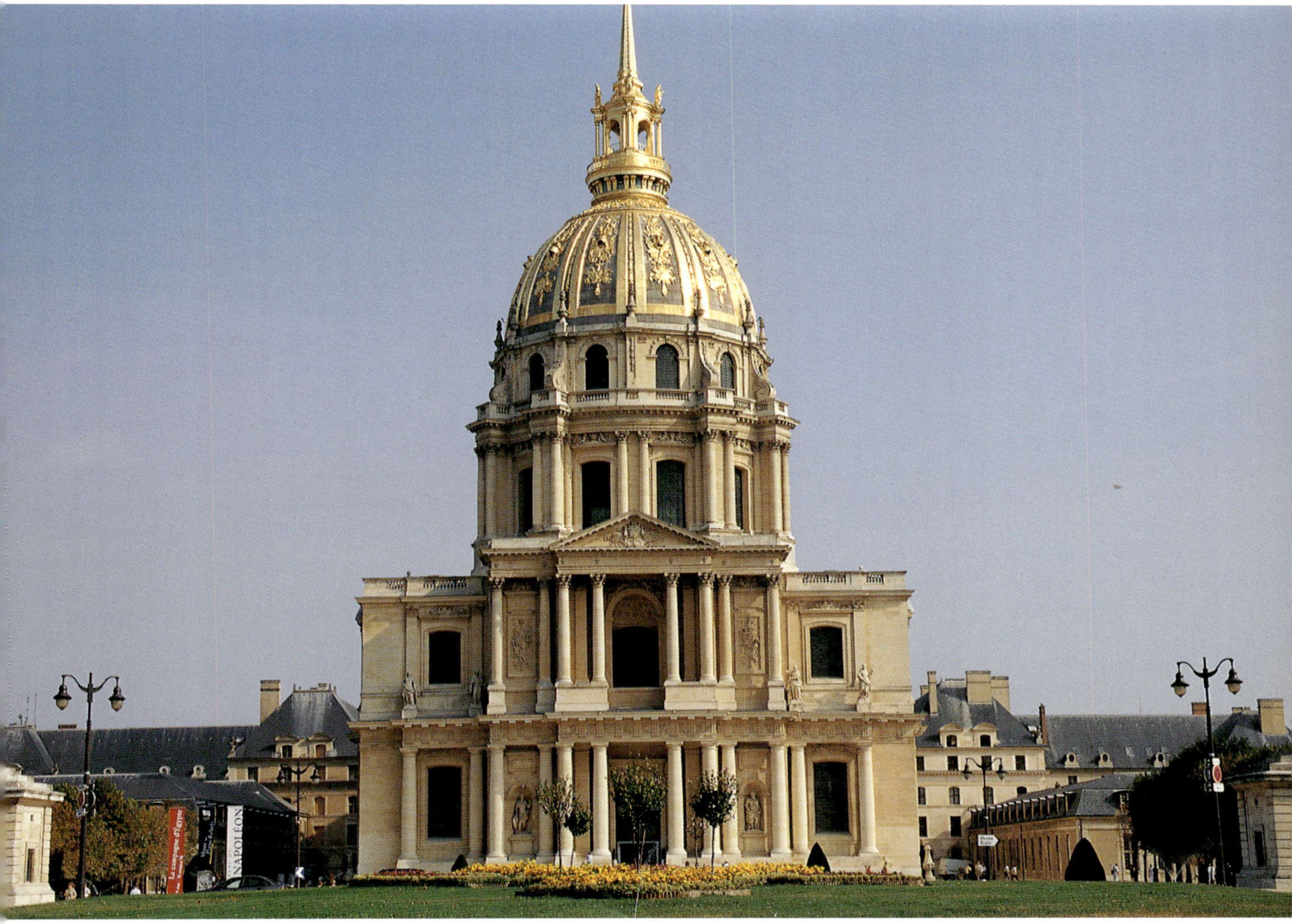
NAPOLEON

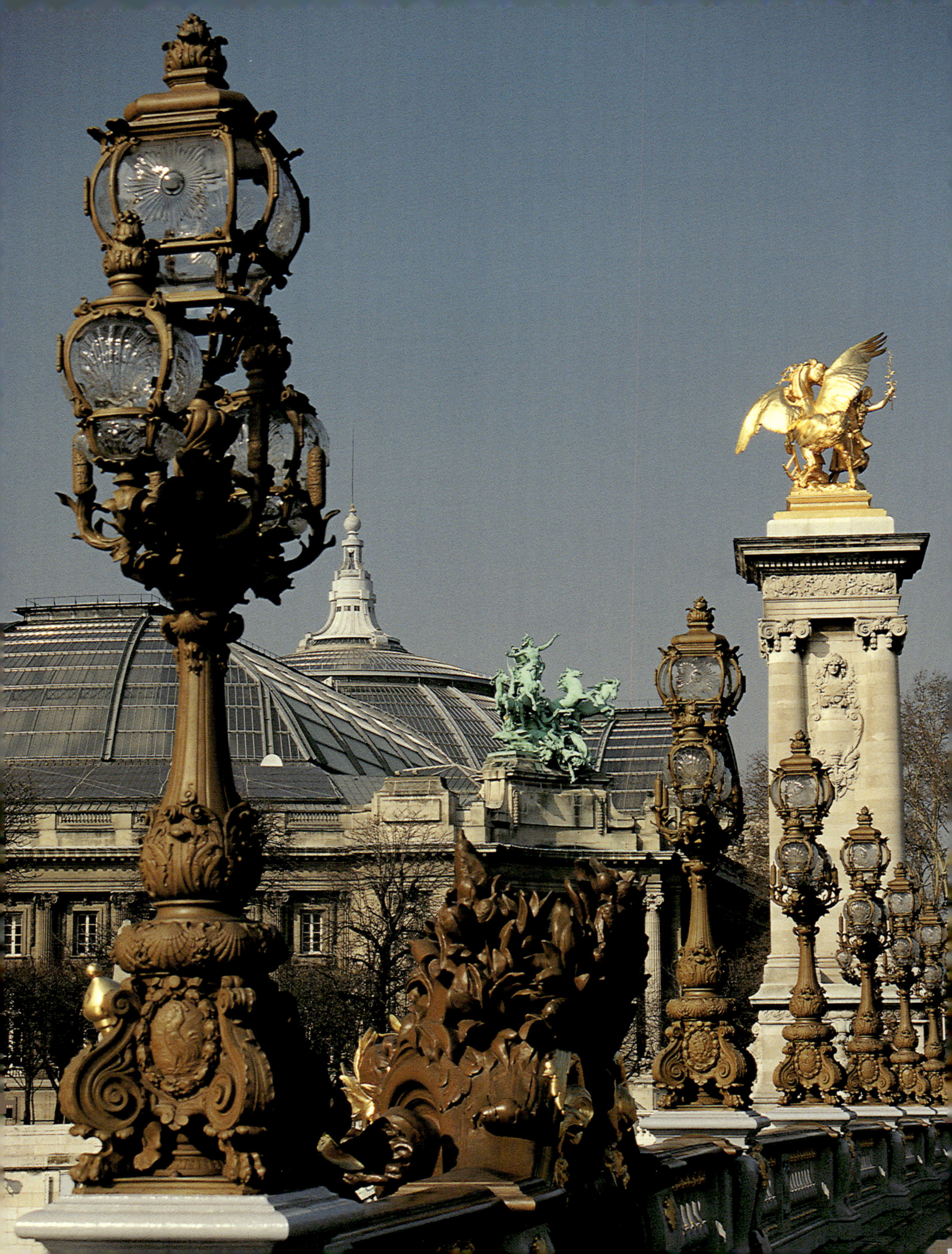

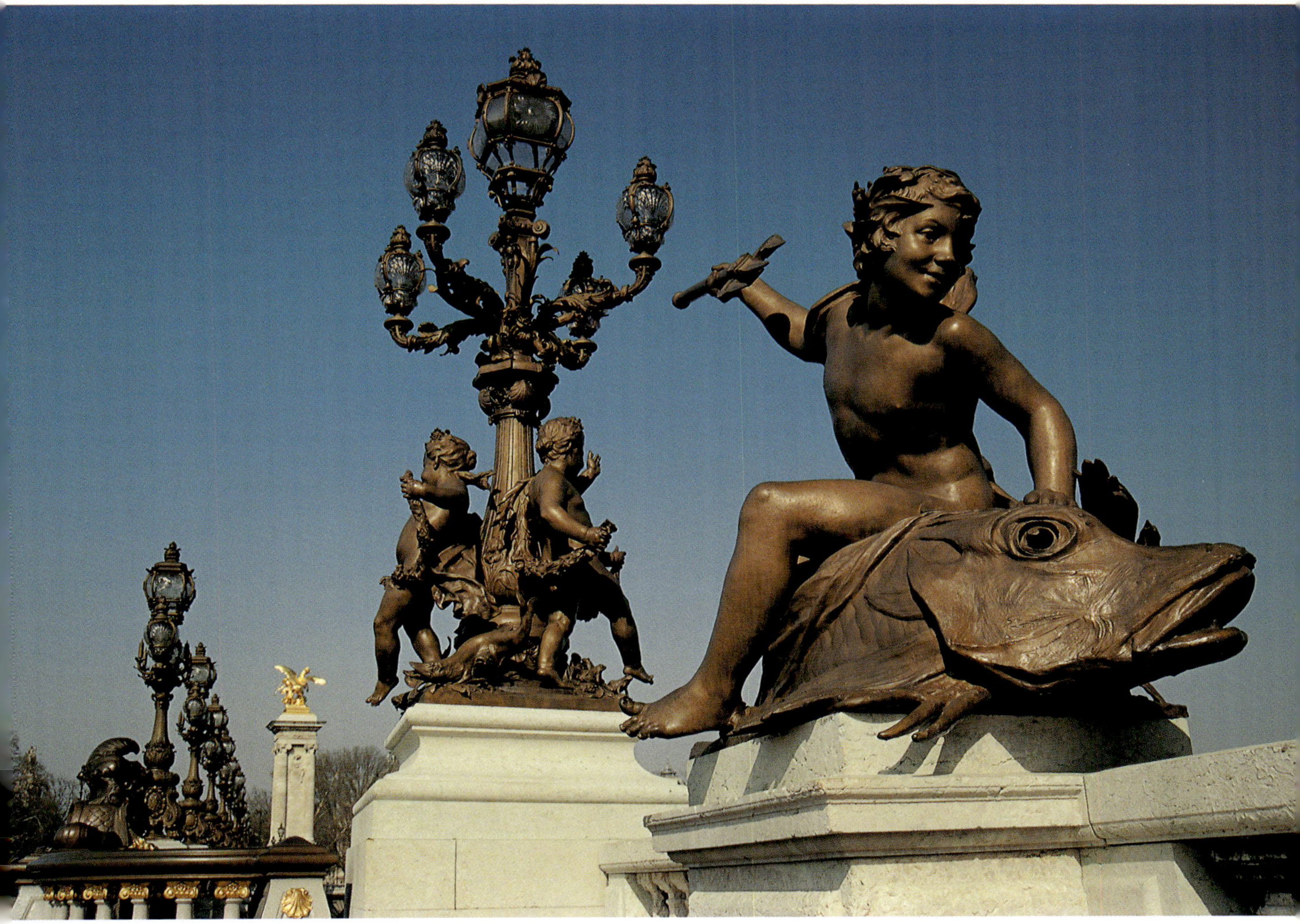

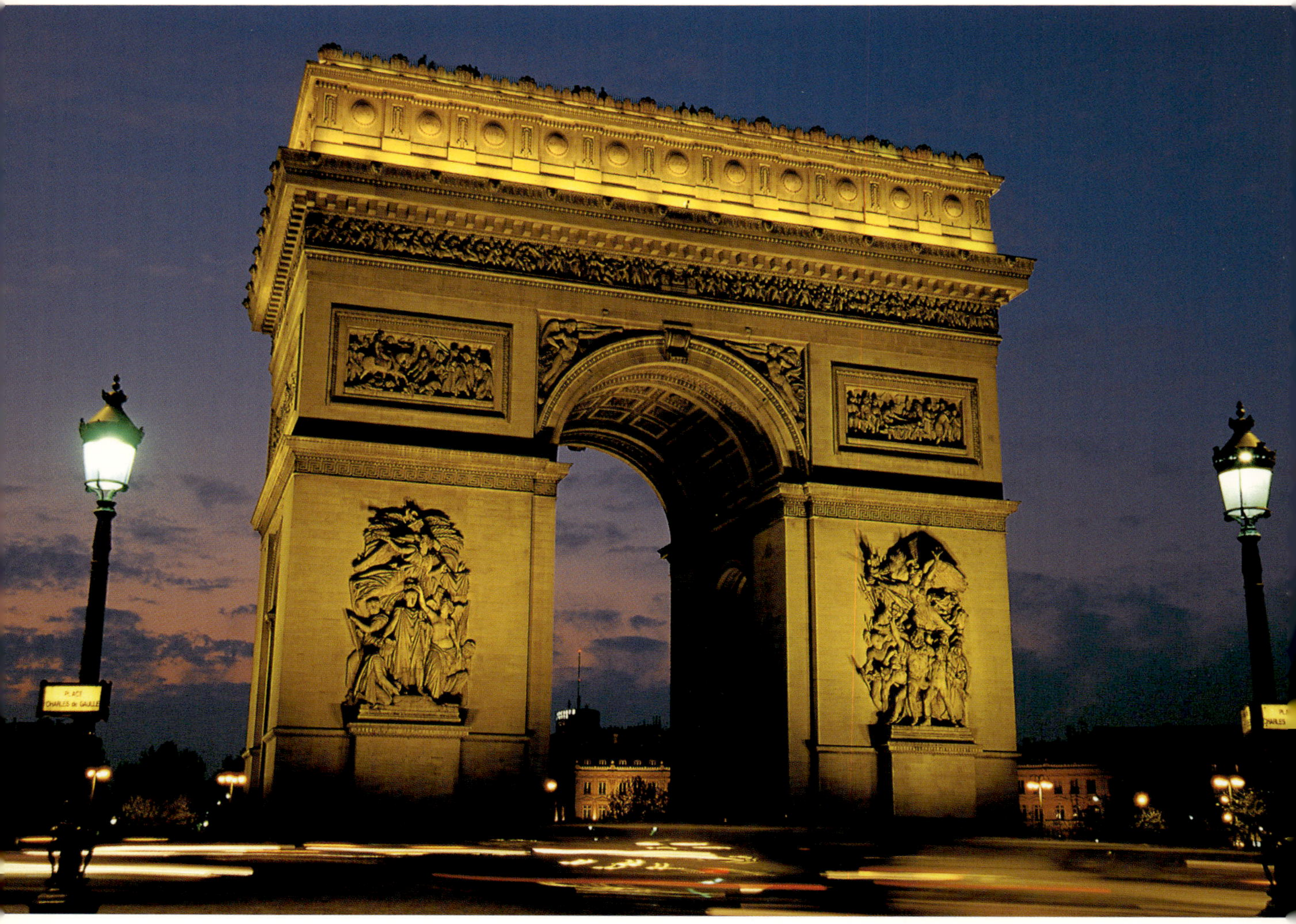

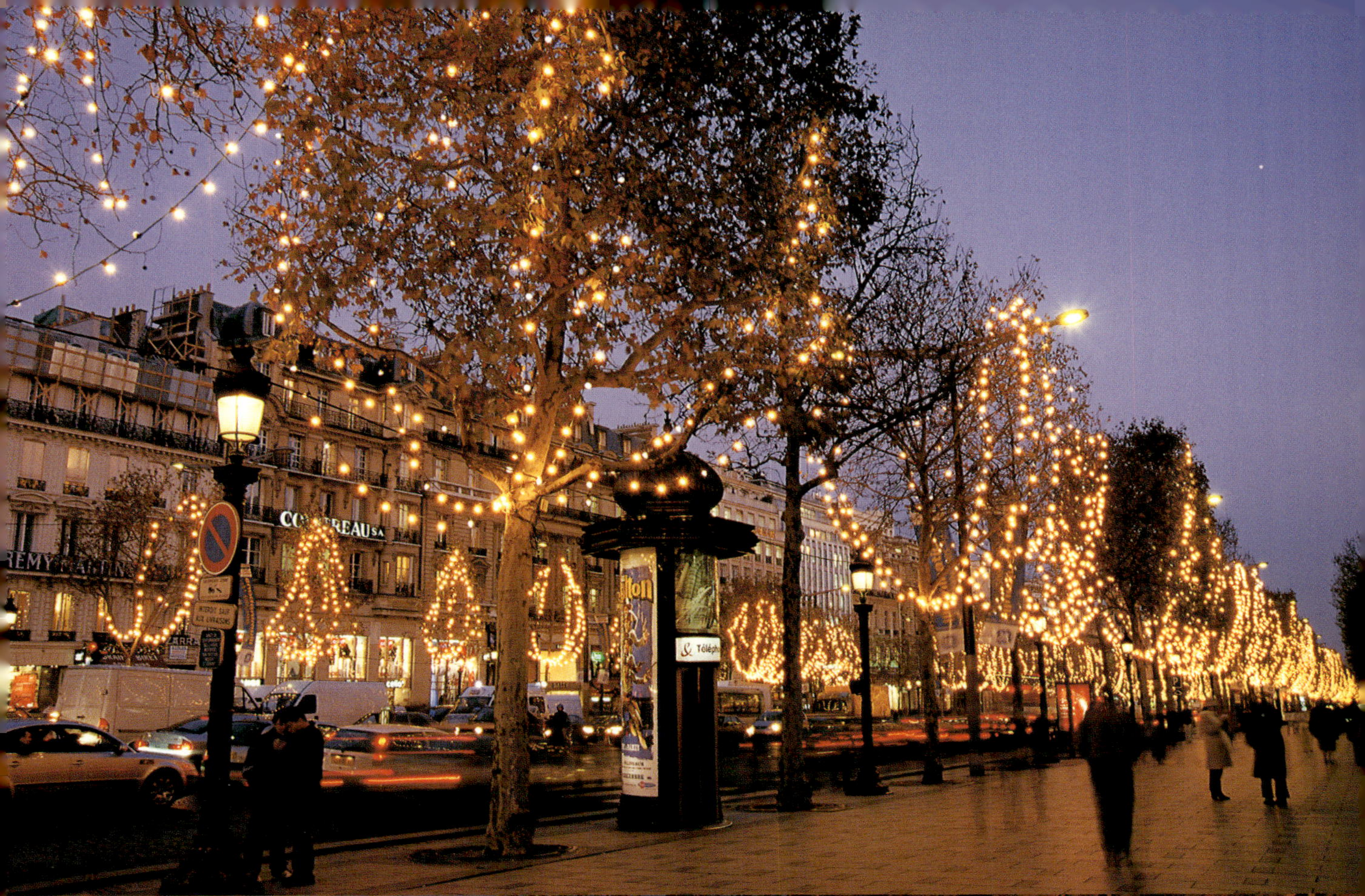

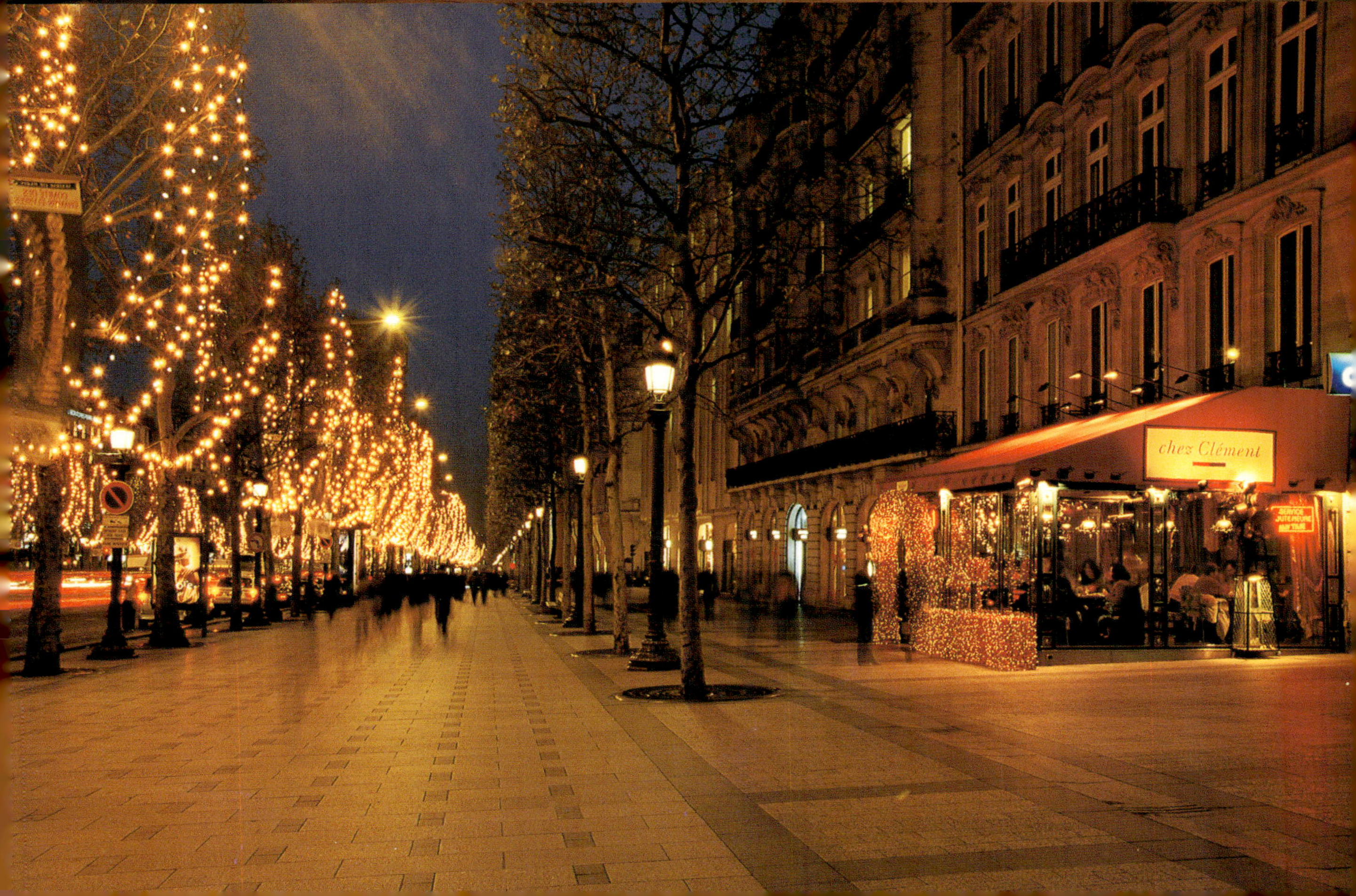
chez Clément

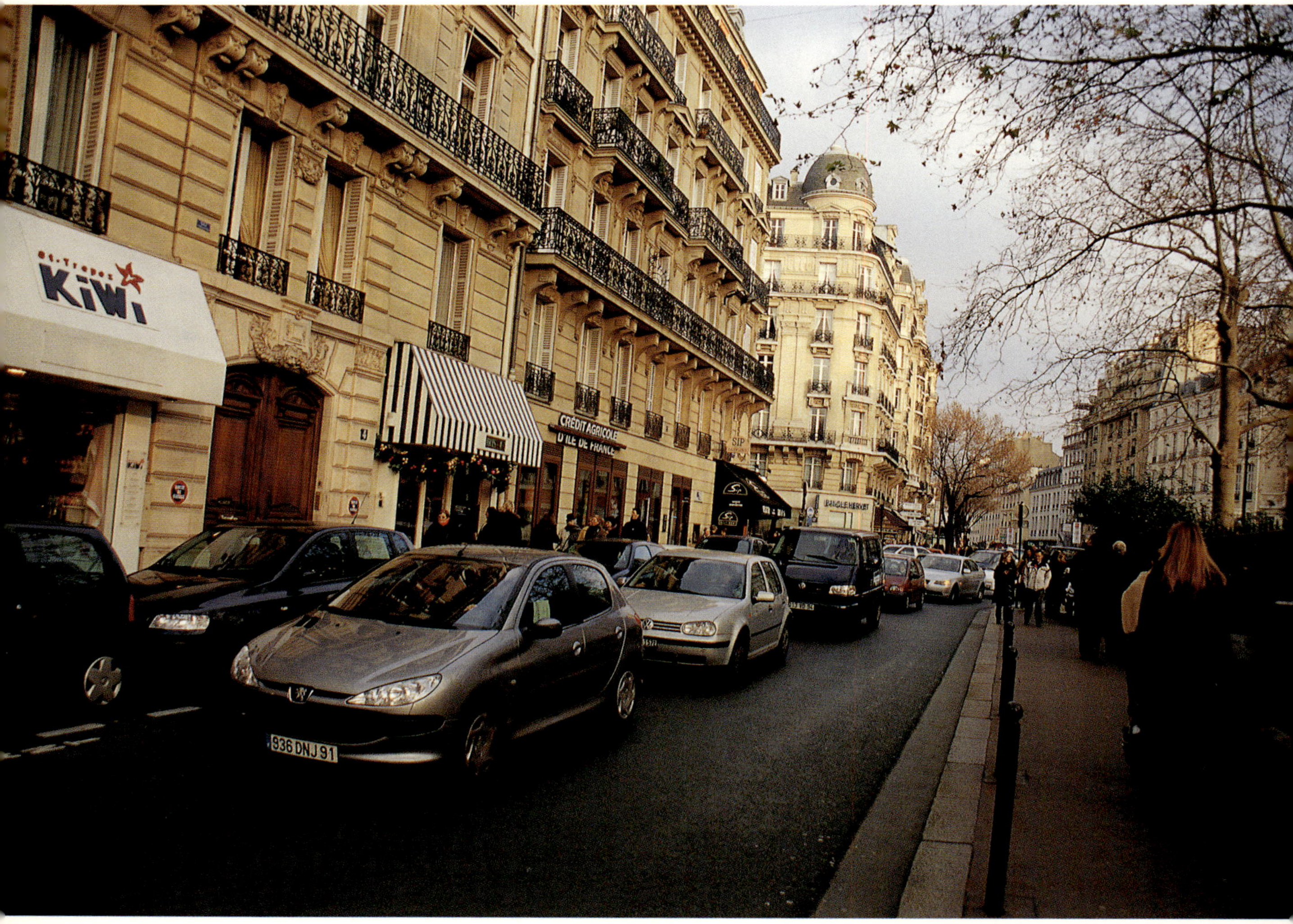
KiWi
CREDIT AGRICOLE
D'ILE DE FRANCE
936 DNJ 91

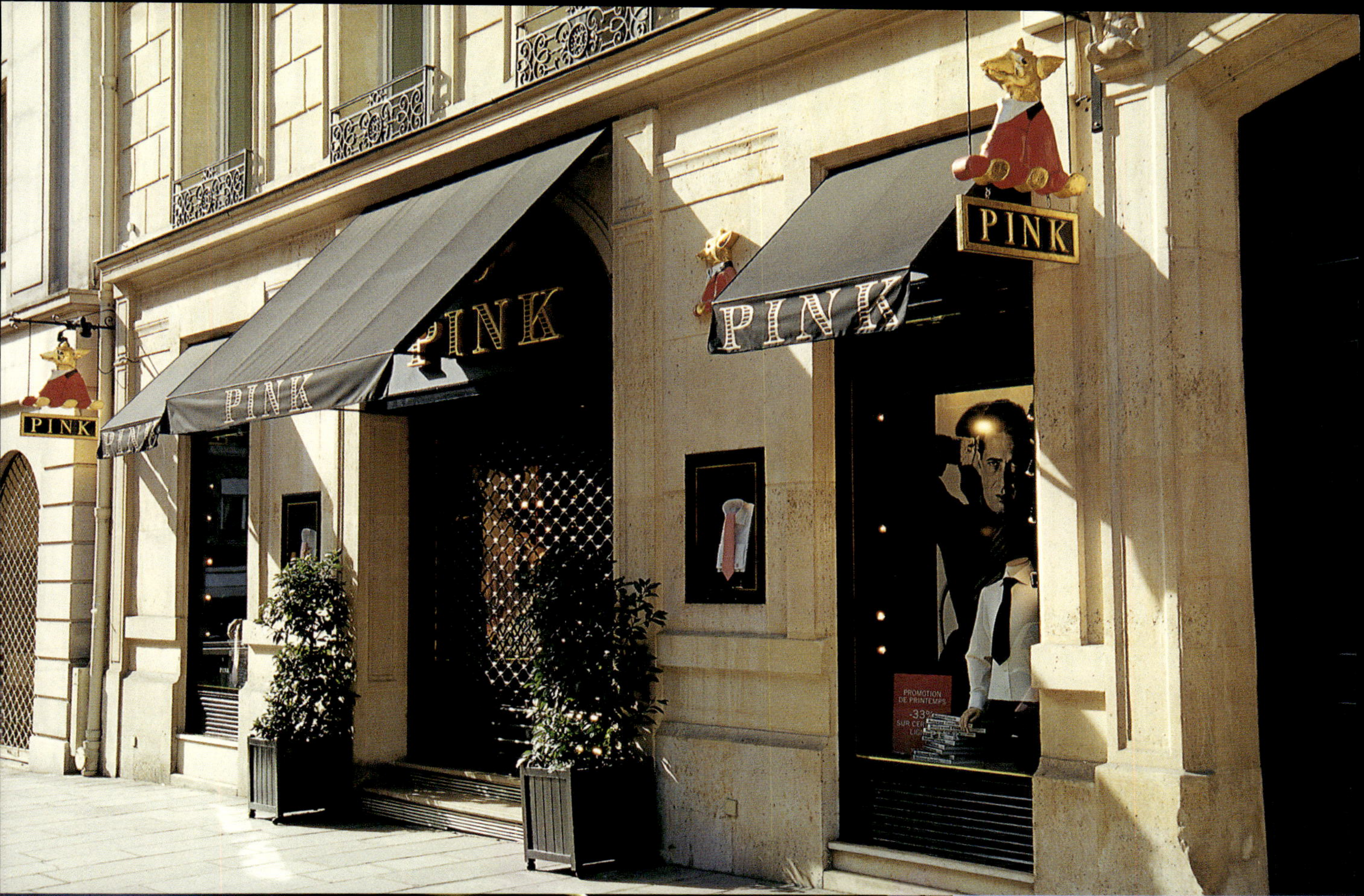
PINK
PINK
PINK
PINK
PINK
PROMOTION DE PRINTEMPS

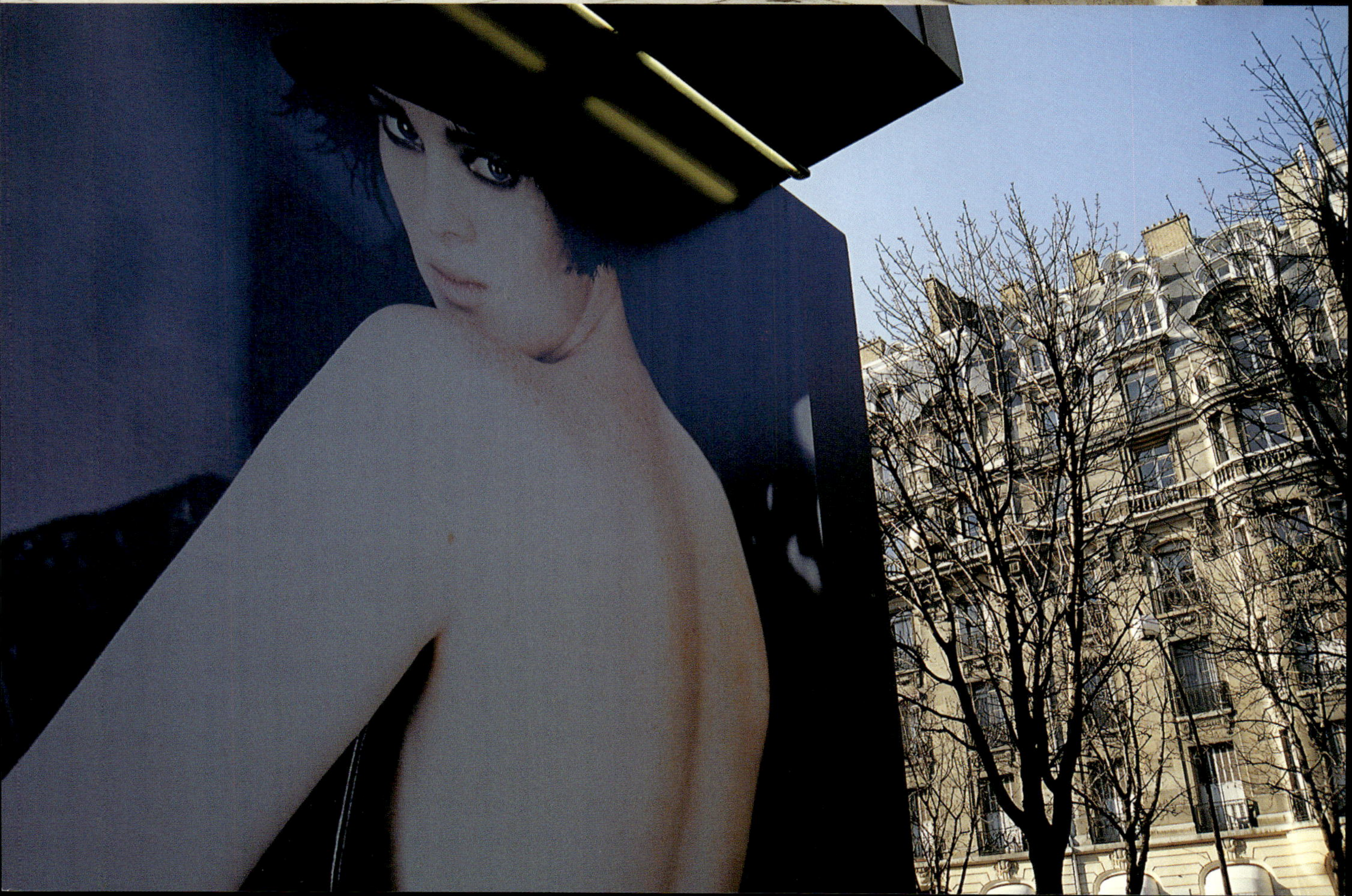

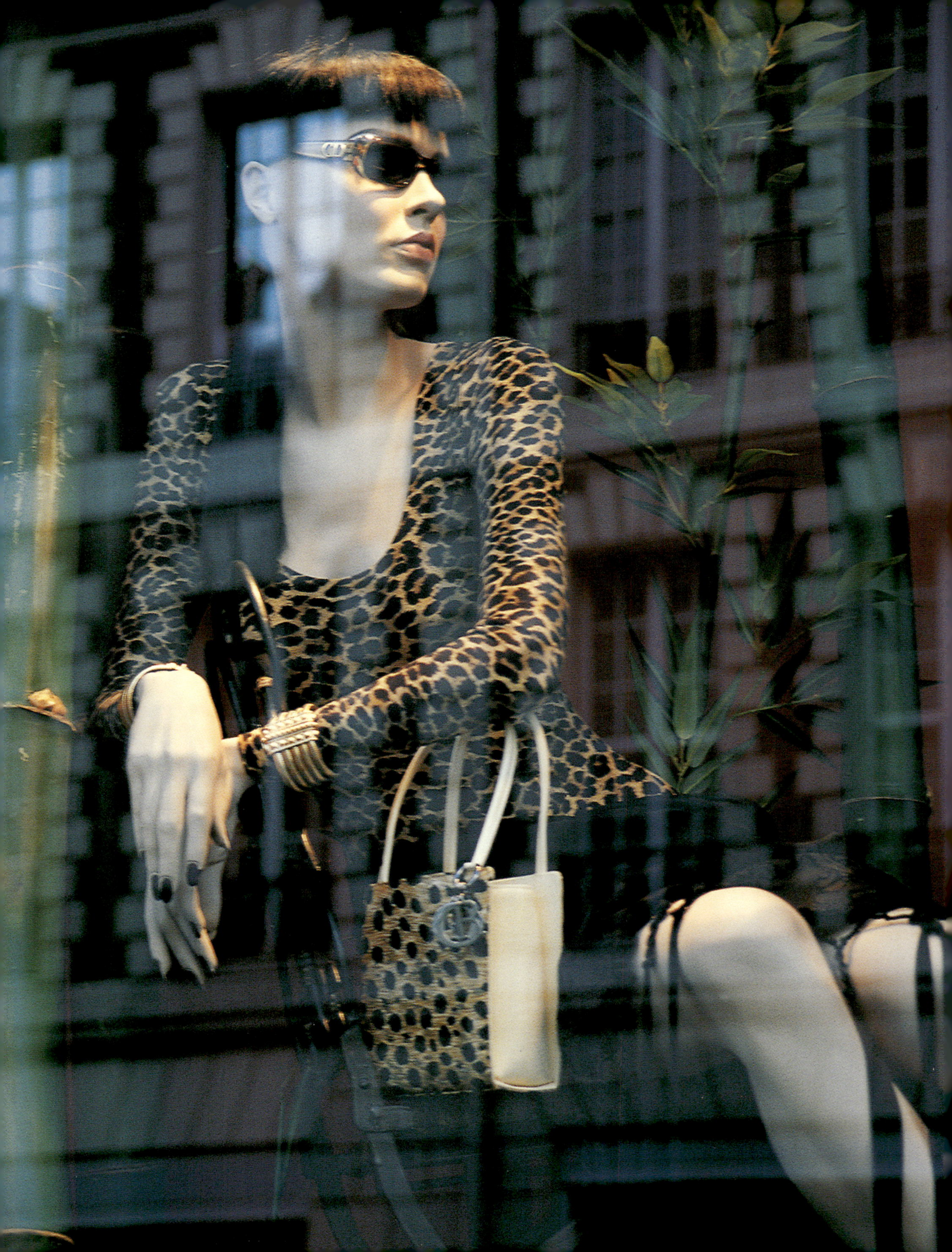

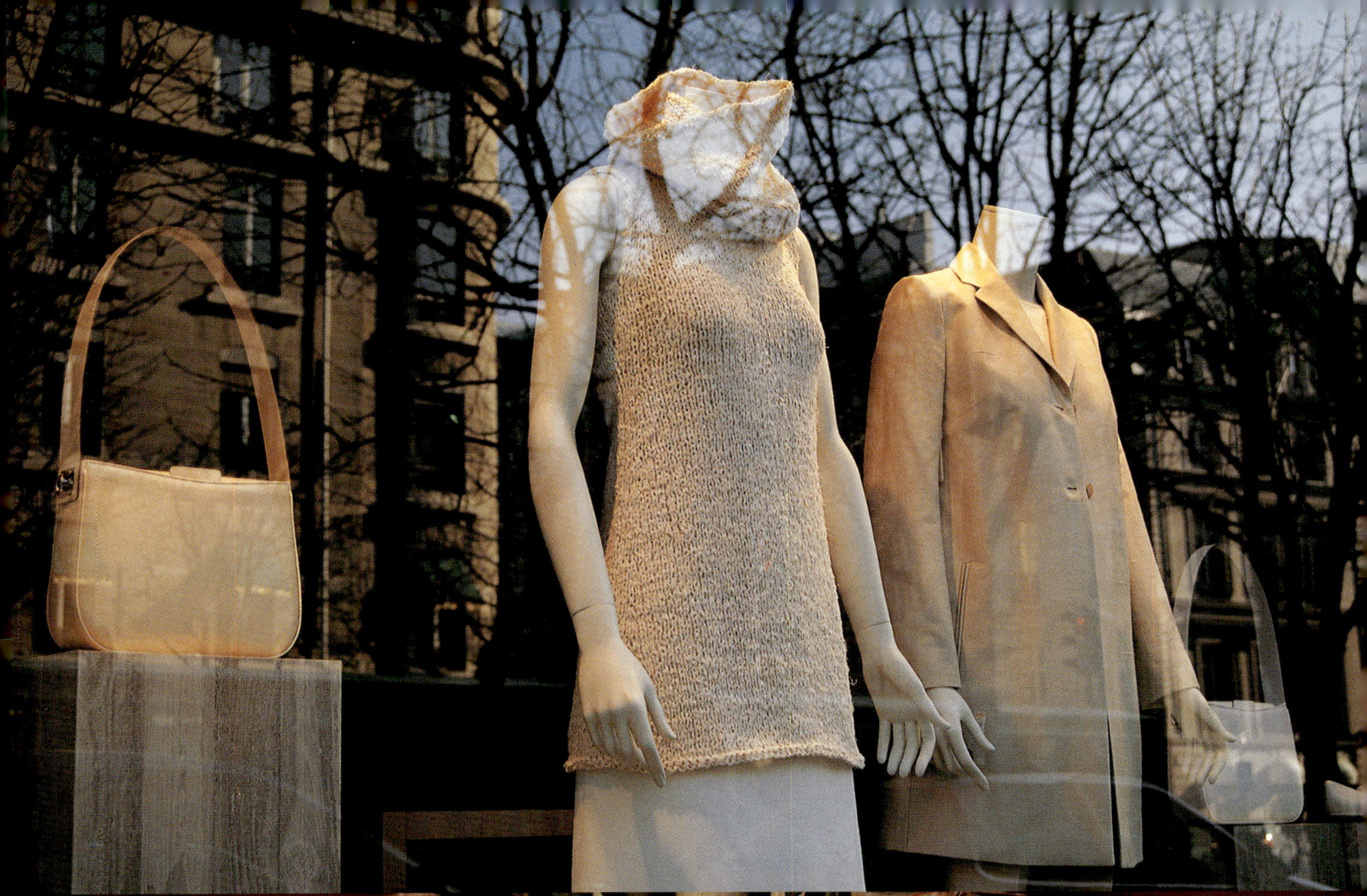

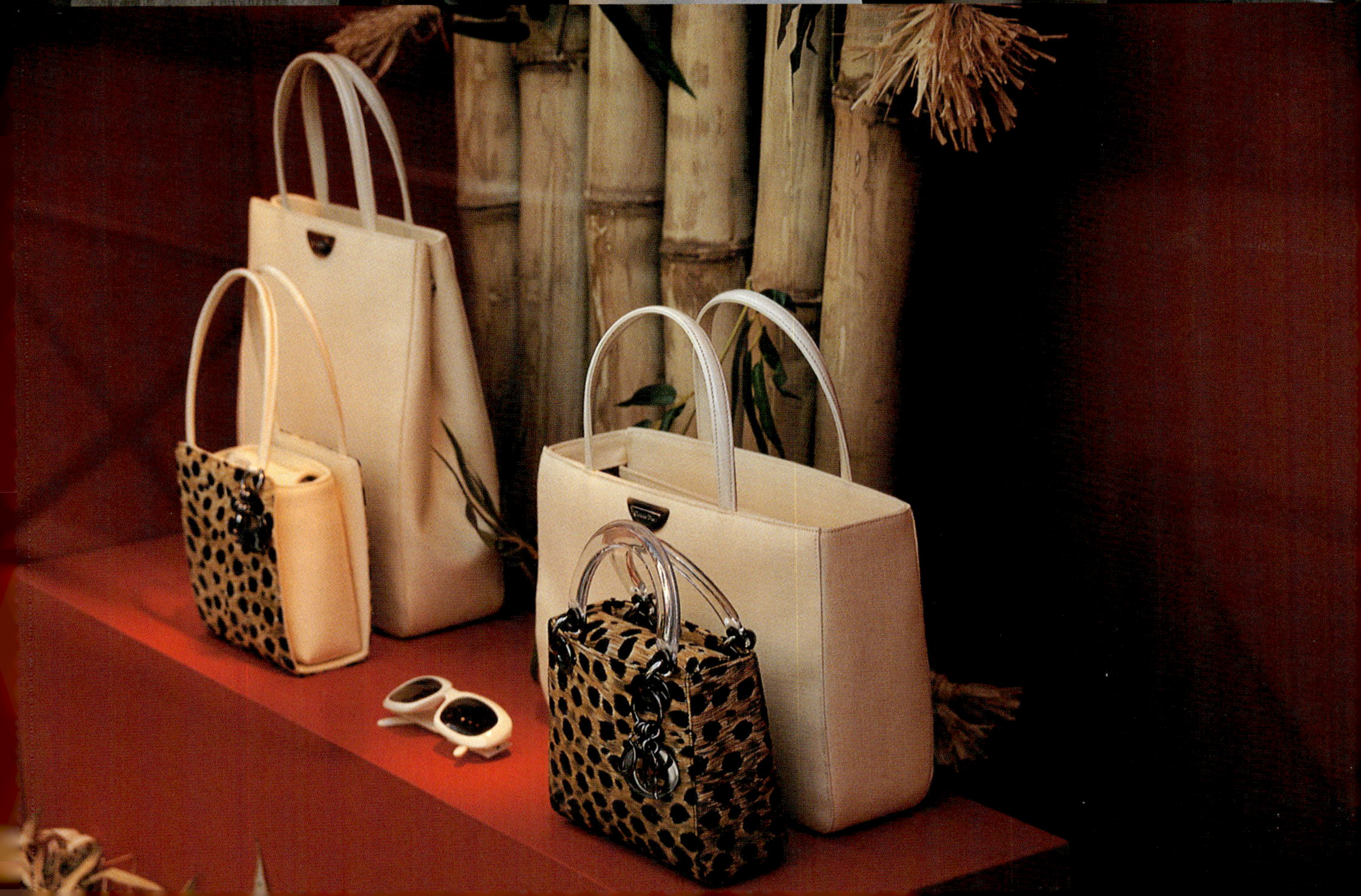

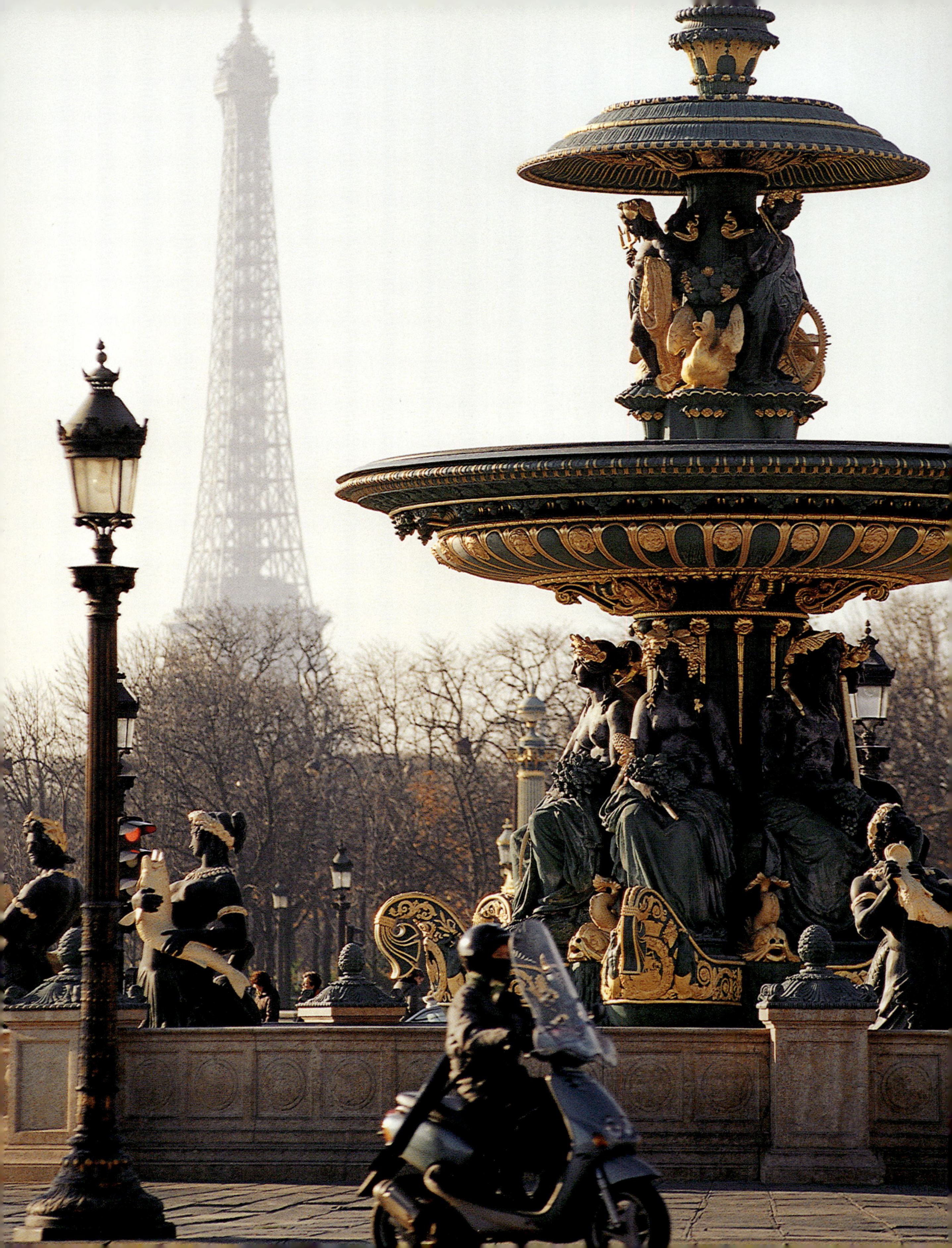

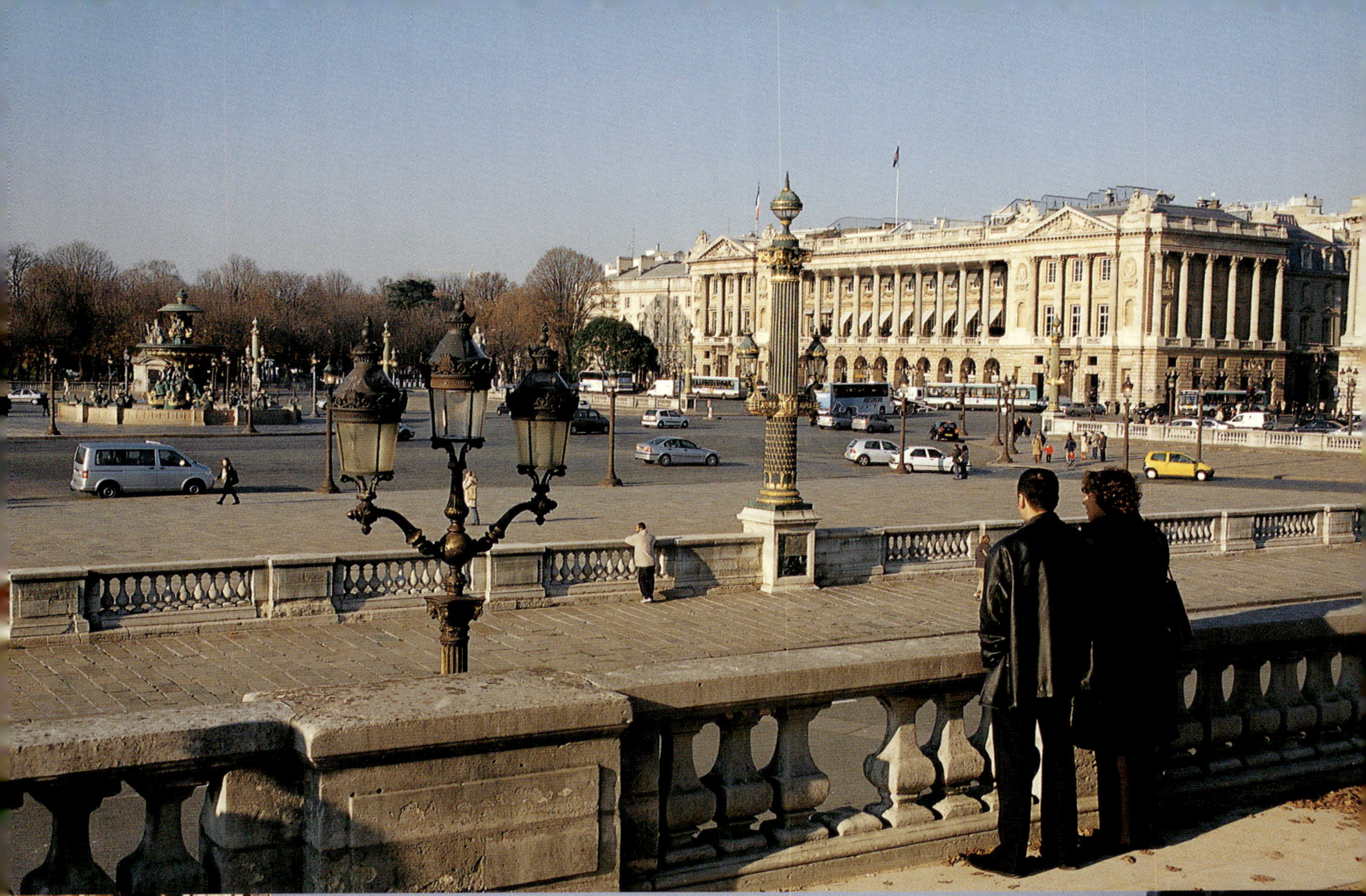

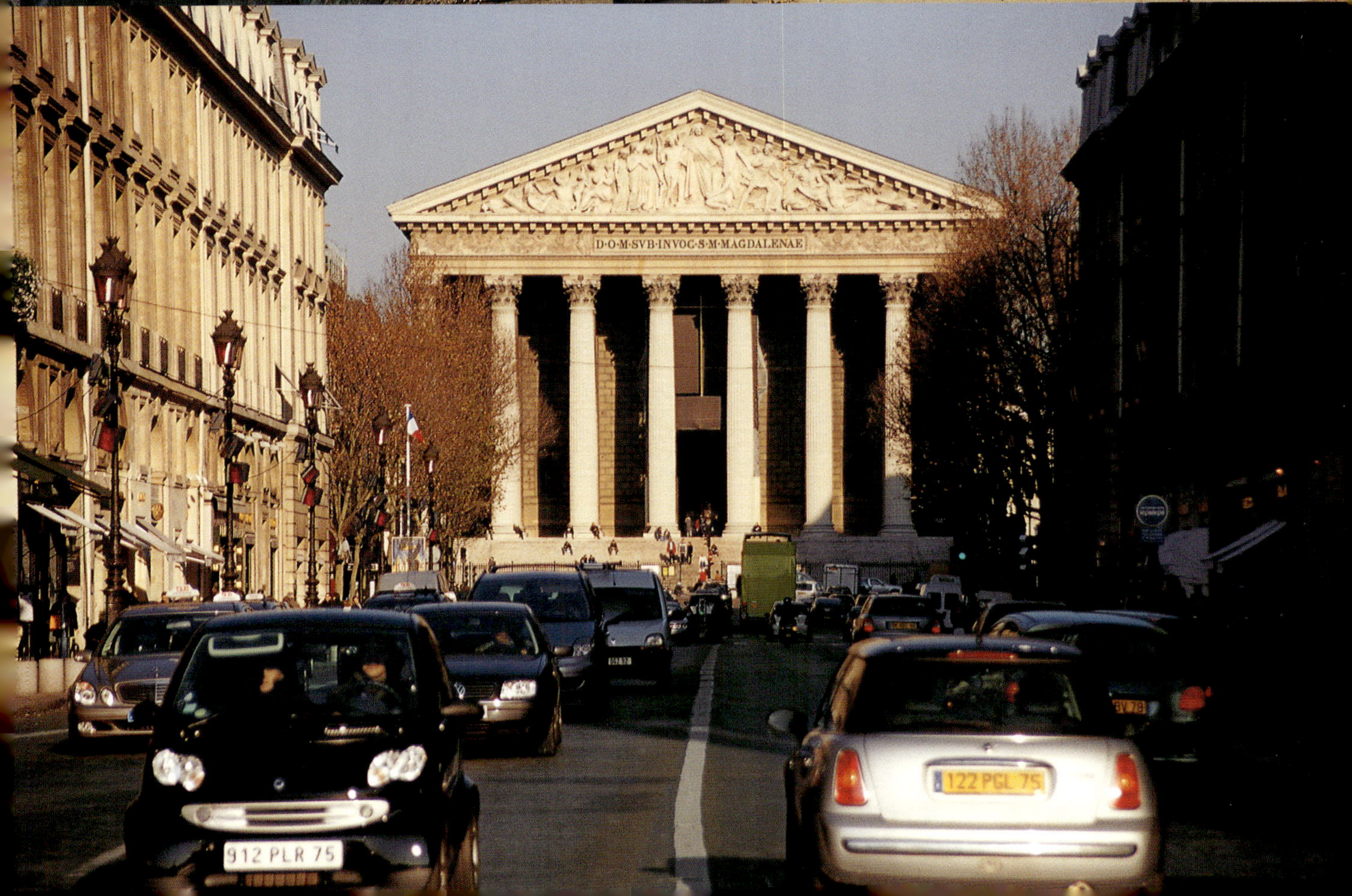
D·O·M·SVB·INVOC·S·M·MAGDALENAE
912 PLR 75
122 PGL 75

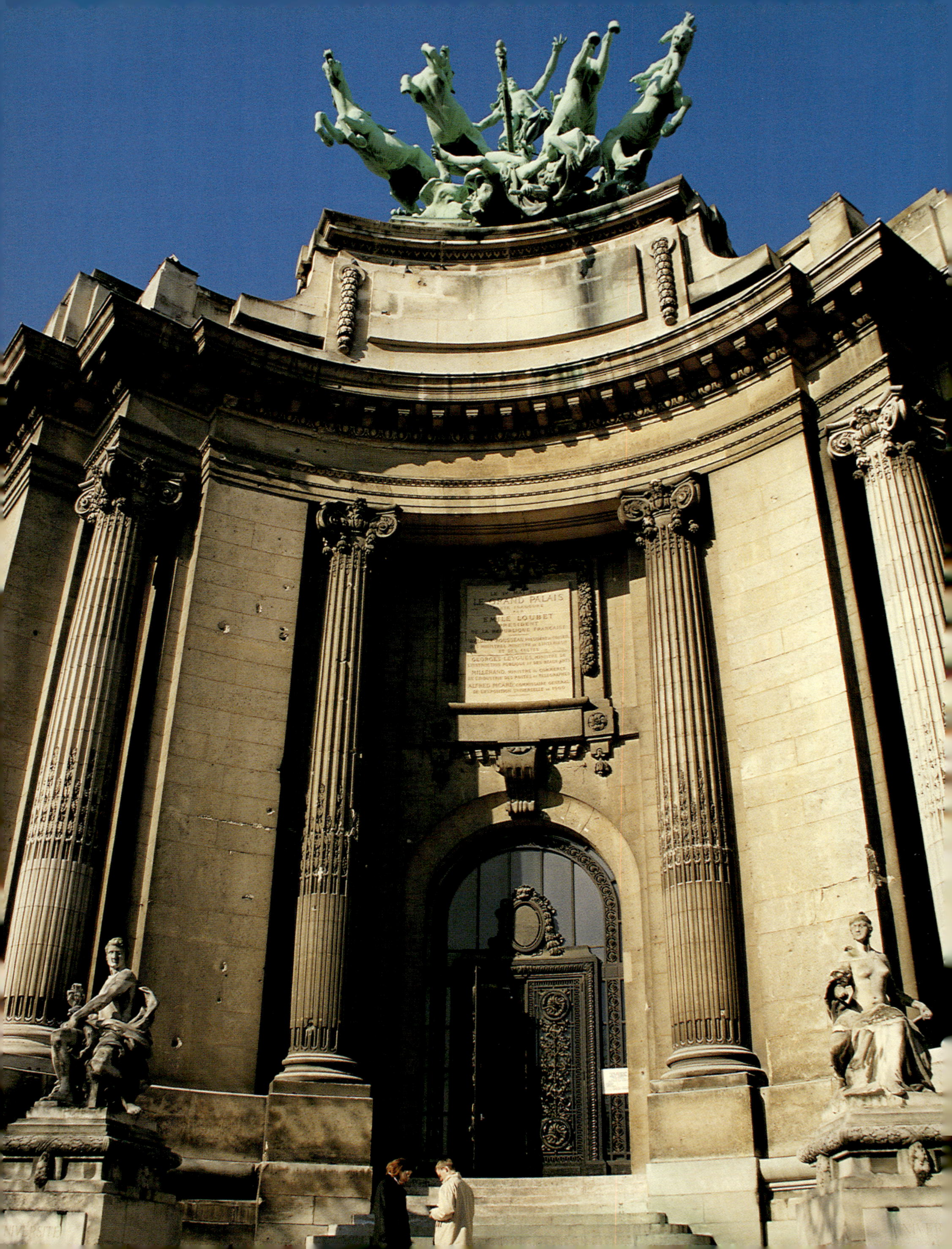
GRAND PALAIS
LOUBET
PRESIDENT
GEORGES LEYGUES
MILLERAND
ALFRED PICARD

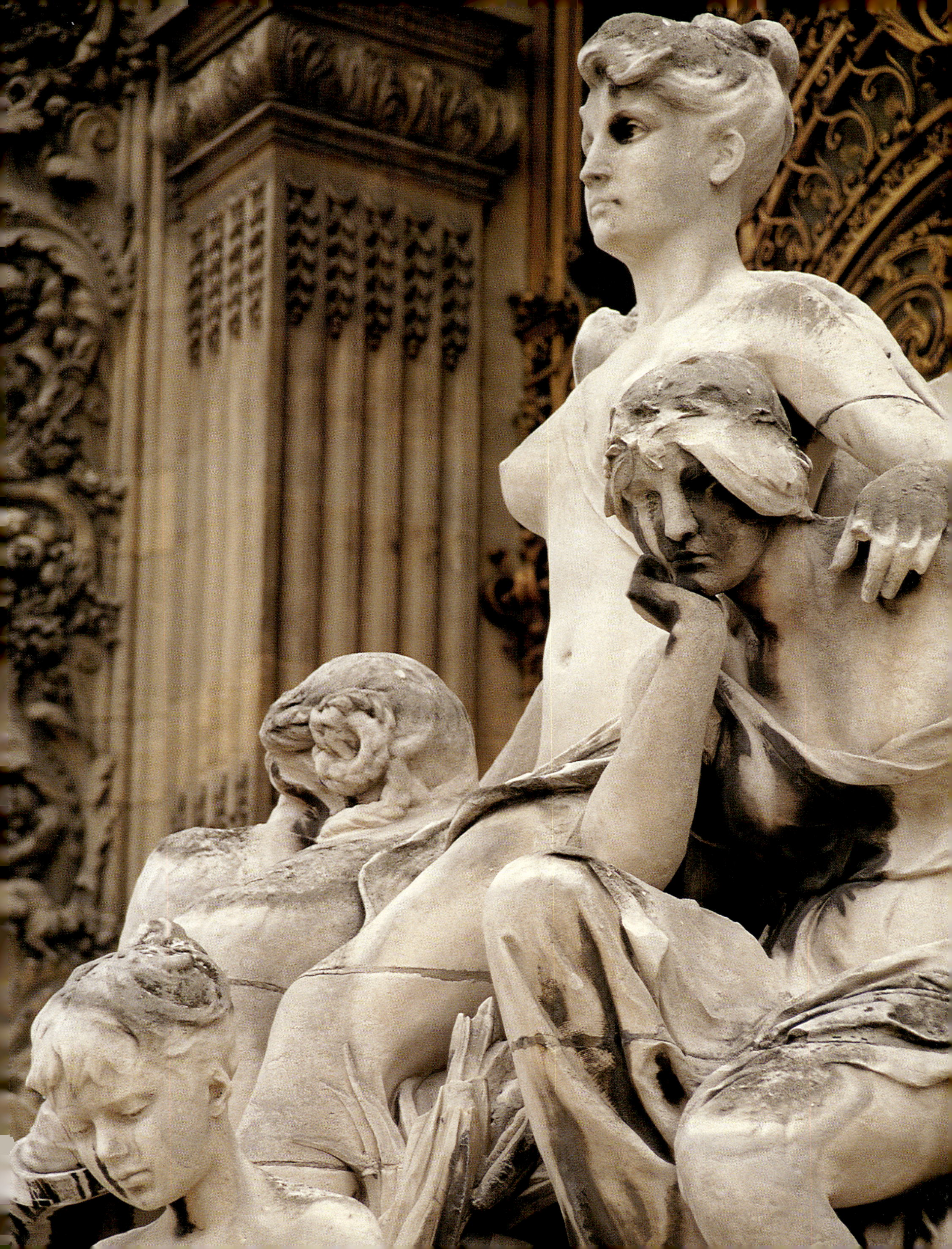

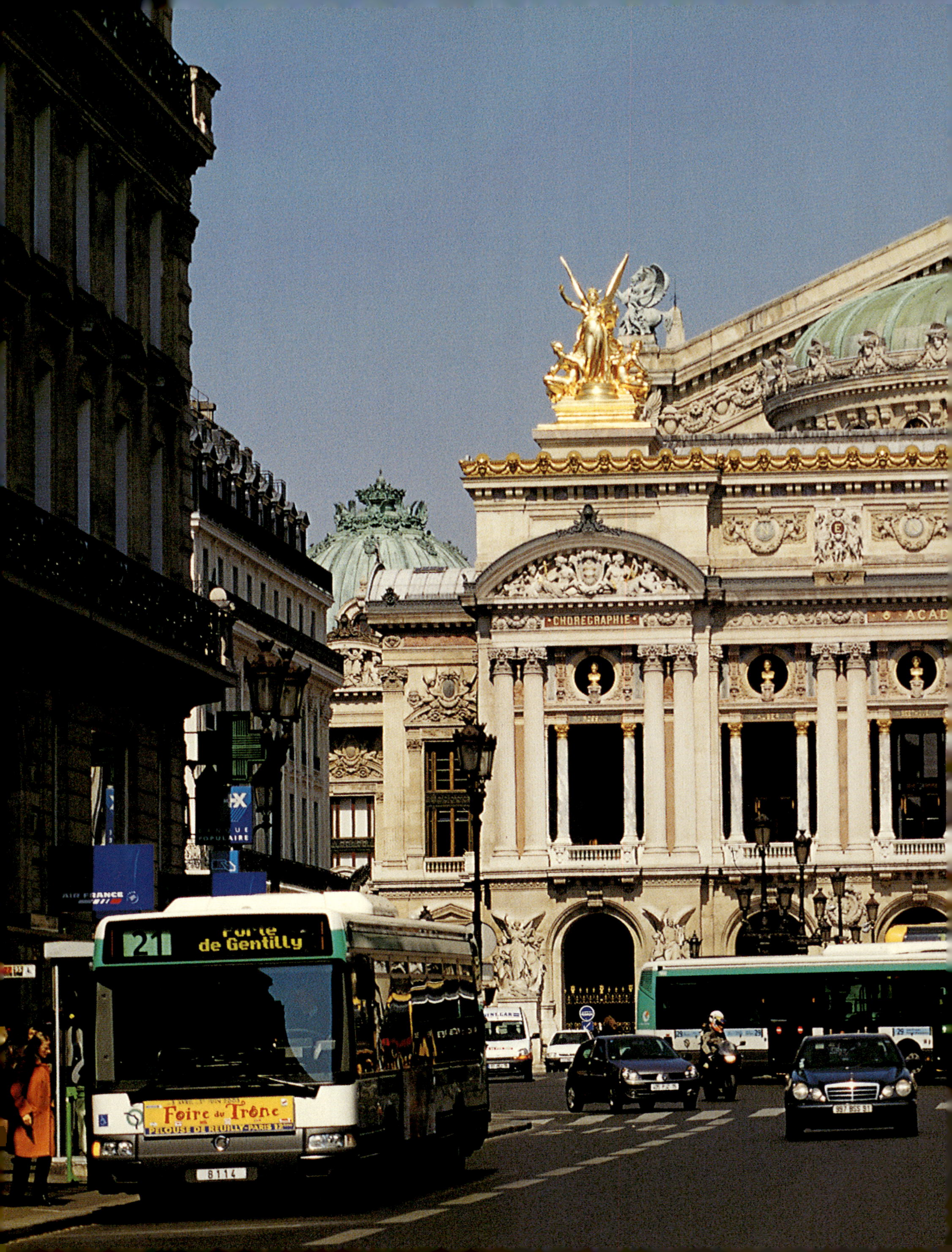
CHOREGRAPHIE
AIR FRANCE
21
Porte de Gentilly
Foire du Trône
PELOUSE DE REUILLY · PARIS 12

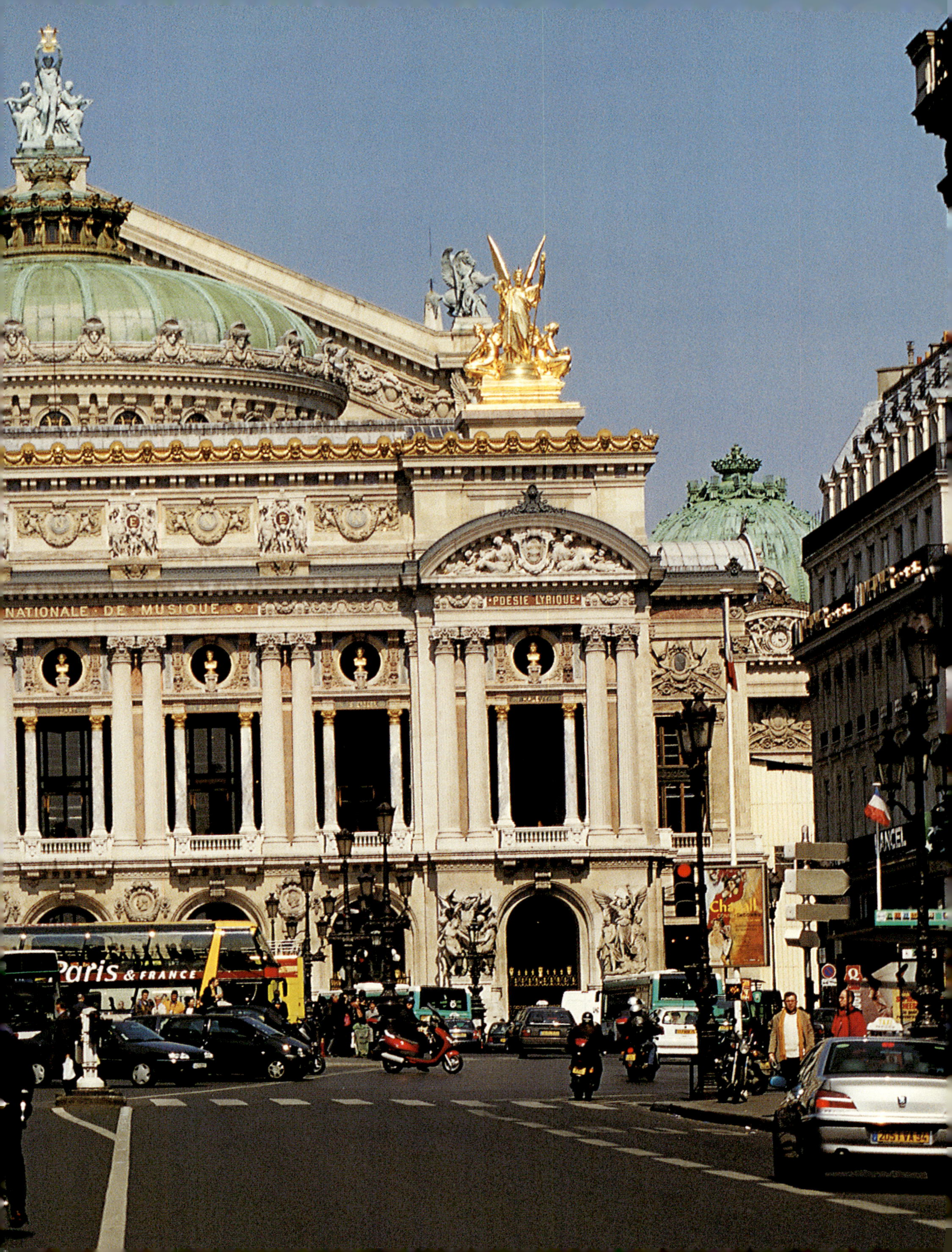
NATIONALE · DE · MUSIQUE
POESIE LYRIQUE
Paris & FRANCE

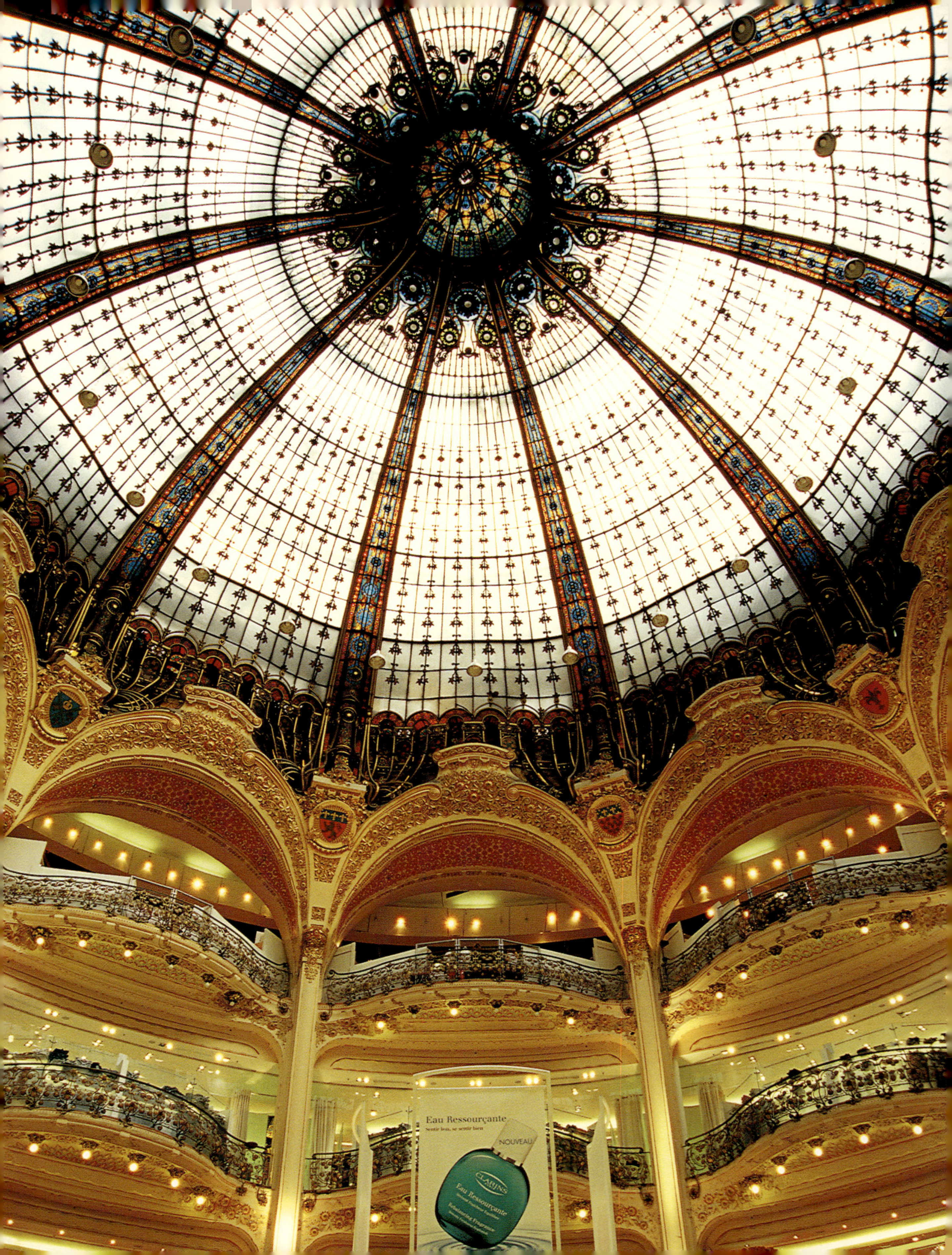
Eau Ressourçante
NOUVEAU
CLARINS
Eau Ressourçante

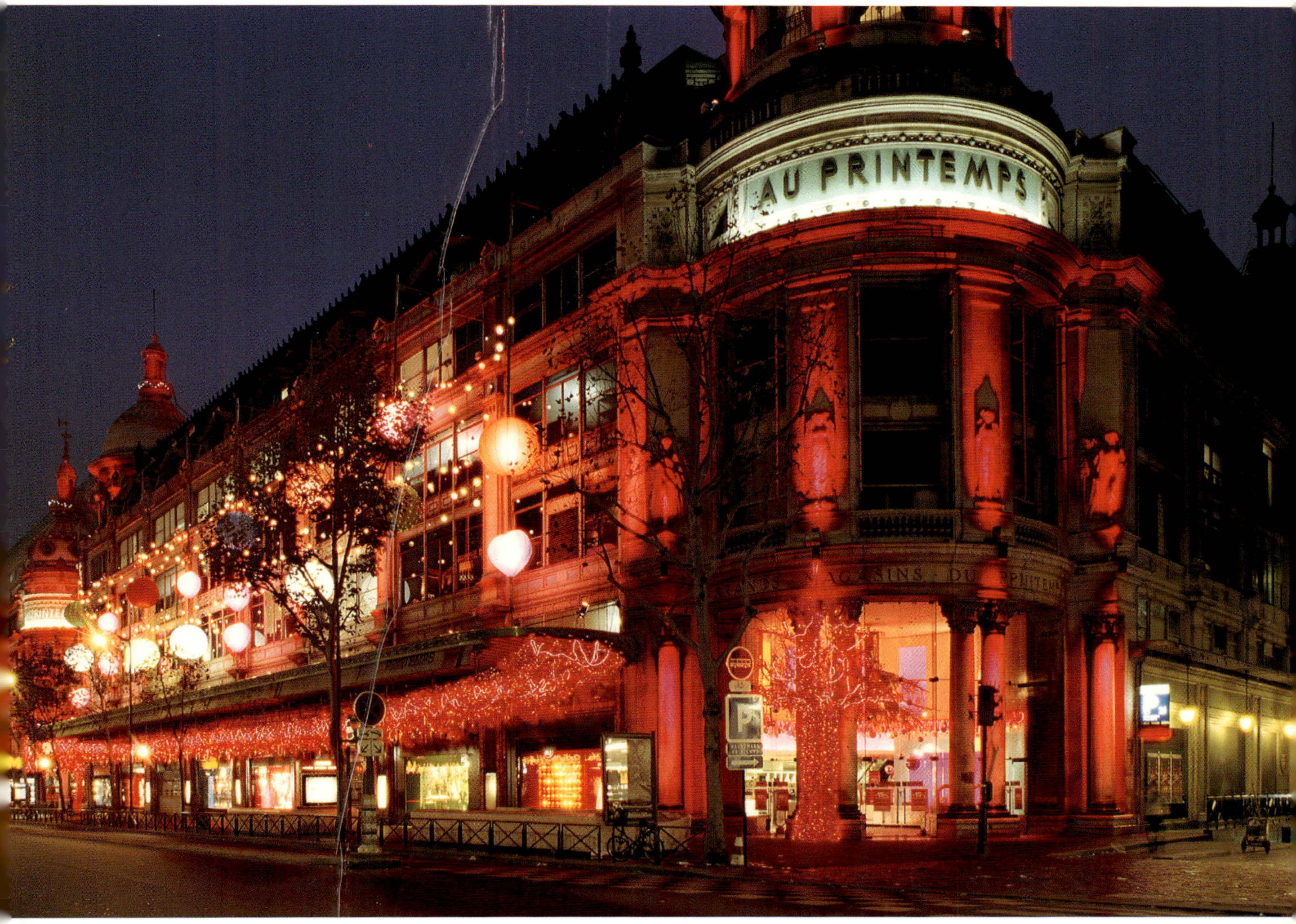
AU PRINTEMPS

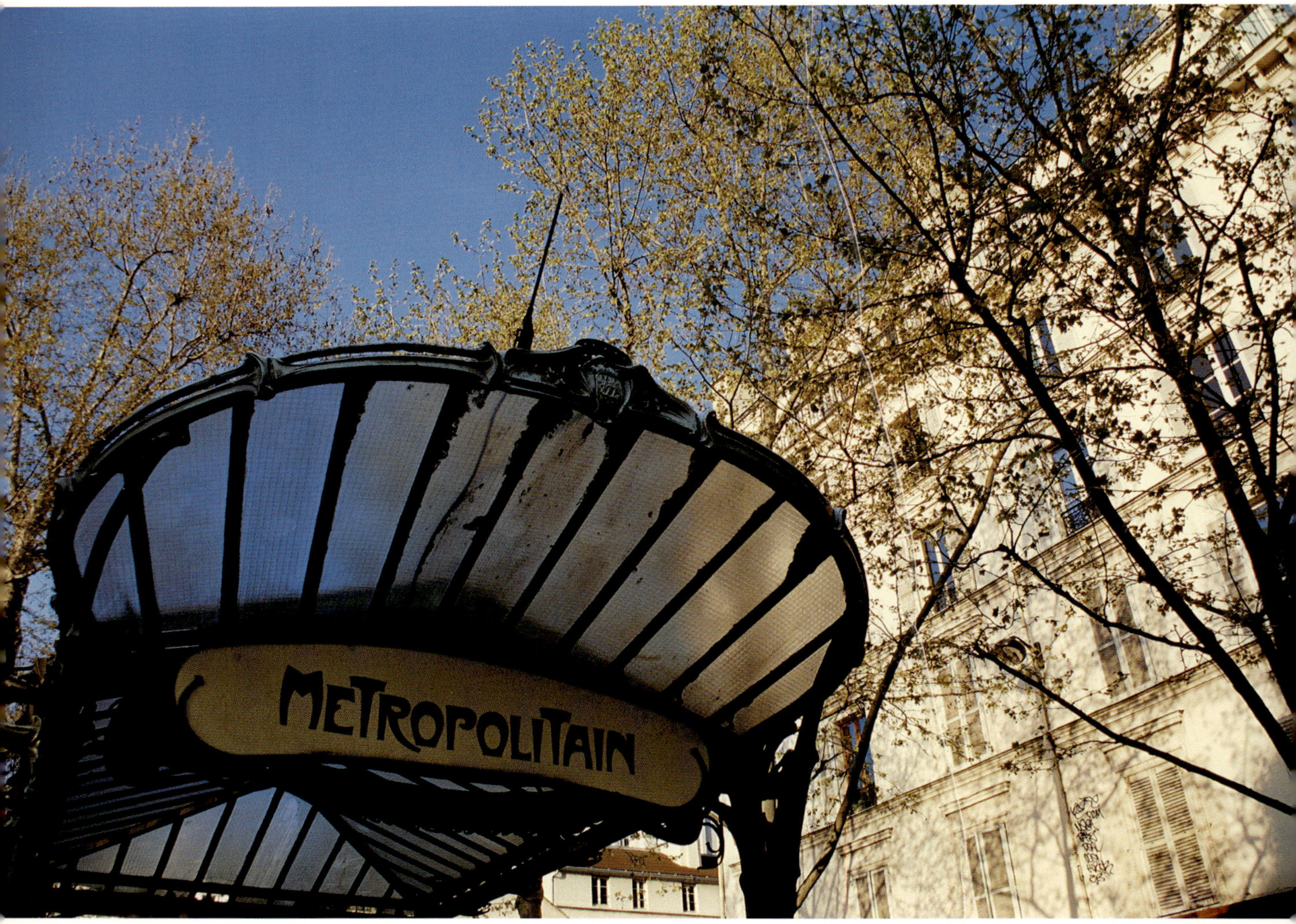
METROPOLITAIN

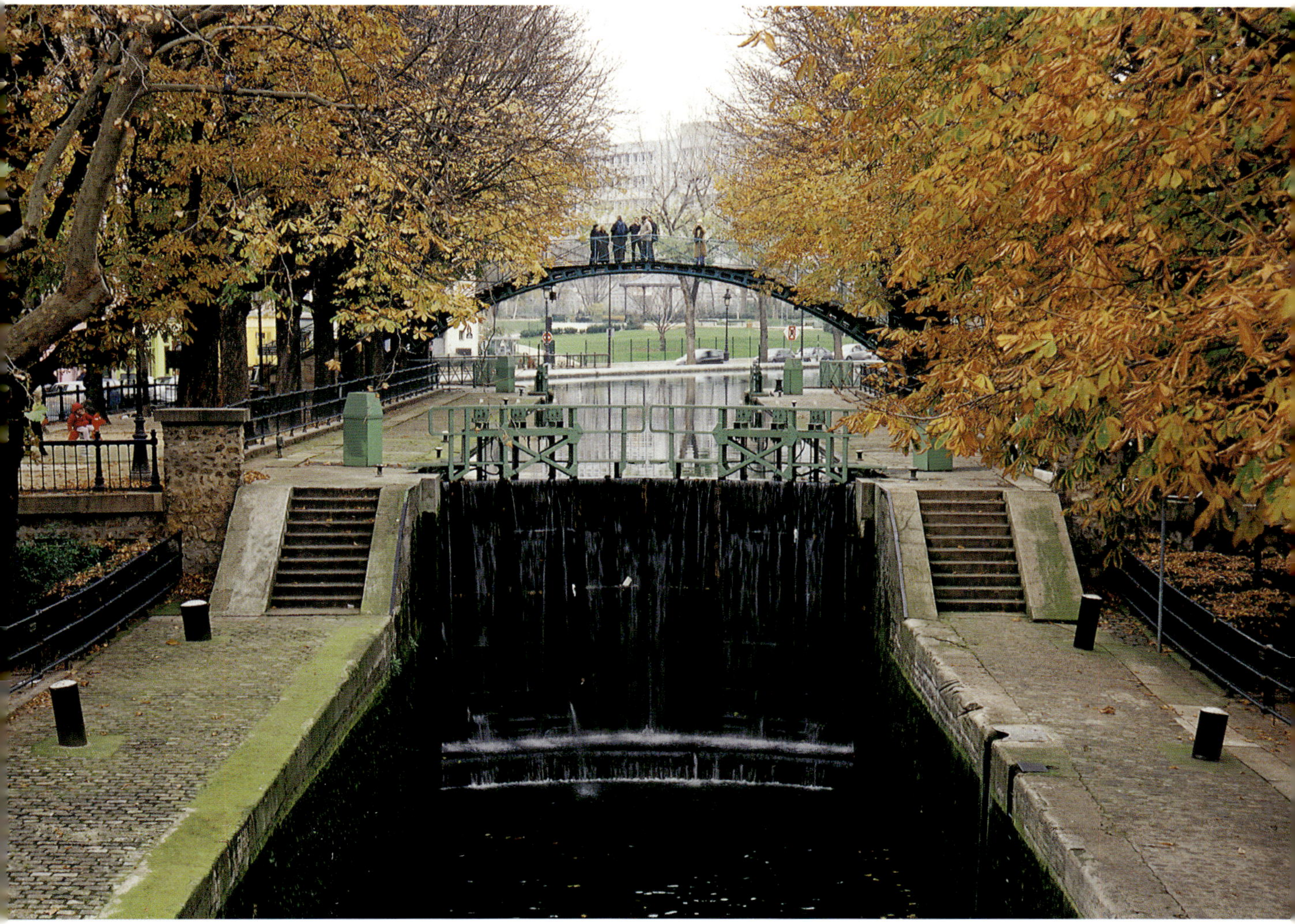

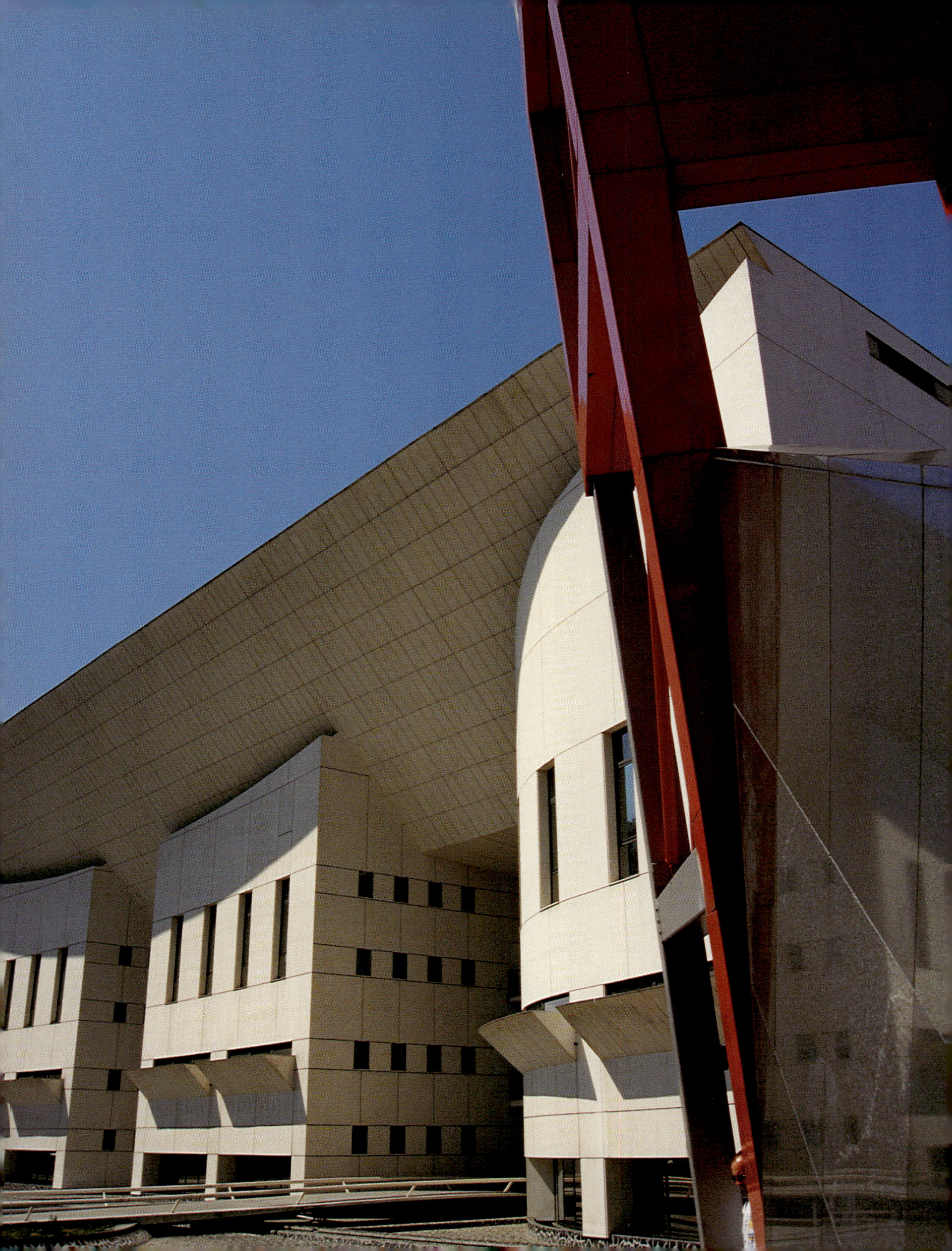

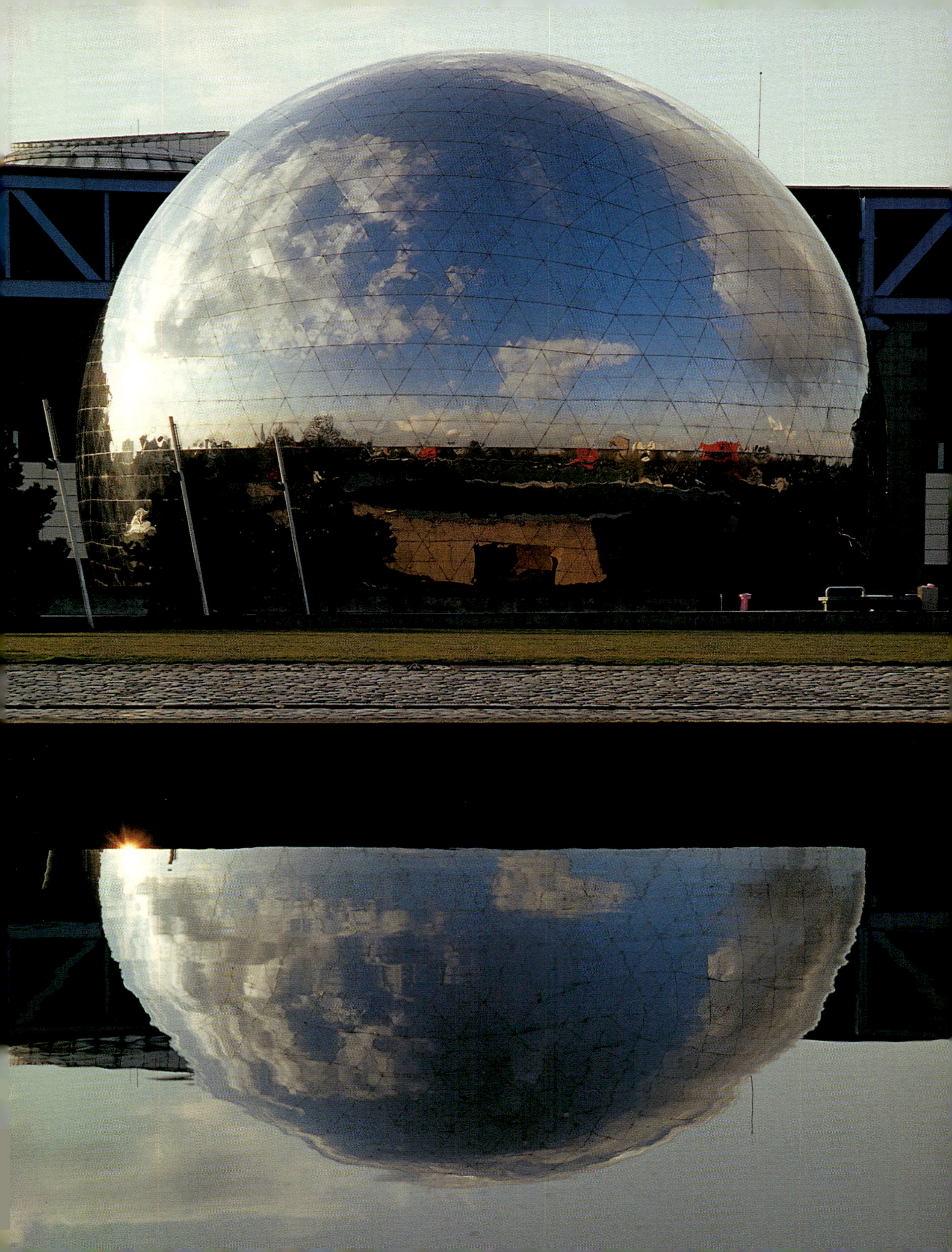

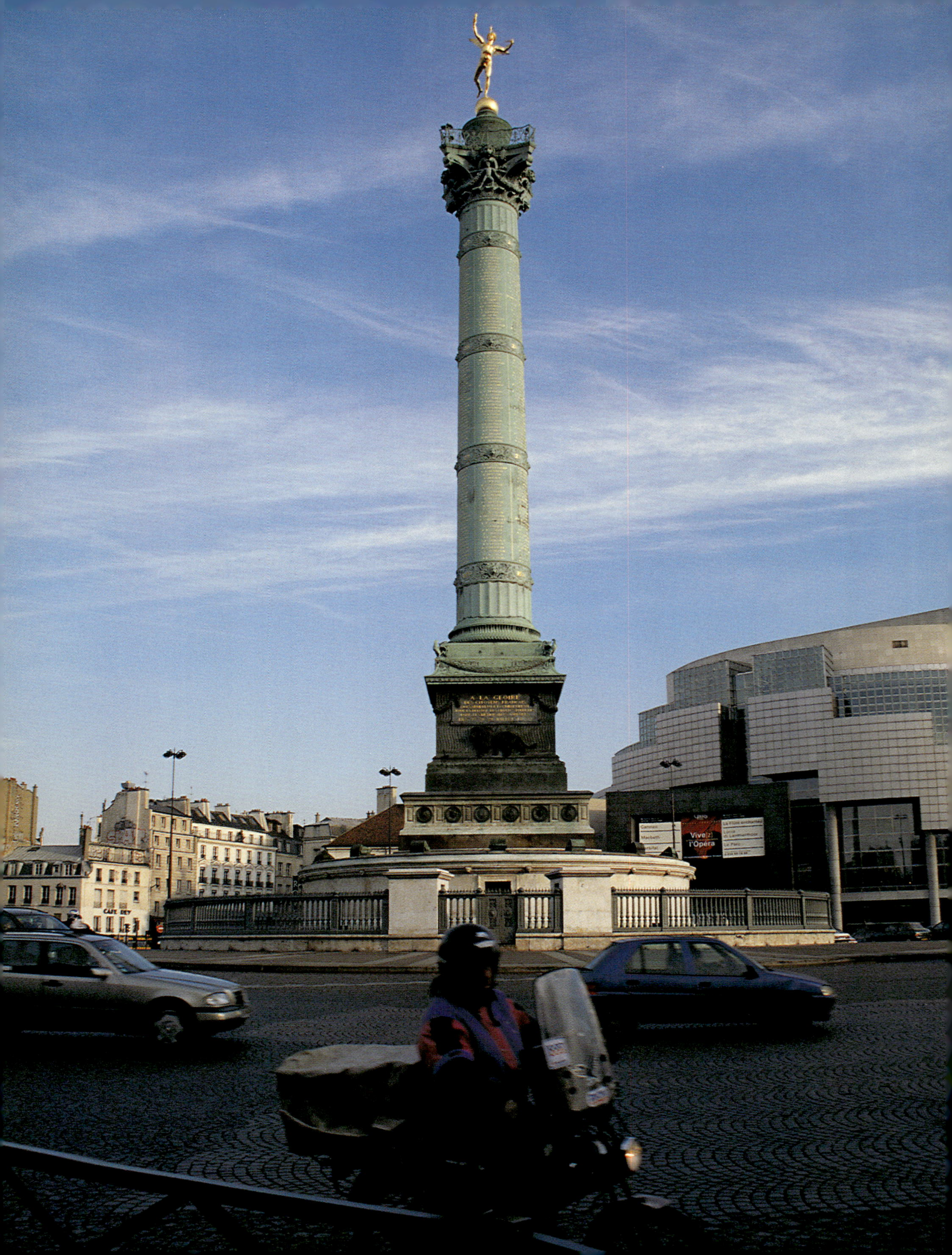

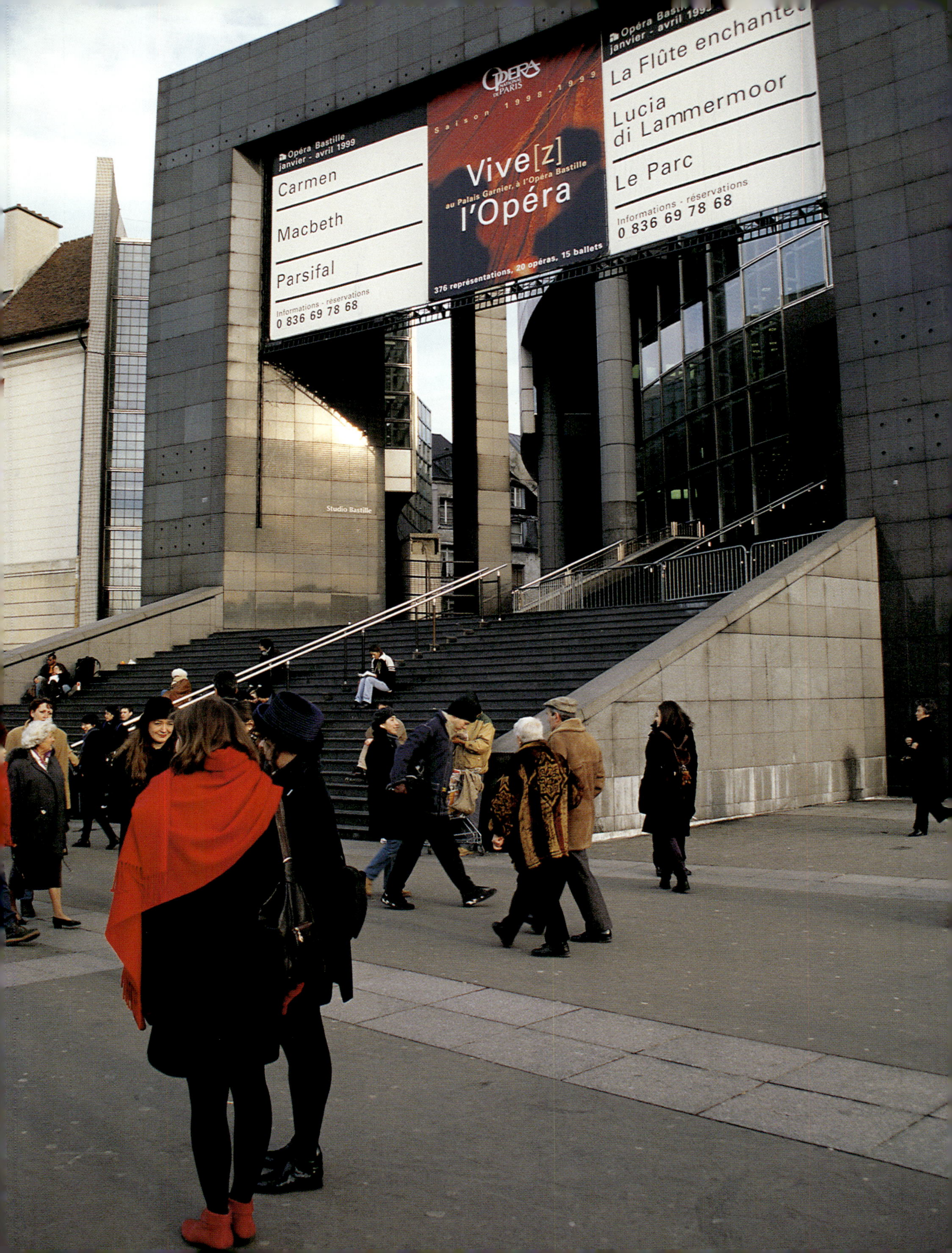
Opéra Bastille
janvier - avril 1999
Carmen
Macbeth
Parsifal
Informations - réservations
0 836 69 78 68
Saison 1998 - 1999
Vive[z]
au Palais Garnier, à l'Opéra Bastille
l'Opéra
376 représentations, 20 opéras, 15 ballets
Lucia
di Lammermoor
Le Parc
Informations - réservations
0 836 69 78 68
Studio Bastille

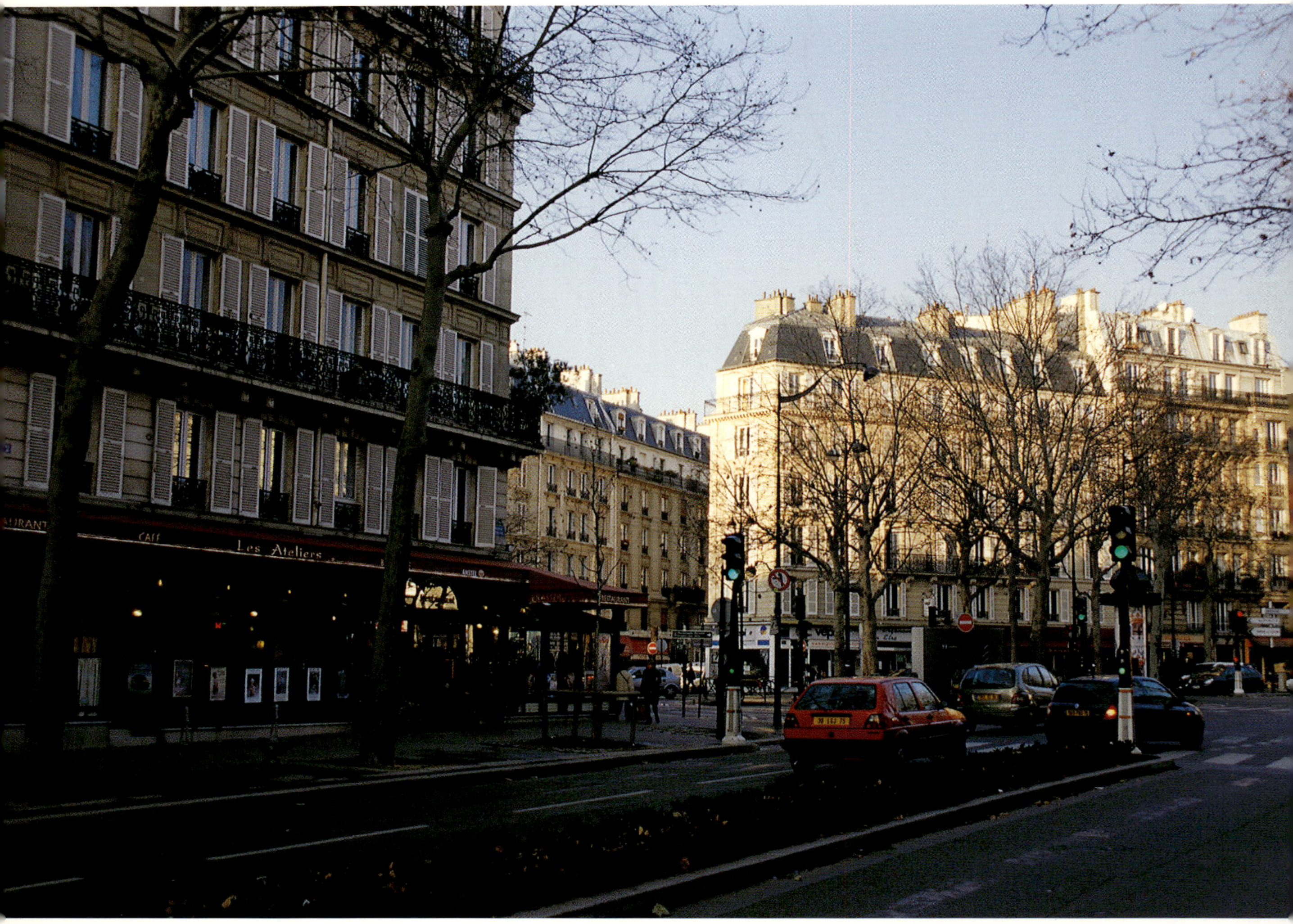
Les Ateliers

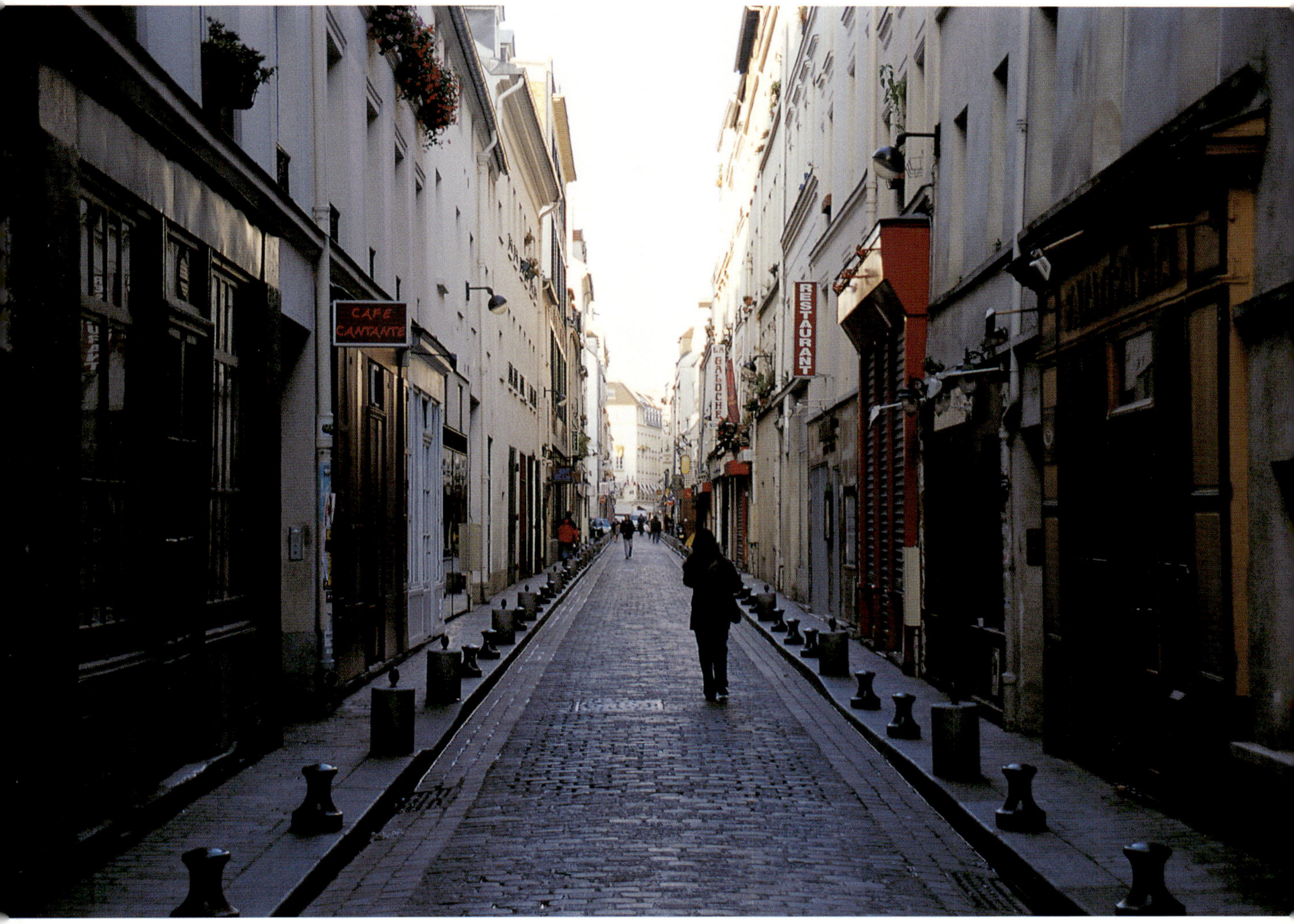
CAFE CANTANTE
RESTAURANT

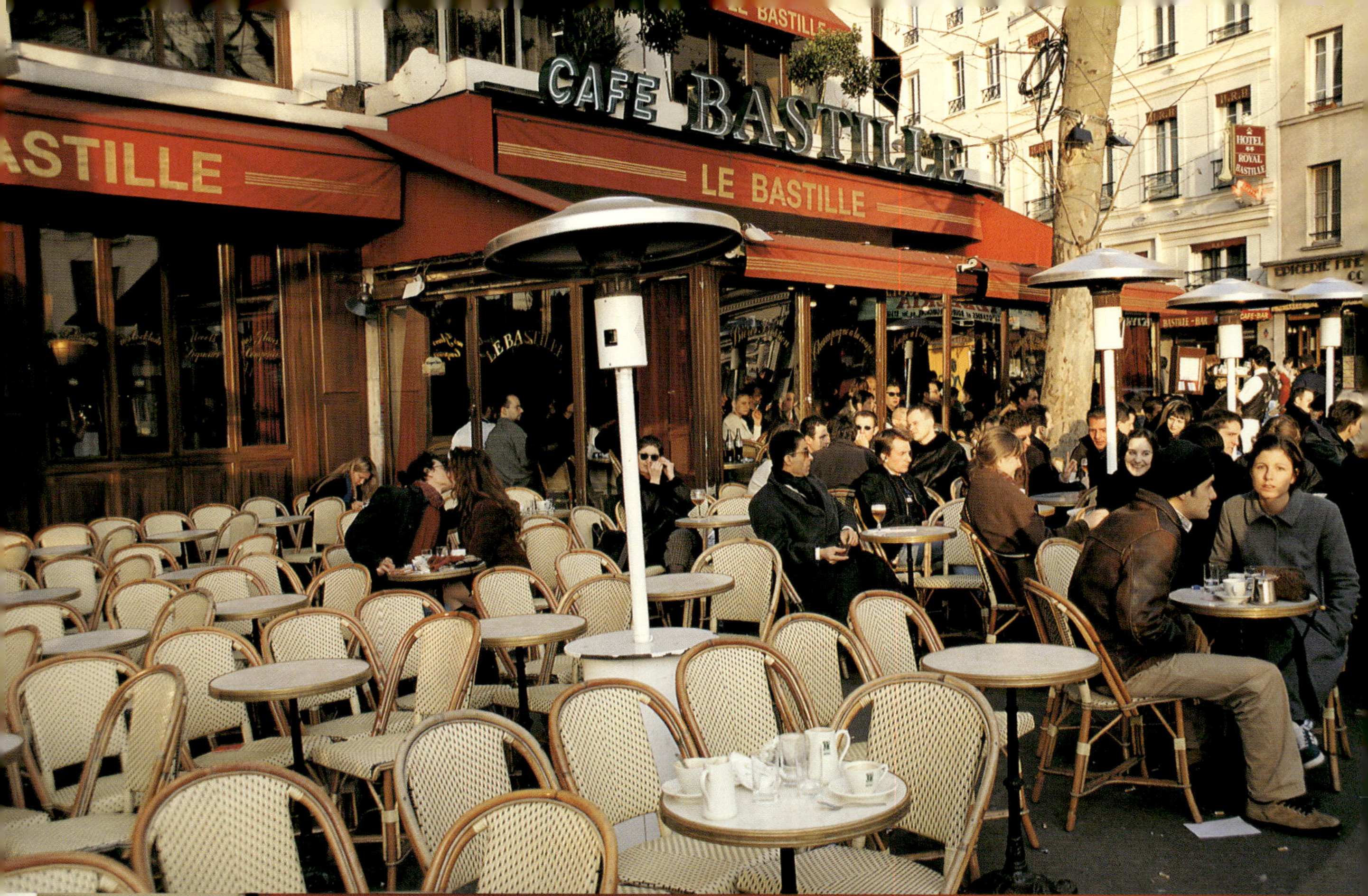
CAFE BASTILLE
ASTILLE
LE BASTILLE

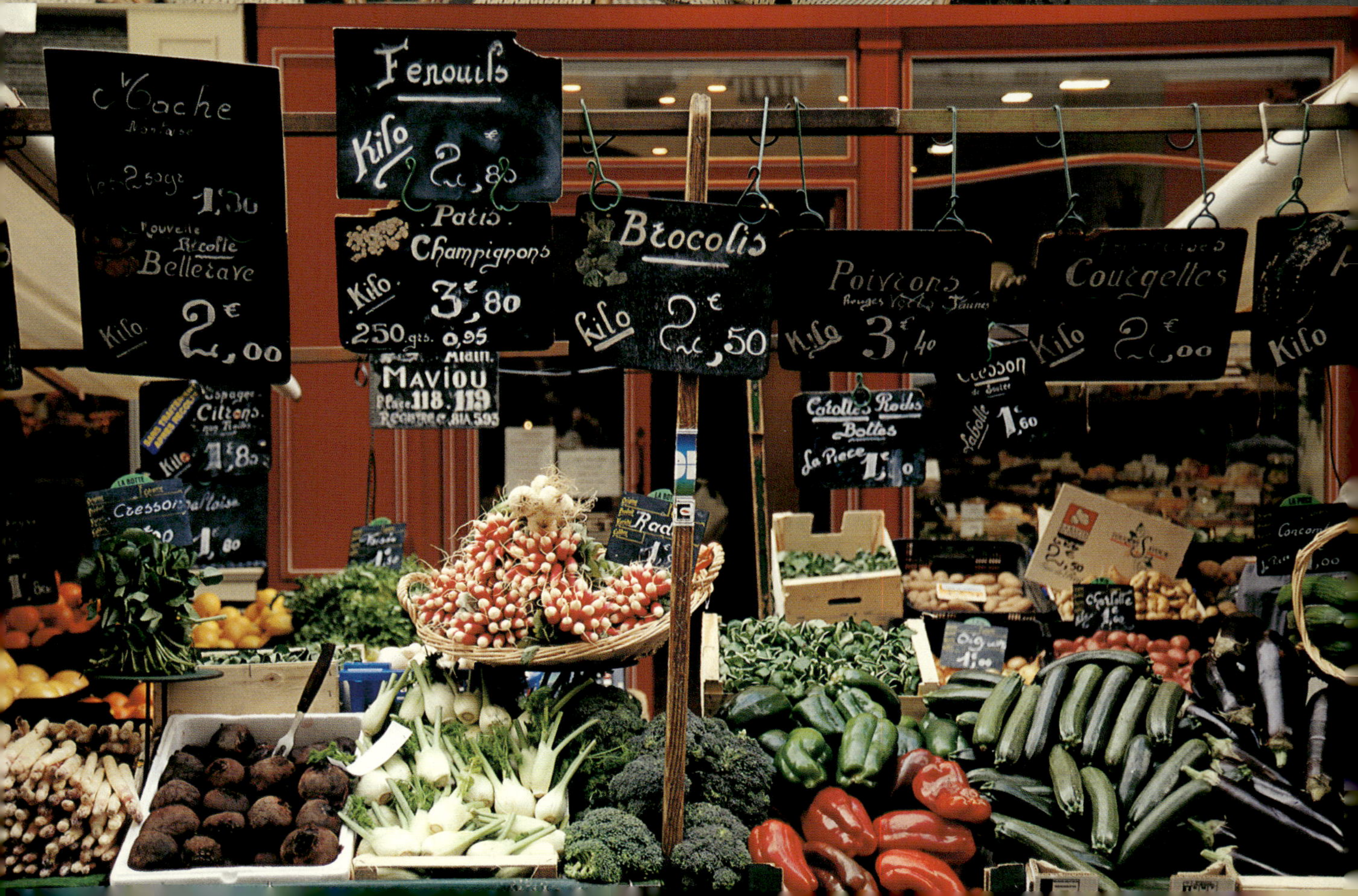
Fenouils
Kilo
Mache
Bellerave
Kilo 2€,00
Paris Champignons
Kilo 3€,80
250 grs. 0,95
Brocolis
Kilo 2€,50
Poivrons
Kilo 3€,40
Courgettes
Kilo 2€,00
Maviou

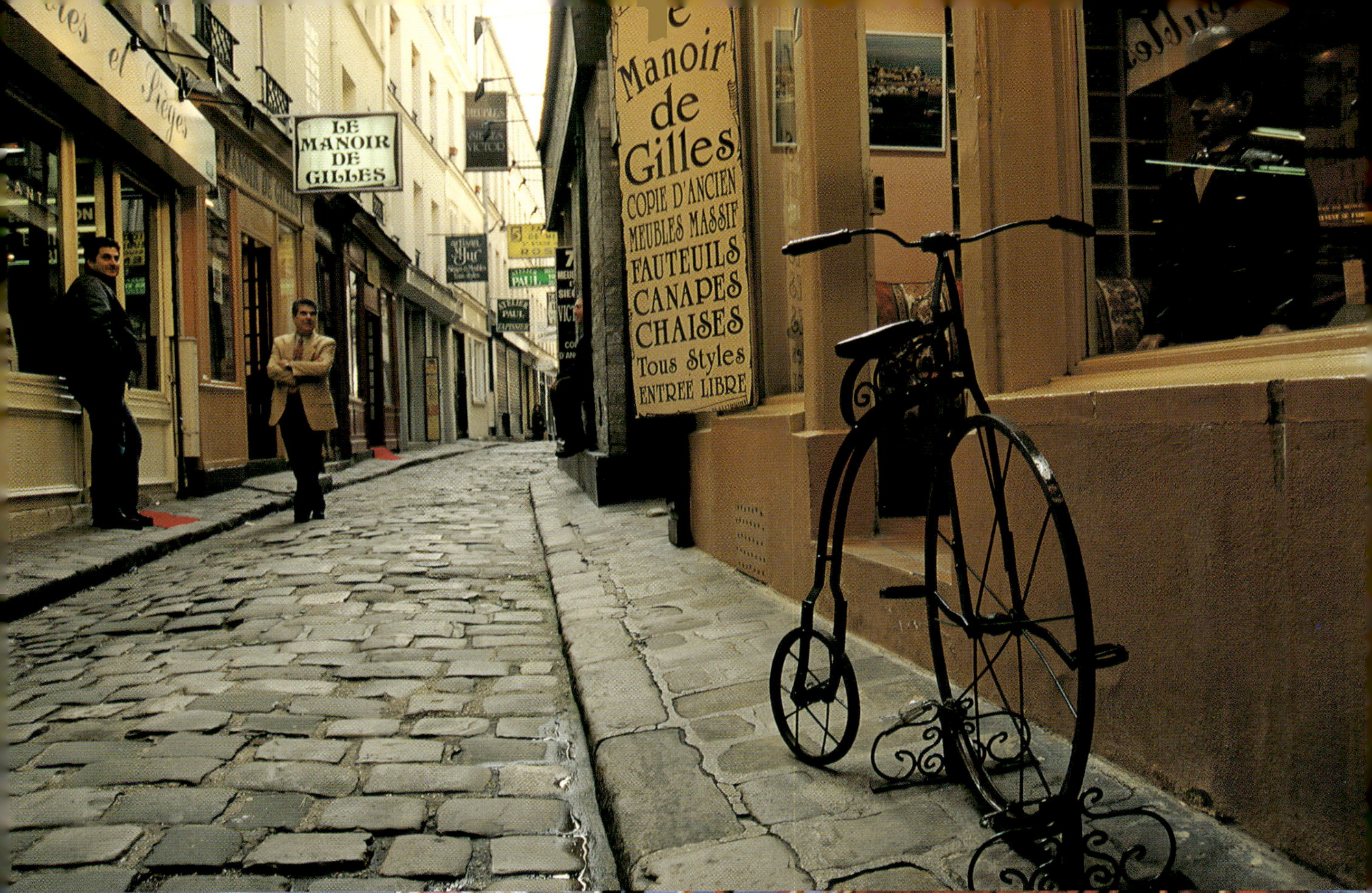
LE
MANOIR
DE
GILLES
Manoir
de
Gilles
COPIE D'ANCIEN
MEUBLES MASSIF
FAUTEUILS
CANAPES
CHAISES
Tous Styles
ENTREE LIBRE

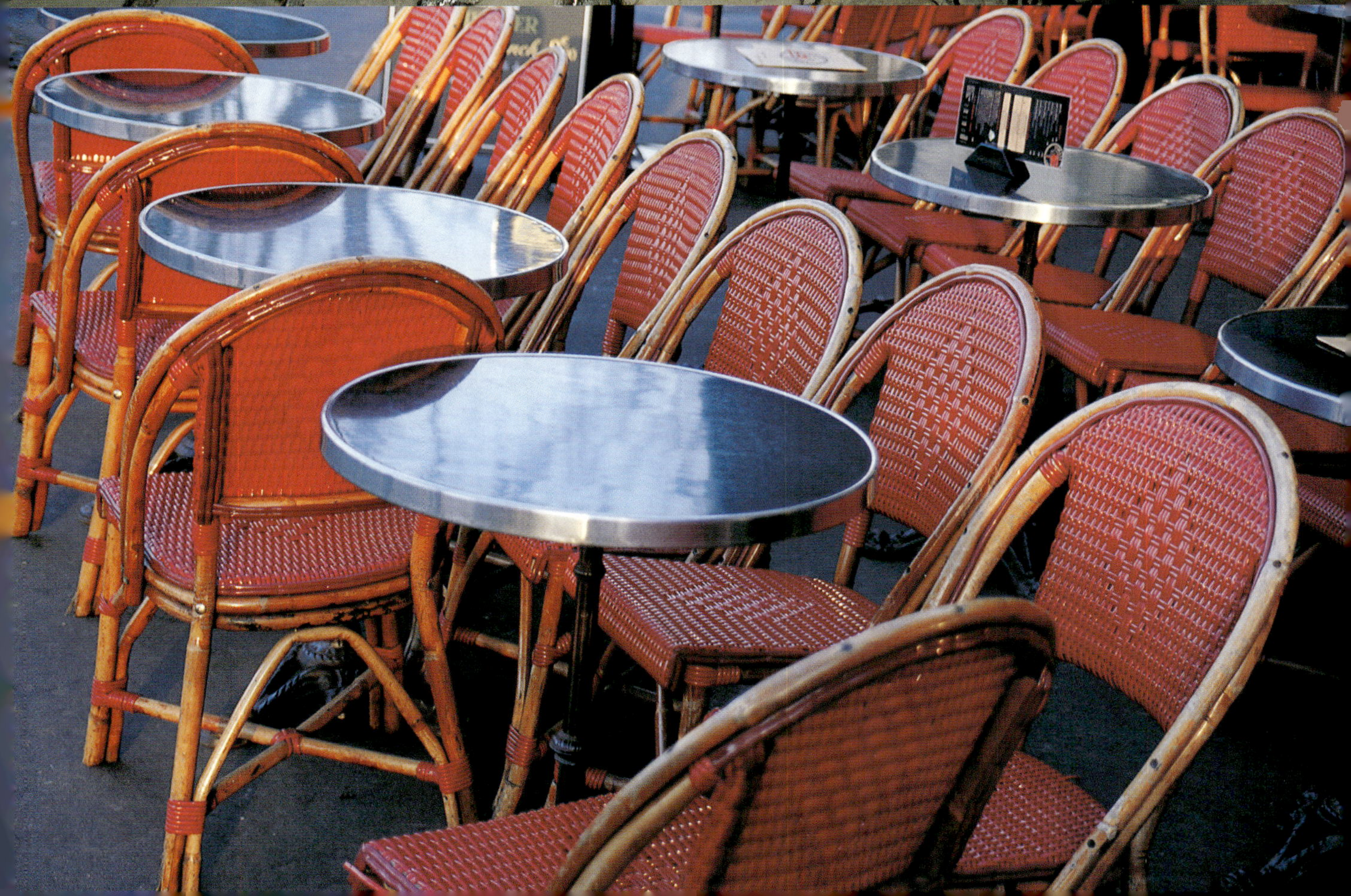

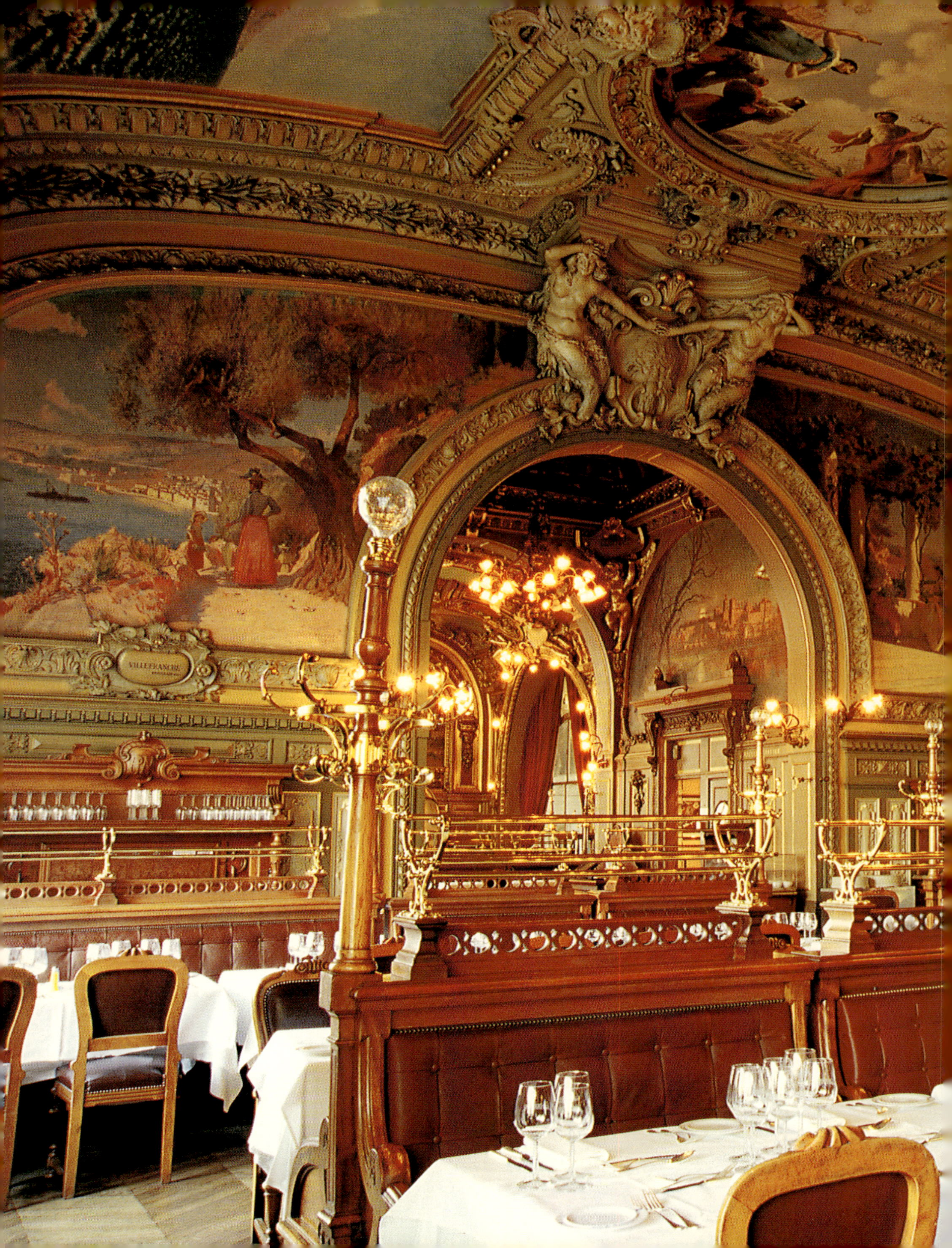
VILLEFRANCHE

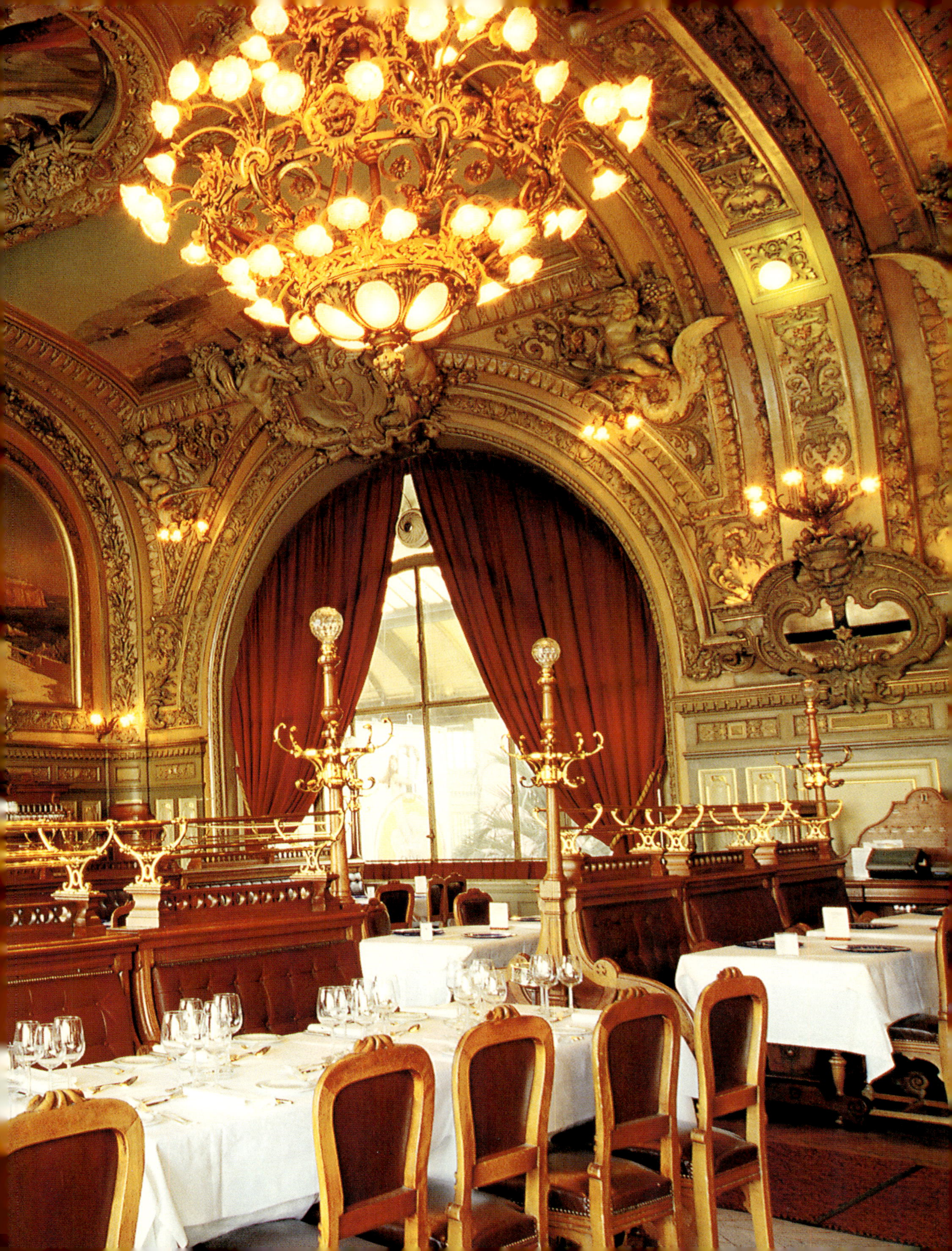

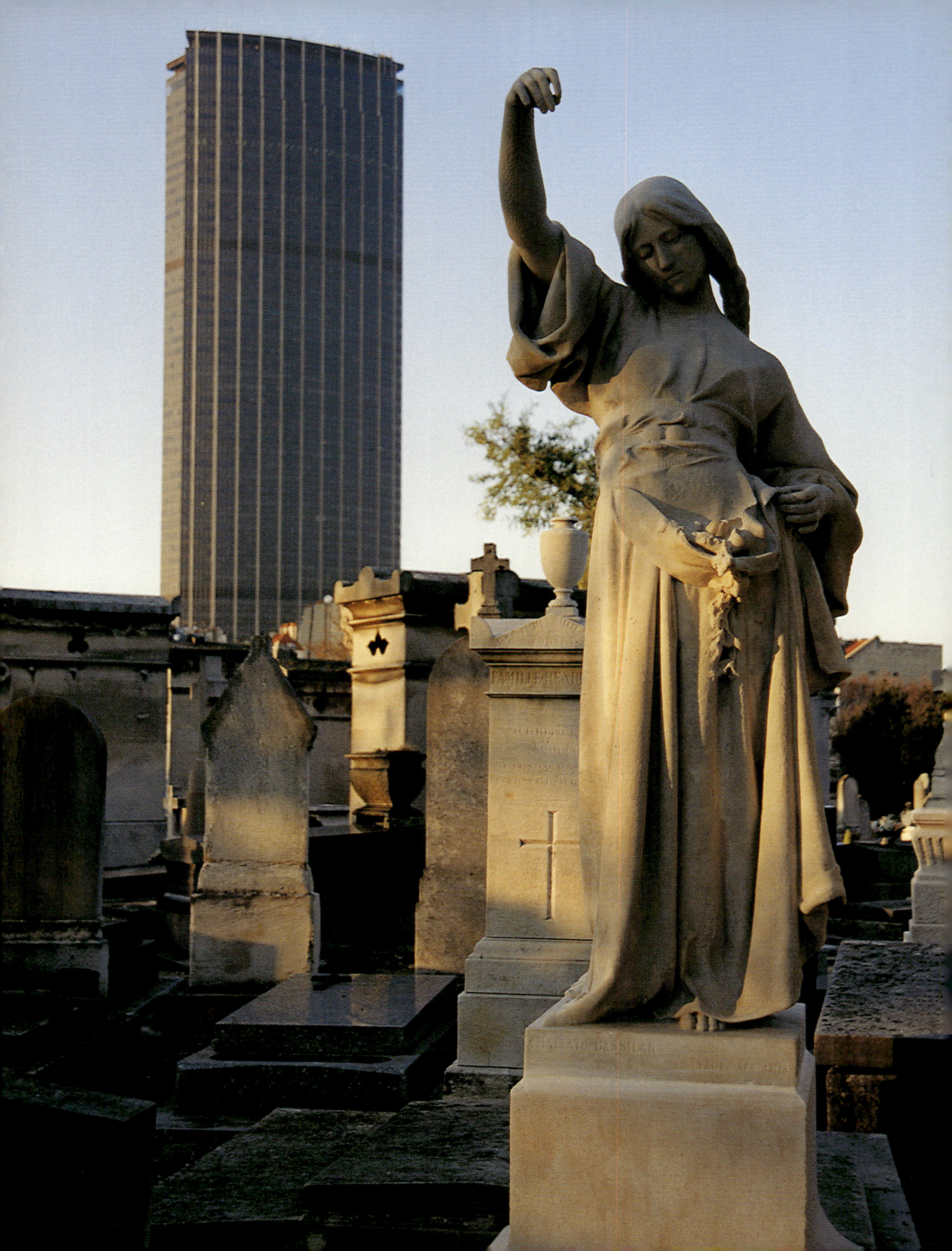

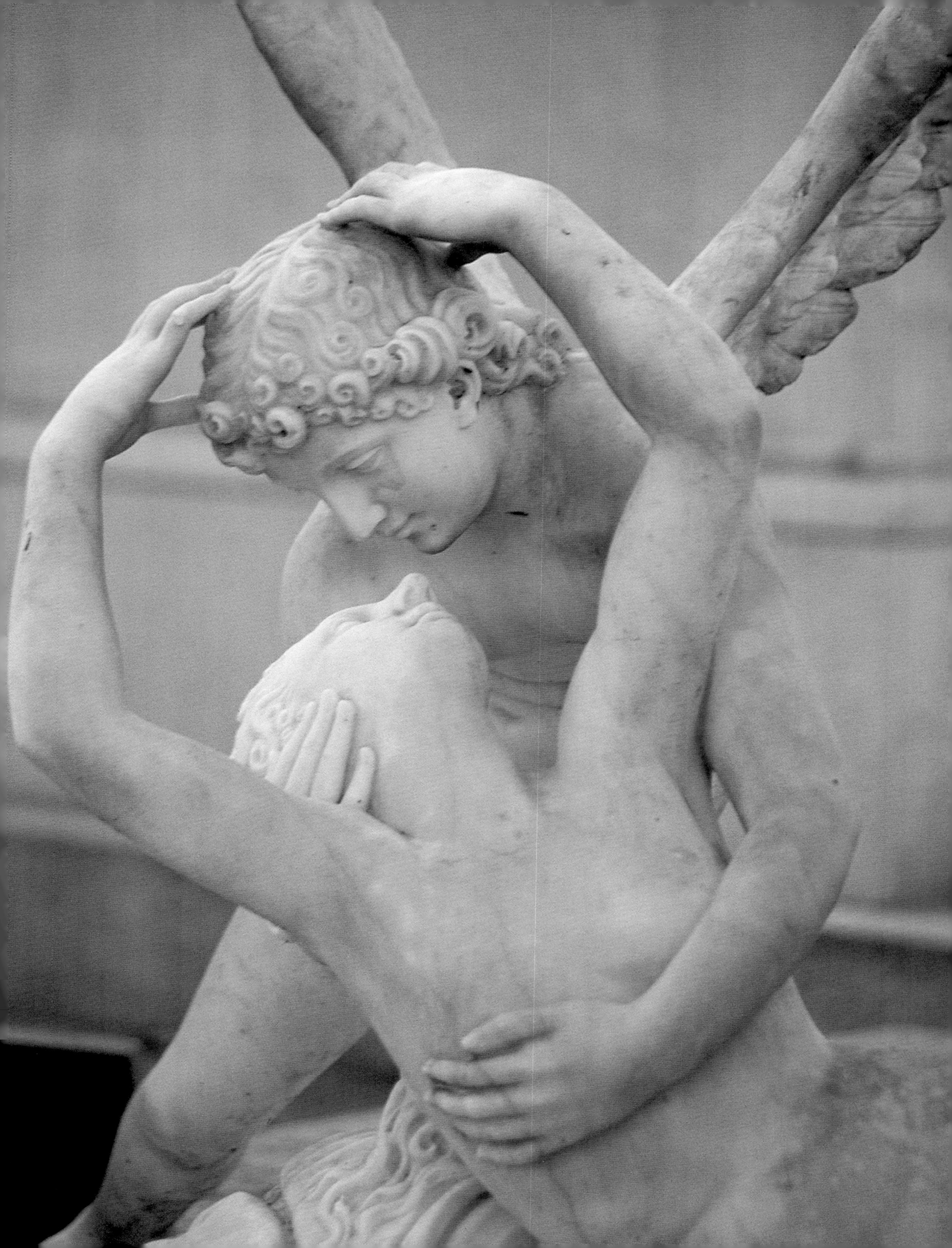

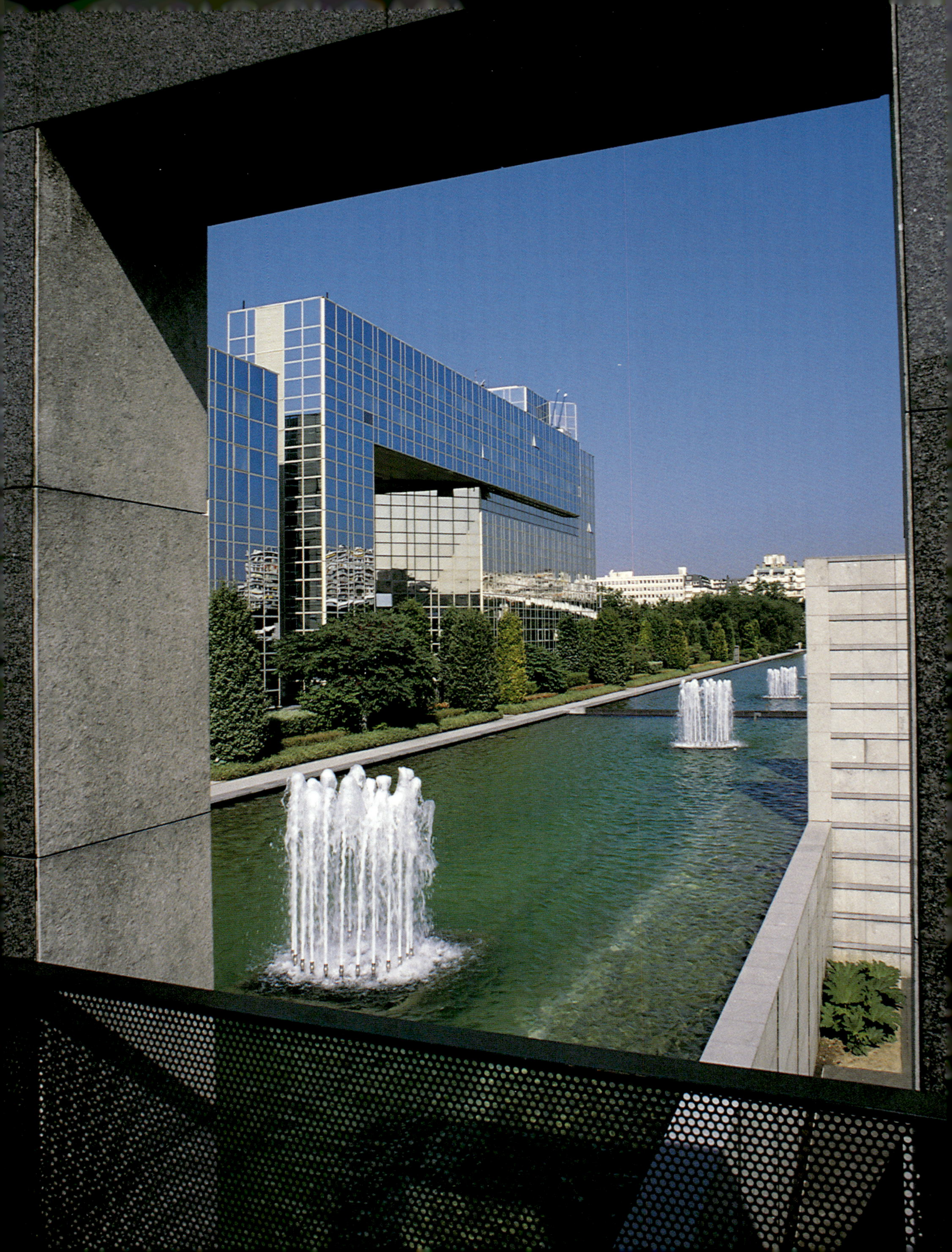

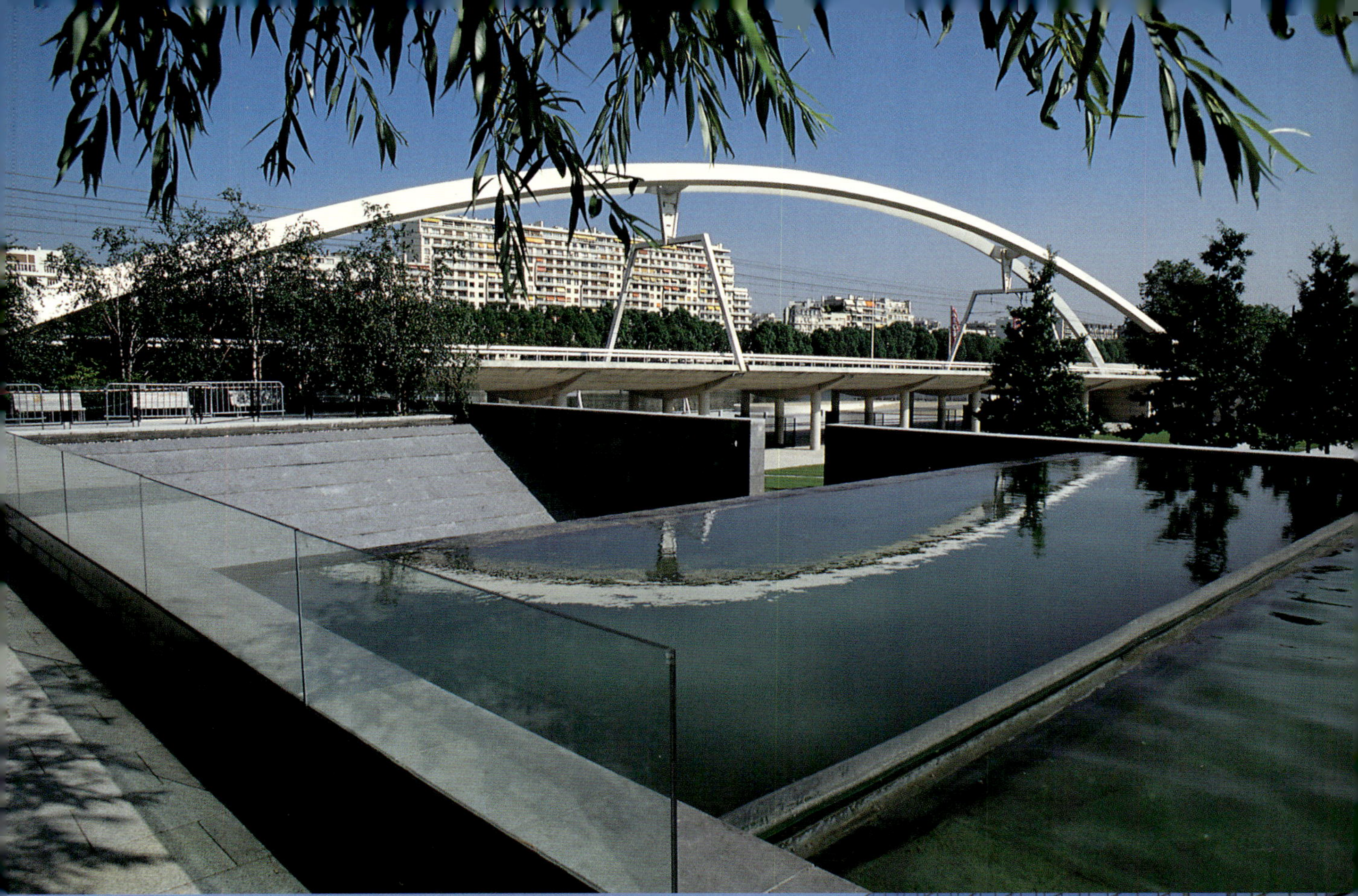

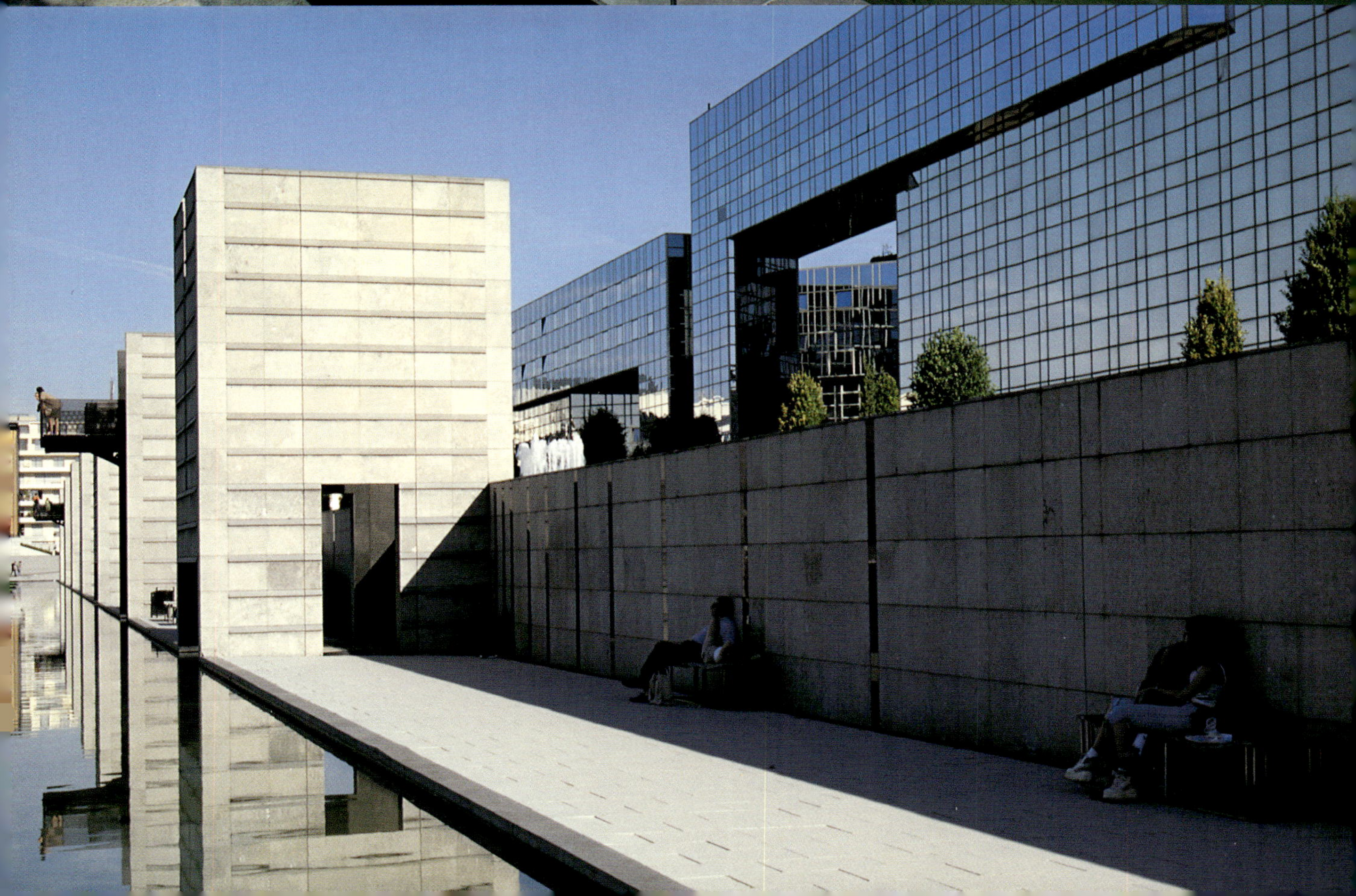

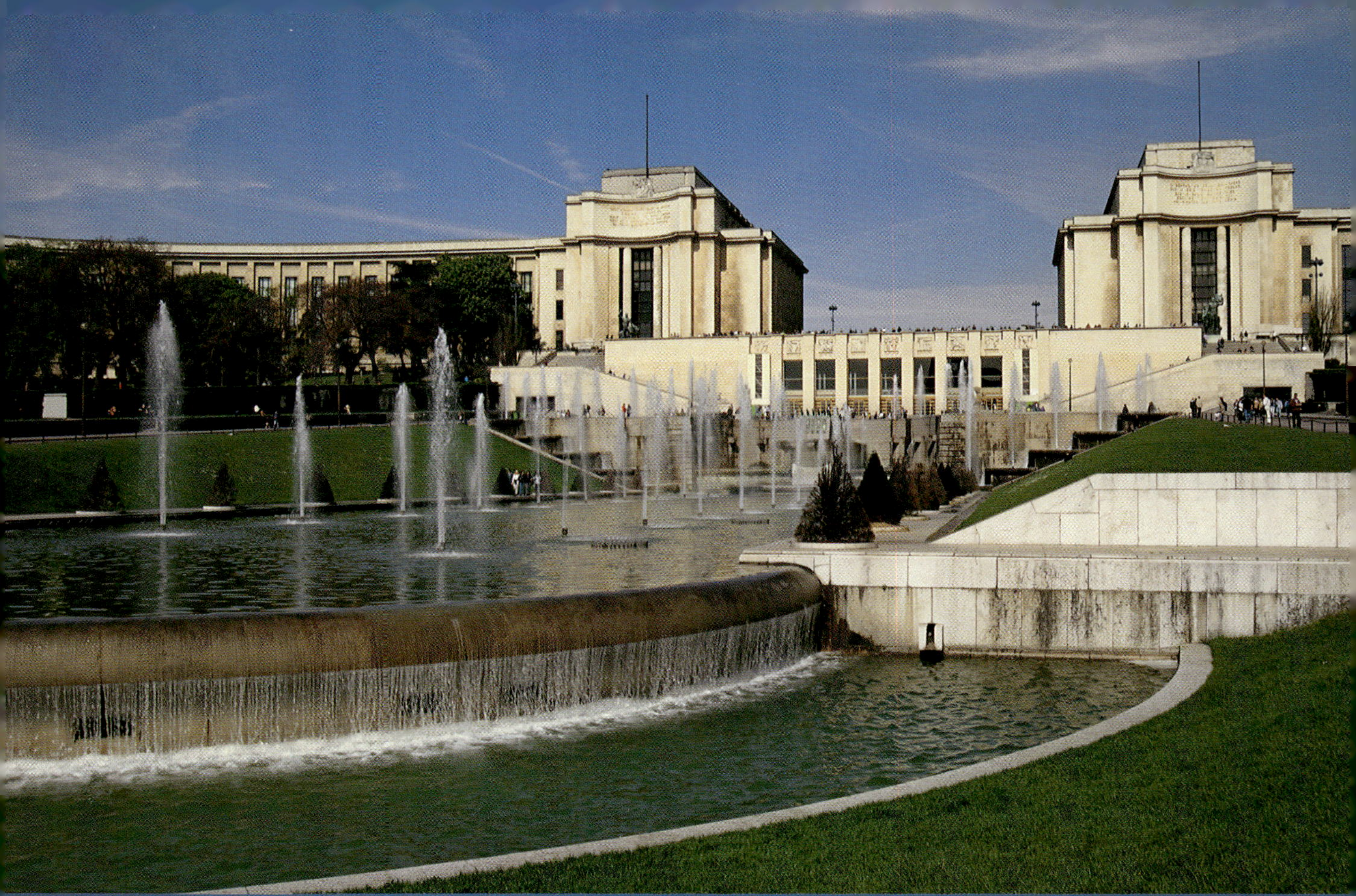

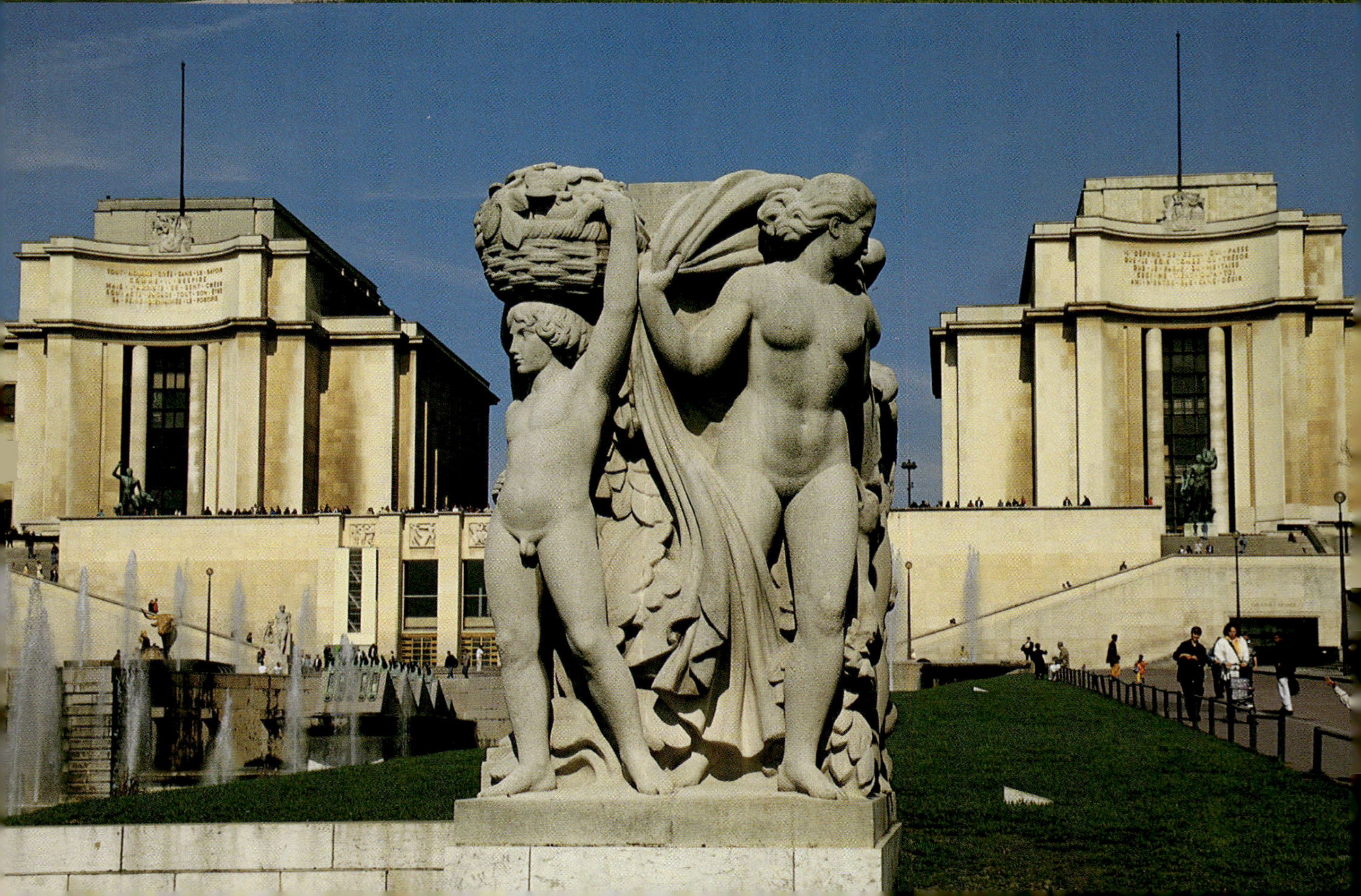

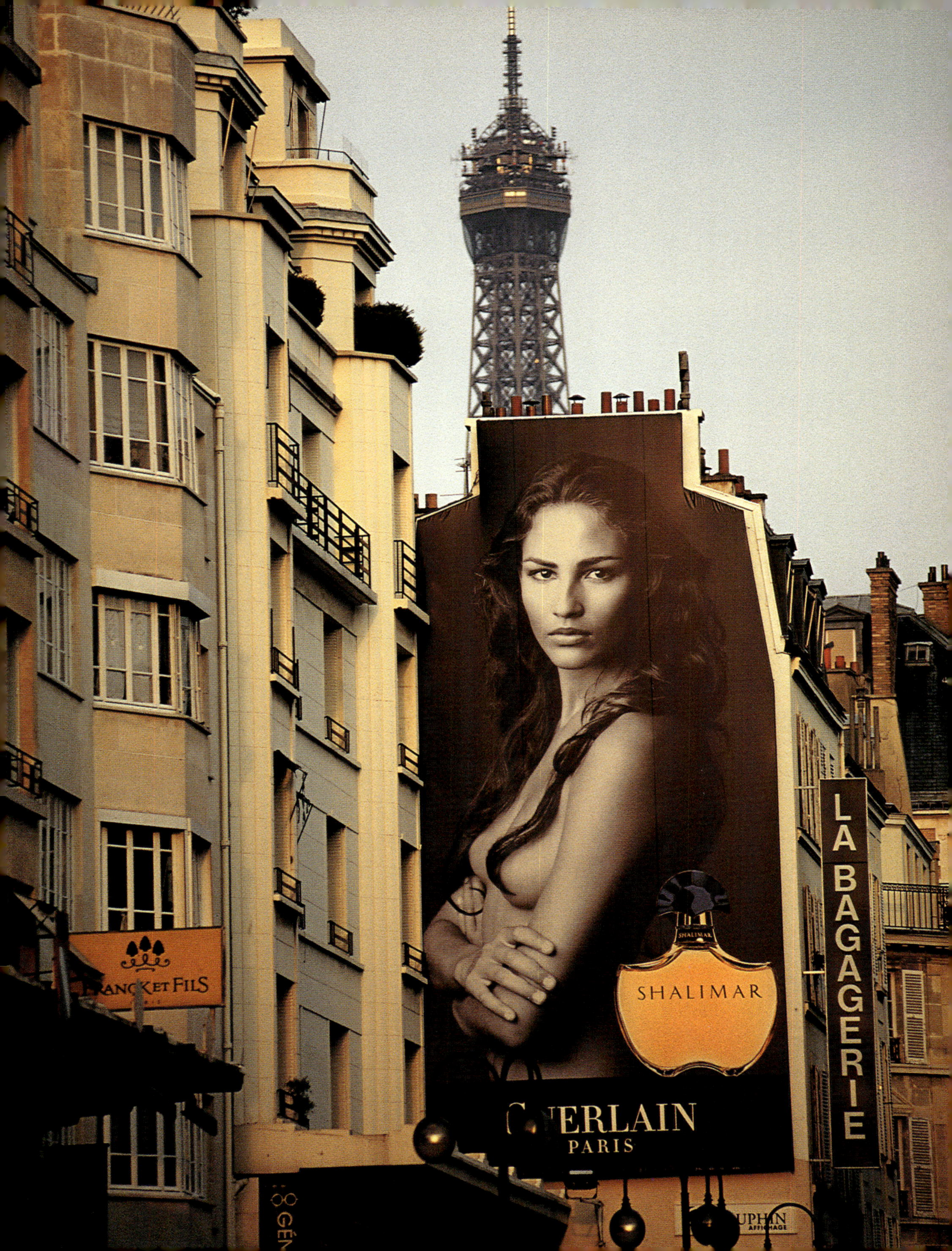
SHALIMAR
PARIS
LA BAGAGERIE

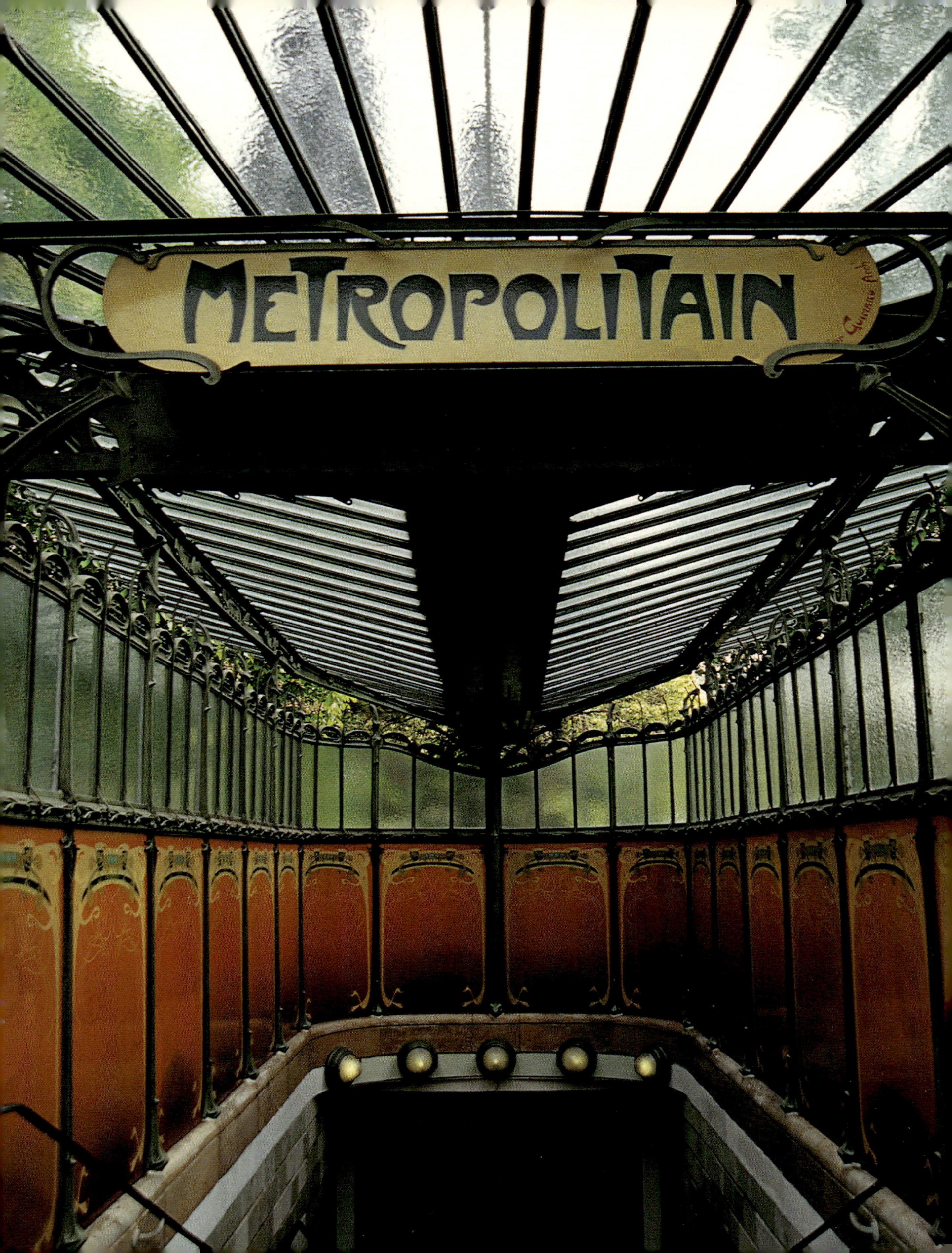
METROPOLITAIN

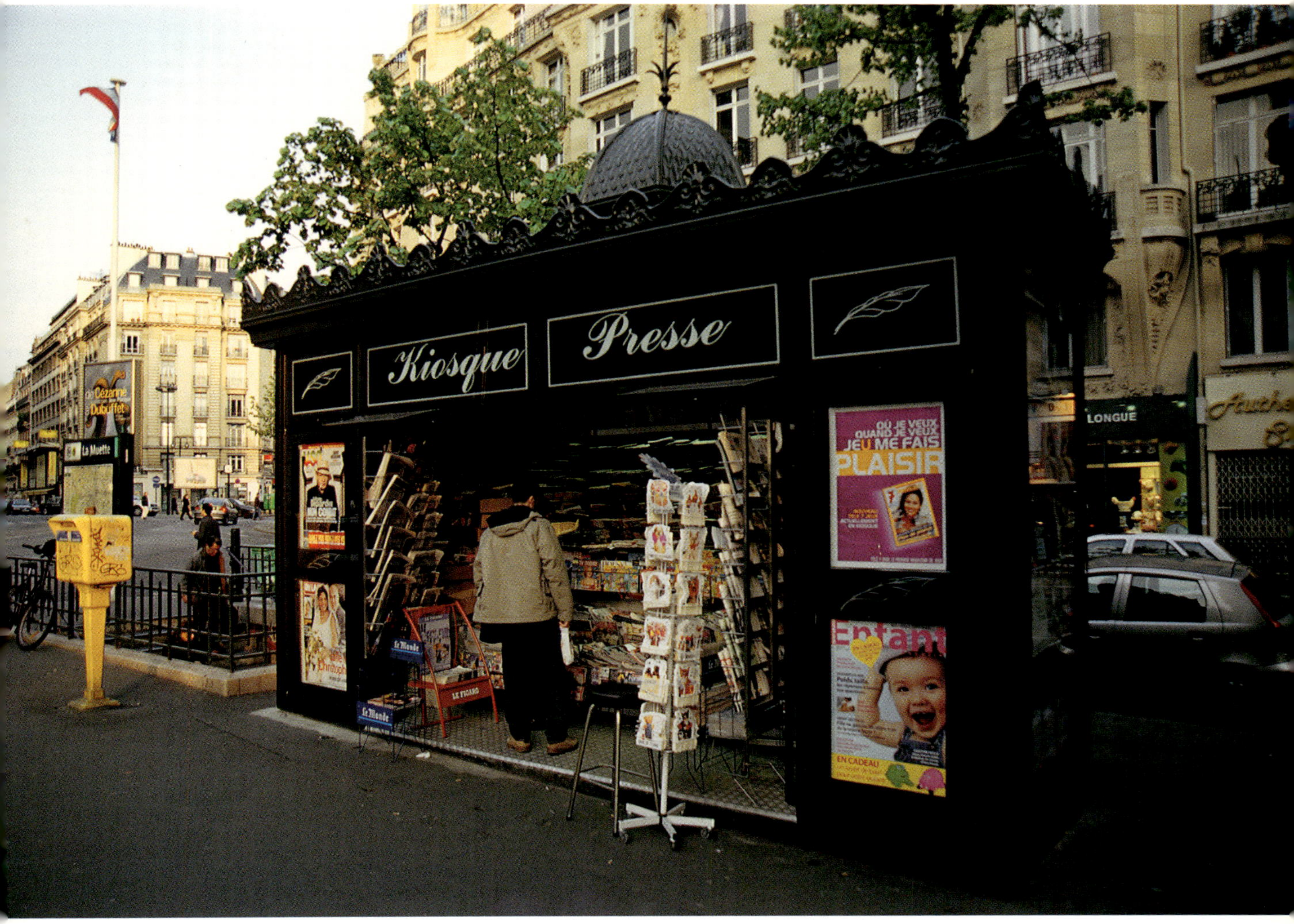
Kiosque
Presse
OÙ JE VEUX
QUAND JE VEUX
JEU ME FAIS
PLAISIR
Enfant
EN CADEAU
La Muette
Cézanne
Dubuffet
Le Monde
LE FIGARO
LONGUE

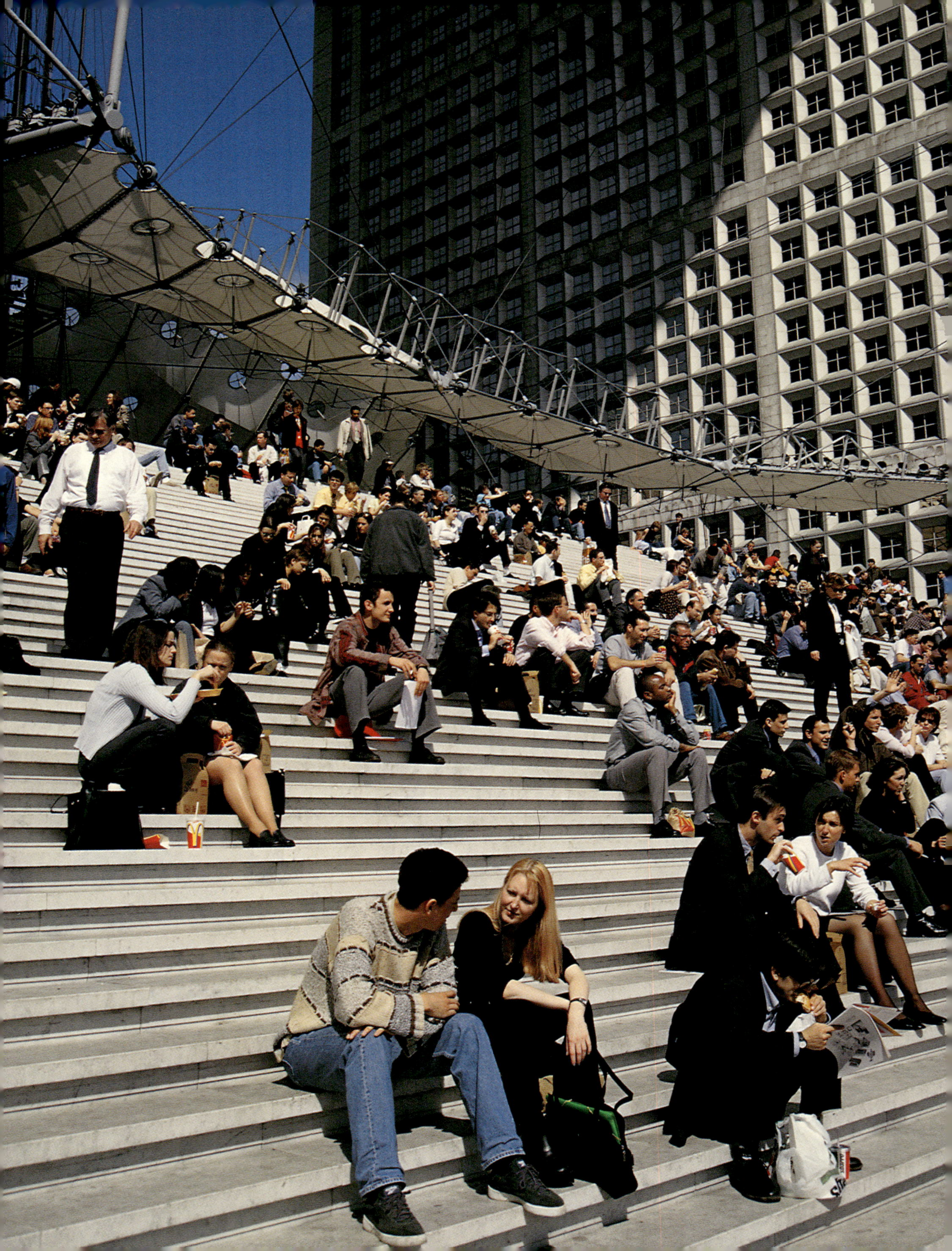

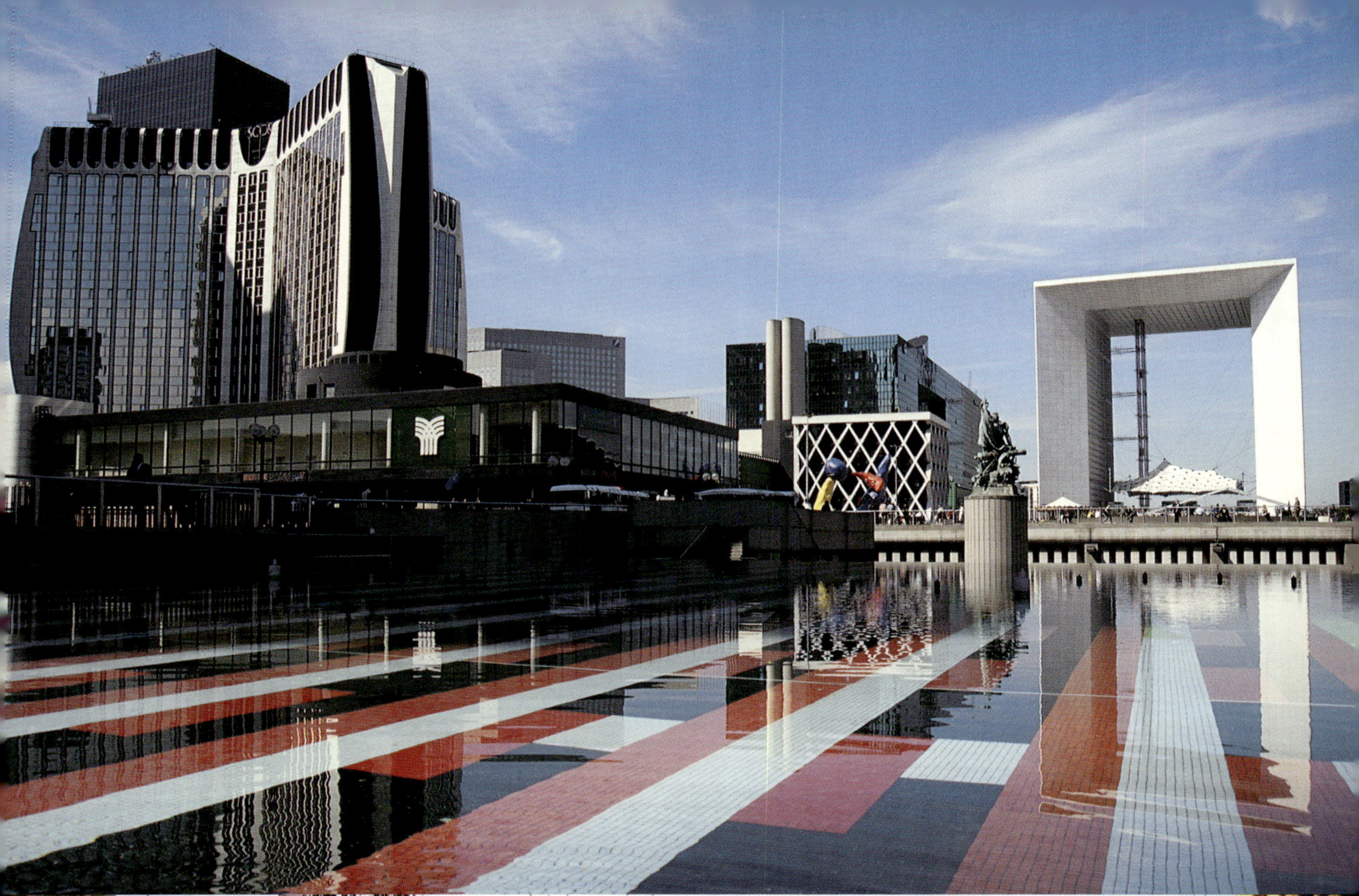

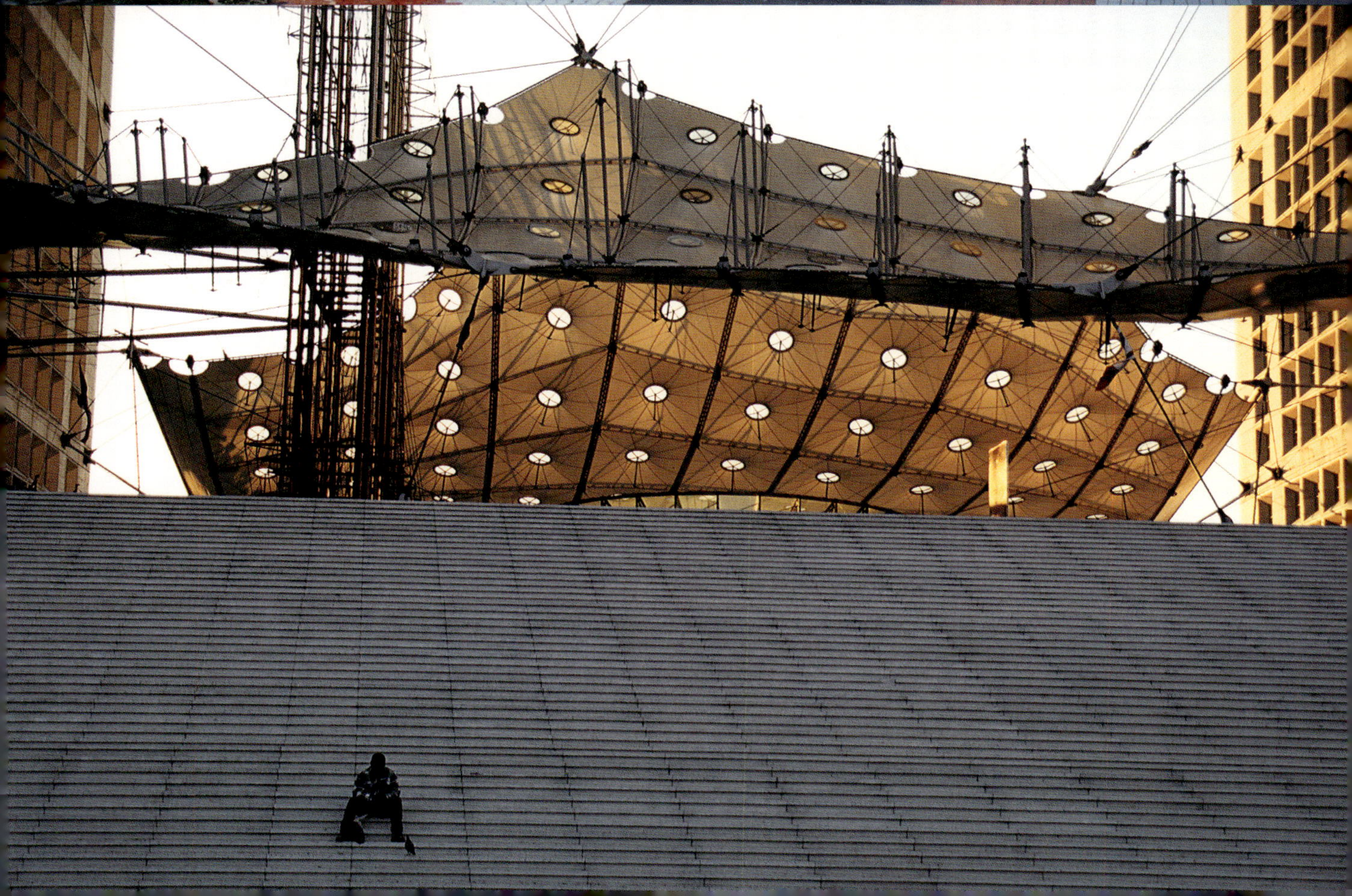

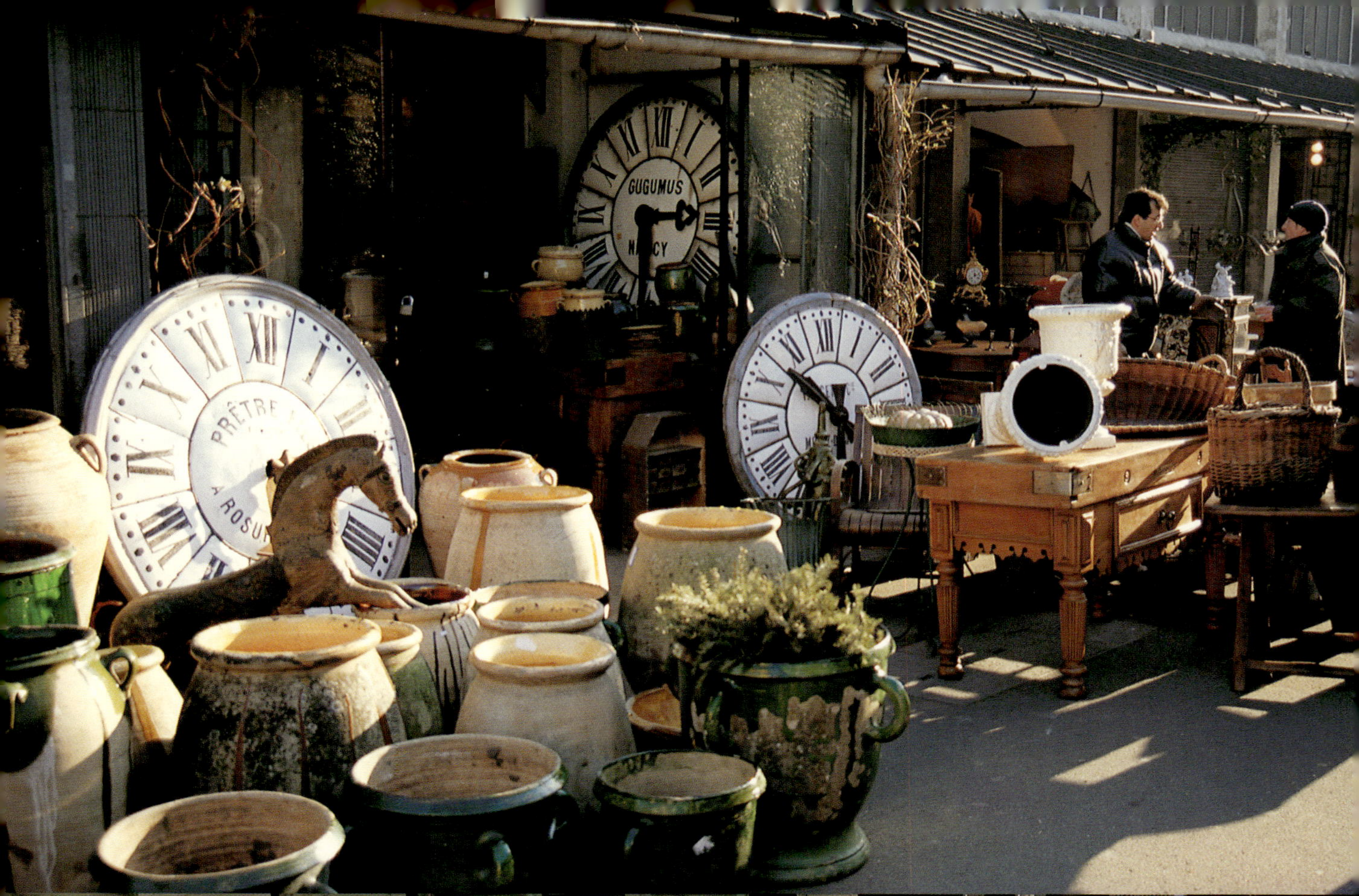
GUGUMUS
PRÊTRE

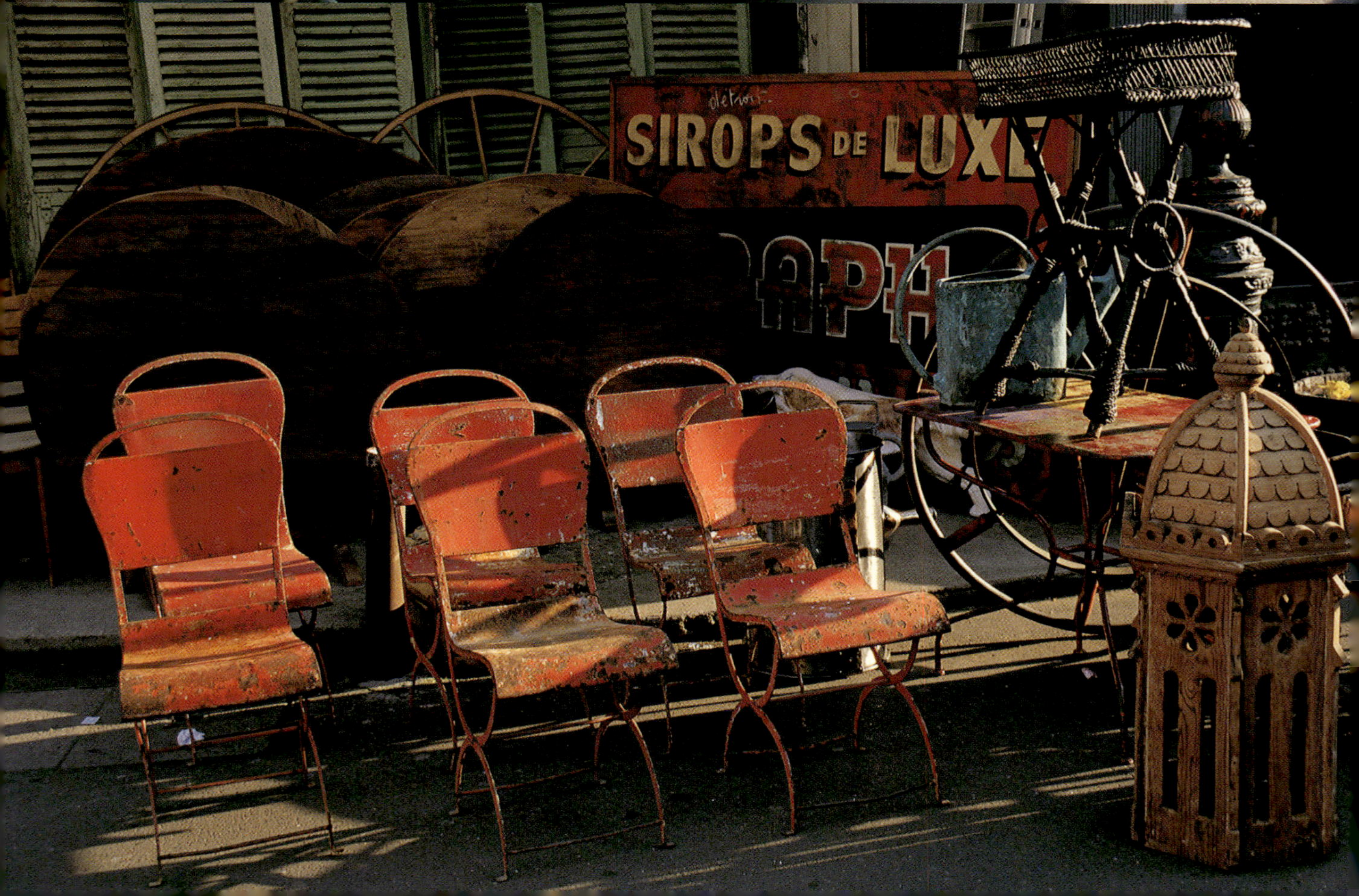
SIROPS DE LUXE

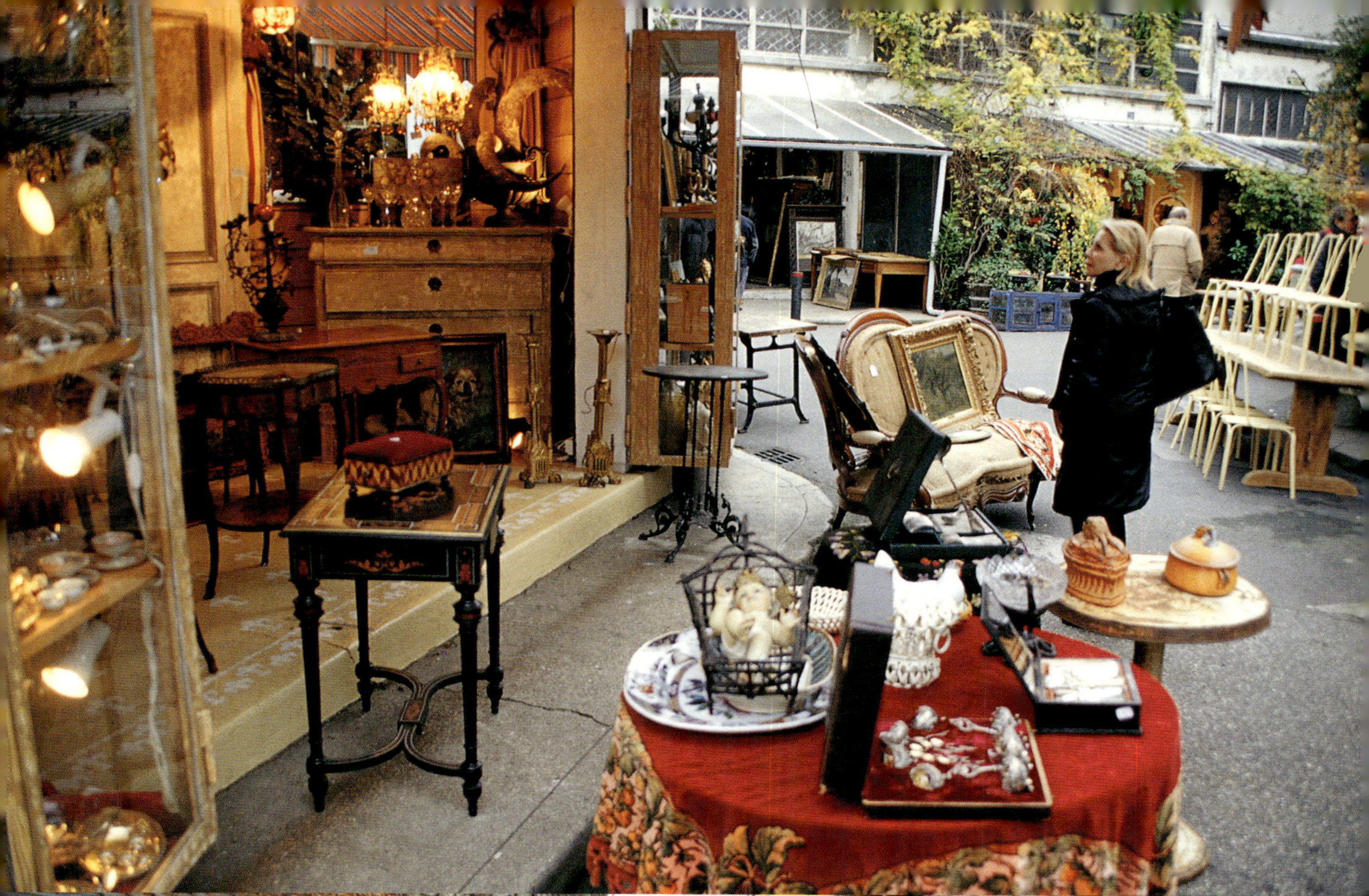

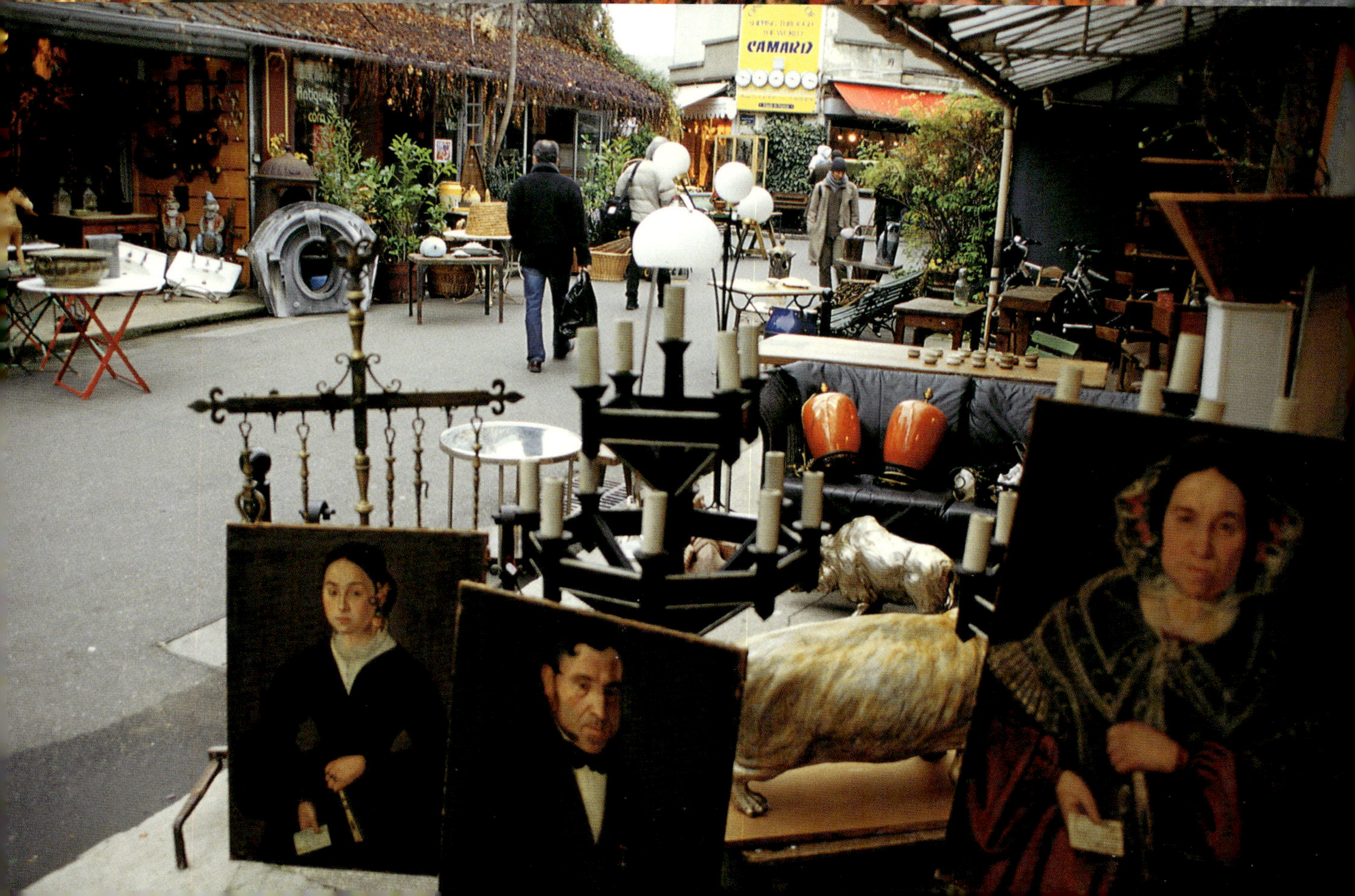
CAMARD

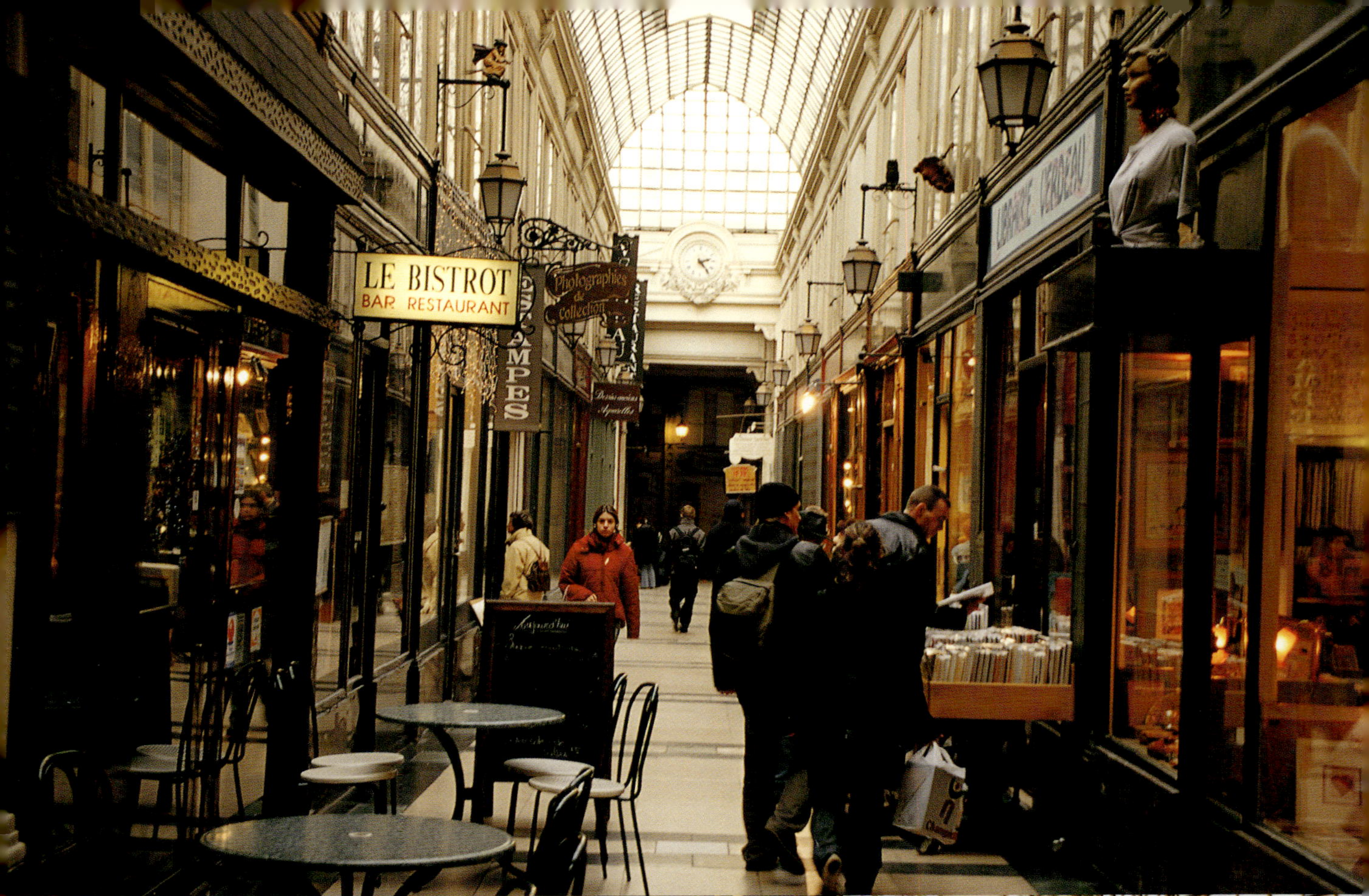
LE BISTROT
BAR RESTAURANT
Photographies de Collection
ESTAMPES

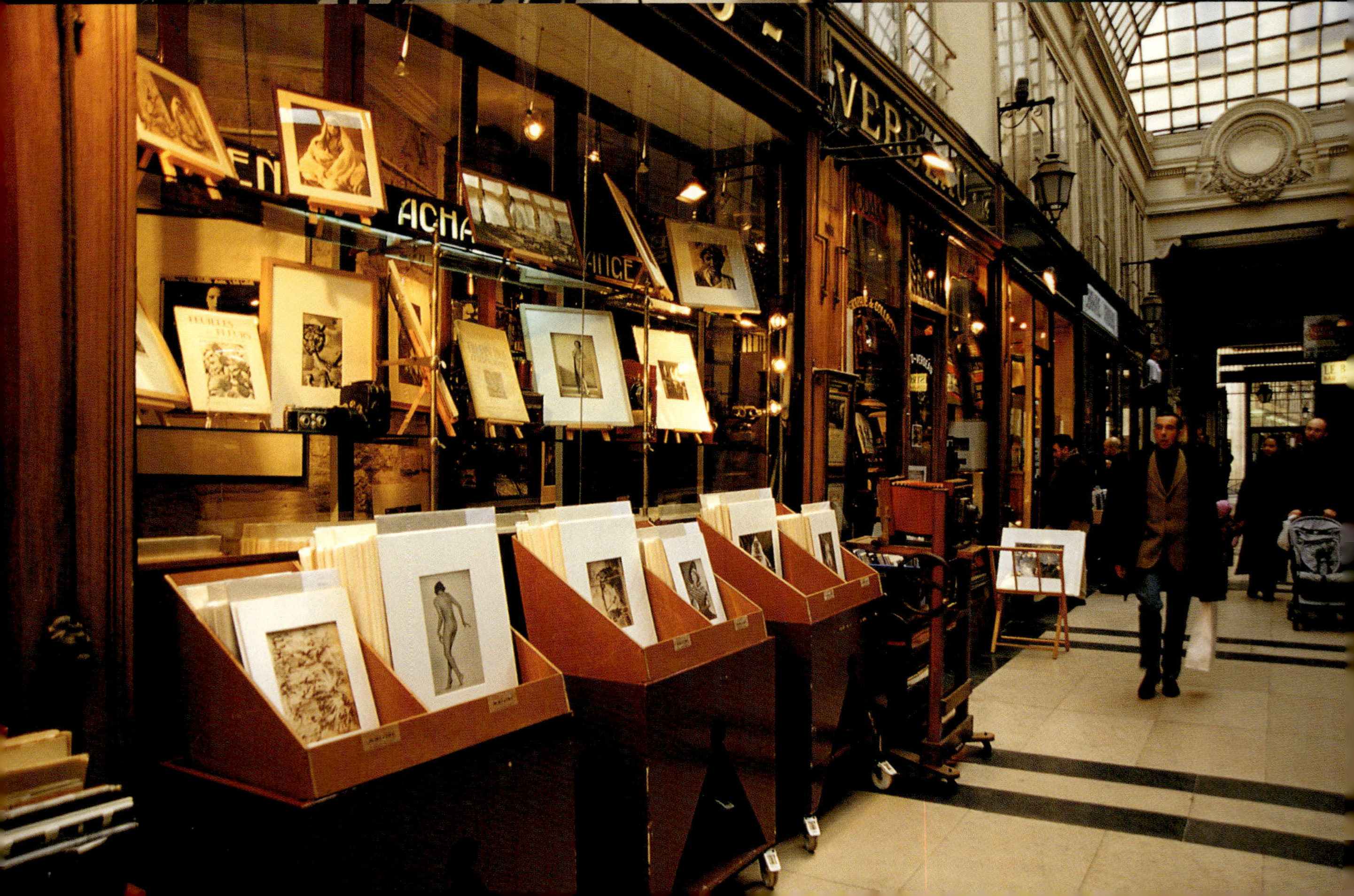

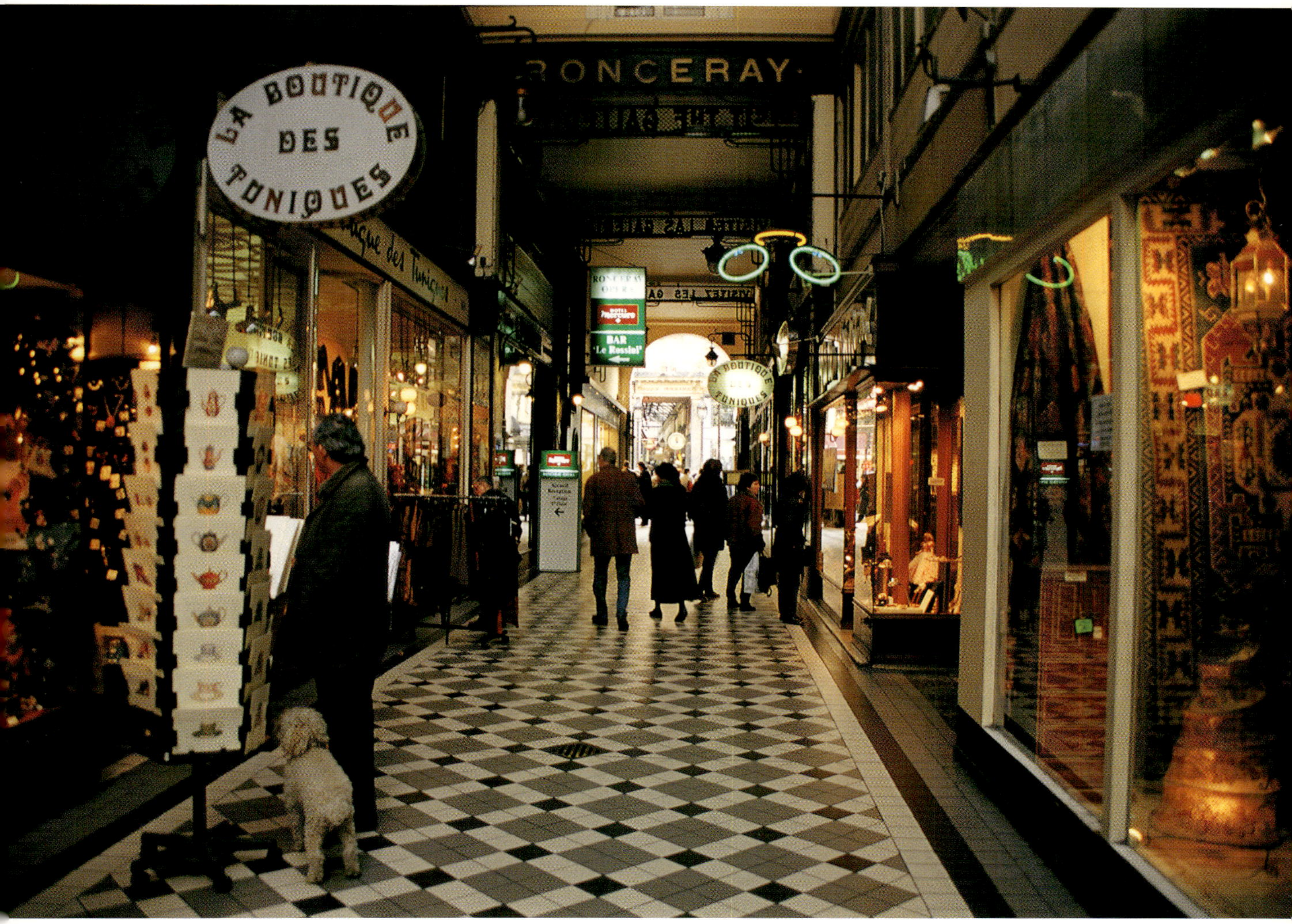
LA BOUTIQUE DES TUNIQUES
RONCERAY
BAR 'Le Rossini'
LA BOUTIQUE DES TUNIQUES

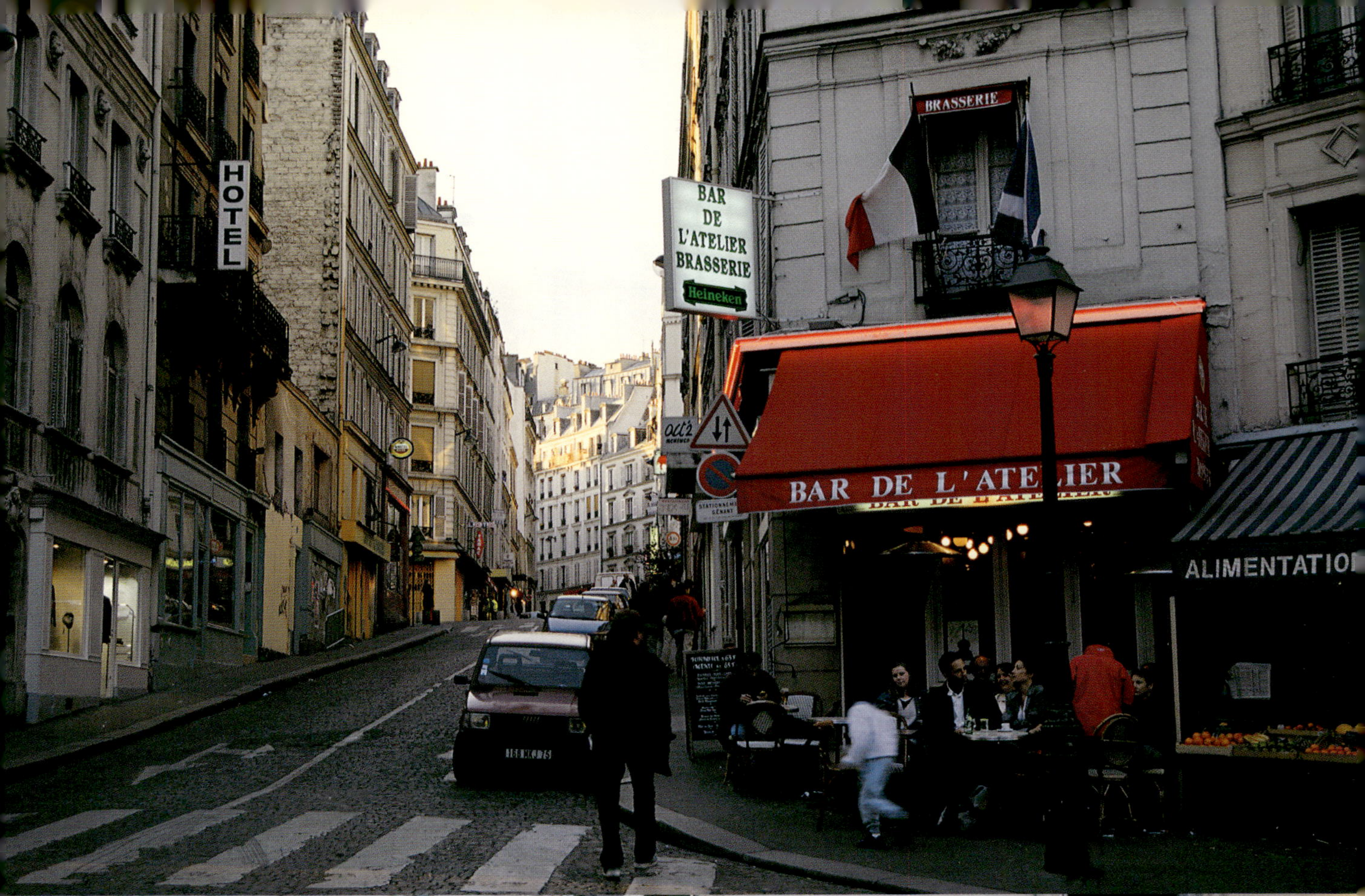
HOTEL
BAR DE L'ATELIER BRASSERIE
Heineken
BRASSERIE
BAR DE L'ATELIER
ALIMENTATIO

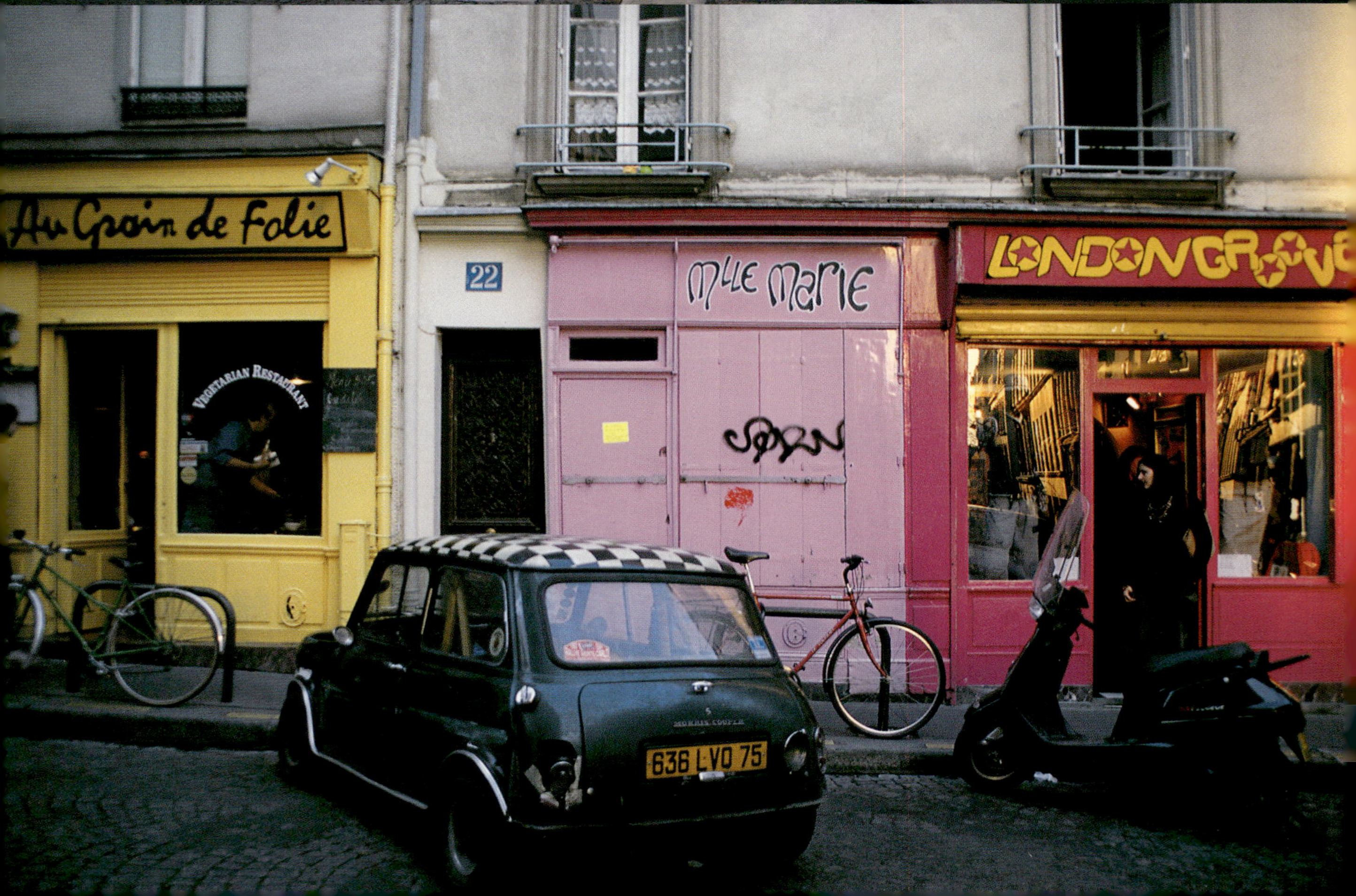
Au Grain de Folie
VEGETARIAN RESTAURANT
22
Mlle Marie
LONDONGROOV
636 LVQ 75

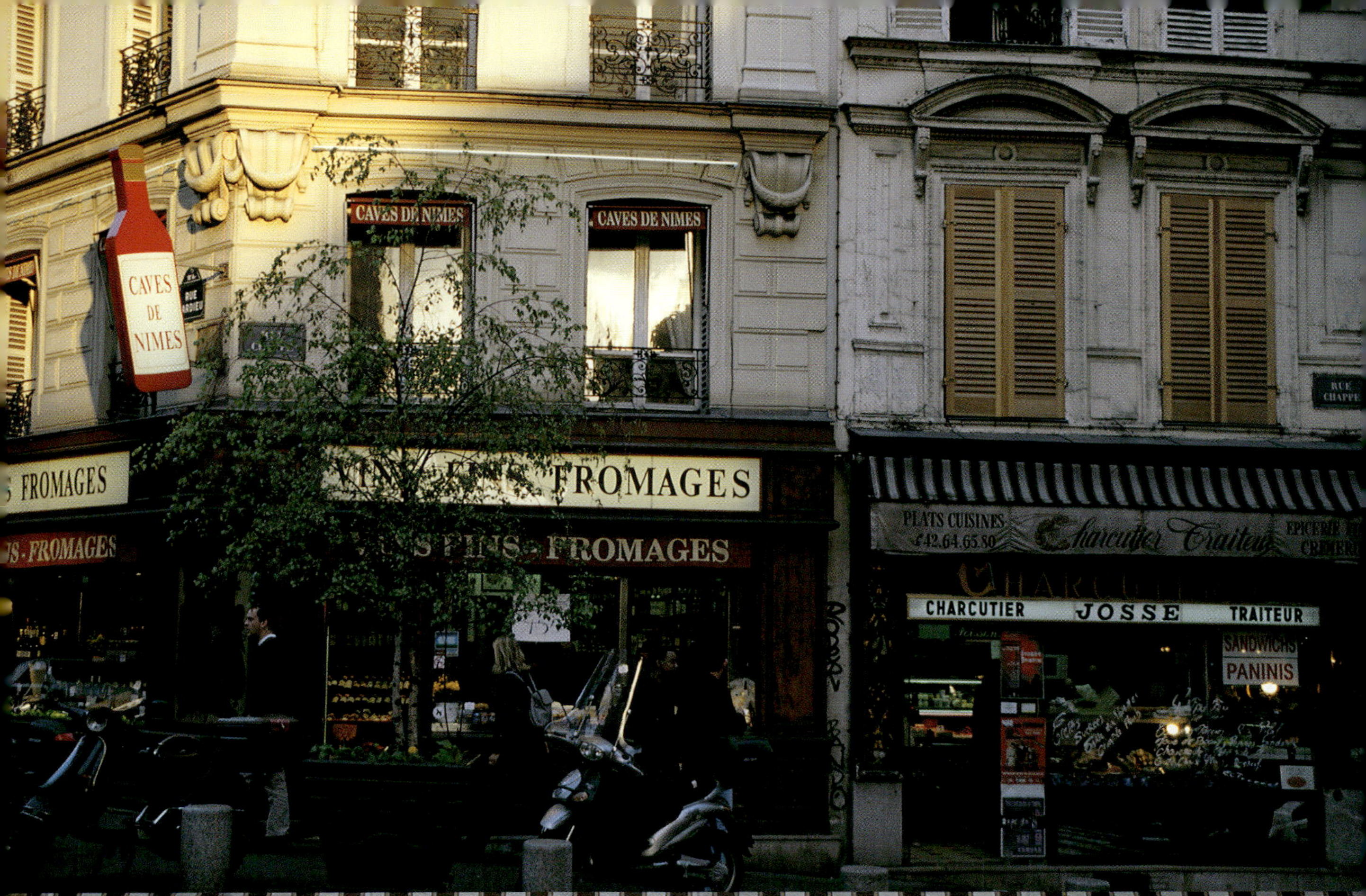
CAVES DE NIMES
CAVES DE NIMES
CAVES DE NIMES
FROMAGES
FROMAGES
FROMAGES
FROMAGES
PLATS CUISINES
42.64.65.80
Charcutier Traiteur
CHARCUTIER JOSSE TRAITEUR
SANDWICHS
PANINIS

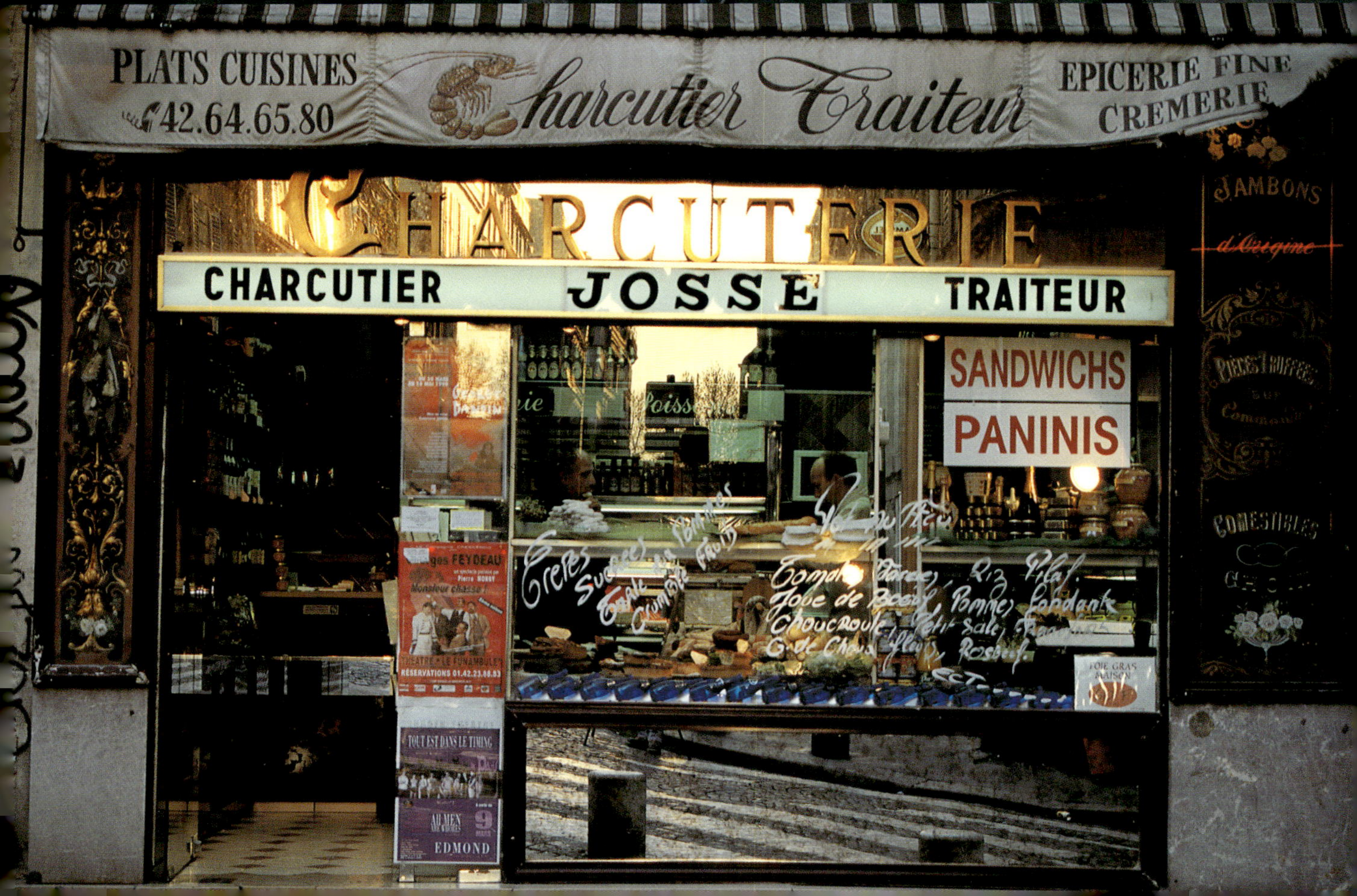
PLATS CUISINES
42.64.65.80
Charcutier Traiteur
EPICERIE FINE
CREMERIE
CHARCUTERIE
CHARCUTIER
JOSSE
TRAITEUR
SANDWICHS
PANINIS
JAMBONS
COMESTIBLES
TOUT EST DANS LE TIMING
EDMOND

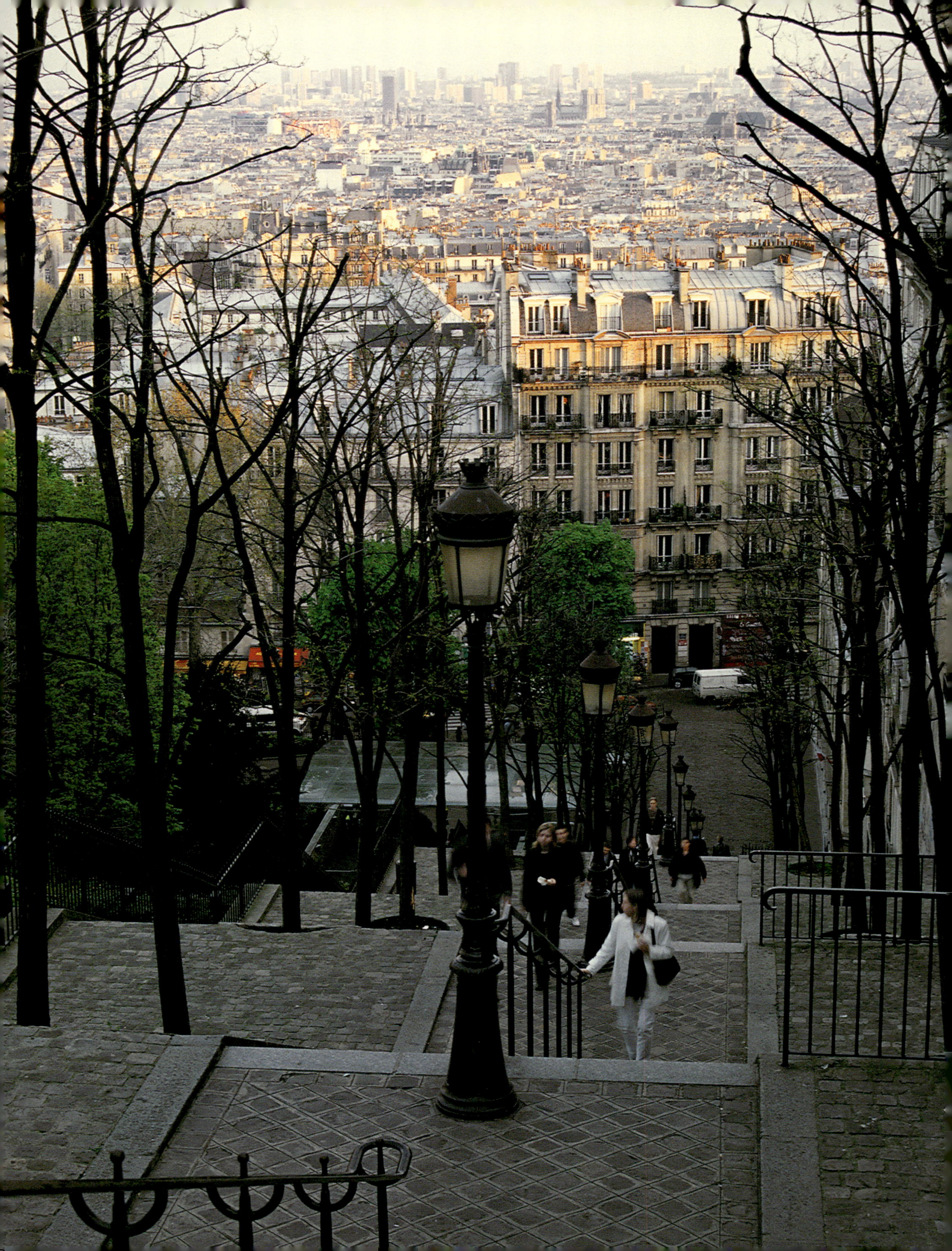

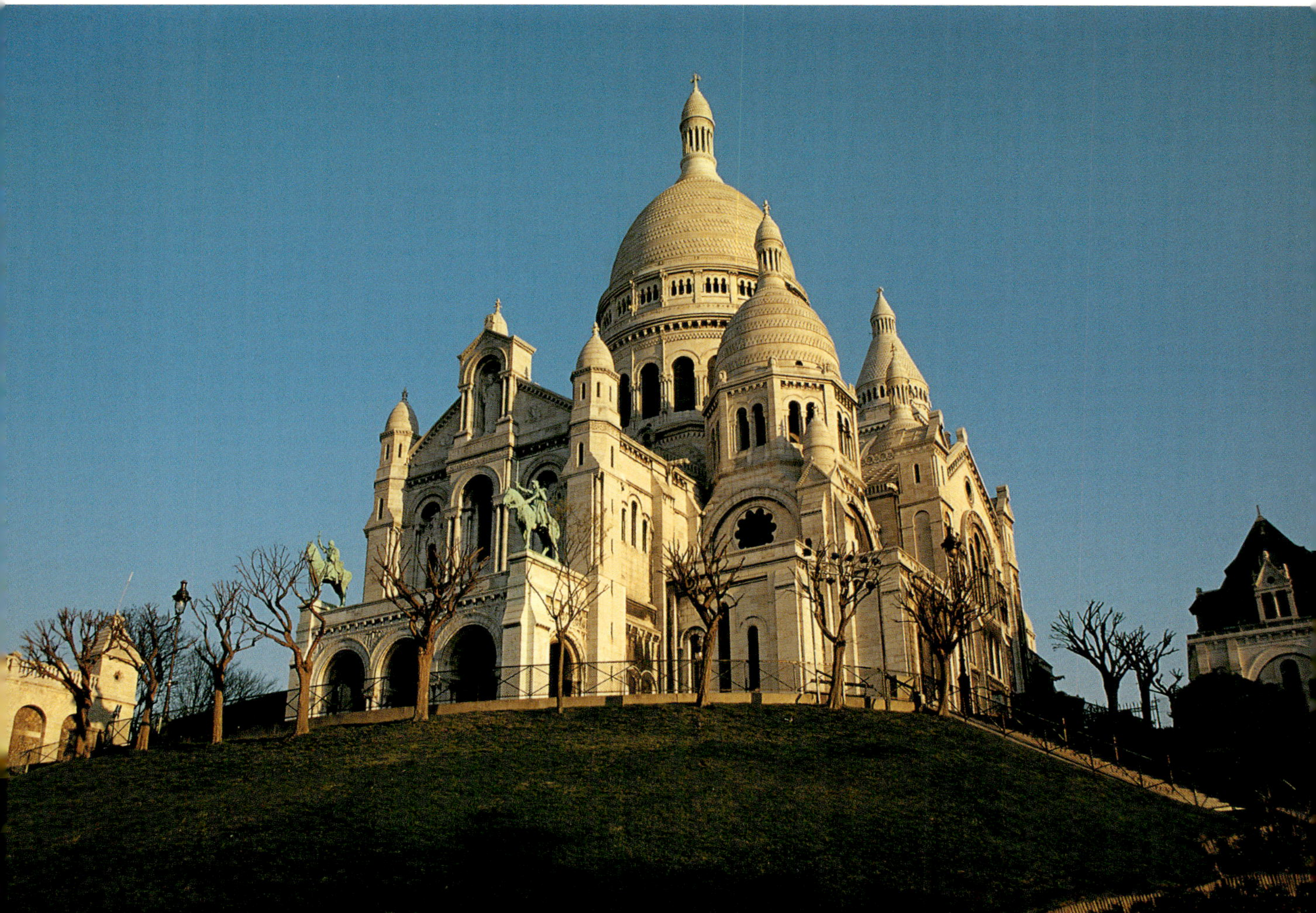

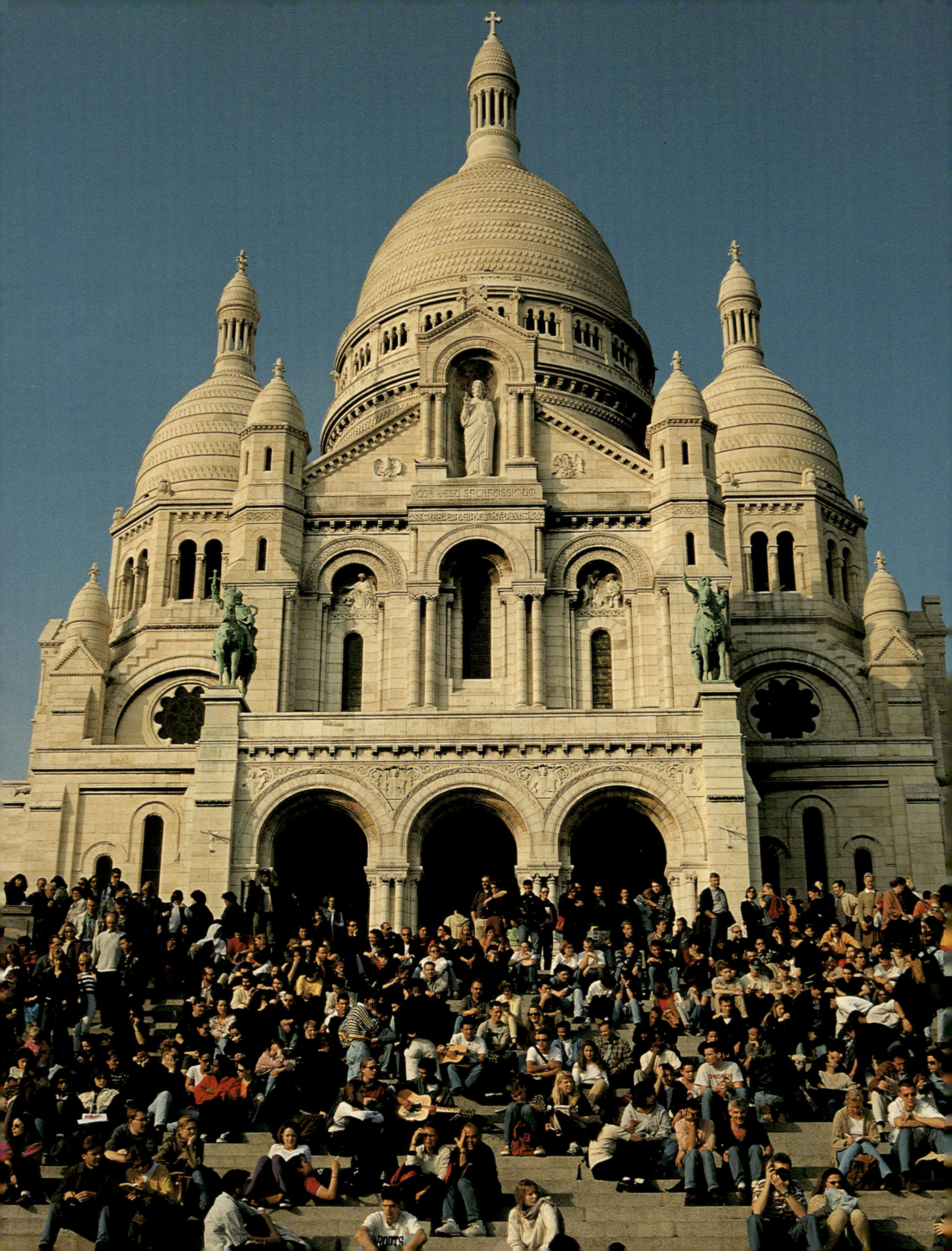
COR JESU SACRATISSIMUM

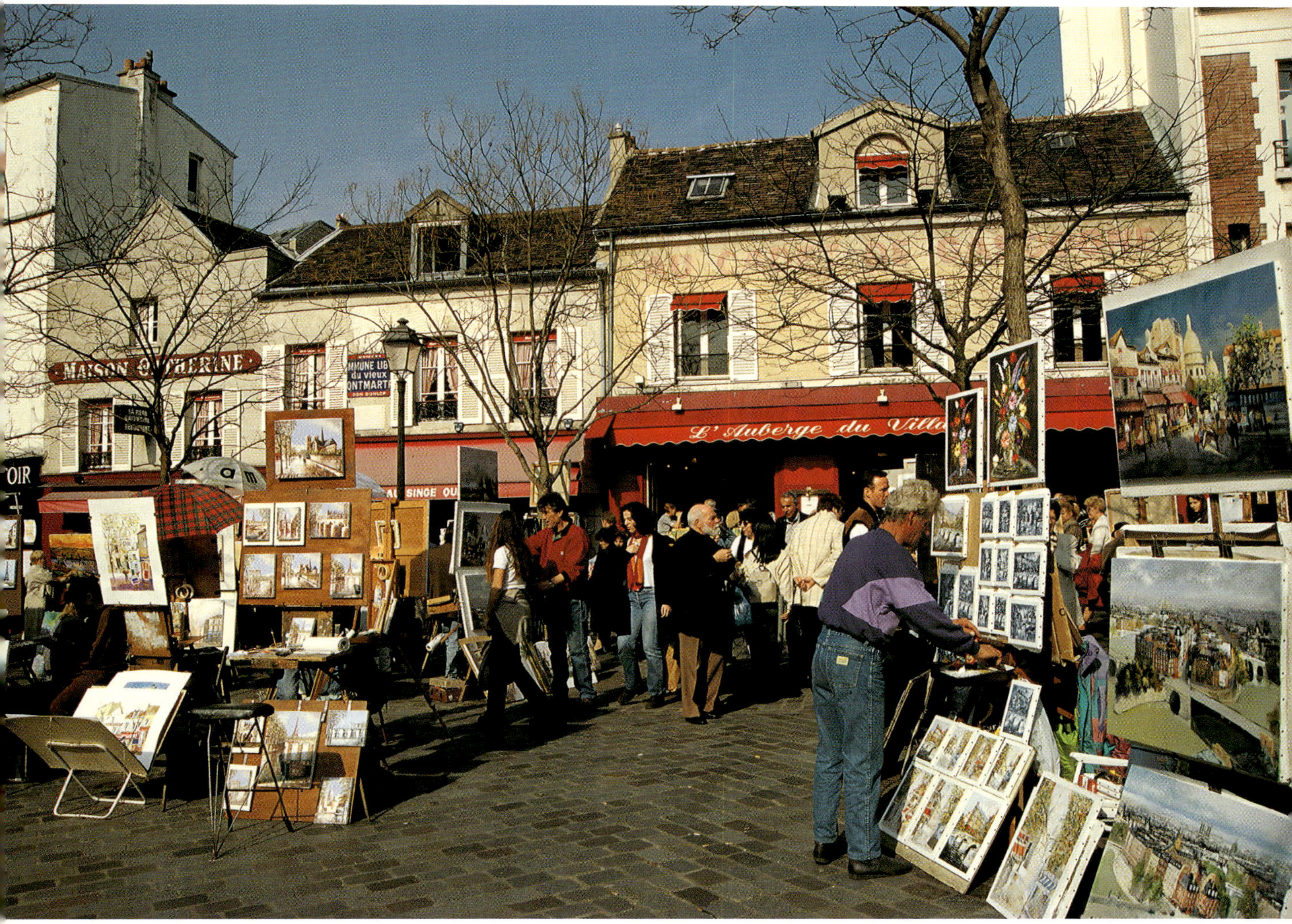
MAISON
du vieux
L'Auberge du

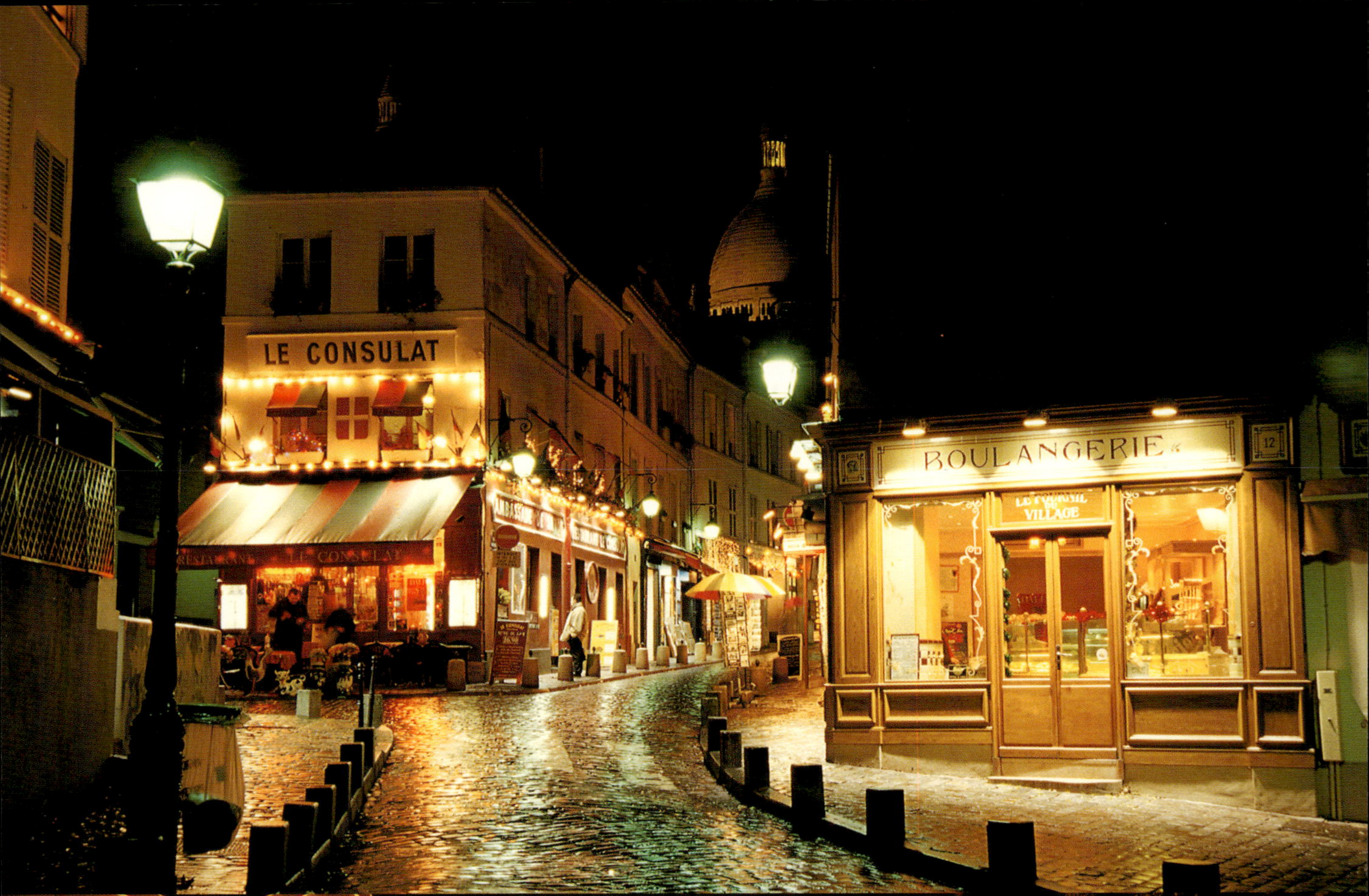
LE CONSULAT
BOULANGERIE
LE FOURNIL DU VILLAGE

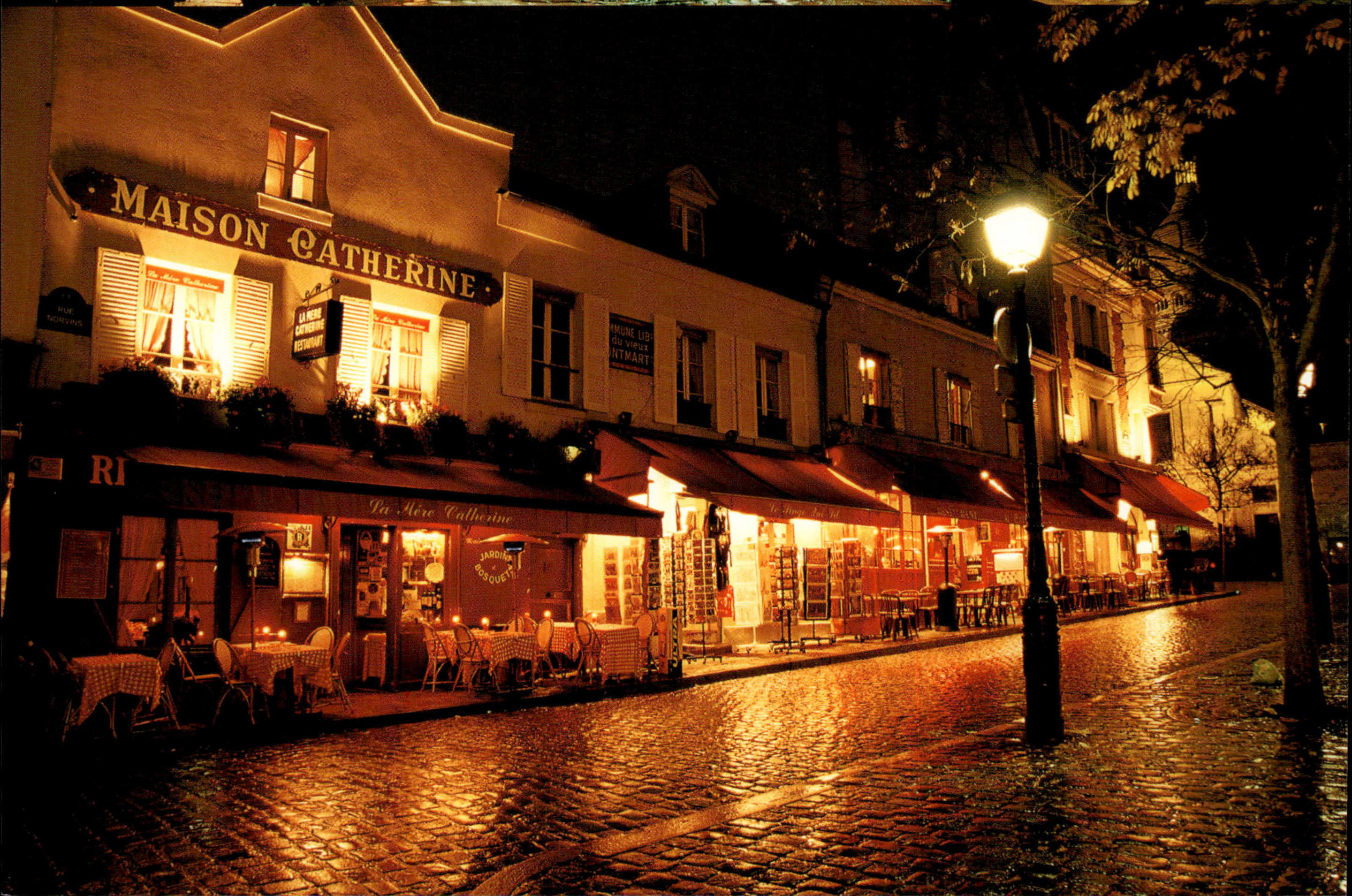
MAISON CATHERINE
LA MERE CATHERINE RESTAURANT
La Mère Catherine
JARDINS & BOSQUETS

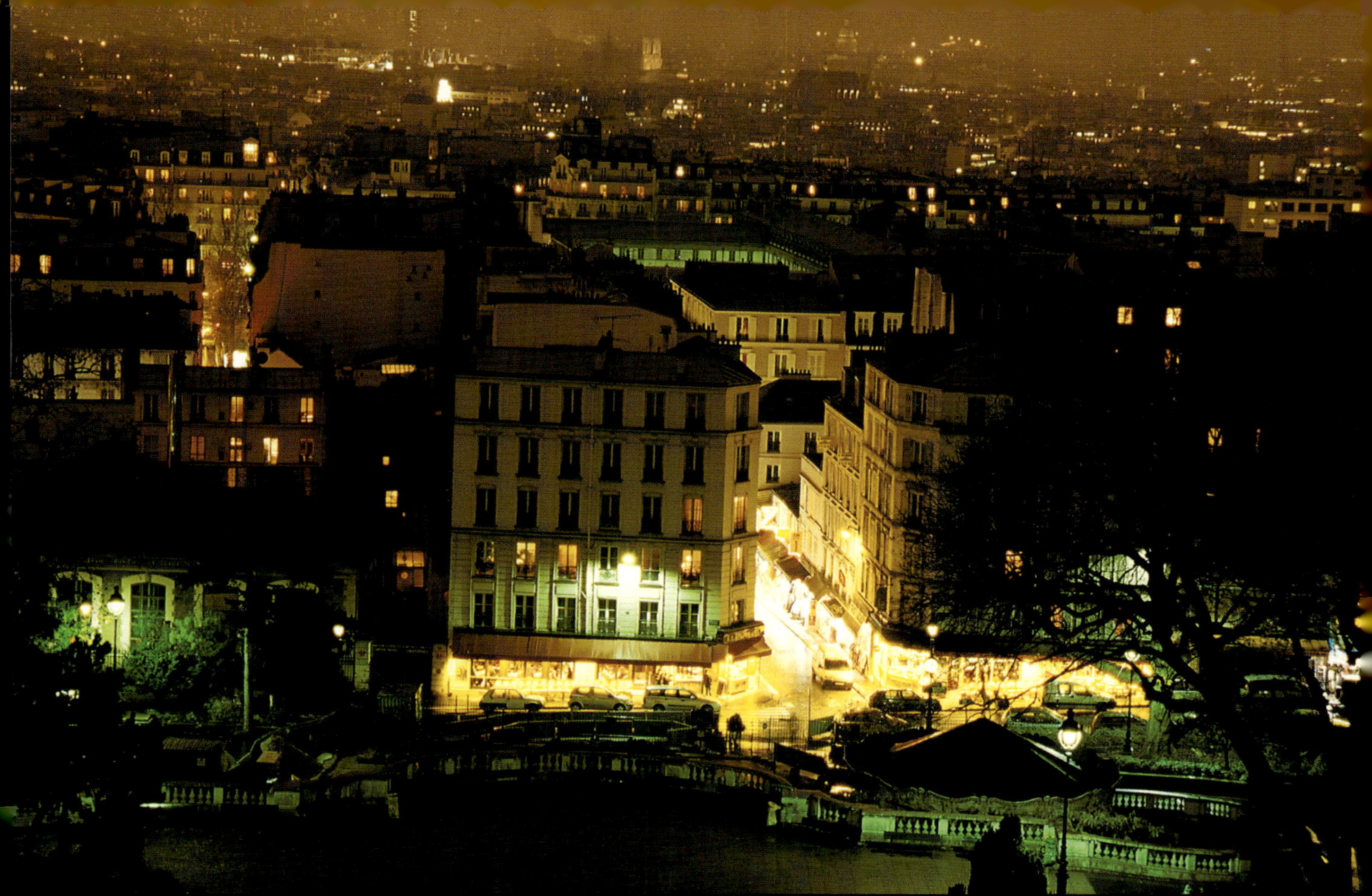

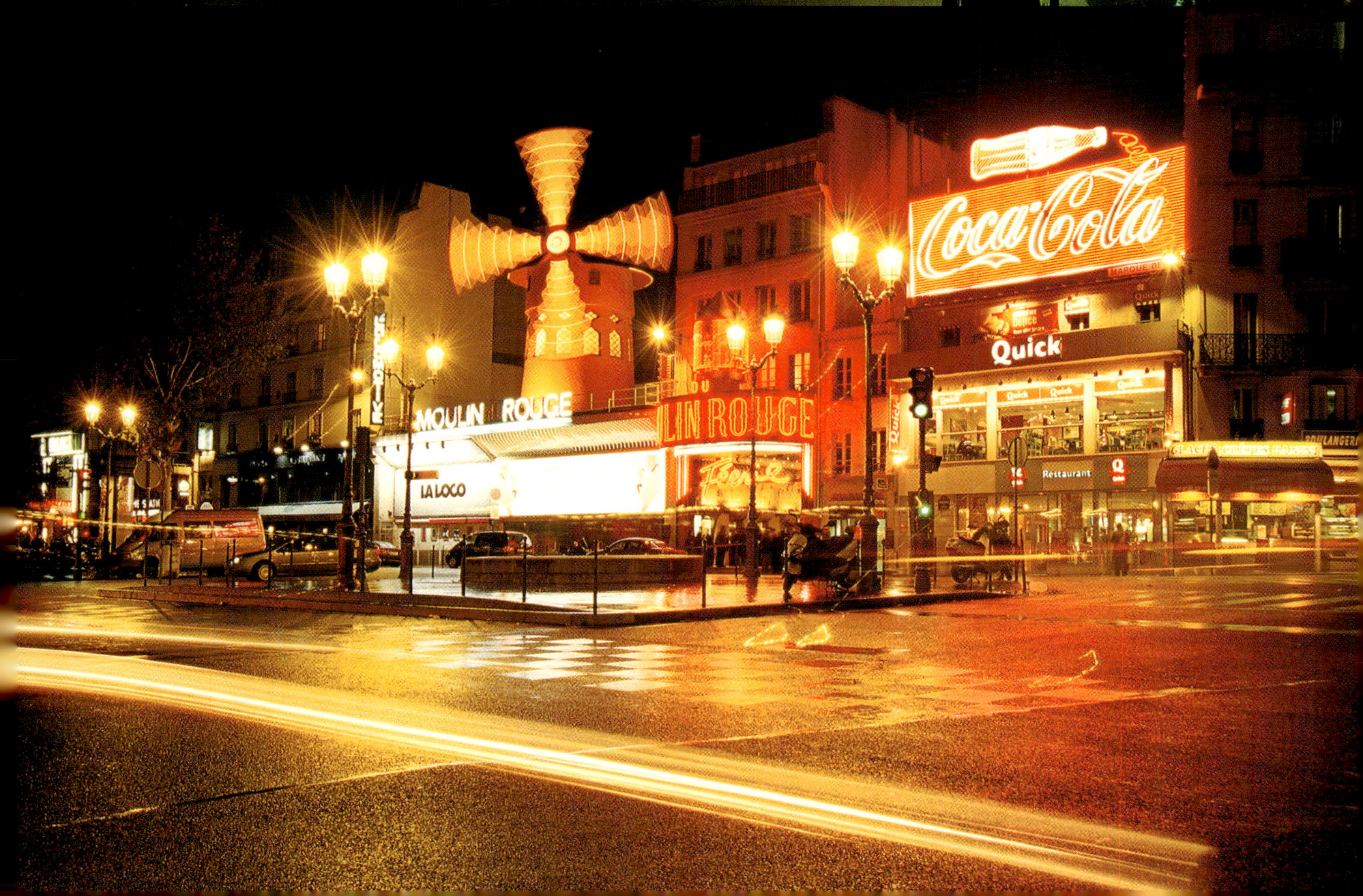
Coca-Cola
Quick
MOULIN ROUGE
LIN ROUGE
LA LOCO
Restaurant

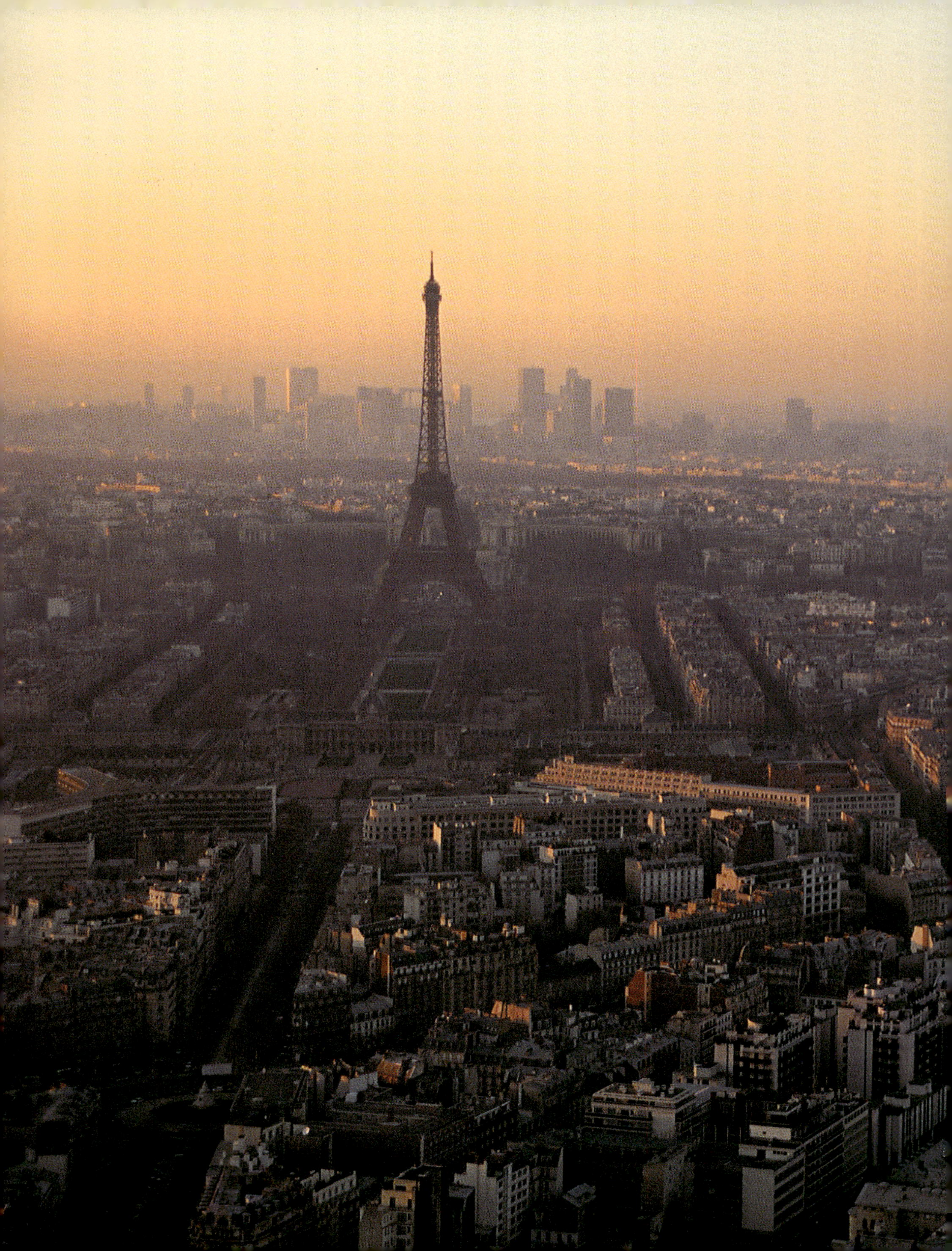

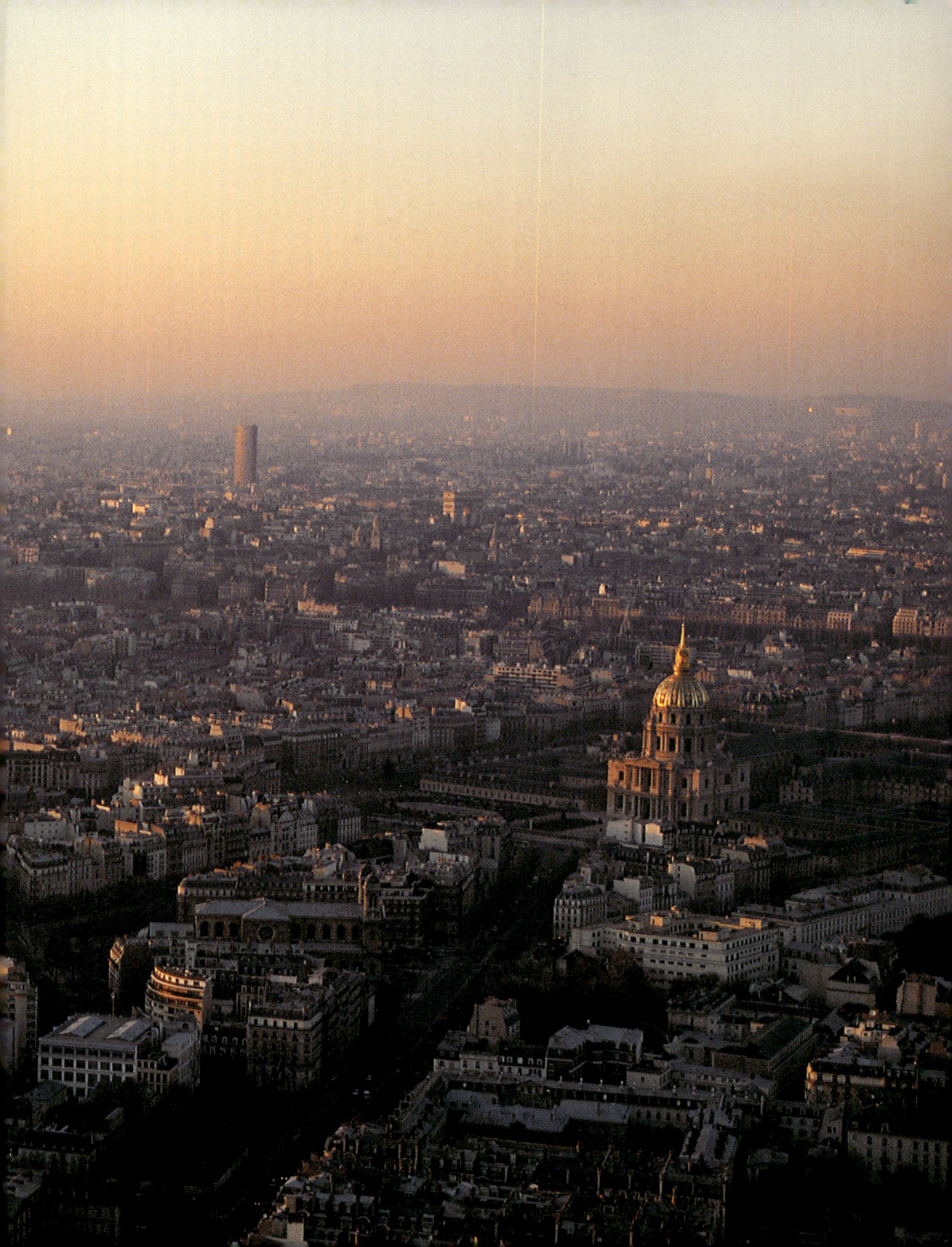

Table des matières Directory Verzeichnis Directorio Indice delle materie

76 Quartier Latin, Rue des Prêtres-Saint-Séverin (5e Arr.)
Saint-Germain-des-Prés (6e Arr.)

77 Place du Petit-Pont, Cafés (5e Arr.)
Quai des Grands Augustins, « Café Lapérouse » (6e Arr.)

78 Saint-Germain-des-Prés, Rue Bonaparte (6e Arr.)
Rue de Rennes (6e Arr.)

79 Boulevard Saint-Germain (6e Arr.)
Boulevard Saint-Germain (6e Arr.)

80 Jardin du Luxembourg (6e Arr.)
Jardin du Luxembourg (6e Arr.)

81 Jardin du Luxembourg (6e Arr.)

82 Saint-Germain-des-Prés, Saint-Sulpice (6e Arr.)

83 Boulevard Saint-Germain, « Café de Flore » (6e Arr.)

84 Saint-Germain-des-Prés, Marché (6e Arr.)

85 Saint-Germain-des-Prés, Café « Les Deux Magots » (6e Arr.)
Saint-Germain-des-Prés (6e Arr.)

86 Tour Eiffel (7e Arr.)

87 Tour Eiffel (7e Arr.)
Tour Eiffel (7e Arr.)

88 Musée d'Orsay (7e Arr.)

89 Hôtel des Invalides (7e Arr.)

90 Pont Alexandre III (7e Arr.)

91 Pont Alexandre III (7e Arr.)

92 Arc de Triomphe (8e/16e/17e Arr.)

93 Avenue des Champs-Élysées (8e Arr.)
Avenue des Champs-Élysées (8e Arr.)

94 Rue de Babylone (7e Arr.)

95 Avenue Montaigne (8e Arr.)
Avenue Montaigne (8e Arr.)

96 Avenue Montaigne (8e Arr.)

97 Avenue Montaigne (8e Arr.)
Avenue Montaigne (8e Arr.)

98 Place de la Concorde (8e Arr.)

99 Place de la Concorde (8e Arr.)
La Madeleine (8e Arr.)

100 Grand Palais (8e Arr.)

101 Petit Palais (8e Arr.)

102/103 Opéra Garnier (8e Arr.)

104 Galeries Lafayette (9e Arr.)

105 Printemps (9e Arr.)

106 Station du métro « Abbesses » (18e Arr.)

107 Canal Saint-Martin (10e Arr.)

108 La Villette, Cité de la Musique (19e Arr.)

109 La Villette, Geode (19e Arr.)

110 Place de la Bastille (4e Arr.)

111 Opéra Bastille (12e Arr.)

112 Bastille, Rue de Lyon (12e Arr.)

113 Bastille, Rue de Lappe (11e Arr.)

114 Bastille, « Café Bastille » (12e Arr.)
Bastille, Place d'Aligre (12e Arr.)

115 Bastille (12e Arr.)
Place de la Bastille (4e Arr.)

116/117 Gare de Lyon, Restaurant « Le Train Bleu » (12e Arr.)

118 Cimetière de Montparnasse (14e Arr.)

119 Cimetière de Montparnasse (14e Arr.)

120 Parc André Citroën (15e Arr.)

121 Parc André Citroën (15e Arr.)
Parc André Citroën (15e Arr.)

122 Palais de Chaillot (16e Arr.)
Palais de Chaillot (16e Arr.)

123 Passy (16e Arr.)

124 Station du métro « Porte Dauphine » (16e Arr.)

125 Passy (16e Arr.)

126 La Défense, Grande Arche

127 La Défense
La Défense, Grande Arche

128 Marché aux Puces Paul Bert, Saint-Ouen
Marché aux Puces Paul Bert, Saint-Ouen

129 Marché aux Puces Paul Bert, Saint-Ouen
Marché aux Puces Paul Bert, Saint-Ouen

130 Boulevard Montmartre, Passage Verdeau (9e Arr.)
Boulevard Montmartre, Passage Verdeau (9e Arr.)

131 Boulevard Montmartre, Passage de Jouffroy (9e Arr.)

132 Montmartre (18e Arr.)
Montmartre (18e Arr.)

133 Montmartre, Rue Chappe (18e Arr.)
Montmartre, Rue Chappe (18e Arr.)

134 Montmartre, Rue Foyatier (18e Arr.)

135 Sacré-Cœur (18e Arr.)

136 Sacré-Cœur (18e Arr.)

137 Montmartre, Place du Tertre (18e Arr.)

138 Montmartre, Rue Norvins (18e Arr.)
Montmartre, Place du Tertre (18e Arr.)

139 Vue de Montmartre
Moulin Rouge

140/141 Vue de la Tour Montparnasse

Front cover: Panthéon, Café
Back cover: Place de la Concorde

www.herzig-foto.de

Photographs by Tina and Horst Herzig
Design by Robert Kuhlendahl, teNeues Verlag
Introduction by Pierrette Stephan-Letondor
Translation by SAW Communications,
Dr. Sabine A. Werner, Mainz
Dr. Suzanne Kirkbright (English)
Ulrike Brandhorst (German)
Gemma Correa-Buján (Spanish)
Nicoletta Negri (Italian)
Editorial coordination by Sabine Wagner, teNeues Verlag
Production by Sandra Jansen, teNeues Verlag
Color separation by Medien Team-Vreden, Germany

Bibliographic information published by Die Deutsche Bibliothek. Die Deutsche Bibliothek lists this publication in the Deutsche Nationalbibliographie; detailed bibliographic data is available in the Internet at http://dnb.ddb.de

ISBN 3-8327-9044-6

Printed in Italy

Published by teNeues Publishing Group

teNeues Book Division
Kaistraße 18
40221 Düsseldorf
Germany
Phone: 0049-(0)211-99 45 97-0
Fax: 0049-(0)211-99 45 97-40
e-mail: books@teneues.de
Press department: arehn@teneues.de
Phone: 0049-(0)2152-916-202

teNeues Publishing Company
16 West 22nd Street
New York, N.Y. 10010
USA
Phone: 001-212-627-9090
Fax: 001-212-627-9511

teNeues Publishing UK Ltd.
P.O. Box 402
West Byfleet
KT14 7ZF
Great Britain
Phone: 0044-1932-403509
Fax: 0044-1932-403514

teNeues France S.A.R.L.
4, rue de Valence
75005 Paris
France
Phone: 0033-1-55 76 62 05
Fax: 0033-1-55 76 64 19

www.teneues.com

teNeues Publishing Group
Kempen
Düsseldorf
London
Madrid
New York
Paris

teNeues